EINSTEIN
IN AMERICA

EINSTEIN IN AMERICA

The Scientist's Conscience in the Age of Hitler and Hiroshima

by Jamie Sayen

CROWN PUBLISHERS, INC.
New York

Published by Crown Publishers, Inc.,
One Park Avenue, New York, New York 10016 and
simultaneously in Canada by General Publishing Company Limited
CROWN is a trademark of Crown Publishers, Inc.
Manufactured in the United States of America

Library of Congress Cataloging in Publication Data

Sayen, Jamie.
Einstein in America.

Bibliography: p.
1. Einstein, Albert, 1879–1955.   2. Physicists—
Biography.   I. Title.
QC16.E5S285. 1985   530'.092'4 [B]   84=20033
ISBN 0-517-55604-9

Design by Jacques Chazaud

10 9 8 7 6 5 4 3 2 1

First Edition

CONTENTS

Acknowledgments   *vii*

Introduction   *1*

1. "Noch Ungehängt" (Not Yet Hanged) (1933)   *5*
2. "Impudent Swabian" (1879–1914)   *23*
3. "Moral Fidelity" (1914–1932)   *35*
4. Demigods and Paradise   *61*
5. The Scientist and the Institute   *81*
6. Refugees   *97*
7. "Against Necessity No One Can Fight and Win"   *117*
8. A Private Life   *125*
9. Hitler's War   *141*
10. "Music of the Spheres"   *153*
11. "Ticket of Admission"   *167*
12. "Between Anarchy and Tyranny"   *181*
13. The Road Toward General Annihilation   *201*
14. A Princeton Landmark   *217*
15. "Jewish Saint"   *233*
16. Enemy of America   *249*
17. "Enfant Terrible"   *267*
18. "Beware of Rotten Compromises"   *281*
19. "Even Age Has Beautiful Moments"   *293*
20. Morning Air   *301*

Notes   *307*

Index   *329*

ACKNOWLEDGMENTS

The act of writing is necessarily a solitary endeavor, yet the finished work is the product of the labors of countless others besides the one whose name appears on the dust jacket. This is especially true of this book. Unfortunately space permits mention of only a few of those to whom I am most deeply indebted.

First, there is Einstein, whose life resonates with integrity and wisdom, and who has served as an unfailing source of inspiration and challenge to me.

Next, I wish to express my gratitude to the late Helen Dukas who took me more seriously than I took myself in the early stages of this project. She was nurse, guide, and guardian of my early researches, and was always volunteering ideas and leads. She was also a true friend, who is sorely missed.

Margot Einstein first introduced me to the writings of her father and brought to life for me the poetic nature of his soul.

Otto Nathan enjoyed a unique perspective on Einstein's political actions and ideas, and, like Helen Dukas, he has aided me in innumerable ways, both tangible and intangible. His encouragement, advice, and assistance have been indispensable.

Valentine and Sonja Bargmann have been like second parents to me. They have willingly shared their knowledge of Einstein and his times, saved me from countless erroneous notions, and restored my flagging spirits more times than I care to remember. Sonja Bargmann has spent hundreds of hours translating material from the Einstein Archives for me. She can never know how great is my debt to her.

I wish to thank all who granted interviews, answered my queries, or volunteered information and leads. The list is far too long to recite here.

Jake Goldberg, my editor at Crown, has been the ideal person to work with. He is as much friend as editor.

My agent, Ray Lincoln, showed patience and kindness above and beyond the call of duty. More important than her valued skills as an agent is her integrity, judgment, and unfailing good humor.

I wish to thank Bill Guthrie and Wells Drorbaugh for encouragement and advice at critical stages of this lengthy project. And special thanks to Bill Guthrie for introducing me to Ray Lincoln.

Sonja and Valentine Bargmann and Otto Nathan kindly read the entire manuscript. Robert Goldman, Kate Sayen Leader, John B. O'Neil, and Louise F. Sayen read significant portions. All offered criticisms and advice which greatly improved upon my efforts and for which I am profoundly grateful. Naturally, any shortcomings are mine alone.

Ehud Benamy of the American Friends of the Hebrew University graciously handled arrangements to permit me to quote material, both published and unpublished, from the Einstein Archives now in the possession of the Hebrew University of Jerusalem.

My typist, Alice Kass, showed great good humor and patience with my deadlines and barely legible scrawl.

Other friends who have made indispensable contributions are Robert Goldman, Robert Axelrod, John O'Neil, H. H. Ashley, Jr., and Leona Stewart.

Finally, I would like to thank my family for love, support, and moral guidance.

Grateful acknowledgment is made to those publishers and individuals who have permitted the use of extracts from the following materials in copyright.

The Life and Work of Sigmund Freud, Volume 3: The Last Phase, 1919–1939, by Ernest Jones. Reprinted by permission; copyright © 1957 Basic Books, Inc.

"Einstein and Israel" by Sir Isaiah Berlin in *Albert Einstein: Historical and Cultural Perspectives: The Centennial Symposium in Jerusalem,* ed. Gerald Holton and Yehuda Elkana, Princeton University Press, copyright © 1982 by permission of Sir Isaiah Berlin.

"Reflections on Einstein's 100th Birthday," by Hyman Hartman, *The Bulletin of the Atomic Scientists,* December 1979. Reprinted by permission of *The Bulletin of the Atomic Scientists,* a magazine of science and public affairs. Copyright © 1979 by the Educational Foundation for Nuclear Science, Chicago, IL 60637.

Prometheus Bound by Aeschylus, trans. David Grene in *Greek Tragedies: Volume I,* ed. David Grene and Richmond Lattimore, copyright © 1960, by permission of The University of Chicago Press.

Stephen S. Wise: Servant of the People, Selected Letters, ed. Carl Hermann Voss, copyright © 1969. This material is copyrighted by and used through the courtesy of The Jewish Publication Society of America.

Walter Lippmann and the American Century, by Ronald Steele, copyright © 1980, by permission of Little, Brown and Company.

"The Great Foreigner," by Niccolo Tucci. Reprinted by permission; copyright © 1947, 1975 Niccolo Tucci. Originally in *The New Yorker.*

The Brothers Karamazov, by Fyodor Dostoevsky, trans. David Magarshack, copyright © 1970. Reprinted by permission of Penguin Books Ltd.

The Winning Weapon: The Atomic Bomb in the Cold War 1945–1950, by Gregg Herken, copyright © 1980. Reprinted by permission of Alfred A. Knopf, Inc.

Einstein: His Life and Times, by Philipp Frank, copyright © 1947. Reprinted by permission of Alfred A. Knopf, Inc.

From *The Politics of Rescue: The Roosevelt Administration and the Holocaust,* 1938–1945, by Henry L. Feingold. Copyright © 1970 by Rutgers University, the State University of New Jersey.

From *Albert Einstein: Creator and Rebel*, by Banesh Hoffmann and Helen Dukas. Copyright © 1972 by Banesh Hoffmann and Helen Dukas. Reprinted by permission of Viking Penguin, Inc.

Excerpts reprinted from *Autobiographical Notes: A Centennial Edition*, by Albert Einstein, translated and edited by Paul Arthur Schilpp, by permission of The Open Court Publishing Company, La Salle, Illinois, © 1979 by The Open Court Publishing Company.

Special thanks to the Hebrew University of Jerusalem for permission to quote unpublished as well as previously published material from the Einstein Archives.

EINSTEIN
IN AMERICA

INTRODUCTION

The life of Albert Einstein appears to be a paradox. On the one hand, here is Einstein, the scientific genius who desired nothing more than the opportunity to pursue his investigations into the nature of things in solitude; on the other hand, there is Einstein, champion of numerous unpopular political and social causes, aggressively striving to abolish war, to secure a national homeland for the Jewish people, to place nuclear weapons under international control, and to protect the right of each individual to develop his unique human potential.

The paradox dissolves when we consider something he wrote, but never finished, in the last week of his life:

> In matters concerning truth and justice [he wrote in April 1955] there can be no distinction between big problems and small; for the general principles which determine the conduct of men are indivisible. Whoever is careless with the truth in small matters cannot be trusted in important affairs.
>
> This indivisibility applies not only to moral but also to political problems; for little problems cannot be properly appreciated unless they are understood in their interdependence with big problems.[1]

Einstein's belief in man's ethical imperative to practice truth in all dealings with his fellow man was uncompromising. It was not enough merely to be a critic of those who were careless with the truth; each individual was obliged to work against untruth, injustice, and oppression. Silence was complicity. Einstein's public life was an enactment of this powerful conviction. Never was this truer than in the final decade of his life, which coincided with the first decade of the nuclear age.

1

In an era of uncontrolled nationalism, Einstein was an internationalist. He despised the competition between nations which ultimately led to war; he detested nationalist chauvinism, exploitation, and oppression of one group by another. His willingness to speak his mind on these and many other controversial issues and his uncompromising insistence on truth in even the smallest matters often brought him into conflict with champions of causes he wholeheartedly supported. At various times his outspoken ways upset pacifists, Zionists, socialists, and, on occasion, even scientists who viewed him as their most esteemed colleague. To the causes he supported, Einstein was always willing to give generously of his time and energy. And yet, withal, he was ever a man set apart.

In his relations with other people there was a warmth, geniality, and compassion that was the same for friends and strangers, the famous and the anonymous alike. He had several close and loyal friends but he remained a solitary figure; not even those closest to him could fully penetrate his inner world. This quality is, of course, universal, but Einstein's detachment from ordinary matters was, nevertheless, extraordinary. It manifested itself early in his life and resulted in his lifelong study of the objective physical world beyond the influence of mortals. At the celebration of the sixtieth birthday of the great physicist Max Planck in 1918, Einstein attempted to explain Planck's motives for entering the "temple of science." Not surprisingly his explanation tells us as much about Einstein as about the man he wished to honor:

> . . . I believe with Schopenhauer that one of the strongest motives that leads men to art and science is escape from everyday life with its painful crudity and hopeless dreariness, from the fetters of one's own *ever shifting* [italics added] desires. A finely tempered nature longs to escape from personal life into the world of objective perception and thought: this desire may be compared with the townsman's irresistible longing to escape from his noisy, cramped surroundings into the silence of high mountains, where the eye ranges freely through the still, pure air and fondly traces out the restful contours *apparently built for eternity* [italics added].[2]

All his life Einstein sought to escape the world of ever-shifting desires and to take refuge in "something eternal that lies beyond reach of the hand of fate and of all human delusions."[3] In this realm the scientist, poet, or philosopher tries to make for himself, in a manner uniquely his own, a simplified and intelligible picture of the world which to some degree he then attempts to substitute for the world of experience as a means of overcoming the fetters of his personal life.

In another context he once told a friend, the Austrian novelist Hermann Broch, that in selling himself "body and soul" to science, he had fled from the "I and WE to the IT."[4] His escape from the "merely personal" world of desires, ambitions, and competition was not a means of avoiding his responsibilities as a member of society. In fact, it was his escape from the self-absorption of the "merely personal" that permitted him to approach these questions with independence, detachment, and courage.

His favorite philosopher, perhaps the historical figure he most admired, was the excommunicated Jew, Baruch Spinoza, who lived and died in relative obscurity in Holland in the seventeenth century. Spinoza was a solitary figure who chose poverty and independence over an appointment as a professor of philosophy at Heidelberg University. He earned a meager, but adequate, wage as a lens grinder and died at the age of forty-five from consumption, doubtless aggravated by the fine dust of the ground lenses. Einstein cherished the image of his beloved Spinoza laboring in obscurity and motivated solely by a love for truth. In 1920 he composed a whimsical poetic tribute to the great philosopher which begins:

Wie lieb ich diesen edlen Mann (Oh, how I love this noble soul
Mehr als ich mit Worten sagen kann. More than words can e'er extol.
Doch fuercht ich, dass er bleibt allein I fear though he'll remain alone
Mit seinem strahlenden With shining halo of his own.)
 Heiligenschein.[5]

In his *Ethics* Spinoza wrote: "So far as men live in conformity with the guidance of reason, in so far only do they always necessarily agree in nature."[6] For Einstein, the answers to all questions were to be found in nature. As a youth in Italy he had enjoyed his first taste of freedom walking in the Alps. Later, in the Swiss mountains, his bond with nature deepened and throughout his years in Berlin and Princeton, he remained a worshiper of fields and forests, lakes and mountain streams, the earth and the sky. He turned to nature for consolation, for strength, and for insight. When absorbed in scientific labor (as he always was), he frequently wandered alone on some back road or in some nearby wood, oblivious to his surroundings, but quickened by the serene atmosphere of the natural world, far removed from the troubles of men.

With this love of nature came an insatiable yearning to understand "the great, eternal riddle"[7] of the working of the universe. Curiosity coupled with stubborn persistence drove him to seek the most fundamental properties of light, energy, gravity, and matter. But his gaze was not, in a manner of speaking, fixed upon the heavens alone. As is common with members of the brotherhood of science, he would, while walking in the woods, ask questions such as, "How do we explain the meandering of rivers?"; when by the sea, he wondered, "Why is sand solid when wet but muddy when submerged in water?"; and, "Why does the wind die down at sunset?" This last question had a particular significance for Einstein, whose only other form of recreation besides walking was sailing.

Alone in nature he experienced a liberating and tranquilizing sense of happiness that was, to use his own word, "marvelous" for thinking. Solitude, for one like Einstein, was essential. "Whether it be a work of art or a significant scientific achievement," he wrote in 1934, "that which is great and noble comes from the solitary personality."[8] He would have been happy, he claimed, living as a lighthouse keeper. There, isolated from the world of men, surrounded by sky and the rhythmic wash of the sea, he would have been able to pursue his scientific investigations and reveries without disturbance. In addition, he would be performing a useful service to society and he would enjoy independence from academic pressure to produce results. Spinoza, the lens grinder, was his model. Most scientists need contact with colleagues and peers; Einstein enjoyed the contact, but did not require it. After he became world famous, this yearning for solitude grew in proportion to the ever-increasing demands upon his time and energy that attended fame.

In nature were to be found peace and harmony, the incessant, hypnotic rhythms of the wind, the waves, and the swaying trees. In nature, too, there is an elemental force, a fury that reminds man of his place in the scheme of things. While crossing the Atlantic to spend a term at the California Institute of Technology, Einstein recorded in his travel diary on December 10, 1931:

> Never before have I lived through a storm like the one this night. . . . The sea has a look of indescribable grandeur, especially when the sun falls on it.
> One feels as if one is dissolved and merged into Nature. Even more than usual, one feels the insignificance of the individual, and it makes one happy.[9]

This primal force of nature, which manifests itself in storms, earthquakes, and floods, has a counterpart in the life of every human being. When Einstein's son-in-law, Rudolf Kayser, writing under the pseudonym of Anton Reiser, published the first reliable Einstein biography in 1930, Einstein wrote in the preface:

> I found the facts of the book duly accurate, and its characterization, throughout, as good as might be expected of one who is perforce himself, and who can no more be another than I can.
> What has perhaps been overlooked is the irrational, the inconsistent, the droll, even the insane, which nature, inexhaustively operative, implants in an individual, seemingly for her own amusement. But these things are singled out only in the crucible of one's own mind.[10]

These remarks point to the inherent deficiencies in the art of biography: We are all strangers to the inner world of another, and although this biographical study attempts to understand the whys and the wherefores of Einstein's nonscientific activities, it is the work not of Einstein but of "another."

The primary focus of the following pages will be upon the nonscientific life of Einstein during the Princeton years. Of particular interest is his response to the events of his time, especially the rise of Nazism, the destruction of European Jewry, the Second World War, the development and use of atomic weapons, the Cold War, and McCarthyism. An integral element of this study is the public image of Einstein—that is to say, the Einstein myth. What is its basis? When is it essentially valid? When is it misleading? When is it false? And how did it influence his actions and his effectiveness? The private life, insofar as it can be studied from Einstein's writings and the testimony of close friends and colleagues, will also be examined to see what light it may shed on his values and actions.

Einstein was a unique phenomenon: a theoretical scientist whose area of expertise was far removed from the everyday concerns of his fellow mortals, a man without interest or training in the workings of politics who, nevertheless, by the sheer force of his character, came to play a critical role in the public life of his epoch as preeminent moral figure of the Western world.

1

"Noch Ungehängt" (Not Yet Hanged) (1933)

The story of Albert Einstein's life in Princeton, New Jersey, from 1933 to 1955, begins on an inauspicious note. In August 1932 the newly founded Institute for Advanced Study, which would commence operations in Princeton in the autumn of 1933, announced that Einstein had accepted a life appointment and would spend six months of every year in Princeton. In October 1932 the California Institute of Technology announced that Einstein would be visiting the Pasadena, California, institution for the third consecutive winter term.

On his previous visits to America, the celebrated physicist had traveled on a special visa as a representative of the Weimar Republic. By late 1932 the democratic Weimar experiment was dead, and Germany, in the throes of the depression, would soon turn to Adolf Hitler for salvation. Einstein, therefore, applied for a visa to the United States as a private citizen.

In November the Woman Patriot Corporation, a group of women who had fought against women's suffrage, notified the Department of State that Einstein was a member of more Communist groups than Stalin himself. The patriotic ladies, since the defeat of their original cause, had turned their energies against the child labor amendment; they had also drawn up a speakers' blacklist for the Daughters of the American Revolution, and had supported the effort to keep undesirable aliens out of the United States. Among their targets were the grandson of Karl Marx and Albert Einstein, who, they charged, was a "German Bolshevik."

Einstein's outspoken support of pacifism, Zionism, and human rights had antagonized the most conservative elements in America on his earlier visits. The prospect that this alien might become a semipermanent resident of the United

States by virtue of his affiliation with the Institute for Advanced Study provoked the Woman Patriot Corporation to action.

On November 22, 1932, Mrs. Randolph Frothingham, the president of this group, submitted a sixteen-page brief outlining the legal basis of their request that Einstein be barred from entering the country, stating that Einstein was the leader of the "anarcho-communist" program to "shatter" the "military machinery" of the existing governments as a "preliminary condition" for a worldwide people's revolution. They charged that he was affiliated with at least three anarchist and Communist organizations: the World Congress Against Imperialist War, the Workers' International Relief, and War Resisters International, a group they characterized as "Revolutionary Radicals."

The patriotic women noted that, although his scientific and religious views could not be used to prevent his entry into America, he had "promoted 'lawless confusion' to 'shatter' the Church as well as the State—and to leave, if possible, even the laws of nature and the principles of science in 'confusion and disorder' and subject to revision with every new proclamation of an 'Einstein theory!' " His "frequently revised theory of 'relativity,' " Mrs. Frothingham wrote, "is of no more practical importance than the answer to the old academic riddle, 'how many angels can stand on the point of a needle if angels do not occupy space.' "

She noted that he "apparently cannot talk English," and that he "promotes 'confusion and disorder' [her definition of anarchy], doubt and disbelief, and advises, advocates, or teaches individual 'resistance' to all accepted authorities *except Einstein,* whether it be a question of peace or war, government or religion, mathematics or anthrolgy [*sic*]!"[1] Einstein's pacifism was especially offensive to Mrs. Frothingham's group, and his flippant suggestion that "the patriotic women ought to be sent to the front in the next war instead of the men" could only have strengthened their resolve to bar his return to the United States.

After Einstein learned of the attack by the Woman Patriot Corporation, he issued the following reply on December 3, 1932:

> Never yet have I experienced from the fair sex such energetic rejection of all advances; or if I have, never from so many at once.
>
> But are they not quite right, these watchful citizenesses? Why should one open one's doors to a person who devours hardboiled capitalists with as much appetite and gusto as the Cretan Minotaur in days gone by devoured luscious Greek maidens, and on top of that is low-down enough to reject every sort of war, except the unavoidable war with one's own wife? Therefore give heed to your clever and patriotic womenfolk and remember that the Capitol of mighty Rome was once saved by the cackling of its faithful geese.[2]

The story does not end at this juncture. The State Department, faithfully following proper bureaucratic procedures, passed the accusation on to the U.S. Consulate in Berlin, which was responsible for the decision to issue visas to German citizens traveling to the United States.

As luck would have it, the American Consul, George Messersmith, was away from Berlin during the week of December 3–9, 1932, and the task of granting a visa to Einstein and his wife, Elsa, fell to Messersmith's assistant, Raymond B. Geist.

On December 5 Einstein was called to the consulate to answer a series of questions regarding his application. Although this was a standard procedure, Einstein had previously been spared this formality, and he did not understand that Geist was merely discharging his duty.

"What is your political creed?" Geist asked. Einstein could give no answer.

"Are you a member of any organization?"

"Oh, yes! I am a War Resister."

"What is the purpose of your visit to the United States?"

"I want to do some scientific work," Einstein replied with growing exasperation. At this point he asked testily, "Do you gentlemen believe I have to go to the United States? It is not necessary."

The interview lasted approximately forty-five minutes, until Consul Geist asked: "What party do you belong to or sympathize with?" Einstein did not understand the question. "For instance," Geist continued, "are you a Communist or an anarchist?"

The *New York Times* reported the next day that Einstein exploded. "What's this, an inquisition? Is this an attempt at chicanery?" Reminding his interrogator that he had not asked to go to America but, rather, American scientists had begged him to visit, he stated that if he was to enter the United States as "a suspect" he would prefer to cancel the trip. He refused to answer any further questions and issued an ultimatum that his visa be granted by noon the following day or he would remain in Berlin.

Later that day, his sense of humor returned, and he told a newsman, "Wouldn't it be funny if they wouldn't let me in? Why, the whole world would laugh at America." By this time the press had picked up the story and the consulate became a target of international ridicule. The visa was issued the next morning, and Einstein could now laugh over his encounter with red tape.[3]

Einstein was in Pasadena on January 30, 1933, the day President von Hindenburg appointed Adolf Hitler Chancellor of Germany. Einstein had long been vilified in the Nazi press as one of the leaders of the "Jewish world conspiracy," and though it would be some weeks before Hitler successfully completed his "legal" seizure of authority in the aftermath of the highly suspicious burning of the Reichstag building on February 27, Einstein's sojourn in Pasadena was fortuitous because in the violent atmosphere which accompanied the Nazis' swift rise to power, Einstein, the most loved and the most despised living Jew, might have been a prime candidate for assassination.

Einstein never set foot on his native soil after Hitler seized control of Germany. He remained in Pasadena until the middle of March 1933, maintaining a guarded silence to avoid providing the Nazis with ammunition in their anti-Semitic campaigns. In February he informed the Prussian Academy of Science that he would not deliver a lecture scheduled shortly after his return. He still did not know where he would go when, on March 10, he broke his public silence by granting a newspaper interview. "As long as I have any choice in the matter," he told Evelyn Seeley of the *New York World Telegram and Sun,* "I shall live only in a country where civil liberty, tolerance and equality of all citizens before the laws prevail." Speculating that he would probably go to Switzerland, he added, "My citizenship is a strange affair. Although my real citizenship is Swiss, I am a German citizen on account of my official position. However, for an internationally minded man citizenship of a specific country is not important. Humanity is more important than national citizenship."[4]

Albert and Elsa Einstein left Pasadena on March 11, traveling by train first to Chicago and then to New York. At both stops he engaged in Zionist and pacifist activities, but on a subdued scale. They were scheduled to sail for Europe on the evening of March 17. That morning they motored to Princeton for lunch with Princeton University mathematician Oswald Veblen, who had preceded Einstein as one of the charter faculty members at the Institute for Advanced Study.

Upon the Einsteins' return to Manhattan, they had to prepare for a dinner at the Waldorf-Astoria which was designed to draw attention to the scheduled publication of a collection of his pacifist writings entitled *The Fight Against War.* At a question-and-answer session at the dinner, he made his first direct public criticism of Hitler's regime by criticizing the German Academy of Art for its treatment of such prominent artists as Heinrich Mann and Käthe Kollwitz who, early in February 1933, had signed a public letter calling on socialists and Communists to rise above their long-standing feud and pool their resources in the upcoming March elections to prevent Germany from "sinking into barbarism."[5] Einstein also pointed out that pacifists were now considered enemies of the state.

Hitler's swift seizure of absolute authority in February and March was supported by monarchists and key figures in industry and bathed in an aura of legality. Five days after assuming the chancellorship, Hitler instituted press censorship. On March 23, while Einstein was still at sea, the Reichstag passed the Enabling Act in which it surrendered all its powers to Hitler, making him Germany's dictator. He had already put the police under the control of Nazi thugs, and personal liberty had been suspended after the Reichstag fire. Anyone "disturbing the peace" could be arrested and disposed of at the Führer's whim.

Eight days later, the war against the Jews began. As a reaction to scattered anti-Nazi economic boycotts outside Germany, Hitler decreed a three-day boycott of Jewish businesses because, the Nazis asserted, "international Jewry" was responsible for "atrocity propaganda."[6] On the first day of the boycott, the flight of German Jews began. Among them was Helen Dukas, Einstein's secretary since 1928. On April 7 Hitler promulgated laws that excluded Jews and Communists from holding positions in the civil service, the universities, and the legal profession. Eighteen days later the "Law Against the Overcrowding of German Schools and Institutions of Higher Learning" limited the Jews to a quota of 1.5 percent of the places in German schools. The first book burnings of Jewish and liberal authors took place on May 10.

The response of the German Jews to this wave of persecution was a mixture of horror and disbelief. In 1933 there were 500,000 Jews in Germany, approximately one-fifth of whom were Eastern European. In the first year of the Nazi reign, 37,000 emigrated to Western Europe, the United States, and Palestine, although in 1933 the Zionists excluded anti-Zionists from Palestine. Most of the emigrants were intellectuals, civil servants, the affluent, and leftist Jews, who would have been incarcerated in the newly constructed concentration camp at Dachau. Those who remained in Germany either could not afford to emigrate, could not secure a visa to another country, or, in the vast majority of cases, simply did not believe that the crude violence of the Nazis could last very long. Assimilated Jews in particular initially responded to Nazi nationalism by emphasizing their own German identity. Until 1938, because of the mistaken belief that the Nazis could be accommodated, emigration never exceeded 25,000 in one year.[7]

While Einstein was on the Atlantic the Nazis raided his summer villa at Caputh, outside Berlin, claiming that they had reason to suspect that arms might be hidden there. From shipboard, Einstein denounced the raid "by an armed crowd" as "but one example of the arbitrary acts of violence" that had resulted from "the government's overnight transfer of police powers to a raw and rabid mob of the Nazi militia."[8] A few days later his bank account was seized to prevent its being used "for treasonable purposes."

On March 29 he disembarked at Antwerp, drove to Brussels to surrender his German passport, and then wrote a letter of resignation to the Prussian Academy of Science, which was on the verge of expelling him for having spread "atrocity stories" about Germany at a time when, the academy maintained, it had been his duty to defend Germany against such "absurd" fabrications. Although disappointed by the action of the academy, he was not surprised, and on April 7 he composed a poem addressed to that distinguished body which contains these verses:

Wer da Greuelmaerchen dichtet, (Whoever writes grim fairy tales
Grimmig wird von uns gerichtet, Will end up in our harshest jails.
Wenn er gar die Wahrheit spricht, But if he dares the truth to tell,
Dann verzeihen wirs ihm nicht. We'll cast his soul down into hell.)

* * *　　　　　　　　　　* * *

Mutig sind wir dann und wann, (Courageous are we now and then
Wenn uns nichts passieren kann, When danger doesn't threaten,
Doch vor maecht'gen Poebels Knute But when the mob begins to rage
Wird uns manchmal schwach We sometimes lose our courage.)
zumute.[9]

Severing ties with the officials of the academy may have had its amusing side, but a letter from Einstein's close friend and colleague, Max Planck, "our beloved Planck," telling Einstein that his resignation had "spared Einstein's friends immeasurable grief," jolted him to the unpleasant realization that even his friends were prepared to bow to Nazi pressure on this issue. On April 6 Einstein, obviously deeply hurt, wrote to Planck denying the accusation of "atrocity-mongering" and warning, "There will come a time when decent Germans will be ashamed of the ignominious way in which I have been treated."

> I cannot help but remind you [he continued] that, in all these years, I have only enhanced Germany's prestige and never allowed myself to be alienated by the systematic attacks on me in the rightist press, especially those of recent years when no one took the trouble to stand up for me. Now, however, the war of annihilation against my defenseless fellow Jews compels me to employ, in their behalf, whatever influence I may possess in the eyes of the world.

The letter concluded on a conciliatory note to the effect that "in spite of severe pressures from without, the relationship between us has not been affected."[10] At this moment Einstein must have reflected upon the many attractive offers of academic chairs outside Germany he had turned down after 1918 because of his promise to Planck and other friends that he would remain in Berlin as long as political conditions permitted.

By virtue of his scientific eminence Planck was one of the leading figures of the German scientific community. Bonds of friendship, both professional and personal, were strong between Einstein and Planck, but Einstein found his colleague's conservative and nationalistic outlook unpalatable. Although Planck disliked the National Socialists, he found it very difficult to oppose them publicly. When Otto Hahn (the scientist whose splitting of the uranium atom in 1938 marked the onset of the nuclear age) approached Planck shortly after the Nazi takeover with a petition protesting the treatment of German professors, the elder scientist refused to sign because he feared the opposition would probably be able to gather many more signatures in support of Hitler's policies.

In May 1933, as President of the Kaiser Wilhelm Institute, Planck paid a courtesy call on the new head of state. He took this opportunity to try to persuade Hitler to stop the purge of Jewish scientists because it was endangering the superiority of German science. Hitler worked himself into a frenzy, equating Jews with Bolsheviks and then asserted that if it were necessary to annihilate "contemporary German science, then we shall do without science for a few years!" The intimidated Planck fell silent, and German scientists, cognizant of Hitler's tirade, never openly challenged Nazi science.[11]

Einstein's response to his expulsion from the Prussian Academy was based less upon feelings of the injustice done to him personally than upon feelings of disgust with the behavior of the "representatives of the scientific world [who] have failed in their duty to defend intellectual values because they have completely lost their passionate love of them."[12] Although he missed the scientific environment of Berlin, he was not particularly upset at leaving Germany itself; in fact his friend and biographer, the physicist Philipp Frank, suggests that in some respects he experienced a "psychological liberation."[13] Even the seizure of his private property, although reprehensible, was ultimately of no great consequence to Einstein.

The moral cowardice of the intellectual community in response to Nazi violence aimed at the Jews and the destruction of the rights of the individual, however, was intolerable to him.

Einstein derived a slight measure of consolation from the actions of his colleagues Max von Laue and Walter Nernst, who defended him from attacks by the Prussian Academy. Einstein especially esteemed Laue, who remained in Germany, continued to associate with Jewish friends, and openly ridiculed Nazi policies, particularly their perverted "Aryan science."

It took the Nazis less than half a decade to tear out the heart of Weimar culture by killing or driving into exile a great number of the outstanding scholars and artists of pre-Nazi Germany. Party membership became the most important criterion for appointment to a university. Individuals like Philipp Lenard gained control of the sciences and, by promoting racial dogma and hysteria, emasculated the great German scientific tradition. Lenard, the 1905 Nobel Laureate in Physics, had become psychologically unhinged by the German defeat in the First World War, and was one of the first intellectuals to support the rising Nazi Party. Since 1920 he had joined with anti-Semitic scientific hacks to attack Einstein's theories and character, and in 1922 he protested the award of the Nobel Prize to Einstein. When Hitler came to power, Lenard's scientific philosophy gained prominence. Like most Nazi rhetoric, his diatribes today read like self-parody, but in 1933 he was deadly serious, and he was supported by the ignorance and hatred th' sustained the Nazis in power. Writing for the Nazi paper, *Völkischer Beobachter,* Lenard proclaimed:

> The most important example of the dangerous influence of Jewish circles on the study of nature has been provided by Herr Einstein with his mathematically botched-up theories consisting of some ancient knowledge and a few arbitrary additions. *This theory now gradually falls to pieces, as is the fate of all products that are estranged from nature* [italics added].[14]

Lenard reproached German scientists who allowed relativity to be taught in Germany "because they did not see, or did not want to see, how wrong it is, outside the field of science also, to regard this Jew as a good German."[15] The elements of Einstein's work that were irrefutable, for instance, $E = mc^2$, Lenard ingeniously declared, had been promulgated by Friedrich Hasenohrl, a gifted Austrian physicist of non-Jewish stock who had died in the war. Hasenohrl had derived the relationship $E = mc^2$ for the specific case of a cavity of radiation, but he would have been disgusted by Lenard's action, which sought to elevate this martyr of Aryan science to the status of Galileo (not Newton, because Lenard detested the English almost as much as the Jews).

Another guiding light of the Nazi philosophy of science and education was Ernst Krieck, whom the Nazis installed as rector of the University of Frankfurt. Mincing no words, Krieck asserted: "It is not science that must be restricted, but rather the scientific investigators and teachers; only scientifically talented men who have pledged their entire personality to the nation, to the racial conception of the world, and to the German mission will teach and carry on research at the German universities."[16] Since pure-blooded German youth could be taught only by pure-blooded teachers, the first step was to purge the schools and universities of Jewish teachers, professors, and students. As a result, 25 percent of the German physicists for the academic year 1932–1933 were dismissed, and many non-Jews, as well, fled Germany.

Where could these scholars go? They were of all ages and stages in their careers. A few, like Einstein, had little difficulty securing positions in England, the United States, or elsewhere. Most, however, were lesser known or just starting out in their careers, and the demand for these intellectual workers was slight. The worldwide depression exacerbated the situation, making for a scarcity of new jobs, and parochialism often ensured that refugee scholars would be less than welcome whenever it appeared that they might be taking jobs away from indigenous scholars.

Shortly after his return to Europe Einstein settled in the small Belgian seaside resort of Le Coq-sur-mer, near Ostend, where German U-boats had been based in the First World War. There, with Elsa, daughter Margot, Helen Dukas, and Walter Mayer, his mathematical assistant, he witnessed the collapse of German culture while enjoying the serene beauty of Le Coq. Margot Einstein, who, like Miss Dukas, had escaped from Germany around the time of the boycott, later recalled two images of her father during that summer. She remembers his amused response to a rather homely little six- or seven-year-old girl who regularly waited for him to appear on his walks. Each time he passed she would rudely call him a "dope." Miss Einstein also remembers the suffering on his face. "When he was with his work, thinking . . . his expression was so quiet, and he was far away, but when he was suffering inside, you could see it in his face."[17]

Einstein spent the summer of 1933 in Le Coq doing what he could to assist the first victims of the Nazis, his refugee status symbolic of the collapse of civilization in Germany. Friends and strangers alike turned to him for consolation, and to one acquaintance, a musician from Munich, he wrote on April 5, 1933:

> . . . Read no newspapers, try to find a few friends who think as you do, read the wonderful writers of earlier times, Kant, Goethe, Lessing and the classics of other lands, and enjoy the natural beauties of Munich's surroundings. Make believe all the time that you are living, so to speak, on Mars among alien creatures and blot out any deeper interest in the actions of those creatures. Make friends with a few animals. Then you will become a cheerful man once more and nothing will be able to trouble you.
> Bear in mind that those who are finer and nobler are always alone—and necessarily so—and that because of this they can enjoy the purity of their own atmosphere.[18]

Although his whereabouts in Belgium were supposed to be a secret, numerous refugees made their way to Le Coq to seek advice and assistance from the man who had become the symbol of the Jewish victims of the Nazis. To them he was the *Wunderrabbi*.[19] He was particularly distressed by the plight of the unknown scholars; "my heart aches at the thought of the young ones,"[20] he wrote to his friend, the physicist Max Born, in May. The situation was all the more painful for him because he had been showered with offers from Paris, Madrid, Leiden, and Oxford, where he already held a part-time position. Despite his previous commitments, he accepted the French and Spanish offers because he saw them as gestures against Hitler's policies, and he felt obligated to reciprocate these acts of good will. To Maurice Solovine, a compatriot from the happy days in Berne, he confessed his dilemma: "I have more professors' chairs by now than reasonable ideas in my head. The devil take it all!"[21]

In response to the crisis of the younger scholars he briefly toyed with the idea of starting up a liberal university in England or America to assist the unknown refugees. Another avenue of hope was Hebrew University in Jerusalem, but to his regret, it was trying to attract well-known scholars, whereas Einstein felt that the Jewish University in Palestine—a land of refugees—ought to give shelter to those who were most in need.

Einstein had severed connections with Hebrew University in 1928 in a dispute over the management and direction of the academic aspects of the university, refusing all reconciliatory overtures until his proposed reforms had been implemented.[22] There had been no change in the situation when, in April 1933, Chaim Weizmann, president of the World Zionist Organization, invited Einstein to join the faculty at Hebrew University. Einstein declined, citing "devastating" criticisms of the administration. Then in an interview with the Jewish Telegraphic Agency he repeated his criticisms and divulged for the first time his resignation from the Academic Council in 1928. An angry Weizmann wrote him from Cairo that under the circumstances Einstein's criticisms were ill-timed and not entirely fair. Einstein admitted on May 7 that he had been rude to Weizmann, but repeated his criticisms and said that as long as Chancellor Judah Magnes remained in charge of academic matters, he could not think of coming to Jerusalem.

Early in June Weizmann tried another ploy: Would Einstein help create the physics department at the institute Weizmann was founding at Rehovot (now called the Weizmann Institute)? Einstein again refused, adding that a new institute was superfluous and that it was unwise to separate the sciences from the existing university. In most speeches during this period Weizmann mentioned Einstein's name. In America on June 29 at a meeting of the American Jewish Physicians Committee he told a questioner that he still had hopes of luring Einstein to Jerusalem. Einstein then told the Jewish Telegraphic Agency that Weizmann had misled the public and "he knows, too, under what circumstances I would be prepared to undertake work for the Hebrew University."[23] Weizmann chose to interpret this statement to mean that if the necessary changes were made Einstein would at last come. He announced, therefore, three days later, that Einstein had agreed to accept a position at the university. He then set about organizing a commission of inquiry into the university, somehow convincing himself that Einstein would now be satisfied. Einstein, however, had stated his position and he refused to reconsider. A survey commission, created in October, subsequently echoed Einstein's criticisms, and in 1935 reforms were implemented which pleased Einstein immensely.

In the spring of 1933 Jews outside Germany were confronted with the sensitive issue of how best to respond to acts of terror against German Jews. While there was great danger that any critical statements made by Jews would be used as an excuse to intensify the existing oppressive measures, silence was impossible. Einstein realized that the Western democracies would be more likely to take measures against Hitler because he was rearming Germany than because he espoused anti-Semitic policies. Consequently, Einstein urged leading American Jews and others sympathetic to the plight of the Jews to concentrate their activities in well-organized, behind-the-scenes efforts to educate the American government and media about the rearmament in Germany, where factories were working night and day, millions of men were undergoing military training, and secrecy was being enforced by means of terror. Einstein supported the creation of a commercial blockade against Germany, which might cause the collapse of Hitler's government without recourse to bloodshed.

Einstein had taken refuge in Belgium at the invitation of King Albert and Queen Elizabeth. He first met "the Kings" (his way of referring to the royal couple) in 1929 and a lasting friendship had developed. In May 1933 he visited the royal palace in Laeken on at least three occasions, during which he and the queen played string quartets. She had been born in Bavaria and was an accomplished artist. King Albert was beloved by his subjects for his courageous stance against Germany in the First World War. Einstein found them simple, modest, informal, and highly intelligent. King Albert died in a mountain-climbing accident in 1934, but throughout Einstein's lifetime he maintained a correspondence of rare beauty with Elizabeth.

While he strolled along the beaches of Le Coq with Walter Mayer, working on his unified field theory, Einstein was struggling in his conscience over the issue of pacifisim. In spite of such statements as the one he had given to a Czechoslovakian journal in 1929 that in the event of another war, "I would unconditionally refuse all war service, direct or indirect, and would seek to persuade my friends to adopt the same position, regardless of how I might feel about the causes of any particular war,"[24] the advent of Hitler forced him to reconsider. In June a French pacifist, Alfred Nahon, urged him to appear as a defense witness for two Belgian conscientious objectors who were soon to stand trial for violation of the conscription laws. Even before he received Nahon's request, Einstein had shifted away from absolute pacifisim. In May he wrote to Rabbi Stephen S. Wise, a leading American Zionist, that an internationalization of military force was necessary to prevent war. On July 1, he advised Lord Ponsonby, a British pacifist, "in the present situation we must support a *supranational* organization of force rather than advocate the abolition of all forces."[25]

King Albert, when he learned of Einstein's possible intervention in the trial of the conscientious objectors, discreetly arranged to meet with him on an off-the-record basis. What they discussed can only be inferred from the exchange of letters that took place afterward. Undoubtedly, the king emphasized that the army of a small country like Belgium was defensive in nature, and in light of the events of

1914–1918 and the current rapid rearmament of Germany, it was essential that Belgium be prepared to defend itself against a new invasion. The discussion may also have touched upon alternate forms of service for conscientious objectors, and it is possible that the king gently reminded his friend that as a guest of Belgium he ought to be careful about intervening in its judicial affairs.

Finally, on July 20, Einstein wrote to tell Nahon of his decision:

> What I shall tell you will greatly surprise you. Until quite recently we in Europe could assume that personal war resistance constituted an effective attack on militarism. Today we face an altogether different situation. In the heart of Europe lies a power, Germany, that is obviously pushing toward war with all available means. This has created such a serious danger to the Latin countries, especially Belgium and France, that they have come to depend completely on their armed forces. As for Belgium, surely so small a country cannot possibly misuse its armed forces; rather it needs them

Einstein with King Albert of Belgium, 1933. King Albert died in a mountain-climbing accident the next year. (Courtesy of Margot Einstein)

desperately to protect its very existence. Imagine Belgium occupied by present-day Germany! Things would be far worse than in 1914, and they were bad enough even then. Hence I must tell you candidly: Were I a Belgian, I should not, in the present circumstances, refuse military service; rather, I should enter such service cheerfully in the belief that I would thereby be helping to save European civilization.

This does not mean that I am surrendering the principle for which I have stood heretofore. I have no greater hope than that the time may not be far off when refusal of military service will once again be an effective method of serving the cause of human progress.[26]

Reaction was swift and emotional. A leading British pacifist sadly noted it was "a great blow to our cause." One pacifist organization branded Einstein an apostate who had "done unutterable harm to the fight against militarism." Lord Ponsonby, in defense of pacifism, wrote to Einstein: "Hitler's methods may be insane and criminal, but I am firmly convinced he is not such a fool as to think he could gain anything for Germany by waging war against another country." The French pacifist Romain Rolland accused Einstein in his diary of "weakness of spirit" and of irresponsibility "for having indoctrinated blind and confident youth without sufficient consideration of all implications." Conceding Einstein's scientific genius, Rolland nevertheless accused him of being "weak, indecisive and inconsistent outside [science]."[27]

Einstein remained a pacifist at heart, but his realistic appraisal of the danger posed by the Nazis compelled him to act as he did because, as he wrote to one of his critics, "in the hope of avoiding war, I cannot go so far as to accept the permanent destruction of all our intellectual and political traditions."[28] The editors of *Einstein on Peace* perceptively note that "he never failed to distinguish between strategy and principle."[29] After 1933 he remained true to the principle of a world free from war, but he abandoned the strategy of individual resistance to war when he realized that such a policy ensured the destruction of civilization.

The letter to Nahon marks a turning point in Einstein's political thinking. In 1933, Einstein's world collapsed. He was summarily cut off from the extraordinary collection of Berlin scientists and forced to uproot himself and family at an age when such forced changes are no longer easily adapted to. But his personal tragedy paled in light of the growing threat against his fellow Jews. He was one of the first people to recognize the intentions of the Nazis toward both Jews and Europe itself. Firsthand knowledge of their hatred, their irrational appeal to the dispossessed of Germany, and Hitler's mastery of mass political psychology convinced Einstein that only organized force could thwart Hitler's movement. Einstein's earlier pacifism had been a deeply personal expression of his antipathy to all forms of killing, and of his conviction that war could be abolished by a rational process of education and an appeal to men's finer instincts. Prior to 1933, he had believed, perhaps naïvely, that the example of enlightened individuals, notably his fellow intellectuals, could educate the masses to the need to abolish war. The rise of Hitler taught him to appreciate the vulnerability of the individual and the necessity of a more organized approach to political problems. In 1915, he had written that the state played no greater role in his life than his life insurance company. In 1933, he acknowledged that prevention of war would require a more explicitly political approach: a unification of national forces rather than the abolition of force.[30]

A few days after writing the letter to Nahon, Einstein paid a brief visit to England. He visited Churchill at Chartwell and was greatly impressed. "He is an eminently wise man," Einstein wrote to his wife; "it became very clear to me that these people have made their plans well ahead and are determined to act *soon*. . . ."[31] Einstein could not foresee that Churchill was to be excluded from the cabinet by the appeasers until after Hitler had invaded Poland.

The Belgian government had provided Einstein with two bodyguards, a state of affairs which both amused and annoyed him. As the summer wore on Elsa became more and more worried about her husband's safety. In Germany the Nazis had circulated a book of photographs of enemies of the state, and under Einstein's picture was the ominous caption "Noch Ungehängt" (not yet hanged). When he learned that a bounty of 20,000 marks ($5,000) had been placed upon his head he laughed. "I did not know it was worth so much." He did not take the threats seriously because, he joked, "When a bandit is going to commit a crime he keeps it a secret."[32] Nevertheless, on September 9, at Elsa's request he again crossed the Channel to England, where he spent his last month on European soil in the solitude of the country home of a member of Parliament.

Late in September, Einstein received yet another bitter piece of news from the Continent. The physicist Paul Ehrenfest, possibly Einstein's closest friend in the preceding two decades, had died in Holland at fifty-three under the most tragic circumstances. The two men had met in Vienna in 1912 and had become "true friends" within a few hours, "as though our dreams and aspirations were meant for each other," Einstein wrote in 1934. By all accounts, Ehrenfest was a "lovable character" who was full of optimism and enthusiasm. He and Einstein loved to talk and argue physics in person and by mail. He shared Einstein's internationalist outlook. Einstein enjoyed the happy family life of the Ehrenfests in Leyden, and the two men played piano and violin duets whenever they were together.

Einstein described Ehrenfest as the best teacher of physics he had ever met, a brilliant but unconventional lecturer who was passionately committed to the welfare and development of his students. Ehrenfest believed that discussions and arguments were an essential part of science, and his greatest talent lay in his ability to "strip a theory of its mathematical accouterments until the simple basic idea emerged with clarity." He conducted his "Socratic" discussions with exuberant wit, characteristic gestures and intonation, without fearing to ask stupid questions. On occasion he was rude and could give the impression of arrogance yet, Einstein wrote in a moving obituary, "his tragedy lay precisely in an almost morbid lack of self-confidence. He suffered incessantly from the fact that his critical faculties transcended his constructive capacities. In a manner of speaking, his critical sense robbed him of his love for the offspring of his own mind even before they were born." Einstein blamed much of Ehrenfest's exaggerated self-criticism on ignorant and selfish teachers.

Ehrenfest was loved by friends, students, and colleagues, yet he was an unhappy man, because, Einstein wrote, "he did not feel equal to the lofty task that confronted him." The extraordinary development of physics in the mid- and late twenties exacerbated this condition; Ehrenfest was tortured by the necessity of learning and teaching things which he could not "fully accept in [his] heart." "Added to this," Einstein poignantly contends, "was the increasing difficulty of adaptation to new thoughts which always confronts the man past fifty. I do not know how many readers of these lines will be capable of fully grasping that tragedy."

Ehrenfest was devoted to his family and friends. The upheavals in Europe and especially the tragedy of many of his most cherished friends in Germany, on whose behalf he had labored indefatigably, had left him a profoundly depressed man. A "fateful partial estrangement" from his venerated wife and collaborator proved to be more than he could endure. On September 25, 1933, Paul Ehrenfest shot and blinded his retarded younger son and then took his own life.[33]

On October 3, a week before sailing for America to begin his work at the Institute for Advanced Study, Einstein made his first public appearance in Europe since Hitler's accession to power. He addressed a mass meeting at the Royal Albert Hall in London chaired by the great British physicist Ernest Rutherford,

Paul Ehrenfest, Paul Ehrenfest, Jr., and Einstein at the Ehrenfest home in Leiden, Holland, ca. 1921. Photograph by Willem J. Luyten. (Courtesy of American Institute of Physics Niels Bohr Library)

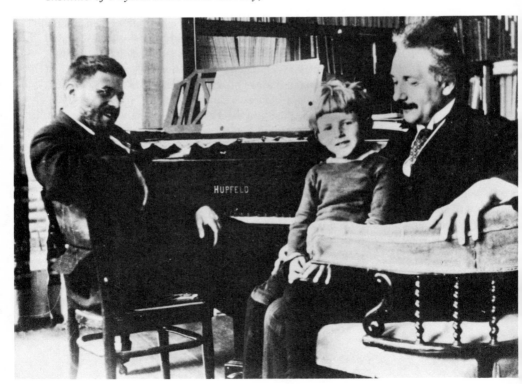

which was sponsored by the Refugee Assistance Fund, an assortment of agencies which had banded together to help refugees. In his talk he avoided direct mention of Germany and spoke instead about the dangerous times and the need to preserve the intellectual and individual freedoms upon which civilization's development and survival depended. In the middle of his speech he extemporaneously interjected the following characteristic idea: "When I was living in solitude in the country, I noticed how the monotony of a quiet life stimulates the creative mind. There are certain occupations, even in modern society, which entail living in isolation and do not require great physical or intellectual effort. Such occupations as the service of lighthouses and lightships come to mind." Could we not, he wondered, place young mathematicians, scientists, and philosophers in such positions? This would help alleviate the crisis existing among the unemployed refugee scholars and, of even greater significance to Einstein, it would permit young people the rare "opportunity to devote themselves undisturbed for any length of time to problems of a scientific nature," while still performing a useful service to society. In this way, they would escape the pressures normally brought to bear upon young research workers to produce results within a given period of time.[34]

In the midst of an otherwise rather ordinary expression of his thoughts on the world crisis, the quintessential Einstein unconsciously slipped in, just as, in his later years, when, speaking in English, he would unconsciously slip into German—the only language he ever felt comfortable speaking.

The comment about the lighthouse is a most revealing, but potentially misleading, statement. It reflects Einstein's attitude to thinking and his approach to theoretical physics. To him, thinking was a very personal endeavor best done in isolation. Late in life he once expressed amazement to a young assistant, Ernst Straus, when they solved a problem by thinking together as though on the same wavelength. He had truly believed this to be impossible. He also had strong reservations about being paid for doing research, in part because he found it peculiar to be paid for doing what came so naturally, so pleasurably; he also felt that the extra demands of teaching and preparing classes distracted from the researcher's freedom of thought. (During the McCarthy era, he would later note, this line of work might subject the individual scholar to interference from political forces attempting to control the values of the creative thinker.)

The years in the Patent Office at Berne from 1902 to 1909 had been a golden period of his life. There he had performed a useful social function, doing a job he enjoyed that challenged his mind in a fruitful way, which was nonetheless entirely removed from the areas of research he was engaged upon in his spare time and, of course, he had performed some of his most important early scientific work. After leaving the Patent Office, he rose to the top of his profession in five years, and for the last forty years of his life he enjoyed the most ideal conditions for research imaginable; and, yet, whether because of the external pressures the positions in Berlin and Princeton subjected him to, or because of some yearning for a lost youth in prewar Switzerland, when he had come of age and enjoyed his first period of discovery in an environment undisturbed by war, injustice, fame, and vilification, he always viewed the days in Berne as a time of innocence and discovery.

The image of a lighthouse keeper, then, represented a genuinely felt desire on his part and, rather innocently, he believed it might appeal to many another young researcher as both a practical and idyllic solution to a hopeless employment situation. It may never have occurred to him that few other scientists and mathematicians could thrive in such extreme isolation. It should be noted that, despite this recurring sentiment, Einstein usually had one or more assistants working with him on a daily basis, and he enjoyed and benefited from contact with the eminent physicists and mathematicians in Princeton and, especially, in Berlin.

Retreat to a lighthouse certainly represents an extreme response to a difficult situation, and Einstein's public expression of such sentiments, coming as it did in October 1933 on the eve of what was to become a permanent, self-imposed exile from Europe, during the first year of the most tragic experience in the history of the Jewish people, and barely a week after the despairing self-destruction of his beloved friend Ehrenfest, presents, indeed, a poignant image. One can only sense the desolation which, despite his long-ago flight from the suffering of the "merely personal," must have gripped him in this hour of fate.

We know Einstein the solitary thinker, the man without roots anywhere, an outsider by choice, belonging with his whole heart to no group, not even his family, and the temptation is overpowering to conclude that here is a lonely figure.

Einstein and Madame Curie, probably outside Geneva, ca. 1929. (Courtesy of AIP Niels Bohr Library)

In fact, he was a solitary figure called to a solitary vocation, but he was not lonely. Even in his later years he enjoyed very close relations with his sister, his step-daughter, and a circle of special friends and co-workers. Nonetheless, he relished his solitude. It is in this connection that his lifelong flight from the I and WE to the IT can be understood. Ernst Straus has stated that when Einstein wished to give fatherly advice, he would say that to be happy one must hitch one's fate to a goal (the IT) not to other things and people (the I and WE). "I think his connection of his life to his goal was a passion so intense," Straus continues, "that by comparison any relation to people certainly pales. . . . I have never seen a relation among human beings that would approach the passion of Einstein's relation to his goal."[35]

Long ago, in a more innocent time, Einstein had committed his destiny to the struggle to understand the laws of the physical world. Now, in October 1933, as Nazism moved to eclipse European civilization, Einstein, in a netherworld between the old life in Europe and the new in America, sought comfort in the notion of retreat to a lighthouse, far removed from the clamor of mortals, where he could, in peace, pursue his goal. Despite the personal anguish and feelings of loneliness he must have suffered in this hour, his response was no bitter, eremitic renunciation of his fellow mortals. Rather, it was the act of an instinctive loner, a scientific dreamer, in search of an environment conducive to healthy, creative thought, who throughout his life had turned to nature for consolation and understanding. Einstein, like the great Spinoza, knew the "liberating feeling"[36] of being alone in the country. His elder son, Hans Albert Einstein, speaking on the BBC in 1965, said, "He did not care for large, impressive mountains, but he liked surroundings that were gentle and colourful and gave one lightness of spirit":[37] rolling hills, rounded mountains, brooks, streams and lakes, the wash of the sea tides—a soothing monotony undisturbed by the world of men bound up in their frantic search for the gratification of personal desires; a realm in which man is the humble visitor, and where God and nature begin to reveal the wonder and majesty of existence.

On October 7 Einstein left Europe forever.

Before commencing the story of Einstein's years in America, let us review very briefly his life from 1879 to 1932 in order that we may acquire an appreciation of the forces and events that shaped his ideas and values.

2

"Impudent Swabian"
(1879–1914)

Albert Einstein was born in southern Germany on March 14, 1879, during an epoch of convulsive technological and industrial development. Germany had been united politically less than a decade earlier under the authoritarian and feudal Prussian monarchy. In little more than a generation Germany was transformed from a rural to an industrial society. The Napoleonic Wars had aroused the first stirrings of defensive nationalism and by 1871, with the unification of Germany, nationalism became a menace to European peace. Basking in the political and economic successes of the second half of the nineteenth century, Germans viewed their great victory over the French as a reward for cultural and moral excellence, a prelude to still greater triumphs. Lost in the excitement was the voice of young Friedrich Nietzsche, who suggested that the true cause of the victory in the Franco-Prussian War had been that the German army exhibited superior organization and technical proficiency.

The Germany of Einstein's youth, dominated by Chancellor Otto von Bismarck, placed the highest value upon militarism and materialism. The Constitution of 1871 contained neither a Bill of Rights nor even a declaration of fundamental liberties. Religious and educational institutions served to buttress the status quo, and those who were viewed as a threat to authority suffered overt and covert repression. While Bismarck ruled he was able to orchestrate the anachronistic government he had shaped, but when he fell from power in 1890, his system, which had stifled every progressive tendency, came under the control of the hotheaded Kaiser and his shortsighted military advisers.

Einstein's ancestors had settled in the south German region of Swabia before 1750. The ancient city of Ulm, where he was born, was small, quiet, and, as yet, unaffected by the industrial and urban revolutions of the nineteenth century. Unlike the sober Prussians, Swabians were simple country folk. They were reflective and speculative, loved art and music, and despised regimentation. Situated near Switzerland, they were peace-loving, moderate, and inclined toward Swiss-German democracy.

A year after Einstein's birth the family moved to Munich, the burgeoning capital of Bavaria. Until the First World War Munich was a cultural center which in many respects surpassed austere Berlin. In the 1880s and 1890s Munich benefited from the growth and prosperity of the era, but its citizens enjoyed a climate of humanism, tolerance, and democracy, which, combined with its natural beauty, made it a haven for artists and writers. In the period after the war, Munich became a refuge for misfits like Adolf Hitler and the other founders of the Nazi Party. The city was more than four-fifths Catholic and, although Einstein was not subjected to the worst excesses of the anti-Semitism of the day, he clearly experienced a sense of not belonging because of his Jewishness.

His parents, Hermann and Pauline (née Koch), like so many of their generation, had turned away from Orthodox Judaism, and although their neglect of the Jewish dietary laws and the father's scoffing at religion upset young Einstein for a period as a boy, the parents provided Albert (the assimilated version of Abraham) and his younger sister Maja (her given name was Maria) a secure and happy environment. Through his parents, Einstein learned to love the best of German culture: the poetry of Heine and Schiller and the music of Mozart, Bach, and Beethoven. Early in his life he developed a deep love of nature on the frequent family excursions to the mountains or upper Bavarian lakes. Hermann Einstein and his business partner, his brother Jacob, an engineer, stimulated the boy's interest in mathematics and science.

Despite the "entirely irreligious"[1] attitude of his parents, Einstein grew up in an environment infused with Jewish values. At the core of Jewish ethics is a love and respect for all that is living; the Jewish tradition teaches that the world depends on justice and that the universe is orderly and rational. For centuries the Jews, disenfranchised and homeless, were called "The People of the Book" because of the value they placed on education, knowledge, and understanding the sacred writings of the Torah.

The emancipation of European Jews from the ghetto in the nineteenth century owed much to the "religion of humanity" of the Enlightenment. Throughout Western Europe, the Enlightenment had led people to question the legitimacy of authority; only Germany had escaped this liberalizing influence.

The experience of homelessness had the effect of turning many Jews away from the narrow nationalism that was the scourge of Europe to a more cosmopolitan and international outlook. Within Germany, as nationalism and the displacement of traditional society by rapid industrialization overwhelmed certain segments of society, anti-Semitic attacks focused upon the *undeutsch* (un-German) qualities of the Jews. Liberation from the ghetto and the accompanying intoxication with new opportunities stimulated the Jewish drive for success and, in the eyes of the anti-Semites, Jews came to symbolize the most ruthless aspects of capitalism. They were alleged to be materialistic, devoid of spirituality and feeling, ultrarationalists who could have no sense of beauty. Historian Lucy Dawidowicz has written that what the Germans hated and feared most in themselves, they projected onto the Jews.[2]

The details of Einstein's childhood are well known. He only started to talk at age three, and his parents were so worried by his slow development that they consulted a doctor. He was a solitary and dreamy child who disliked games and sports, and even when other children were present he tended to play alone. When he did join in their activities, it was as an arbiter and peacemaker who mediated their quarrels. When Albert was four he was taken to see the Royal Guards parade through Munich in their splendid uniforms. While most boys at that time dreamed of becoming soldiers, Einstein wept at the sight of grown men who were forced to wear ridiculous clothes and march in unison.

German schools taught discipline, order, obedience to authority, and a distorted picture of German history. Not surprisingly, the sensitive and independent young Einstein failed to impress his early teachers, although the popular notion that he was a poor student is untrue.

Until he was nine years old Einstein attended a Catholic elementary school where the students were hit on the palms of their hands with a ruler as they learned to count and multiply; this exercise was supposed to teach them the discipline necessary to become obedient citizens of the Reich. Einstein was reticent and considered dull-witted because he required extra time to think and was a poor calculator. He was, however, patient, persevering, and gifted at problem-solving. At the elementary school he encountered anti-Semitism for the first time. "Physical assaults and insults were frequent on the way to school," he wrote in 1920, "though for the most part not really malicious. Even so, however, they were enough to confirm, even in a child of my age, a vivid feeling of not belonging."[3]

In October 1888 he transferred to the Luitpold Gymnasium, a grammar school that, in the humanist tradition, emphasized Latin and Greek instead of science and mathematics. The clear and logical structure of Latin appealed to Einstein, but he found Greek and modern languages very difficult because of his poor memory. His Greek teacher told him he would never amount to anything. Discipline was rigorous, some of the teachers were anti-Semitic, and shy Albert apparently had only one friend in school. All young Germans were expected to enter military service, and school provided the early discipline necessary for that calling.

When he was ten or eleven, his school required its students to study religion, and Einstein turned to a distant relative for tutoring at home. He was deeply impressed by the Proverbs of Solomon in the Old Testament and by the Ethics of the Fathers in the Talmud, and for a year or two he strictly adhered to the rituals of Judaism, refusing, for instance, to eat pork. He also wrote and set to music songs praising God, which he performed at home and in the street. In his *Autobiographical Notes* he described this brief period of orthodoxy:

> Even when I was a fairly precocious young man I became thoroughly impressed with the futility of the hopes and strivings that chase most men restlessly through life. . . . As the first way out there was religion, which is implanted into every child by way of the traditional education-machine. Thus I came . . . to a deep religiousness which, however, reached an abrupt end at the age of twelve. Through the reading of popular scientific books I soon reached the conviction that much in the stories of the Bible could not be true. The consequence was a positively fanatic [orgy] of freethinking coupled with the impression that youth is intentionally being deceived by the state through lies; it was a crushing impression. Mistrust of every kind of authority grew out of this experience. . . .[4]

His disillusionment with formal religion left him feeling that Jewish students who were compelled to attend religious services at the synagogue, whether or not they had any interest, suffered the same sort of coercion as military conscripts.

It would be many years before he would again acknowledge religious feelings. In the meantime, he turned almost all his attention to his independent studies in mathematics, natural science, and philosophy and, shortly thereafter, his lifelong love of music blossomed. Although it would be misleading to claim that music replaced the discarded religion, the timing of the two events should not be considered mere coincidence. Years later Einstein told Anton Reiser that religious feelings carry over into art, especially in the case of music.[5] Music filled a void in his emotional life at this time, and throughout his life served as a creative means of releasing inner tension and relaxing the spirit.

> "I took violin lessons from age 6 to 14," he remembered, "but had no luck with my teachers for whom music did not transcend mechanical practicing. I really began to learn only when I was about 13 years old, mainly after I had fallen in love with Mozart's sonatas. The attempt to reproduce, to some extent, their artistic content and their singular grace compelled me to improve my technique, which improvement I obtained from these sonatas without practicing systematically. I believe, on the whole, that love is a better teacher than sense of duty—with me, at least, it certainly was."[6]

After he began his serious study of mathematics, physics, and philosophy as a teenager, music served as his only distraction. With his mother accompanying him on the piano, he played Mozart and Beethoven sonatas and sometimes he improvised on the piano by himself. These musical interludes relaxed him from his thinking, and often he would arise from his playing and exclaim, "There, now I've got it"[7]—the solution to some problem had suddenly occurred while he was absorbed in the music.

Einstein's real education took place at home, where curiosity and discovery were not thwarted by discipline and achievement marking. In his *Autobiographical Notes* Einstein attributed much of his early fascination with natural phenomena to two events. When he was four or five his father showed him a compass, which defied his childish understanding of the behavior of objects and filled him with a sense of wonder. "Something deeply hidden had to be behind things," he wrote years later. When he was twelve he experienced "a second wonder of a totally different nature" when his father presented him with a little book of propositions and proofs of Euclidean plane geometry. This "Holy Geometry booklet" enchanted the boy, and he would work for days trying to devise his own proofs of Euclid's propositions. It contained assertions that "though by no means evident—could nevertheless be proved with such certainty that any doubt appeared to be out of the question. This lucidity and certainty made an indescribable impression upon me."[8] To the mature Einstein the miracle of science was that methods existed for ordering the mysterious and apparently chaotic world of appearance, or, as he once wrote, "the eternal mystery of the world is its comprehensibility."[9]

After his disillusionment with religion, his second attempt to escape the world of the "merely personal" led him to the study of the physical world. "Out yonder," he wrote, "there was this huge world, which exists independently of us human beings and which stands before us like a great, eternal riddle, at least partially accessible to our inspection and thinking. The contemplation of this world beckoned as a liberation, and I soon noticed that many a man whom I had learned to esteem and to admire had found inner freedom and security in its pursuit. . . . Similarly motivated men of the present and of the past, as well as the insights they had achieved, were the friends who could not be lost."[10] The laws of nature, Einstein learned at an early age, enjoyed universal applicability: If they were true they were true regardless of the time, the place, or the perspective and condition of the individual scientist. Knowledge of natural laws provided a much surer sense of security than was offered by the laws and society of man.

Einstein and Professor Adolf Hurwitz and daughter in Zurich, ca. 1912. (Courtesy of Margot Einstein)

Einstein's most important childhood friend was Max Talmey, a Munich medical student from Eastern Europe, who joined the Einstein family for a meal every Thursday for five years. Despite the difference in their ages, he and Talmey shared a love of science, and the latter brought the boy the popular scientific books which eventually undermined his orthodox beliefs. Between the ages of twelve and sixteen, under his friend's guidance, Einstein devoured books on natural science that provided "excellent popular exposition";[11] he deepened his study of mathematics by teaching himself the principles of differential and integral calculus, and he read much in philosophy. His development was so rapid that by the time Albert was fifteen, Talmey, burdened by his own studies, could no longer keep up with his protégé's progress in mathematics and science.

In June 1894 business failure caused the Einstein family to move to Italy, leaving Albert behind to complete his final year at school. Disliked by his teachers and miserably lonely, he convinced a sympathic doctor to provide him with a certificate stating that he suffered from nervous exhaustion and his health required the sunnier climes of Italy. Shortly before his departure for Pavia, where his parents had moved in early 1895, his Greek teacher summoned him and "expressed the wish that I leave the school. To my remark that I had done nothing amiss he replied only 'your mere presence spoils the respect of the class for me.' " Einstein had resented the "dull, mechanized method of teaching" by which the student learns to "gabble by rote" and, no longer the reticent adolescent, he apparently had relieved his frustration and misery with schoolboy impertinences that offended the school's code of discipline.[12]

Einstein had another reason to escape to Italy. At the age of seventeen he would have become eligible for the draft, and he could not bear the prospect of military service in Germany. Before Hermann Einstein departed for Italy, he had, at Albert's request, taken the necessary legal steps to renounce his son's German citizenship. At the same time the younger Einstein severed his formal ties with the Jewish religious community because, one biographer wrote, he "wanted to avoid having his personal relationship to the laws of nature arranged according to some sort of mechanical order."[13]

While in Italy he managed to appease his worried parents by detailing a plan of self-study designed to prepare him for entrance to the Swiss Federal Institute of Technology (ETH)* in Zurich. His sister later wrote that his method of working was quite peculiar: In the midst of a large company of people he could sit on a sofa with paper and pen and become so immersed in a problem that the conversation stimulated rather than distracted him.

In Italy he enjoyed freedom for the first time in his life, and this had the temporary effect of transforming him into an extrovert liked by everyone. For six months he explored the ancient towns of northern Italy with their museums, churches, palaces, and gardens. Often he went on outings with young friends into the hills and vineyards where they mingled with the country folk. On one occasion

---

*ETH: Eidgenossiche Techniche Hochschule.

he crossed the Apennine Mountains with a friend—a trip of several days' duration. He relished the contrast between the light and gay Italian temperament and the harsh regimes he had left behind. This left an indelible imprint upon him, and half a century later he recalled with fondness, "The happy months of my stay in Italy are very beautiful memories. . . . Days and weeks without anxiety and tension."[14] All his life he retained a special love for Italian food and music.

He left for Zurich in the autumn of 1895, intending to enroll in the ETH. He scored impressively in the mathematics and physics entrance examinations, but because of failures in languages and history he was obliged to spend another year in high school. This extra year turned out to be his happiest school experience. He attended the Swiss Cantonal School in Aarau and lived with the family of Jost Winteler, who taught German and history. Winteler, an excellent teacher, was also a dedicated ornithologist and he was happy to be sidetracked from the prepared lessons. Einstein frequently accompanied the Winteler family on long excursions into the Swiss mountains. The caliber of instruction at Aarau was excellent, and the relaxed, informal, and democratic atmosphere ideally suited Einstein's temperament. The teachers treated their students as individuals and encouraged them to develop independent lines of thought through work in laboratories, visits to museums, and trips into the countryside. In contrast to their German counterparts, they gained the respect of their pupils through strength of character rather than by coercion and fear. As a result of his year at Aarau, Einstein temporarily lost his aversion to school; his general education was significantly expanded and deepened, and he developed several enduring friendships—most notably with the Winteler family, whose son Paul later married Maja Einstein.

During this year, his interest in physics blossomed. He had an excellent teacher and, for the first time, a laboratory for experimentation. On one occasion he was required to write an essay on his plans for the future. "A happy man," he began, "is too contented with the present to think much about the future." Nevertheless, he knew he wished to become a theoretical physicist because, he continued, "[A]bove all is the individual disposition for abstract and mathematical thought, the lack of fantasy and of practical talent. . . . Besides, there is also a certain independence in the scientific profession that greatly pleases me."[15] While still at Aarau he asked himself, "What will happen if a man tries to catch a light ray?" Within this naïve question is contained the seed of his work on special relativity.

A half-century later, Hans Byland, a classmate at Aarau, described Einstein as an "impudent Swabian, whose original nobility already distinguished him from all the others." He was "sure of himself," a "restless spirit," "unhampered by convention," and the "sarcastic curl of his rather full mouth with the protruding lower lip did not encourage the Philistines to fraternize with him." He gave the impression of being a "laughing philosopher" whose "witty mockery pitilessly lashed any conceit or pose," and "[h]e made no bones about voicing his personal opinions whether they offended or not." And yet, Byland continues, "One day we met in the delightful school refectory to play Mozart sonatas. When he began to play his violin, the room seemed to broaden out. For the first time I was listening to the real Mozart in all the Grecian beauty of its clear lines, alternately graceful and magnificently powerful. 'That is heavenly,' he said, 'we must play it again.' What fire there was in his playing! I no longer recognized him. So this was the genius and the unregenerate mocker. He could not help himself! He was one of those split personalities who knew how to protect, with a prickly exterior, the delicate realm of their intense emotional life."[16] As he matured and came to a deeper understanding of human nature and the nature of things, he acquired an inner calm and sureness that brought an end to the need for this "prickly exterior"; many a fool, however, was to discover that the "impudent Swabian" remained an integral part of his makeup.

Einstein entered the ETH in the fall of 1896. It was the most famous institute of technology in Central Europe outside Germany. Zurich was, at this time, a haven for revolutionaries; it attracted many Eastern Europeans because of its political tolerance and its democratic institutions. But the happy experience at Aarau was not repeated at the ETH, although Einstein did enjoy sufficient independence to conduct his own scientific investigations.

He intensified his work in physics, neglected mathematics, which did not appeal to him, and spent long hours in the physics laboratory "fascinated by the direct contact with experience."[17] He did not enjoy quite such direct contact with his professors, in part because of the formalities which limited intercourse between professor and student to the classroom and laboratory and, in part, because of Einstein's innate reticence.

Heinrich Weber, his professor in physics, taught a course on the historical developments in classical physics which ignored the dramatic work of the last decades of the nineteenth century by Maxwell, Kirchoff, Helmholtz, and Hertz. Einstein often cut Weber's classes and embarked on a course of self-study in which he read the works of the neglected physicists, particularly Maxwell. Years later he recalled that he had been "untidy and a daydreamer . . . aloof and discontented, not very popular," a person who made no concessions to tact.[18] He was openly scornful of anything that displeased him, and he antagonized so many of his professors that, despite his acknowledged promise, he was unable to secure an assistantship when he graduated. One exasperated professor told him, "You're a clever fellow! But you have one fault. You won't let anyone tell you a thing."[19] Years later Einstein, while conceding that he had not been a model student, asserted that his teachers had disliked him for his independence.

In the months before graduation in 1900 he had to catch up on years of neglected work. This forced cramming had such an unpleasant effect upon him that, "after I had passed the final examination," he wrote in the *Autobiographical Notes,* "I found the consideration of any scientific problems distasteful to me for an entire year. Yet I must say that in Switzerland we had to suffer far less under such coercion, which smothers every truly scientific impulse, than is the case in many another locality. . . . It is, in fact, nothing short of a miracle that the modern methods of instruction have not yet entirely strangled the holy curiosity of inquiry;

for this delicate little plant, aside from stimulation, stands mainly in need of freedom; without this it goes to wrack and ruin without fail."[20] His cramming had been enormously facilitated by the use of the notes of his classmate, Marcel Grossmann, who had been as diligent as Einstein had been inattentive.

During the two years following his graduation from the ETH Einstein was forced to take on short-term, low-paying tutoring jobs while he desperately sought permanent employment. He was fired from one substitute teaching job when his superior learned that he had convinced his students that the rigor of their school was stifling them. Finally, in June 1902, through the intercession of Marcel Grossmann's father, Einstein began work as a probationary technical expert, third class, at the Swiss Patent Office in Berne. That October, his father, worn down by business failures and his dependence upon relatives for financial support, died of heart failure.

On January 6, 1903, Einstein married Mileva Maric, a Serbian classmate at the ETH, with whom he had often studied. On their wedding night they were locked out of their flat because the groom had forgotten the key. The apartment they lived in was small and cluttered and because they could not afford a servant, Einstein helped with the housework, carried coal from the basement, split wood, and, when he remembered to, did the shopping on his way home from work. In May 1904 Hans Albert ("Aden") was born; the child did not learn proper German until his fifth year because his parents spoke to him only in baby talk. There were regular string quartet sessions and philosophic discussions with friends in the rather bohemian apartment; nonetheless, Einstein managed to do revolutionary scientific work in his spare time. A second son Eduard ("Tetel") was born in 1910, but by 1914 the marriage had failed, and the couple were divorced in 1919. Lasting friendships from this period developed with Maurice Solovine and Michele Besso. Solovine was a Rumanian student of philosophy who later translated several of Einstein's books into French. He, Einstein, and Conrad Habicht, a mathematician, met on a regular basis beginning in 1902 to discuss philosophy, physics, literature, and anything else that interested the young participants; they called themselves the "Olympia Academy." Michele Besso married one of Professor Winteler's daughters and worked alongside Einstein at the Patent Office. Einstein corresponded with Solovine and Besso all his life, and these letters are among the most revealing and beautiful of his writings.[21]

The Patent Office job allowed him sufficient free time to work on his own investigations and calculations, which he discreetly hid when his superior appeared. According to Einstein's sister, Maja, this sympathetic gentleman "benevolently turned a blind eye or even two" to his employee's extracurricular activities because the young clerk always discharged his duties faithfully. Anton Reiser presents a rather different account. He maintains that Einstein's superior had a low opinion of speculative work and would have held his clerk up to ridicule.[22] In 1905 these furtive calculations resulted in five papers which were published in the prestigious *Annalen der Physik,* including his work on the photoelectric effect, for which he was subsequently awarded the Nobel Prize in physics for 1921, and his first paper on special relativity. This work would have been astonishing for any scientist, but the fact that it was performed by an obscure twenty-six-year-old patent examiner in his spare time was without precedent since the time of Newton.

Einstein characterized his scientific work of this period as *Gelegenheitsarbeit* (a casual or odd job). While it was to have an immense effect upon the world of physics, there was little immediate change in his own life. He continued to work at the Patent Office for another four years and, as late as November 1905, was still giving private lessons in electricity. A few physicists, notably Max Planck and Max von Laue, quickly understood the importance of Einstein's work, but he did not receive an appointment to a university until 1909, when he became Associate Professor of Theoretical Physics at Zurich University. Years later he quipped that he had not met a real physicist until he was thirty years old. While the gist of this remark is true, it should be noted that he was visited by Max von Laue in Berne in 1906.

The job at the Patent Office had been a great blessing because it had freed him from the academic pressures to produce and publish results that so often compel young scientists to "write a lot of superficial stuff and become a busybody in order to get ahead."[23] Instead he was able to work at his own pace, motivated only by the "pure joy of learning." Michelle Besso's son later recalled that during these years Einstein was "always in a good mood, he was amusing and jolly."[24]

From Zurich Einstein moved to Prague in 1911 and sixteen months later he returned as a full professor to his alma mater, the ETH, which only a decade earlier had refused to hire him as an assistant. He did not remain long in Zurich. He was now recognized as Europe's greatest young physicist, and he received offers from universities all over the Continent. In 1913 Max Planck and other leading German scientists arranged for him to be elected, at the extremely young age of thirty-four, to the Royal Prussian Academy of Science, with one of the few endowed chairs. He was also named a professor at the University of Berlin, where he was free to lecture as little or often as he chose, without the burden of administrative duties; and, in addition, he was named director of the newly created, but as yet unbuilt, Institute of Physics of the Kaiser Wilhelm Society for the Development of Sciences. It was an irresistible offer, and in April 1914 he moved to Berlin.

"I accepted this peculiar sinecure," he confessed to Paul Ehrenfest, "because giving lectures grates so oddly on my nerves. . . ."[25] Nevertheless, his lectures, which he described as "performances on the trapeze,"[26] were well received. His unorthodox style of delivery, a casual naturalness punctuated by occasional good-natured jokes, contrasted sharply with the formality of most of his colleagues. His genuine love for his subject, his desire to be helpful, and his ability to present ideas in an esthetically satisfying manner earned him the respect and affection of his students. However, his need for solitude, his disinclination toward personal relations, and his intense preoccupation with the question of general relativity made regular lecturing an unwelcome distraction.

Einstein at the Patent Office in Bern, ca. 1905, aged twenty-six. (Courtesy of Margot Einstein)

He disliked having to organize a year's worth of material into evenly divided units because he preferred to dwell on topics of interest to him and to skip lightly over less absorbing matters. Thus there was an uneven quality to his lectures, although Philipp Frank, Einstein's successor in Prague and author of the most valuable biography of Einstein written in Einstein's lifetime, testifies that isolated lectures on subjects which interested him were invariably superb. As a teacher he possessed one other enviable talent, the ability to interrupt his work at any moment to receive a student. As soon as the interruption ended, he was able to return to his own work without any disruption in his chain of thought.

The move to Berlin was a mixed blessing. Almost twenty years earlier he had renounced his German citizenship. He despised Prussian militarism, and Berlin was the capital of Prussia. To Besso he confided: "Not without some unease do I see the Berlin venture approaching. . . . The (grown-up) Germans are not wont to take a free and unprejudiced view of things. (Blinders!)"[27] Einstein felt that Prussians were generally cold, mechanical, and overly enamored of formality and ceremony. The other members of the Prussian Academy were older and believed that membership in the academy marked the pinnacle of success. They were accustomed to, and adept at, academic politics and infighting. Einstein disliked this sort of pettiness, was completely unimpressed by the importance attached to membership in the academy, and adopted an open, friendly, and egalitarian air with his younger colleagues.

In the summer of 1914 Mileva returned to Switzerland with the boys. Their departure caused him very great personal pain and caused a strain in relations with his sons which never entirely healed. Throughout Mileva's life, she remained embittered and more than once Einstein made unkind references about her to family and friends. Hans Albert was ten years old at the time, and he was especially unforgiving of his father.

In August the First World War broke out. On August 19, Einstein wrote to Ehrenfest: "Europe, in her insanity, has started something unbelievable. In such times one realizes to what a sad species of animal one belongs."[28] For thirty-five years the world had left Einstein in peace to study the workings of the universe. Abruptly this world collapsed, and Einstein, who had always wanted nothing more than to be left alone, found himself drawn into the struggle to protect and preserve the highest ideals of civilization.

3

"Moral Fidelity"
(1914-1932)

T he outbreak of war on August 4, 1914, was the great tragedy of our age. The agony of the later twentieth century was spawned in the mud of France during the bitter years that followed. Throughout Europe, the advent of war was greeted by frenzied exaltation; visions of romance and glory masked visceral yearnings and hatreds. Nationalist chauvinism swept across class lines in almost every European country.

In Germany, most scholars, especially the historians and philologists, fell sway to this fever. In October 1914 ninety-three prominent intellectuals, including Nobel Laureates Max Planck, Fritz Haber, Walter Nernst, and Wilhelm Roentgen, signed the now-famous "Manifesto to the Civilized World," which denied German war guilt and charges of atrocities in Belgium, deplored the "shameful spectacle . . . of Russian hordes . . . allied with Mongols and Negroes . . . unleashed against the white race," and defiantly asserted, "Were it not for German militarism, German culture would have been wiped off the face of the earth."[1] Einstein not only refused to sign this document but, in his first public political act, became one of the four signers of the "Manifesto to Europeans," which denounced nationalism, called for an immediate end to the war, and for the creation of a united Europe. The "Manifesto to Europeans" was the work of Georg Friedrich Nicolai, a Professor of Physiology at the University of Berlin, a leading German pacifist, and the author of *The Anatomy of War,* written during the war. Nicolai and Einstein were joined by only two others, one of whom, Wilhelm Förster, long the Director of the Berlin Observatory, had come to regret signing the "Manifesto" of the ninety-three.

The shock caused by the war galvanized the previously unpolitical physicist to a social activism that grew in intensity with the years. There is no record of any previous political views, although Maurice Solovine later said that in the prewar years Einstein was "a great liberal of the epoch of 1848," the year of idealistic liberal revolutions led by intellectuals, professors, students, and workers against the autocratic governments of Central and Western Europe.[2]

Einstein viewed the commandment "Thou shalt not kill" as an injunction against all war. His instinctive pacifism reflected his antipathy to all forms of cruelty and hatred and his contempt for what he called the "military mentality." The war poisoned cultural relations between belligerent nations, and as a member of the scientific community whose life depended upon an environment that stimulated creative work, Einstein once asserted, "He who cherishes the values of culture cannot fail to be a pacifist."[3]

He refused to assist the German war effort and worked instead with pacifist organizations. By the time of the armistice in November 1918, he was viewed by his colleagues, not surprisingly, as an "archsocialist." Ironically, it was during the first two years of the war that Einstein completed his most original and far-reaching scientific work—the general theory of relativity. His ability to work productively despite external disruption extended even to war.

Living as a bachelor and absorbed by his scientific work, Einstein was careless about diet and regimen in wartime Berlin, where proper nourishment was exceedingly difficult to obtain. Visiting his apartment at that time, Margot Einstein once discovered him preparing a meal of soup and a hardboiled egg. The uncleaned eggshell had been placed in the boiling soup broth because, as he cheerfully pointed out, he would only need to clean one pot![4]

Einstein became seriously ill with a stomach ulcer early in 1917. The illness persisted for a number of years and required him to follow a strict diet for the remainder of his life. His cousin, Elsa Einstein Löwenthal, whom he had known since childhood, took charge of the patient, cooked his meals, and arranged for him to occupy the apartment next door to the rooms she shared with her two daughters, Ilse and Margot. Friendship with Elsa had been renewed shortly before the move to Berlin, and in 1915 Einstein wrote to a friend in Switzerland that his "Cousine" "drew me to Berlin."

By the end of 1918 Einstein was on the mend, although still far from fully recovered. He and Elsa decided to marry as soon as a divorce could be secured from Mileva. They were married on June 2, 1919, and, at the time, he adopted Elsa's daughters. She was devoted to her "Albertle," and Einstein enjoyed being looked after, but he remained something of a stranger in the bourgeois comfort of Elsa's apartment. Unlike her husband, she enjoyed society, reveled in his fame, and cared about social standing and the opinions of others. Often she dragged him to benefits and allowed him to be used as a "museum piece." According to Philipp Frank, she was not popular in Berlin circles. Nevertheless, particularly during the war and the early years of marriage, Einstein enjoyed the company and ministrations of his devoted cousin and wife.[5]

Einstein in his Berlin study in 1916, aged thirty-seven. He was at the peak of his scientific powers and was engaged in his most intense scientific labors, yet he was one of the few in Europe not blinded by the hysteria of the war. Years before his fame gave him an international platform, he was aggressively outspoken in his opposition to the killing. (Courtesy of Margot Einstein)

In the summer of 1918, after years of privation, the German public, believing the propaganda put out by the military authorities, expected imminent victory that would redeem their sufferings. The shock of defeat prostrated the entire society. Even as Germany was signing the armistice on November 11, the Prussian nationalists—the prime architects of the German war effort—frightened by the collapse of the old regime, fearful of a revolution from the Left, and poisoned by a sense of romantic pessimism, translated their fears into aggression by launching a campaign to pass the blame of Germany's humiliation to Jews, pacifists, and socialists.

Under the Weimar Republic, civil equality was guaranteed for the first time in German history; new opportunities for Jews opened up in the bureaucracy and the academic world. The victorious Allies, however, instead of aiding the fledgling democracy, treated it as a pariah, continuing the food blockades for many months, heaping impossible reparation bills upon it and placing full blame for the outbreak of the war upon Germany. The antidemocratic forces from the army, the imperial bureaucracy, and judiciary continued to exercise power under the Weimar regime. They had a field day identifying democracy with the Western powers and then rejecting it as un-German. The secondary schools actually taught that the republican forces had lost the war. Einstein, as an outspoken pacifist, socialist, and enthusiastic supporter of the 1918 German revolution and the Weimar Republic and, after 1919, a world-famous figure and Zionist, was anathema to the reactionary forces.

The extent of Einstein's support for the Weimar Republic can be gauged by his decision not to accept a magnificent offer from the University of Leiden in September 1919. In Leiden he would have been near two of his most beloved colleagues, Paul Ehrenfest and H. A. Lorentz, the physicist whose work in the field of electrodynamics had been invaluable to him, and whose human greatness was a lifelong source of inspiration to Einstein. In Leiden, too, he would have been far removed from the reactionary groups which made public life in Germany frequently violent and unpleasant. Einstein refused this ideal offer because of his sense of obligation to the Weimar Republic and because he had promised Max Planck that he would only quit Berlin if conditions made it impossible for him to remain. "It would be doubly base of me," he informed Ehrenfest, "if, just when my political hopes are being realized, I were to walk out unnecessarily, and perhaps *in part* for my material advantage, on the very people who have surrounded me with love and friendship."[6]

Anti-Semitism had been increasing through the latter half of the nineteenth century in German society. Financial scandals enriched politicans and aristocrats and ruined the lower-middle classes. Jews, acting as middlemen, did not make fortunes, but they became scapegoats for the calamity that befell the ruined groups, and a wave of anti-Semitism swept the young nation.[7] During the years of the empire (1871–1918) the perception of a Jewish "threat" to German culture gradually receded because of a growing fear of Marxism. After the collapse of the empire, reactionary forces tied the alleged Jewish world conspiracy to the Communist revolution, and a new round of anti-Semitism appeared from 1918 onward. It should be noted, however, that anti-Semitism was a fact of life throughout Europe, and German anti-Semitism did not become a serious political problem until 1928 when the Nazis were first elected to the Reichstag. Attacks against Einstein in the early twenties by nationalists and anti-Semites were a consequence of his fame and his support of internationalism, pacifism, and Zionism.

During the war, Einstein had been sensitized to the plight of his fellow Jews by his contacts with the Berlin Jewish community, but he was still uninformed about the modern Zionist movement which had been initiated by Theodore Herzl in 1896 in response to the brutal pogroms in Eastern Europe and the notorious Dreyfus Affair in France in 1895. The goal of Zionism was to end the diaspora—the 1,800 years of Jewish dispersion throughout the Gentile world. Since the Romans expelled the Jews from Jerusalem in the first Christian century Jews had been a despised and persecuted minority wherever they went. Their communities had been confined to ghettos in the Middle Ages and all occupations except small trade had been denied them. England and Spain had expelled all Jews who had refused baptism. The Roman Catholic Church had tried to eliminate Jewish heresies by means of the dreaded Inquisition. At the end of the eighteenth century, the Jews, confined to their ghettos, had no farming class, no political or economic security, and were closed off from the intellectual life of the countries where they lived.

In the half-century after 1789 Western European Jews benefited from the rising tide of democratic liberalism. This period of emancipation liberated the Jew from the ghetto confines but opened a new chapter in his suffering. The forces of assimilation and religious reform (which often led to rejection of religion) undermined the traditional communal bonds. Some of the more successful German Jews tended to convert to Christianity and in other respects adapt to German culture in an ultimately futile attempt to escape from their heritage of homelessness. Many became ardent patriots and frequently turned their backs upon their less fortunate brethren who were still shackled by the ghetto's legacy of poverty. The desperate, misguided, but acutely human attempt by the Jew to achieve a fuller degree of emancipation by submerging his identity in the culture, religion, and society of his nation of birth had a devastating effect upon individual and collective Jewish self-respect. Those who believed they had found security and escape from their tragic past were to discover that in the eyes of the anti-Semites, a Jew—even baptized—remained a Jew. Estranged from his past, often unwelcome in the society of Gentiles, the assimilated Jews of Western Europe were rootless creatures, "slaves in the midst of freedom,"[8] as Ahad Ha'am, one of the leading Zionist writers and thinkers, expressed it.

In Eastern Europe, especially Russia and Poland, where most of the Jews lived, emancipation never came. They remained imprisoned in the ghetto, impoverished, diseased, poorly educated, and despised. Following the assassination of Tsar Alexander II in 1881 a series of pogroms was instituted by the authorities. For the final three and one-half decades of tsarist rule, the Jews of Russia lived in stark terror. One solution was to emigrate to the West, and from 1899 to 1914 more than 1.3 million Jews entered the United States. A great many also settled in Germany, Austria, and Switzerland. Those who remained behind either retreated into a fanatic religious orthodoxy or renounced religion and turned to Zionism or to radical politics, especially socialism and communism. Many of the first Jewish settlers in Palestine had fled the pogroms.

From the start, the Zionists were united by external pressures and divided into internal factions. They agreed that anti-Semitism made large-scale assimilation both impossible and undesirable, and as long as Jews remained an unwelcome minority in a hostile world, Jewish self-respect and the survival of Jewish culture and tradition were imperiled. The Zionists' solution was the establishment of a Jewish national home—a "living society"[9] to which all Jews could belong, in which all could take pride, to whose upbuilding all could contribute, and whose existence would help them endure the hatred of the world. After 1903 the Zionists were united in their determination that the homeland must be in Palestine—a return to Zion, the holy land.

When Zionism was politically weak, its leaders spoke of the social, cultural, and spiritual center they wished to create in Palestine. Few seriously believed that all or even the majority of Jews would actually settle there, but all would partake of the spiritual uplift of the Palestine settlement. The revival of Hebrew, the preservation of the religious tradition of Israel, and the creation of a Jewish university were the means to achieving this uplifting of spirit. When Einstein joined the movement, this was his vision of Zionism.

As the movement gained in strength after 1917, and as the situation in Palestine steadily deteriorated after 1919, Zionism became increasingly political. By the late 1930s the avowed goal of the majority of Palestinian colonizers and ever greater numbers of Zionists elsewhere was a Jewish state or a bipartisan state of Arabs and Jews. The internal schism between cultural and political Zionists was bitter and often had most undesirable consequences.

On November 2, 1917, the British government issued the Balfour Declaration, a statement of policy in which His Majesty's government endorsed the right of Jews to settle in Palestine provided that the civil and religious rights of the non-Jewish residents of Palestine were in no way jeopardized. Overnight this controversial endorsement of Zionist aims added a dimension of legitimacy to Zionism in international politics. It identified Zionism with the British Empire and catapulted a Russian-born British chemist, Chaim Weizmann, into the leadership of the World Zionist Organization. Weizmann's lobbying efforts had been primarily responsible for persuading Prime Minister Lloyd George and Foreign Secretary Arthur Lord Balfour to commit Great Britain's support for the Zionist aims. The Balfour Declaration sowed the seeds for the conflict between Arab and Jew that continues to threaten world peace and security three-score years later.

After the war, the Zionist Union of Germany, in an effort to strengthen cultural Zionist work, compiled a list of prominent Jewish intellectuals whom they wished to recruit to support the cause. Einstein's name, still almost unknown outside scientific circles, was on the list, and in February 1919 Kurt Blumenfeld, director of propaganda for the German Zionists, approached him in Berlin. Blumenfeld discovered that Einstein had scant knowledge of or interest in the movement and was reluctant to become involved. Einstein embraced Zionism only after long deliberation, when he concluded that it was a movement dedicated to winning spiritual freedom for the Jews, and that the colonization process was free of profiteering and exploitation. [10] It was some time before he assumed an active role in Zionist affairs; his early statements were of a general nature as, for example, the 1920 statement that "Only when we [Jews] have the courage to regard ourselves as a nation, only when we have respect for ourselves, can we win the respect of others." [11] A year later he asserted that the goal of the leaders of Zionism was social and cultural but not political.

It is necessary to differentiate between Einstein's attitudes toward Judaism and Zionism. His religious views never changed: He rejected the concept of a personal God and regretted that the ancient Jews had attempted to base the moral teachings of their religion upon the authority of God. To the extent that Judaism defined a moral attitude toward life, he willingly acknowledged his support. "The essence of [the Jewish concept of life] seems to me to lie in an affirmative attitude to the life of all creation. The life of the individual only has meaning in so far as it aids in making the life of every living thing nobler and more beautiful. Life is sacred, that is to say, it is the supreme value, to which all other values are subordinate." [12] Einstein felt the Jews of the world were bound together by ties of blood and a uniquely tragic history as well as by religion. A moral attitude to life, love of justice and knowledge, and a desire for personal independence were the ideals that "make me thank my stars that I belong to [the Jewish tradition]." [13] Another aspect of the Jewish heritage that strongly appealed to his pacifist beliefs was that, unlike almost all national traditions, the Jews had never celebrated the warrior. In place of the usual heroic saga, they honored reason and subtlety; the story of David and Goliath is a case in point. [14] To Einstein, Zionism represented the healthiest means to rescue the Jews of the diaspora from the loss of self-respect, the fatal illusions of assimilation, and the danger and insecurity of anti-Semitic persecution. He did not believe it could cure all the ills afflicting Jews, but it could help them to restore the inner dignity necessary to survive in a hostile world. To him, it was a moral, not a political, movement.

The First World War awakened Einstein to the plight of his fellow Jews. The spectacle of unsuccessful attempts by emancipated Jews to blend into a society which refused to forget their alien heritage impressed him as a case of self-deception that could lead only to estrangement from all groups. "The best in man can flourish," he wrote, "only when he loses himself in a community." [15] It is perhaps surprising to encounter these sentiments in a man who, a quarter of a century earlier, had severed his formal ties with the religious institutions of his fathers. Throughout his adult life he sought (not always successfully) to avoid participation in organized groups. Although he was free of the self-delusory elements of those Jews who attempted to blend inconspicuously into the fabric of German society, he had also lost contact with the community to which his blood tied him. It is of course treacherous going to try to reconstruct the motivations of another, but available evidence leads to the conclusion that his enthusiastic participation after 1919 in Zionist affairs was an expression of his desire to escape the ambiguity of his quasi-assimilated situation and to become a member of a life-giving community.[16]

The armistice signaled an end to the killing and destruction, but the spiritual collapse engendered by the war experiences grew worse. The Treaty of Versailles, with its war-guilt clause aimed at prostrate Germany, fueled the hatred, distrust, and moral decay of both victor and vanquished. Starvation and disease eventually were conquered, but the spiritual wounds never healed. To Einstein it was especially tragic that men of great learning had not been immune to the war poison. International intellectual cooperation, nearly impossible in the war, failed to resume. In the war the teaching of German had been suppressed in many American, British, and French schools, while German schools considered similar bans against the study of Shakespeare. Even in the mid-1920s, British scientists, while respecting their American counterparts, continued to express contempt for German science at a time when the greatest collection of physicists in history lived in Germany.[17]

One of the first steps to the improvement of relations took place in May 1919 when British astronomers, led by Professor Arthur Stanley Eddington, traveled to the South Atlantic to photograph a total eclipse of the sun in an attempt to verify one of the predictions of Einstein's general theory of relativity, which asserted that light passing near the sun would be slightly displaced (popularly, but less accurately, "curved") by the sun's gravitational field. Eddington's measurements were sufficiently close to the theory's predictions to verify Einstein's theory.

On November 6, 1919, the results of the expedition were announced at a joint meeting of the Royal Society and the Royal Astronomical Society in London. It was a moment of high drama and irony. In spite of the prevailing atmosphere of postwar hatred, English scientists had just traveled several thousand miles to verify the theory of a German. This in itself was an extraordinary step in the direction of reestablishing cooperation in intellectual matters between the two bitterly hostile nations. The drama was intensified because the announcement had been made at the Royal Society, where Isaac Newton had served as president for more than twenty years. Newton's portrait looked upon the audience as the announcement was made that his theory of gravitation had been eclipsed by Einstein's masterwork.

The public responded to the announcement with wild enthusiasm. Newspapers proclaimed the bending of light and the curvature of space. Few people even remotely comprehended Einstein's theory, but that only intensified the mysterious fascination it held for the war-weary public. As other claims of the special and general theories of relativity reached the public via popularized and sensationalized reports of the press, Einstein became endowed, in the public mind, with the powers of a sorcerer.

Front row: A. S. Eddington and H. A. Lorentz. Back row: Einstein, P. Ehrenfest, and W. de Sitter. This photograph was taken in Leiden in the 1920s. Einstein revered Lorentz both as a scientist and as a humanist. In later years he quoted the Dutch physicist's comment: "I am happy that I am a member of a nation that is too small to afford big blunders." (Courtesy of AIP Niels Bohr Library)

Overnight he became world famous. The telephone and doorbell did not stop ringing for days, and an avalanche of mail descended upon the modest Einstein apartment, whose baffled occupant would later remark, "I envy the simplest working man. He has his privacy."[18]

Gradually a new image of the sorcerer-scientist took shape as the press devoured his every word and action. He impressed his first interviewers with his modesty, his gentle manner, his playful sense of humor, his "fascinating smile and the twinkle of his penetrating eyes."[19] Other descriptions from this period emphasize his youthful and athletic appearance, the charms of his facial expressions, "which were sometimes meditative and aloof, sometimes lively and playful."[20]

His arresting, somewhat bohemian appearance, coupled with his unusual informality and utter lack of an air of self-importance, increased the fascination he held for the public. Then, when his behavior during the war became known, England, France, and the United States saluted him for his courage and integrity. Although much of what was written about him in these days was exaggeration or pure invention, a moderately accurate impression of his extraordinary human qualities did emerge, and the early adulation slowly deepened into genuine admiration of his human warmth and moral courage.

For the next several years Einstein traveled extensively through Europe and the world, and wherever he appeared, he created a sense of excitement and mystery. Of a lecture in Vienna in 1921, Philipp Frank reported that people were "in a curious state of excitement in which it no longer matters what one understands but only that one is in the immediate neighborhood of a place where miracles happen."[21]

Abraham Pais believes that the cause of Einstein's lasting fame "has everything to do . . . with the stars and with language." In the following passage, Pais eloquently describes the impact of Einstein's scientific discoveries on the collective consciousness of his contemporaries:

> A new man appears abruptly, the "suddenly famous Doctor Einstein." He carries the message of a new order in the universe. He is a new Moses come down from the mountain to bring the law and a new Joshua controlling the motion of heavenly bodies. He speaks in strange tongues but wise men aver that the stars testify to his veracity. Through the ages, child and adult alike had looked with wonder at stars and light. . . . [S]tars had forever been in his dreams and his myths. Their recurrence manifested an order beyond human control. Irregularities in the skies—comets, eclipses—were omens, mainly of evil. Behold, a new man appears. His mathematical language is sacred yet amenable to transcription into the profane: the fourth dimension, stars are not where they seemed to be but nobody need worry, light has weight, space is warped. He fulfills two profound needs in man, the need to know and the need not to know but to believe. . . . The new man who appears at that time represents order and power. He becomes θεῖος ἀνήρ, the divine man, of the twentieth century.[22]

Pais contends that the timing and circumstances of the announcement enhanced the drama of Einstein's emergence as a public hero, but played a secondary role to the mysterious revelations themselves. Undoubtedly Pais is correct as far as he goes. If Einstein's personality had failed utterly to impress the news media, the mention of his name would, nonetheless, have forever excited a sense of mystery. That his character did capture the imagination of the media and the public, and that he experienced lasting public adulation which grew, if anything, stronger with the passage of time, must, in large measure, be credited to his public behavior—to activities on behalf of those less fortunate than himself—which was eminently comprehensible to the layman.

Einstein's appearance upon the public scene one year after the cessation of fighting provided a happy excuse to restore a desperately needed sense of equilibrium in human relations. No family who had lost a son or a father could forget, and few could begin the painful process of forgiveness. Yet, it is not in human nature to sustain, ungoaded, a mass impersonal hatred.

Einstein's obvious goodness and simplicity coupled with his nonsupport of German war aims answered the great subconscious needs of the more enlightened elements of British, French, and American society to escape from the debilitating effects of the war. Perhaps the bitter memory was still too acute to permit the admission of softened feelings toward the recent enemy but, in the person of Einstein, there was an opportunity for the more healthy, more natural human feelings to reassert themselves. Ultimately it would even be possible to admit that the Germans, too, were human.

The circuslike atmosphere which accompanied fame was thoroughly distasteful to Einstein, who would later observe with impatience that there is no such thing as a great man.[23] He could no longer enjoy the anonymity and freedom of movement that his solitary nature required. His "newspaper face" guaranteed that his mere presence would create a commotion anywhere he went, and his privacy was severely curtailed. At first he had been patient with journalists, but soon he discovered the unreliability of a press more concerned with selling papers than printing the truth. At this point Elsa emerged as his intermediary with overzealous reporters, and he was able to resume his interrupted work—although never again completely free of external distractions. To Paul Ehrenfest he complained, "With me, every peep becomes a trumpet solo."[24] When he saw his own picture in the newspapers, he would say, "Bah! What a nasty, fat fellow."[25] Eventually he acquired a philosophic resignation to this unsought fame and adulation, reasoning that "men need hero-worship,"[26] but he never really understood why he was so universally loved. "Why is it nobody understands me," he once asked with a laugh, "and everybody likes me?"[27]

Praise, honors, power, and money meant nothing to Einstein; what mattered were the simple pleasures of his family circle, his violin, his sailboat, and, above all, his unceasing efforts to understand the secrets of the physical world. "The only way to escape the personal corruption of praise," he once said, "is to go on working. One is tempted to stop and listen to it. The only thing to do is to turn away and go on working. Work. There is nothing else."[28] As a result of this attitude his wealth and influence never remotely approached the magnitude of his fame.

Fame, he discovered, did have one redeeming quality: It provided him with an opportunity to use the influence of his name on behalf of the most critical human questions of peace, international reconciliation, justice, and the dignity and independence of the individual. Einstein's early forays into the public realm were generally little more than spontaneous expressions of a concerned individual, but early in 1921 this was to change.

Weizmann was deeply worried about the weakness of the American branch of the Zionist Organization, and in the spring of 1921 he decided to visit the United States for the dual purpose of launching an ambitious fund-raising program and a strengthening of American Zionism. For this delicate task he recognized the enormous symbolic value of Einstein's support. Once again Weizmann dispatched Kurt Blumenfeld to persuade Einstein to accompany the Zionist leader to the United States. Einstein refused to go, saying, "I am no orator. I can add nothing convincing. You will only be using my name."[29] As the disappointed Blumenfeld was leaving he said, "Not Dr. Weizmann, as an individual, but the president of the Zionist Organization has ordered me to persuade you to go to America, and I have the right to expect that you subordinate your considerations to Dr. Weizmann's decision." Much to Blumenfeld's surprise, Einstein agreed: "You are right. If it were left to every one to behave according to his own desires, it would be impossible to accomplish any united enterprise."

On March 15, just days before Einstein and Weizmann departed for America, Blumenfeld wrote Weizmann a long, fascinating letter to advise the Zionist leader how to deal with the famous physicist he had not yet met. Blumenfeld warned Weizmann that Einstein was no Zionist and that efforts to pressure him to join would backfire. Einstein would, however, be available for specific tasks. Blumenfeld noted that Einstein was primarily drawn to Zionism because of his aversion to assimilating Jews, and he was particularly attracted to the socialist aspects of the Palestinian experiment.

The Zionists were paying all expenses for the trip and, according to Blumenfeld, this caused Einstein such discomfort that at one point he suggested in all seriousness to Elsa that they travel steerage to reduce expenses. This led Blumenfeld to request that all money questions be discussed exclusively with Elsa.

Turning to practical considerations, Blumenfeld observed that Einstein's participation would offer the Zionists an excellent opportunity to win many new big-name supporters and a significant increase in pledges. On the forthcoming tour Weizmann expected Einstein to make speeches at the rallies but, Blumenfeld worried, "Einstein is a bad speaker and sometimes out of naïveté says things which are not welcome to us." To prevent such an occurrence, he urged Weizmann to map out any speeches in advance.[30]

The trip took place at a critical moment in Zionist history; by 1920 Zionist finances were depleted and in order to raise money for land acquisition and resettlement in Palestine, the *Keren Hayesod* (the Palestine Foundation Fund) was established. The United States had the largest Jewish community outside Eastern Europe but, at the time, the Zionist organization was still weak, and the leading American Zionists, particularly Justice Louis D. Brandeis, were in open disagreement with Weizmann's philosophy. The trip was designed to inaugurate the *Keren Hayesod* in America, to resolve the dispute with Brandeis, and to organize American Zionism properly. One of Weizmann's fondest dreams was the creation of a Jewish university in Jerusalem. Einstein, the supreme example of the largely untapped possibilities of the Jewish intellect, was the ideal symbol of the university. He shared Weizmann's dream because he had seen too many Jewish professors and students from Eastern Europe discriminated against at the University of Berlin.

In the autumn of 1920 Einstein had received invitations from several American universities, including Princeton and Wisconsin. Shortly before, Einstein had been subjected to a number of right-wing attacks, some of which had been anti-Semitic in nature. At the time of the invitations, he was worried that his situation in Berlin might become untenable. "Dear friends in Holland" (Paul and Tatiana Ehrenfest) strongly advised Einstein to set his demands for remuneration high because, they reasoned, if Einstein were to lose a half-year of valuable research time, he ought to gain financial independence from the venture. Otherwise, the Ehrenfests counseled, remain home and do research. Einstein and the Ehrenfests apparently believed that American universities could afford to pay huge sums of money for Einstein's services, and Einstein requested $15,000 from both Princeton and Wisconsin. In return, he would lecture three times a week for two months at each institution. When several weeks elapsed without any response, Einstein realized that his request might have appeared "somewhat immodest" as, indeed, it was. Later, he discovered that his request had caused "tremendous indignation," and he was relieved that nothing came of it.

In February 1921, after Einstein agreed to accompany Weizmann to America, he wrote to Princeton and other American universities to offer his services without financial conditions, reasoning that this might be beneficial to the Zionist cause.

In March leaders of the Zionist Organization of America cabled Weizmann urging that Einstein's trip be canceled because his negotiations with the universities had aroused so much protest that, they feared, his visit at this time would be disastrous. Weizmann refused to heed the cables and ordered the ZOA to smooth over any problems.[31] Then a problem with Harvard arose and Weizmann received a telegram reading "Harvard absolutely declines Einstein." Whether Harvard declined because of the charges against Einstein or because of his Zionist connection is unknown. However, the following year, Harvard's President A. L. Lowell advocated official quotas on Jewish students "to avoid anti-Semitism on the campus."[32]

Because Einstein offered his services to the universities without remuneration, the charges of exploitation were forgotten and Einstein was well received everywhere. However, this incident added further fuel to the hostile feelings between Weizmann and the American Zionists.

The Zionist contingent arrived in New York harbor on April 2, 1921. Even before they debarked from the boat they were subjected to welcoming speeches, an official greeting committee of famous citizens, and a barrage of newsmen, cameramen, and a moving picture crew. On shore to greet them were also thousands of Jews who had been waiting for hours. Einstein spoke little English, but this did not deter the reporters from firing a series of questions at the baffled scientist who had never experienced this sort of public adulation. They wanted a one-sentence explanation of relativity; how did he like America? (He was still on board ship.) Einstein parried with jokes and smiles that were well received, and the *New York Times* reporter wrote that "he has made an unusual impression of geniality, kindliness and interest in the little things of life on those who have come in contact with him." He was hailed as a "poet in science," and as he left the boat carrying his pipe and violin, "he looked like an artist—a musician."[33]

In the next two months Einstein and Weizmann attended numerous rallies at which several million dollars were pledged. Einstein sat on the stage, exhibited "like a prize ox,"[34] while Weizmann addressed the large crowds. When called upon to speak, he would say in his limited English, "Your leader, Dr. Weizmann, has spoken, and he has spoken very well for us all. Follow him and you will do well. That is all I have to say."[35] Despite his rather nominal participation, Einstein, more than Weizmann, was the focus of the adulation of the excited crowds of Jews. His brilliant achievements were the inspiration which these refugees, only recently liberated from the stifling restrictions of the Old World, needed in their struggle to develop mental and social powers. As a result of the efforts of Weizmann and Einstein, and the enthusiastic support of the Jewish physicians, the medical faculty of the future Hebrew University was assured, and the general fund of the *Keren Hayesod* was successfully launched.

The Jews in America, like those in Germany, were divided between the "uptown Jews," Western European immigrants from the period after 1848 who by 1921 had generally succeeded in assimilating into American society, and the more recent, poorer, unassimilated Jews from Eastern Europe, the "downtown Jews." In many cases, the successful Jews viewed the impoverished immigrants with alarm and contempt. Although they were willing to wine and dine the celebrated Einstein, they did not contribute much to the Zionist cause, and Einstein mockingly labeled them *"haute finance."*[36] The support for the university and the *Keren Hayesod* came from the middle classes, the professionals, and the recent immigrants from Eastern Europe. After the trip, he wrote: "It was in America that I first discovered the Jewish people. . . . [They] came from Russia, Poland and Eastern Europe generally. These men and women still retain a healthy national [Jewish] feeling; it has not yet been destroyed by the process of atomization and dispersion. I found these people extraordinarily ready for self-sacrifice."[37] When Einstein sailed from New York at the end of May, his commitment to Zionism had been profoundly strengthened, and thereafter he assumed a far more active role within the movement.

The American tour had been a moving experience for both Einstein and Weizmann. Years later Weizmann wrote to Einstein that the trip was a "milestone in the awakening of Jewish Americans for Zion."[38] Einstein, despite exhaustion, aggravated by his aversion to the limelight, was also happy. In June he wrote to a friend: "Zionism indeed represents a new Jewish ideal that can restore to the Jewish people their joy in existence. . . . I am very happy that I accepted Weizmann's invitation."[39] The trip also cemented a lasting friendship between Einstein and Weizmann, which, although frequently stormy, remained strong because of the genuine respect the two men developed for each other while traveling together. In later years they would disagree, sometimes sharply, over the direction of Hebrew University, Arab-Jewish relations in Palestine, and the creation of a Jewish state. Vera Weizmann later wrote that during the trip she had found Einstein to be "young, gay and flirtatious."[40]

From time to time Einstein managed to escape from the grueling pace of the fund-raising tour to meet with American scientists. He gave lectures at Columbia University and City College of New York, and in the second week in May, when Princeton is at its loveliest, he was able to leave the tour for several days to deliver a series of lectures on relativity theory at Princeton University. The physicists at Princeton had been among the first in America to express serious interest in Einstein's work and, when he joined the Zionist expedition, he notified the delighted Americans that he would be able to accept their invitation to lecture.

Before his first lecture, the university awarded him an honorary degree in a large and impressive ceremony in the architectural curiosity known as Alexander Hall. The war had been over for two and a half years, yet animosity toward Germany still was fierce. A week earlier Einstein had received a chilly welcome in Washington because he was a Berliner. When it was explained that he was a Swiss citizen, the atmosphere immediately thawed. At the degree ceremony, Andrew F. West, Dean of the Graduate College, greeted Einstein in German, praised his scientific accomplishments, and then continued: ". . . especially would we do him honor for the moral fidelity whereby, amid distressing perils, he refused to join with others in condoning the invasion of Belgium."[41] Einstein was described as a professor at "Leyden" (Holland), a position he had held only since 1920; no mention of his German titles was made. Dean West's speech was followed by the presentation of the honorary degree. One newspaper described the scene: "When Dr. Einstein was supposed to sit down he stood, he sat when he should have stood and finally when the smiling, confused scientist who does not understand English, steered about by little tugs at his sleeve, was to receive his hood of a doctor from President John Grier Hibben he turned his back in the confusion upon the president."[42]

That afternoon in McCosh 50, one of the largest lecture halls on the campus, Einstein delivered the first of four lectures, which were later published by Princeton University Press as *The Meaning of Relativity*. A large crowd of faculty, students, and specially invited scientists filled the hall. Many attended to satisfy their curiosity, and the size of the audience shrank significantly after the first day because the technical content was incomprehensible to the uninitiated, and because Einstein spoke in German. There was no translation, but after each lecture one of the members of the physics department provided a brief English summary. Even the curiosity-seekers were captivated by the evident good will and energy of the lecturer, who impressed one observer with his sincere desire to impart his ideas to his listeners.[43]

At a reception held in his honor, Einstein was informed that Professor Dayton C. Miller had laboriously repeated the famous Michelson-Morley experiments and had detected the presence of ether, a discovery which, if true, would have meant the collapse of Einstein's relativity theory. Later Miller's results would be shown to be erroneous, but Einstein's initial response to the news that his theory might have been refuted has become legend: *"Raffiniert ist der Herrgott,"* he replied,

Einstein and the Princeton University mathematician Oswald Veblen in Princeton, May 1921. Veblen later received the first appointment to the Institute for Advanced Study. (Courtesy of Margot Einstein)

"aber boshaft ist er nicht." (Subtle is the Lord, but malicious He is not.) Oswald Veblen, at that time a member of Princeton's mathematics faculty, heard the remark and jotted it down. In 1930, when the university built Fine Hall (renamed Jones Hall in 1969) to house the mathematics department, Veblen wrote and asked Einstein for permission to inscribe his statement in the marble above the fireplace in the faculty lounge. Einstein quickly assented and explained he had meant "Nature hides her secret because of her essential loftiness, but not by means of ruse."[44] (After settling in Princeton, he once exclaimed to one of his assistants, Valentine Bargmann, "I have second thoughts, maybe God is malicious," by which he meant that God makes us believe we have understood something that in reality we are far from understanding.)[45]

The week at Princeton had been a welcome respite from the arduous tour schedule and the mystifying phenomenon of American hero-worship to which Einstein was subjected everywhere he went. He was astonished by the manner in which Americans would walk up to him and thrust a pen in his face for an autograph; to him autograph hunting was a form of cannibalism. After his brief and hectic visit, it is not surprising that he left the country under the impression—common in European intellectual circles—that capitalist America was materialist and anti-intellectual. In later years, increased firsthand knowledge of America would moderate these views, but in 1921 they provoked a storm after his return to Europe because he had not yet learned to be on guard at all times when dealing with the press. When some careless remarks that he made to an American reporter in Germany were sensationalized, he was acutely embarrassed and hastily issued a clarification. He had told the reporter that in general he found Americans to be friendly, optimistic, and helpful, and he was particularly impressed by the peaceful coexistence of so many different nationalities. The technological progress, tall buildings, and means of communication were clearly superior to Europe's but, he added, too much importance was attached to material comforts and goals. Americans were more group-oriented, less individualistic than Europeans. Visual arts and music were less developed, but scientific research was maturing rapidly. He was especially critical of Prohibition and the damaging influence of the press, which he believed was under the control of vested interests. He also felt that America ought to come forward and assume its proper role in world affairs, especially regarding the question of disarmament and membership in the League of Nations.[46]

The garbled account of this interview, which appeared in the *New York Times* on July 8, quoted Einstein as saying that the people were "colossally bored" and suffered from an "intellectual poverty" which explained the "excessive enthusiasm" they displayed for a scientist whose work they could not comprehend. The *New York Times* editorialist fumed on July 11: ". . . his tirades are received by most Americans, now, as showing the errors of judgment natural in the circumstances to a man of his sort, and particularly to one who, though not German by blood or birth, is a product of training exclusively German. . . . Dr. Einstein will not be forgiven . . . for his boorish ridicule of hospitable hosts."

Einstein quickly repudiated the July 8 article, declaring: "On the contrary, I arrived in Europe overcome by the warmth of my reception in the United States." As to his comments on the foolish response to his theories, he noted that this had happened in every country. Regarding the intellectual climate in America, he stated: "If Americans are less scholarly than Germans, they have more enthusiasm and energy, which cause a wider spread of new ideas among the people."[47] A few days later he told a reporter that he had found Oxford more pleasant than Germany and then added, "But I also found Princeton fine. A pipe as yet unsmoked. Young and fresh. Much is to be expected from America's youth."[48] These comments did not endear him to nationalistic and anti-Semitic circles in Germany.

On his return trip to Germany in June 1921 he visited England, where he received another chilly reception because he was German. His modesty and conciliatory behavior soon won the favor of the British public and press after he emphasized the importance of international intellectual cooperation and praised the contributions to science made by the British since the time of Newton. By the end of his short stay, one English newspaper declared that Einstein's visit "certainly represents a turning-point in the emotions of the post-war period in this country. Science and the arts have no boundaries."[49]

The pattern was repeated the following year when Einstein became the first prominent German to visit France since the war's end. Members of the French Academy threatened to walk out if he were invited to their august chambers because, they maintained lamely, Germany was not a member of the League of Nations. The threatened demonstrations never materialized, and Einstein's good will and desire to end the hatred dividing the two countries won the approval of the more reasonable elements of French society. These visits to the three enemy countries in the early twenties contributed significantly to the reestablishment of cooperation among intellectuals. The visits also helped to complete the transformation of the public image of Einstein from scientific genius to moral leader.

In November 1922 the Einsteins sailed for Japan, where he spent several weeks sightseeing and lecturing. He fell in love with the people and country but not the music, which sounded barbarous to him. The Japanese were particularly impressed by his egalitarianism and his interest in all aspects of the natural world. Einstein was surprised to learn that the Japanese did not question nature in the way Europeans do; instead "they immersed themselves in it." Problems in translation sometimes caused amusing misunderstandings. On one occasion, a wealthy Japanese man was greatly impressed that Einstein did research on "that place high above the clouds called space"—the gentleman assumed "space" meant "heaven." When the Einstein party was shown a sacred horse at the shrine on Miyajima Island, Einstein commented rather irreverently, "I wonder whether or not a sacred horse realizes his sacred function. Probably he's aware of nothing but his appetite. That would make him just like a priest. . . ." Einstein's manner made a strong impression upon his hosts. A Japanese cartoonist, Ippei Okamoto, who accompanied the Einsteins on their travels, wrote: "He has a quiet way of walking, as if he is afraid of alarming the truth and frightening it away."[50]

While he was in the Orient, the Nobel Prize in physics for 1921 was awarded to him for his contributions to theoretical physics and especially for his discovery of the law of the photoelectric effect. Relativity was still too controversial and was, therefore, omitted from the citation.[51] (In July 1923, when Einstein finally delivered his Nobel Prize lecture in Sweden, he ignored the usual practice of speaking about the work mentioned in the citation and lectured on the theory of relativity. He presented the prize money to Mileva.)

After leaving Japan, the Einsteins stopped in Palestine in February 1923. He was received like a head of state. In twelve days he was given a thorough tour of the cities and settlements of the 85,000 Jewish colonists. It was an emotional experience for him and for the colonists who were struggling against poverty, malaria, hunger, the desert, and their hostile Arab neighbors. Arabs constituted approximately 90 percent of the population and had erupted in violence against the Jews in 1920 and again in 1921. In his travel diary he described his visit to the Wailing Wall in Jerusalem, "where dull-witted clansmen of our tribe were praying aloud, their faces turned to the wall, their bodies swaying to and fro. A pathetic sight of men with a past but without a present."[52] He was taken to the future site of Hebrew University on Mount Scopus where he was invited to speak from "the lectern that has waited for you for two thousand years."[53] The university was officially dedicated in 1925. On February 8, 1923, he was named the first honorary citizen of Tel Aviv.

Einstein was greatly impressed by the work of the colonists in reclaiming the desert, and even more pleased by the spirit of solidarity and optimism it had instilled in them. After his return to Germany, he wrote to Solovine: "We liked our brethren in Palestine very much as peasants, as workers and as citizens. On the whole, the country is not very fertile. It will become a moral center, but will not be able to take in a large proportion of the Jewish people. I am convinced, however, that the colonization will succeed."[54] At that time, and again in 1933, pressure was applied on him to accept a position at Hebrew University and settle in Palestine. He resisted, in part because of his preference for life in Europe, and, in part because of the inevitable adulation—"sainthood," as he later described it—that would make normal existence impossible for him. Of the move to Jerusalem, he wrote in his 1923 diary, "The heart says yes, but the mind says no."[55]

A quick glance at Einstein's activities in the 1920s suggests that he was perpetually at the eye of the storm, primarily because of his political activities. In science, too, Einstein's ideas stirred controversy. After 1925 he entertained profound reservations concerning the direction quantum theory was taking. The consuming passion of his later life, his search for a unified field theory in which he sought to discover the underlying relationship between gravitation and electromagnetism, was viewed by much of the physics community with disdain and even scorn.

Disagreement among peers concerning the merit of ideas is a necessary fact of life for a scientist. Whenever a new theory is proposed, it must pass rigorous examination by the scientific community before gaining general acceptance.

In Einstein's case, however, in addition to bona fide scientific discussion of the merits of his theory, the scientist was subjected to abusive attacks on his character and his science by right-wing demagogues. Soon after the announcement by the British eclipse mission in 1919 that the general theory of relativity had been verified, Einstein's theories were attacked by an organization subsidized by anti-Semites who detested Einstein's wartime pacifism. Calling themselves the Study Group of German Natural Philosophers, they organized public meetings to denounce both the theory and its author. The Study Group (Einstein dubbed them the Anti-Relativity Company) was led by an anti-Semitic demagogue who possessed no understanding of science. Philipp Lenard's participation provided this collection of hacks a much-needed air of respectability.

On August 27, 1920, the Anti-Relativity Company staged a rally in Berlin, and Einstein, going along with what he thought was a farce, was in attendance, laughing at the most absurd attacks. Later, still exercising poor judgment, he responded to these character assassins in the press. In another attack at this time Bruno Thurring, author of the scurrilous volume, *Einstein's Attempt to Overthrow Physics,* warned "the Jewish plot to relativize all concepts and values must lead to chaos."[56] A decade later, after the publication of the book *One Hundred Authors Against Einstein,* Einstein was content to point out to a friend that if his theory was wrong, one author would have sufficed.[57]

Distasteful as these public disputes were, life in Berlin was not an unrelieved curse. He continued to be encouraged by the democratic Weimar Republic until, at

Einstein with Jewish settlers in Haifa, Palestine, February 1923. (Courtesy of Margot Einstein)

the end of the decade, world-wide economic collapse wrecked the fragile experiment. In his private life, he was surrounded by sympathetic spirits—family, friends, and colleagues. He relished the weekly Physics Colloquia with Planck, von Laue, Erwin Schroedinger, and many other outstanding physicists of all ages. Conditions for research and collaboration were excellent. Traditional German culture, as well as some aspects of the more experimental and erratic Weimar culture, greatly appealed to him. In Berlin he had endless opportunities to play and listen to classical music. In spite of his dislike of certain fundamental qualities of the German character, he himself was a German by birth, by tongue and, in many respects, by culture. His situation in Berlin, he once told Philipp Frank, resembled that of a man lying in a beautiful bed tortured by bedbugs.[58]

Einstein's international popularity, which grew with every trip abroad, provided the German right-wing with additional ammunition in their steady attacks against him in the 1920s. Acclaim from the Western democracies, the perpetrators of the Versailles Peace Treaty, was further proof, if any had been necessary, that the Jewish rabble-rouser and scientific charlatan was un-German. During this period, German nationalists hated domestic opponents even more than they hated Germany's enemies abroad. On more than one occasion, Einstein's friends and family pressured him to go into hiding or leave the country because of fears that he might be the next assassin's victim.

In the winter of 1928–1929 the German economy, which had enjoyed several years of prosperity after 1924, slipped into a recession, and by the spring of 1929, 1.5 million workers were unemployed. The psychological shock of the depression shattered Germany's faith in the existing world order. Political, moral, and intellectual standards collapsed, and Nazi and Communist extremists soon were engaged in street brawls. Hitler's attacks on Jews, democracy, and internationalism exploited the fears, longings, and resentments of the former middle class and the growing legions of unemployed workers who did not opt for socialism or communism. By 1932 the Nazis had forged a temporary alliance with the traditional antiliberal elements of German society—nobles, officers, civil servants, and large industrialists—which enabled Hitler to seize power legally in January 1933.

Although Einstein's unqualified pacifism of the late twenties may have been based upon utopian presuppositions, his assessment of the German political situation was acute. While crossing the Atlantic in December 1931, on his way to Pasadena, he noted in his travel diary: "I decided today that I shall essentially give up my Berlin position and shall be a bird of passage for the rest of my life."[59] At the time he envisioned something of a gypsylike existence divided between Leiden and Oxford, where he already held appointments, and possibly the California Institute of Technology in Pasadena.

Einstein first visited Cal Tech during the winter term of 1930–1931. He had been invited to work with the cosmologists assembled by Cal Tech's director, the American physicist Robert Millikan. It was his first visit to the United States since 1921, and, coming as it did in the midst of the Great Depression, his presence in

America provided the media and the public with a diversion from the economic catastrophe, and as a consequence, the trip often took on a circus atmosphere.

When word leaked out in November 1930 that he was soon to visit the United States, his Berlin apartment was deluged with invitations from representatives of many of the causes with which his name was publicly identified, as well as offers of thousands of dollars to endorse American products. His arrival in New York on December 11 produced a reaction similar to his reception a decade earlier, and he parried the inane questions of the newsmen with what he referred to in his travel diary as "cheap jokes." While in New York, he told a group of pacifists that if only 2 percent of those assigned to perform military service announced their refusal to fight, governments would be powerless because they would not dare to send so many to jail. The 2 percent speech may have delighted the pacifists, but it had a most unpleasant effect upon the staid, conservative Millikan who was assiduously courting wealthy, even more conservative, financial backers to repair the damage done to his institute by the depression. The Einstein party sailed for California via the Panama Canal, briefly stopping in Cuba in time for the latest revolution.

The two months in California were probably the liveliest in his life. His arrival in San Diego on December 31 set off four hours of parades, ceremonies, speeches, and a tour of the city. In addition to his scientific work, he spent time with the socialist novelist Upton Sinclair and with Charlie Chaplin, Elsa's "matinee idol," who took them to the opening of his *City Lights*. On the train trip to New York they stopped on February 28, 1931, at the Grand Canyon and visited the Hopi Indian Reservation where an embarrassed Einstein was given the name "The Great Relative" while he posed uncomfortably in Indian headdress for the benefit of news photographers.

There was a serious side to his nonscientific activities, but this could hardly have placated Millikan. The tone of his public comments had been set by the 2 percent speech: he was outspoken in support of draft resistance, disarmament, and Zionism. He criticized the United States policy of isolationism which, he asserted, was unworthy of this great nation at this critical moment in history. He became interested in the Mooney-Billings case in California in which two labor organizers had been convicted of a 1916 San Francisco bombing. They were not pardoned until 1939, although key witnesses had long since recanted their testimony and even the prosecutor had come to question their guilt. The following summer Einstein wrote to the governor of California urging an "absolute pardon"; he also wrote to Thomas J. Mooney, saying, "I know full well what strange judicial conditions exist in California and how arbitrarily persons are treated who are repugnant to certain influential groups."[60] In July 1931, from Germany, he supported the protest against the conviction of the "Scottsboro Boys"—eight black Alabama youths who had been convicted of raping two white women in one of the classic cases of Southern injustice.

Millikan was embarrassed by Einstein's political activities and tried to dismiss them as emotional and unrealistic. To an angry conservative philanthropist he wrote that Einstein was "exceedingly straightforward, honest and childlike . . ."

and had been "exploited by all sorts of agencies that had their special axes to grind. Part of these have been of the Charlie Chaplin type and part of the Upton Sinclair type."[61] The conservative Millikan was in a very awkward position. He was building a monument to American science at Cal Tech, and he hoped to attract Einstein as a regular visitor or a permanent member. He also had to keep wealthy, often reactionary, donors happy, and Einstein's outspoken liberalism made his task infinitely more difficult. Millikan was not the first to praise Einstein's noble character and scientific genius while dismissing his political activities as naïve and misinformed.

Einstein returned to Pasadena the next two winters but, at his request, and to the relief of Millikan, both of these subsequent visits avoided publicity. One of the few public functions Einstein did attend during the second Pasadena visit was sponsored by the Los Angeles University of International Relations, a school for diplomats and economists where he delivered a short, serious speech on the need for disarmament and a strong international court of arbitration. He and Elsa were both offended by the atmosphere at this dinner which, Elsa complained, "was treated as a kind of social entertainment," with the chairman cracking jokes. Einstein fumed in his diary: "I too gave a speech, but alas! this was hardly a responsive audience. The propertied classes here seize upon anything that might provide ammunition in the struggle against boredom. . . . It is a sad world in which such people are allowed to play first fiddle. . . ."[62]

Some time during that winter, Einstein was introduced to Abraham Flexner, who was then in the process of recruiting eminent mathematicians to his new Institute for Advanced Study. Flexner, then almost seventy years old, believed higher education in the United States desperately needed an institution exclusively dedicated to theoretical research where postdoctoral students of exceptional ability would enjoy informal and intensive contact with the most outstanding scholars in their field without the pressure to achieve practical results according to a predetermined timetable.

In 1930 he was given $5 million by Louis Bamberger and his sister Mrs. Felix Fuld, who had recently sold their famous department store, Bamberger's, in Newark, New Jersey. They wanted to place the institute in their hometown, but Flexner wisely lobbied for Princeton, arguing that it was essential for the institute to be located in the vicinity of a first-rate university with an excellent library.

Mr. Bamberger and Mrs. Fuld permitted Flexner to organize the institute slowly. He spent 1931–1932 visiting the leading academic institutions in America and Europe to discuss his ideas and solicit advice. Those with whom he consulted encouraged him to begin his experiment with one field of study, and to expand only after his ideas had been given an opportunity to prove themselves. Mathematics was chosen because it was a fundamental subject which required the smallest investment in plant or books, and because Flexner was advised that he could secure greater agreement on the identity of the most eminent mathematicians than in such disciplines as history, literature, or philosophy. It so happened that Princeton University had an outstanding mathematics department, and when

Flexner described his dream to President Hibben, Hibben assured him of cooperation and office space in Princeton's newly constructed mathematics building, Fine Hall.

By the end of 1931 Flexner had completed the first phase of his preparations. The institute was to be small, flexible, quiet, and comfortable. The faculty would enjoy complete intellectual freedom without administrative responsibilities or concerns. There would be no pressures or deadlines, and the scholars were to be provided with proper assistance. Flexner's institute was to be a haven for theoreticians, not technicians, because he believed that scientific knowledge could only be advanced by research and then, only after this was achieved, could it be applied to practical problems. Flexner designed his institute to be neither a graduate school nor a research institute, but a cross between the two. There were to be no regular lectures or courses; the faculty was to be free to choose its subjects, and teaching should be informal and on an individual basis.

Originally, Flexner had planned to issue Ph.D.s, but this idea was abandoned because it was decided that sufficient opportunities for advanced degrees already existed and the institute should concentrate on advanced research. In addition, the formal examinations and paperwork connected with advanced degrees cut into the professors' research time.

To attract the finest scholars and to protect them from the necessity of having to supplement their income with outside jobs (such as positions at other universities), Flexner set faculty salaries at more than three times the median salary of full professors in the United States. He was so devoted to the idea that his professors give full time to the institute that he was infuriated when his successor permitted faculty members to engage in war work in the 1940s.

The "students" of the institute were to be drawn from two sources: younger men and women who had recently taken their Ph.D.s and who wished to extend their research, and members of university faculties on leave from their teaching duties to catch up with the latest advances in their field. The faculty was to select and admit students to their department. There were to be no fixed admissions procedures, and qualified students were to be located by any means necessary. Institute students were called "members" and usually were appointed for one or two terms (three or six months). To insure a steady turnover of members, their stipends were to be kept small.[63]

Flexner later wrote that he had gone to Pasadena to discuss his ideas with Millikan and other eminent mathematicians at Cal Tech, but that he had purposely avoided approaching Einstein because "he was so much lionized." On the day he intended to depart from Cal Tech, Flexner received a telephone call from a Professor Morgan with whom he had already discussed his ideas. Morgan asked him if he had met with Einstein, and when Flexner answered that he had not, Morgan urged him to do so, even taking it upon himself to arrange the meeting. That day Einstein and Flexner met for an hour, and Einstein was so intrigued by Flexner's institute that he agreed to a second meeting at Oxford in May. On this occasion, an offer was made—"You would be welcome on your own terms"[64]—

and the men agreed to meet in Germany in June. At the third meeting shortly after the collapse of the Brüning government on May 30, following a daylong discussion, Einstein agreed to join the institute, making it clear, however, that he wished to retain his position at the Prussian Academy of Science in Berlin and his recent appointment at Christ Church, Oxford. Because of the rapidly deteriorating situation in Germany, Einstein was worried about the plight of his assistant, Walter Mayer, whom he had described in a 1930 letter to Maurice Solovine as "a splendid fellow, who long ago would have obtained a professorship, were it not for his being Jewish."[65] Millikan had been unable to offer Mayer a position; Flexner, after protracted negotiation, eventually assured Einstein there would be a place at the institute for his assistant.[66] With that assurance, Einstein accepted a life appointment to the institute to begin in October 1933. The conversation then turned to salary and, after some thought, Einstein proposed something in the range of $3,000 per year. Flexner suggested that he work out the details with Mrs. Einstein, and eventually Einstein's salary was set at $15,000 per year. As they were saying goodbye, Einstein exclaimed to Flexner, "*Ich bin Feuer and Flamme dafür* [I am full of enthusiasm]."[67]

4

Demigods and Paradise

instein sailed for America on October 7, 1933, aboard the *Westernland* from Southampton, where he had joined Elsa, his secretary, Helen Dukas,[1] and Walter Mayer, who had embarked at Antwerp. The uneventful passage across the Atlantic was disturbed only by Miss Dukas's seasickness. The *Westernland* was scheduled to dock in New York on October 17. The city was in the midst of an election campaign and Mayor O'Brien, running for reelection against Fiorello La Guardia, seized the opportunity to welcome the world's most celebrated Jew with a band, a parade, and speeches. The mayor's visions of capturing the Jewish vote were short-circuited by Flexner, who had arranged for the Einstein party to be discharged at the Battery.

They were met by Herbert N. Maass, a trustee of the institute, who presented Einstein with a letter from Flexner which warned that, after consultation with local and national authorities, he had "no doubt whatsoever that there are organized bands of irresponsible Nazis in this country. . . . [Y]our safety in America depends upon silence and refraining from attendance at public functions."[2] Although Einstein did not share Flexner's sense of danger, he was only too happy to avoid fanfare of the kind that awaited him. And so, while the band played on, and the flowers for Mrs. Einstein wilted in the mayor's arms, the honored refugees were whisked through customs and arrived in Princeton while the *Westernland* was still discharging her less celebrated passengers.

The town of Princeton, located in the rolling hills of central New Jersey, lies fifty miles from both New York and Philadelphia. The first settlers arrived between 1685 and 1697. They were Quakers who were attracted by the fertile land, the streams, the abundant forests, and the chance to build a religious community in solitude. The town was named Princeton in 1724, and by the middle of the eighteenth century, although the region was still sparsely populated, the woods had been cleared away, the land was under cultivation, and frontier conditions no longer prevailed. When the College of New Jersey moved from Elizabeth to Princeton in 1756, the small community of farmers, merchants, and innkeepers was transformed into an intellectual center.

Anglo-Saxon Protestants have dominated both town and gown (the university), but Princeton has always been blessed with an interesting mix of ethnic groups. The late nineteenth and early twentieth centuries saw an influx of craftsmen and laborers from England, Scotland, Russia, Poland, and an especially large contingent from Italy. There had always been a substantial black community, dating from the colonial period when the farms and households depended upon slaves. Princeton's greatest native-born son, Paul Robeson, born in 1898, was the son of a black minister. The great singer and actor devoted his life to the fight against racism and injustice, which he first experienced in his hometown.

In the 1900s the town grew slowly, but until the end of the Second World War Princeton remained a small, quiet college town with beautiful tree-lined streets, large estates and farms and significant tracts of second-growth woods where once there had been fields. The university was the dominant force in the town, and most residents were directly employed by it or were engaged in some kind of service or business which catered to the university community.

Four days before Einstein's arrival, the *Princeton Herald* reported that according to "persistent rumor" he would rent the home of Mrs. William R. Hall at 11 Cleveland Lane. The article continued: "Unless a request is made for protection, Borough police will not supply a guard for Dr. Einstein over whom English police have been keeping a watchful eye because of threats made against him as a result of his attacks upon the Hitler movement in Germany."[3] No such request was ever made. It is ironic that local British and American authorities were willing to provide Einstein with protection from Nazi assassins while their national leaders seemed unable to recognize the Nazi threat to world peace. The *Herald,* like the Nazis, had overestimated Einstein's role among the anti-Nazi forces. Einstein's public "attacks" against Hitler up to this point had been intentionally cautious. The Nazi threats against his life were due to his exposed position as a world-famous Jew, and absolute silence on his part would not have placated them.

While rumors claimed that the Einsteins were staying with an unnamed friend, they quietly settled into the Peacock Inn, an old but comfortable and unpretentious hotel a block from Nassau Street. One of their first visitors was Dr. Otto Nathan, a German economist on the faculty of Princeton University, who had left Germany immediately after Hitler became Chancellor. In the hectic first days after Einstein's arrival he provided invaluable assistance. (Miss Dukas has said, "We would have been lost without Otto Nathan.") Einstein had not known Nathan in Berlin; in Princeton a powerful bond between these two men was quickly forged. They shared a similar outlook on political, economic, and moral issues, and for more than twenty years they fought together in an unflagging effort to implement their ideals. Nathan, an indefatigable worker, possessed the background and expertise in politics and economics that Einstein lacked.

During the first days a circus atmosphere prevailed as newsmen vainly sought the elusive scientist. On October 20 the *Herald* carried a story headlined "Einstein Wears Invisible Cloak" which claimed that he had become the object of the "greatest man-hunt Princeton has ever seen. . . . Persons who were not seeking him out saw him here, there and everywhere. Persons who looked high and low for him were unable to locate him."

On the eve of Einstein's arrival Flexner had issued a polite but firm warning to the press which asserted, "Professor Einstein will give no interview, issue no statements and make no public appearance at this time, since his one desire is to resume his scientific activity. . . ."[4] Princeton University apparently did not get the message and, unbeknownst either to Einstein or to Flexner, the university scheduled a photographic session for his second day in town. When Einstein learned of this, he and Mayer slipped out a back door of Fine Hall while the newsmen fidgeted in front.

The Einstein party remained at the Peacock Inn for about ten days while Mrs. Einstein searched for a suitable home. The house on Cleveland Lane was not

112 Mercer Street in Princeton, ca. 1980. Helen Dukas is approaching the front door. Einstein lived here from September 1935 until his death. It remains a private residence and, at his request, it has not been turned into a museum or public shrine; it is hoped it never will be. (Courtesy of Margot Einstein)

taken, and eventually they settled upon a two-family house at 2 Library Place across the street from the Princeton Theological Seminary. For a while they were pestered by a steady stream of curiosity-seekers and newsmen. Mrs. Raymond Leslie Buell, whose family occupied the other half of the house which had its entrance on Mercer Street, recalls that sometimes when uninvited guests appeared, Mrs. Einstein would don her hat and coat and pretend she was on her way out. She then walked around the corner, knocked at the Buells' door, and in this way became acquainted with her neighbor while dodging the curious.

Princeton society was primarily composed of two groups. In addition to the academic community associated with the university, there were a significant number of wealthy, business-oriented people, many of whom were alumni of the university, who had settled in Princeton because of its rural beauty and proximity to New York and Philadelphia. At first, both groups showered the Einsteins with invitations to tea or dinner. Most were politely declined, and their early socializing was confined to becoming acquainted with their neighbors and colleagues from the institute and university. The *New York Times* kept a watchful eye out for news-worthy activities involving Einstein (almost anything involving Einstein was considered newsworthy), and there were occasional reports of musical evenings in those first months. As time passed, the invitations, especially from the alumni and business faction, diminished when it became clear that Einstein was simply not interested in socializing.

Shortly after settling in Princeton, Elsa wrote a friend in Europe that "the whole of Princeton is one great park with wonderful trees."[5] Her husband recorded somewhat more acute first impressions of his new home in a letter to Queen Elizabeth of Belgium dated November 20, 1933. "Princeton is a wonderful little spot," he reported, "a quaint and ceremonious village of puny demigods on stilts. Yet, by ignoring certain social conventions, I have been able to create for myself an atmosphere conducive to study and free from distraction. Here, the people who compose what is called 'society' enjoy even less freedom than their counterparts in Europe. Yet, they seem unaware of this restriction since their way of life tends to inhibit personality development from childhood." Later, after he had become more adjusted and comfortable in Princeton, he is reputed to have said that going to Princeton was a "banishment to Paradise."[6]

An aura of mystery, saintliness, absurdity, and confusion soon surrounded Einstein in Princeton. Halloween occurred a few days after they moved into the house on Library Place, and on that night they were visited by a group of twelve-year-old schoolgirls who intended to play a trick on a celebrity, but as one of the pranksters later recalled with some "discomfort," "Einstein seemed to have been warned that some response was expected, and he came out on the stoop and played the violin for us. We were all torn between pleasure and shame that so generous a response should have been made by this great man to these nasty little girls that we 'slunk' off. It was a peculiar and uncomfortable feeling for all of us; I don't think any of us had had that kind of feeling before."[7]

A visit by another group of youngsters in November led to an unpleasant scene with Flexner. One Saturday a group of boys from Newark, who had named their science club in honor of Einstein, called upon their hero with a drawing of him made by one of the boys which they wanted him to autograph. He received them graciously and offered them encouragement, little realizing that the gentleman posing as their adviser was a newsman. The resulting article in the *Newark Star-Ledger* offended Mrs. Fuld and Mr. Bamberger, who concluded Einstein was a publicity hound.

On another occasion that same autumn, Mrs. Einstein and Miss Dukas went shopping in New York. They were escorted by a distant relative of Elsa's who had taken it upon himself to notify the press of the outing. They were overwhelmed by newsmen and photographers and when the *New York Times* printed something quite harmless about the incident, Flexner took exception. He also objected when Einstein played his violin at a Jewish benefit and tactlessly expressed disapproval of Einstein's involvement in Jewish functions. He claimed that such activities would provoke an increase of anti-Semitism in the United States. It is more likely that he was concerned about adverse publicity for the fledgling institute, whose survival depended upon the largesse of donors whose views on Zionism and politics did not necessarily coincide with Einstein's.

Flexner took it upon himself to refuse all requests addressed to Einstein for interviews, dinners, benefits, and lectures. In general, Einstein appreciated the protective shield the director of the institute had thrown up around him, but protection gave way to meddling when Flexner declined, in Einstein's name, an invitation to visit President Franklin D. Roosevelt at the White House. The idea for a White House visit for Einstein originated with Rabbi Stephen S. Wise, Einstein's most direct link with the leaders of American Jewry. The day after Einstein's arrival in Princeton, Wise wrote to Judge Julian Mack, another Jewish leader: "Could not F.D.R. be moved to invite Einstein to visit him in the White House? We have had nothing but indifference and unconcern up to this time. Perhaps we can have something of help. . . . It would make such a fine impression if the President were, at the instance preferably of some Christian friend . . . to invite Einstein . . ." Mack replied that unless Einstein were spared publicity Flexner would oppose the invitation. On October 20 Wise shot back: "We are not doing it for the sake of publicity. Einstein has nothing to gain. F.D.R. has not lifted a finger on behalf of the Jews of Germany, and this would be little enough, and to have Einstein at the White House is at least as honoring to F.D.R. as to Einstein." The same day Wise passed his suggestion along to Charles Burlingham, one of Roosevelt's advisers, and soon an invitation was extended.[8]

On November 3, 1933, Flexner informed the President that Einstein required seclusion for his scientific work and that it was "absolutely impossible to make any exception which would inevitably bring him into public notice. You are aware," Flexner continued, "that there exists in New York an irresponsible group of Nazis. In addition, if the newspapers had access to him or if he accepted a single engagement or invitation that could possibly become public, it would be practically impossible for him to remain in the post which he has accepted in this Institute or in America at all. With his consent and at his desire I have declined in his behalf invitations from high officials and from scientific societies in whose work he is really interested."[9] The unhappy implication of the final phrase is that Einstein was not *really* interested in the work Roosevelt was doing. Why Flexner behaved as he did on this occasion remains a mystery. One biographer, Ronald Clark, speculates that Flexner was worried that Roosevelt might exert pressure upon Einstein to align himself with both the institute and Millikan's Cal Tech. While it is true that before Hitler had come to power, Einstein was planning to come to Princeton every year only during the October–April term at the institute, and Flexner and Millikan had had a somewhat bitter exchange concerning Einstein's affiliation with the institute, it appears to be more reasonable to assume that Flexner's irrational behavior was provoked by his strong personal dislike of Roosevelt and his own tendency toward autocratic behavior.

Only a chance remark by Mrs. Roosevelt to Henry Morgenthau, then Undersecretary of the Treasury, expressing her disappointment, exposed Flexner's interference. When Einstein learned of Flexner's action he wrote Mrs. Roosevelt: "You can hardly imagine of what great interest it would have been for me to meet the man who is tackling with gigantic energy the greatest and most difficult problem of our time." After explaining that he had known such an invitation was intended but, he assumed, had been abandoned, he concluded: "I am writing this letter because it means a great deal to me to avoid the ugly impression that I had been negligent or discourteous in this matter."[10] A second invitation was immediately extended—directly to Einstein—and he and Elsa spent the night of January 24, 1934, in the White House. On that wintry evening the conversation ranged from a mutual love of sailing and Einstein's friendship with Queen Elizabeth of Belgium to the tragedy in Europe. Einstein undoubtedly took the opportunity to emphasize the desperate plight of Hitler's victims and perhaps put in a discreet word about America's policy of isolation. But it was a friendly, informal occasion and serious discussion of politics probably was avoided. Each man came away from the meeting with lasting respect for the other. Einstein later told friends, "I'm so sorry that Roosevelt is President—otherwise I would have visited him more often."[11]

Einstein was furious at Flexner. In November, when he learned of the director's interference, he informed Rabbi Wise; the return address on the letter read "Concentration Camp, Princeton."

In a long letter to the board of trustees of the institute written either in December 1933 or January 1934, he complained: ". . . Mr. F[lexner] has interfered several times in my private affairs, and that in a very tactless way. . . . [H]e has written insulting letters to my wife and myself." A list of six specific grievances followed: (1) Flexner had attempted to prevent Einstein's appearance at the Royal Albert Hall; (2) letters and telegrams of great importance had not reached Einstein in his first days in Princeton; (3) Flexner had written an insulting letter after the *Newark Star-Ledger* article and had never apologized for his "incorrect behavior"; (4) he had bungled the White House invitation; (5) he had interfered with a Jewish benefit, claiming Einstein "was doing all such things driven by pure vanity"; and (6) he had told a rabbi that Einstein's behavior would make it impossible for Flexner to invite any more Jews to the institute (Flexner was an "uptown Jew"). Einstein stated he would resign from the institute if Flexner did not leave him alone. The director, who had explained to one defender of Einstein that his actions were motivated by a belief that "in my judgment, he does not understand America,"[12] immediately terminated his almost daily admonitions and memos, and his next letter to Einstein is dated several years later. Although there were to be some bitter disagreements between the two men concerning institute policy toward the end of the decade, relations between them improved markedly after this episode.

Einstein's presence in Princeton had a subtle but profound effect on his neighbors, and soon a spontaneous folklore sprung up around him. His innocence of American mores endeared him to Princetonians and often provoked their laughter. Except for sailing, the only recreation he enjoyed was walking, usually with his head bowed, lost in thought. The sight of this man walking along some side street in Princeton was an exciting event, much as the sight of an animal in the forest thrills the city dweller. He quickly achieved the reputation of being an absent-minded professor, largely because of popular stories that he could not remember where he lived. During Einstein's first winter in Princeton one university undergraduate recalls: "Twice I heard (from two different girls who lived in Princeton) about his sense of direction. Each said that Einstein had approached her on a side street several blocks off Nassau Street asking for directions to Nassau Hall. In each case Einstein explained that the only reason he wanted to get to Nassau Hall was that he knew his way home from there. Both girls asked him where his home was and, on finding out, suggested more direct routes. He thanked them both but said he would go via Nassau Hall."[13]

On another occasion in the mid-1930s, he was invited to dinner at the home of his close friend and colleague at the institute, the art historian Erwin Panofsky. Mrs. Panofsky had requested that he be punctual because the guest of honor, a noted pianist, was performing in concert that night. That afternoon Einstein and his assistant Leopold Infeld became absorbed in some problem which they continued to discuss as they walked to the Panofskys', on the other side of town. When they reached the street, Einstein suddenly realized he had forgotten where the house was, and since Infeld did not know the Panofskys, they knocked on a door to ask directions. By this time he had forgotten Panofsky's name and could remember only that he was an art historian. Eventually they were directed to their destination, only slightly tardy. He was too embarrassed to tell his host and hostess what had happened for fear they might take it amiss but, in fact, they were highly amused when they learned of the story much later.[14] After living in Princeton for a short while, he became perfectly adept at navigating about town. It is true that often he did not pay careful attention to details, so that he sometimes appeared to be absent-minded, but this image has been exaggerated, and in important matters he had a fine memory.

In the thirties, Princeton society, whether academic or business-oriented, was decidedly formal. Einstein's unruly hair, his careless style of dressing, his sock-lessness, and his freedom from social constraint soon spawned the now-familiar stories of the Einsteinian mythology. Humorous anecdotes, which purported to reveal his peculiar nature, abounded, although most owed their origin to a fertile imagination or the exaggeration of some slight incident. Some of the stories merely attempted to convey a humorous glimpse of the great but simple man; others smacked of gossip tinged with envy. While wives of the "puny demigods" exchanged tales of Einstein's and his wife's alleged social gaffes, the stolid husbands amused themselves with smug appraisals of the great man's simple-minded political views. More often, however, the stories, real or imagined, were harmless attempts to capture a sense of the spirit of the distinctive, often funny, physicist.

Those who came to know him personally quickly saw beyond the superficialities of appearance. They saw the kindness in his eyes, the mischievous smile of innocent delight from hearing a funny story; they heard the quiet and calming voice speaking softly, often pausing thoughtfully for the correct phrase. Frequently, particularly in later years, he would begin to speak in English and, in the middle of a sentence, would slip unconsciously into German. Sometimes with a twinkle in his eyes he would break out in strong and free laughter that burst from deep within. Those who knew him understood that the absentmindedness and seeming eccentricity in dress were not a pose but the consequence of his desire to liberate himself from the details of existence. His life was proof of Thoreau's contention that "a man is rich in proportion to the number of things which he can afford to let alone." Einstein is reputed to have said, "It would be a sad situation if the bag was better than the meat wrapped in it."[15]

One individual who knew him well described him with the German adjective *"bedächtig,"* which can be translated as "circumspect, discreet, prudent, cautious, deliberate, slow." Since earliest childhood he had had a dreamy disposition. His speech, movements, and manner were slow and thoughtful, yet firm and decisive. When considering a matter of importance, he gave fullest attention to all significant circumstances and possible consequences before reaching a conclusion. Only then would he act, prepared to defend his decision with unyielding stubbornness.

Einstein's unusual appearance made an especially strong impression upon Princeton children. When walking around town, or on his way to and from his office, he would always greet them, pat them on the head, and babble with the babies. His one source of vanity, which he delighted in showing off to children, was his ability to wiggle his ears. Invariably, they wanted to know why he did not wear socks. One little girl even warned him, "Your mother will be afraid you'll catch cold." To a group of small boys who posed the question, he replied, "I've reached an age when if somebody tells me to wear socks, I don't have to."[16] To others he claimed that he objected to someone having to mend the holes in his socks.

It was his hair that most baffled and delighted the young. One little boy, fascinated by the unruly white mass of hair, referred to him as "the man with soap in the hair." Einstein was so pleased that he signed a letter to the boy with this name. Another boy was so confused by Einstein's long hair that he asked his nurse, "Why doesn't *he* cut *her* hair?" Still another, seeing him pass by on the street, asked, "Is that Mrs. Einstein?" Once, before a young mother took her son to visit the Einsteins, she described to the boy what Einstein looked like. When they arrived, he was taken upstairs to say hello. A few moments later he came rushing downstairs calling, "Mother, he *does* look like a lion!"[17]

One child who lived on the route Einstein took to the institute (after the move to Fuld Hall in 1939) described, many years later, the "vivid memory" of his first encounter with Einstein: "The memory is of a wraith-like figure wrapped in an ancient overcoat reaching nearly to the ankles, a woolen sailor's cap afloat on long white hair, baggy pants reaching nearly to scuffed shoes but betraying the absence of socks, and the most angelic face I had seen before or since. . . . It was one of those sights about which one had to inquire of one's parents. Whereupon I learned that the vision was that of Albert Einstein en route to work. When, infrequently, his walk to work coincided with my presence in the front yard, I would wave and call out and he would wave and respond. The memory of my first encounter remains, as you can see, intense."[18]

The growing legend of Einstein, a mixture of genius and benevolent clown, precipitated zany behavior in others. One undergraduate in the thirties recalls observing a classmate, who was struggling to pass his science course, act out the following scene: "One winter morning I was the delighted observer of this new version of Einstein's progress [across the campus to his office in Fine Hall]. There had been a fresh fall of snow that night, and Einstein's footsteps on the duckboards were the first to be printed there. Behind him about a dozen paces was my friend Eddie who had patiently waited for the famous man. Then very carefully he was planting his feet in Einstein's tracks, hoping, presumably, to capture some of his vibes—as you young people say. Eddie followed his leader until I could see the pair no more."[19]

Once Hans Panofsky chauffeured his father, Erwin, and Einstein to an art collection outside Philadelphia. On the return trip, to the chagrin of the younger Panofsky, who was driving with an expired California license, a policeman stopped the car. He had no interest in the driver but, rather, simply stopped the car to be sure that he had indeed spotted the great Einstein.[20]

The institute did not have a building of its own until 1939; prior to that time its scholars maintained offices in Fine Hall, along with the mathematicians of the university. A great many people erroneously assumed Einstein was affiliated with the university. When he first arrived, a number of right-wing alumni vehemently protested his alleged affiliation with their alma mater, because they felt he was a Communist. In the confusion over his status, Einstein sometimes received bizarre letters, including one, written in 1934, that warned of a plot afoot to poison Princeton undergraduates in the dining hall.

Occasionally he participated in undergraduate activities on campus. A year after his arrival he addressed the Princeton Anti-War Society and the International Relations Club, where he impressed the students with his "warm, genial and exceedingly patient . . . comments and responses to our questions."[21] In November 1934 he delivered his first lecture in English at Professor John Stewart's undergraduate astronomy class. His lecture was not announced in advance and, to complicate matters, the class was at 8:30 A.M. the Monday after a major football victory. As a result, less than half of the hundred students enrolled in the course attended, a detail the *New York Times* dutifully reported. One student who did attend recalls that although an interpreter was present, Einstein's command of English proved to be quite good. ("The undergraduates could have used some help on the substance, however.") He spoke on special relativity, filling the blackboard with a number of clocks traveling away from each other at velocities approaching the speed of light. "Einstein's manner was charming," Laurence Fenninger remembers, "so much so that no one left when the bell rang even though there could not have been ten people in the room (including Einstein and Stewart) who really knew what he was talking about. At the end of the affair, some ten minutes after the bell, he smiled, shrugged his shoulders, and said in a heavy German accent, 'Gentlemen, that's all there is to it.' We were all properly dumbfounded to think that we'd heard 'all' from the originator of the theory, and applauded enthusiastically."[22]

From time to time he was the guest speaker at Friday night religious services for Jewish students at the university, which were held to satisfy the compulsory chapel requirement. They were informal sessions that discussed aspects of Jewish history and problems Jewish students encountered at Princeton. In an effort to improve these often less than inspiring sessions, the students sought and received permission to invite guest speakers: professors from the philosophy department, rabbis and, eventually, Einstein, who is remembered for his informality and unpretentiousness—he was the only person who appeared without a necktie. At one meeting he was asked if he believed it was permissible for Jews to marry out of the faith. He replied with "a hearty guffaw," "It's dangerous—but then *all* marriages are dangerous."[23] In the two decades he was at Princeton, he attended these Friday night services once every two or three years.

As Einstein settled into his new life in Princeton, he found that, despite the initial fuss made over him, he was able to lead a relatively quiet existence which allowed him to get on with his work. Princetonians soon came to accept him as, if not one of them, at least one among them, and except for newsmen and occasional out-of-town curiosity-seekers, and the steady stream of refugee scholars who came to him for encouragement, advice, and sometimes assistance, he was generally accorded the privacy he desired. Originally he had intended to return to Europe in April 1934 to his positions in England and Holland, but events in Europe continued to worsen almost daily, and as the plight of the Jews in Germany deteriorated, Einstein's status as symbol of the Nazi victims grew. If he returned to Europe that summer he knew he would be drawn into the political crisis. In Princeton he was able to do just as much for the refugees as he could do for them in Europe, and in Princeton it could be done with much less public fuss. (The danger of assassination worried Elsa, but it is unlikely that it disturbed him.) He remained a European in spirit always, but the European civilization to which Einstein belonged, the Europe of Shakespeare, Spinoza, Goethe, and Mozart, was in eclipse.

By March 1934 Einstein had decided to spend a quiet summer somewhere near water. ("Why should an old fellow like me not enjoy relative peace and quiet for once?" he asked Max Born.)[24] He rented a house in Watch Hill, Rhode Island, which he shared with the family of his close friend Dr. Gustav Bucky. Bucky had been the head of the X-ray department in a Berlin hospital. On April 1, 1933, the day of the Nazi boycott against the Jews, he left Germany and returned to the United States, where he was a citizen. He was a talented inventor and he and Einstein loved to tinker together (once they took out a patent on a camera they had

Einstein and Dr. Gustav Bucky, ca. 1934. (Courtesy of Margot Einstein)

developed). Like Einstein, he was tireless in his efforts to assist refugees from Germany.

The Einsteins had chosen Watch Hill because it was too far from New York or Princeton for visitors to come for the day. It was a coastal town which, despite the often heavy fog, was a delightful place for Einstein to sail. He never mastered the changing tides, and on more than one occasion he and Dr. Bucky ran aground. While Bucky fidgeted, the schoolboy at the tiller would laugh and say, "Don't look so tragic, Bucky. They'll wait for me at home—my wife is used to this."[25] Despite the news from Europe it was a peaceful summer in Rhode Island.

In May word was received that Elsa's older daughter, Ilse Kayser, was desperately ill in Paris. Einstein resisted all attempts by his wife to persuade him to accompany her to France, saying he could be of no use. Elsa sailed alone for Europe on May 19 and arrived shortly before her daughter died, a blow from which she never recovered. Margot, Elsa's younger daughter, had nursed her sister throughout the final illness, and after Ilse's death, she accompanied her distraught mother to America.

Ilse had been married to Rudolf Kayser, a prominent German writer who, in the decade before Hitler's rise to power, was editor-in-chief of Germany's foremost literary magazine, *Die Neue Rundschau*. He was the author of numerous books, including biographies of Stendhal, Spinoza, and Kant, and in 1930, under the pen name of Anton Reiser, he wrote the first reliable biography of Einstein. Kayser was responsible for saving Einstein's Berlin papers and Elsa's family furniture. He took the papers from the Berlin apartment to the French Embassy, where one of the high-ranking officials arranged to take them out in the diplomatic pouch which would not be opened by Nazi border guards. Kayser also succeeded in shipping the family furniture out of Germany and, eventually, to Princeton. He had to name himself as addressee because anything sent to Einstein from Germany would have been confiscated. When the furniture arrived in Princeton, a customs agent, detached to process the shipment, was dumbfounded to learn that Kayser did not live at the address on the crates. "But where is Mr. Kayser?" he kept repeating. It took a long time to explain to him that Einstein was a proscribed man in Germany and that subterfuge was necessary when dealing with the Nazis.[26] In 1935, most Americans simply did not understand the seriousness of the Nazi threat.

Elsa and Margot brought with them from Paris several boxes and trunks filled with Einstein's papers. On board the *Westernland* Elsa recognized some neighbors from Princeton, Professor and Mrs. Blackwood. He was a professor of homiletics at the Princeton Theological Seminary and they were returning from Jerusalem. Elsa, mourning Ilse's death, was afraid that she would be unable to get the boxes and trunks through customs because she was not an American citizen. She asked the Blackwoods if they would claim them, and when they reached New York, Professor Blackwood put on his customs declaration that they had been "acquired in Europe for scholarly purposes."[27] Upon their arrival, Elsa and Margot joined

Einstein, Margot Einstein, and Elsa Einstein, probably taken at Watch Hill, R.I., in late summer 1934. (Courtesy of Margot Einstein)

Einstein at Watch Hill while the Blackwoods generously arranged to safeguard the "contraband" in a shed behind their house in Princeton until the Einsteins returned to town in the autumn.

Late in December 1934 Elsa suffered an attack of sciatica. A group of young members of the First Presbyterian Church had a tradition of singing Christmas carols outside the windows of people who were ill, and one evening shortly before Christmas, about a dozen carolers, accompanied by a violinist, assembled in front of 2 Library Place. One of the carolers described the scene: "With snow coming down all over the place, just like an old Christmas card scene, we went over and started singing unannounced, when the front door opened and Dr. Einstein came out. He was obviously touched; he thanked us and asked if he could accompany us on our violin. We thought that was great and Jane Lewis presented him with her violin, and we sang Christmas carols for quite a few minutes. He played with the snow coming down and very graciously thanked us. I don't think he'd been exposed to this before. He was just a lovely person, and it made an impression on all of us. It was one of those little vignettes that you always remember."[28] Although the faces change with the passing of years, the tradition of serenading the Einstein home at Christmastime continues to this day.

Einstein's presence in Princeton had a significant impact upon the town, and if it is something of an exaggeration to claim that he put Princeton on the map (as has been suggested), it is true that after 1933 the town gained an international reputation it had never previously enjoyed. The Princeton area absorbed a substantial number of refugees from European fascism. Intellectuals like Einstein, Thomas Mann, Hermann Broch, and Erich Kahler were attracted by the academic and intellectual life and the quiet beauty of the town and its environs. There were also a great many nonintellectuals who settled in this region, happy to be alive, and grateful for any opportunity to work. In the depression years three factors combined to make the Princeton area especially attractive to refugees: the intellectual opportunities, the excellent farming land in the outlying districts, and the fact that Princeton's economy had been buffered from the worst of the depression by the stability of the university and the wealthy landowners and alumni. Furthermore, Princeton was the home of Einstein, the most celebrated of all refugees.

Before the influx of these refugees, Princeton society had been conservative and somewhat insular. Old Princeton was forced to make certain adjustments to the refugees, most of whom were Jewish. The wife of a prominent faculty member who had regular dealings with Einstein, had grown up in a small town in Pennsylvania where there had been only one Jewish family. As the refugees began to arrive in Princeton, she confided to a friend that she was somewhat "appalled at this invasion and what it was going to do to the community."[29] When the Einsteins bought a house in 1935, the real estate agent, as a matter of course, asked the woman next door if she would object to having a Jew move in; she did not.[30] A daughter of one of the great estate owners in the time of Woodrow Wilson said of the "invasion": "Oh, it made it a much more interesting place to live. Although the

Princeton I grew up in was a nice, happy, cozy place, I think it did Princeton a lot of good. Princeton was too small, too smug. That gave it a big lift."[31]

There was very little open anti-Semitism in town. The university was known to have an admission quota that limited the percentage of Jews in any one class to approximately the percentage of Jews in the population of the United States. In 1933 there were only three Jewish faculty members, one of whom was Otto Nathan. Einstein was convinced that Nathan's appointment was terminated in 1935 because of anti-Semitism. Some professors were upset by the influx of foreign scholars and jealous of the attention and salaries reputedly being paid to the newcomers; but this sort of disgruntlement is common to any society and, in general, these feelings were neither widespread nor overtly expressed. Miss Dukas recalls, "We personally didn't notice it. We were only told there was [anti-Semitism] before coming. Not active, but snobbish. . . . Really we never experienced anything, but we were told it was a reactionary town."[32] Compared to the atmosphere in Germany, however, Princeton certainly was paradise.

In February 1935 Einstein sent condolences to Queen Elizabeth (now Queen Mother) of Belgium after the death of King Albert, who had been killed in a mountain-climbing accident in 1934. "Among my European friends," he wrote, "I am now called 'The Great Stone Face' [*Der grosse Schweiger*], a title I well deserve for having been so completely silent. The gloomy and evil events in Europe have paralyzed me to such an extent that words of a personal nature do not seem able to flow any more from my pen. Thus I have locked myself into quite hopeless scientific problems—the more so since, as an elderly man, I have remained estranged from the society here. . . ."[33]

Einstein had come to Princeton because of the opportunities the institute afforded him as a scientist. Science was always the first priority in his personal life and during the early years in Princeton he was particularly successful in immersing himself in his work. He had many good reasons for avoiding publicity, and despite Flexner's earlier insinuations about his improper handling of the flood of publicity, he generally was successful in maintaining a low profile. A measure of this success can be gauged from the fact that the *Princeton Herald,* ever alert to local doings, did not mention Einstein after his arrival in 1933 until it reported his attendance at a YMCA function in 1939. As Princetonians became more comfortable around their celebrated neighbor, the stereotyped image of the absentminded professor with long hair began to give way to an image of simplicity and good will. Incidents of no great significance in themselves revealed, time after time, genuine thoughtfulness and consideration for others. One such incident was the occasion for the only interview he granted to a "newsman" in his first years in Princeton.

A teacher at Princeton High School offered the grade of "A" to anyone in the journalism class who successfully interviewed Einstein. Henry Rosso, recognizing his chance to raise his "C" average to more respectable heights, took up the challenge. The direct approach failed when Mrs. Einstein refused to permit him in the house. As he was retreating in dejection, the milkman sympathetically asked him why he wanted to see the professor. When he learned of Rosso's objective, he told the boy that Einstein walked past the Springdale golf course on his way to Fine Hall at nine-thirty each morning. The following morning, with his teacher's blessing, Rosso slipped away from school and positioned himself along Einstein's path. Almost immediately Einstein came along lost in thought. The young would-be reporter stepped up, startled him, and nervously explained his mission. Rosso describes what followed:

> He looked me over and started to draw away but, in deference to my youth, I suppose, he stopped and turned toward me.
> "I don't give interviews," he said.
> I explained, hurriedly, that I was just a high school student, that our students were most eager to know about our new neighbor in Princeton and that, gosh, I just had to have the interview.
> "But if I give you an interview, then other newsmen will seek an interview. Further, what appears in your newspaper will appear in others."

Rosso earnestly explained that other newsmen would not read the high school paper, and that he would copyright the story as a protective measure. Einstein relented. "All right, young man, ask your questions"—and the interview took place as Einstein walked to his office. Rosso continues: "In the first several moments of our discussion, I got to learn that I knew little about the interview procedure. But he was a kind and tolerant man. He led the way, offering topics for discussion, suggesting emphases for the interview. When we parted at the door of [Fine Hall] I felt that I had been in the presence of a great and gentle man."[34]

After writing the article, Rosso returned to Library Place to secure Einstein's approval. Again he was frustrated in his efforts to enter the house, until Einstein appeared. A week later, despite the "copyright," the story was reprinted in a Trenton paper. Rosso, quite upset, called on Einstein to apologize; Einstein graciously assured him that he understood the ethics of American journalism and did not hold Rosso responsible.

No matter how carefully he kept out of the limelight, he could not avoid the daily visits of the mailman. There was always a steady stream of mail, and, after every controversial public statement, he would be inundated with letters of praise or censure. (A quarter of a century after his death, the institute still receives an occasional letter addressed to him.)

In addition to responses to his public statements and letters from European refugees seeking assistance, he received a large number of scientific manuscripts written by amateurs, most but not all of which, were either "stupid or crazy."[35] Two such manuscripts were titled "Sex in Celestial Objects" and "The Sun Is Not Hot." Many other letters dealt with questions of religion and the meaning of life; he also received a number of abusive, anti-Semitic postcards and numerous evangelical appeals to convert to Christianity and save his soul. He tried to answer all the sincere and coherent letters, although there always was a folder of un-answered letters to torment his conscience. Often he drafted his reply on the back

Einstein and Judge Irving Lehman with unidentified small boy at Port Chester, N.Y., ca. 1940. (Courtesy of Margot Einstein)

of the letter as he was reading it; later Miss Dukas would type up his answer. After one particularly large mail delivery, he wrote, in mock despair:

Brieftraeger bringt uns allemal	(The postman brings me every day
Haufen Post zu meiner Qual	Piles of mail to my dismay.
Ach warum denn denkt sich keiner	Oh, why does no one ever reason
Wir sind viel' und er nur einer.[36]	That he is one while we are legion.)

Aside from the sheer volume of his mail, Einstein was oppressed by the underlying assumption in most of the unsolicited letters that he was the smartest man in the world and was capable of resolving almost any problem.

Some of the most delightful letters were written by children, who asked such questions as: Do geniuses always go insane? Do you ever make any mistakes? and, Do you really exist? One South African girl wrote him to express her surprise that he was still alive because she had always thought he was Newton's contemporary. Einstein replied, "I have to apologize to you that I am still among the living. There will be a remedy for this, however." A second letter soon followed in which she confessed she was not a boy, as Einstein had mistakenly assumed. He responded, "I do not mind that you are a girl. But the main thing is that you yourself do not mind. There is no reason for it."[37]

Einstein's affection for children is well known. Once the wife of Eugene Wigner brought Einstein something from her husband. Einstein inquired after the children, and she answered that they were all right except they had the chicken pox. "Where are they?" he asked. "They are in the car outside, but they are quarantined." "Oh, I had that disease." He laughed and insisted on going out to visit with the youngsters.[38]

Everyone has heard some version of the story of the little girl who asked Einstein to help her with her arithmetic. It happened in the late thirties when Adelaide Delong was in the third or fourth grade at Miss Fine's School in Princeton. The Delongs lived on Mercer Street about a half-mile beyond the Einsteins'. One day her mother pointed out the Einstein house and said it was the home of the world's greatest mathematician. At the time Adelaide was struggling with arithmetic, and she decided to take advantage of her good fortune as Einstein's neighbor. One afternoon, instead of returning directly home from school, she stopped at the Einsteins'. When Miss Einstein answered the door, Adelaide requested an audience with the professor. Usually a formal appointment was required, but an eight-year-old is a special case, and when he appeared, she cheerfully extended a handful of fudge to him. He accepted the offering, but gently refused to help her do her arithmetic because he felt it would be unfair to the teacher and the other children. Despite the failure of her mission, Adelaide became a favorite of the ladies of the house and, for a while, she was a regular Sunday visitor. Years later, after the story had become celebrated and elaborated upon, John Kemeny, then Einstein's assistant, asked him if it were true. Einstein laughed. "Oh yes, I remember her vividly. She was a very naughty girl. Do you know she tried to bribe me with candy?" "He just loved that," Kemeny recalls. "The idea of a little girl coming over, not just to ask for help with homework, but to offer him some of her candy, he thought it was marvelous . . . although he pretended to be very annoyed with her for offering bribery." The feigned annoyance must have vanished quickly because, as Adelaide was leaving, Einstein gave her some cookies as partial compensation for her unsuccessful mission.[39]

By 1935 he had decided to settle permanently in America. In May he sailed for Bermuda with Elsa, Margot, and Miss Dukas to apply for a permanent visa, as a necessary preliminary step before taking out naturalization papers. In August they bought a home in Princeton at 112 Mercer Street, less than two blocks from their rented home on Library Place. It was an old wooden-clapboard, two-story white house set at the front of a thin strip of property bordered by hedges. The long narrow backyard shaded by several tall trees afforded a great deal of privacy. The neighborhood, then as now, presented an interesting mix of academic and nonacademic families who lived together quietly and privately. The Einstein family was spending the summer in Old Lyme, Connecticut, where Einstein was again able to indulge his passion for sailing. Elsa, who was supervising the renovations being done to the new house, made frequent trips from Old Lyme to Princeton. The most significant alteration involved the removal of a large section of wall at the rear of the house on the second story; it was replaced by a large picture window and this room became Einstein's study. From the window, he could look down the garden and up the hill to the Cleveland Tower at the Graduate College upon a peaceful neighborhood dominated by trees.

When they returned from Old Lyme the Einsteins moved into the new house. On the day of the move the first symptom of Elsa's fatal illness—a swelling around the eyes—was discovered. Initially it was thought to have been caused by the strain of the move, but by Christmastime she was in a New York hospital, suffering from what was described as a heart condition. By the spring of 1936 she appeared to be improving, and the family engaged a cottage for the summer on Saranac Lake in New York's Adirondack Mountains. During the summer and autumn her condition worsened and any hope for her recovery vanished. The Polish physicist Leopold Infeld had recently begun to collaborate with Einstein, and a few years later he wrote: "Einstein gave his wife the greatest care and sympathy. But in this atmosphere of coming death Einstein remained serene and worked constantly."[40]

On December 20, 1936, Elsa died after a painful bout with heart and kidney disease. Her three years in Princeton had been darkened by the death of her daughter Ilse, her own wasting disease, and the strain of uprooting her home and family late in life under the most tragic circumstances. She had been deeply attached to Berlin and hated to leave it. She had borne these sorrows with resignation and had continued to safeguard her husband's privacy, a task that was not easy and occasionally was unpleasant. She was the one who generally had to say no to people who sought entrance to the great man's inner sanctum. Often the very people who were delighted by her husband's eccentricities ridiculed hers. But she was a strong individual who bore criticism with stoicism. Once, however, she admitted, "It is not ideal to be the wife of a genius. Your life does not belong to you. It seems to belong to everyone else. Nearly every minute of the day I give to my husband and that means the public."[41]

In the beginning Einstein was very much in love with Elsa, but with the passage of time the marriage proved to be less than perfect. Frau Einstein reveled in her husband's fame and often allowed him to be used at benefits despite his aversion to this form of idolatry. With the passage of time Einstein became less tolerant of Elsa's domineering and bourgeois qualities, and occasionally he rebelled in tactless fashion. On one occasion shortly after they settled in Princeton, Otto Nathan, not yet an intimate friend, witnessed an embarrassing scene. The Einsteins had been invited to the home of President and Mrs. Dodds and Elsa told him he must dress. Einstein refused, a quarrel ensued, and although he eventually yielded, he adamantly refused to don his socks because, as he explained to his uncomfortable visitor, he could not stand to have his wife or secretary mend the inevitable holes.[42]

In fairness to Elsa, Einstein was not an easy husband. He appreciated her care and her protection from the public, and he enjoyed the gaiety of her daughters; but he remained aloof, independent, and absorbed in his work. As Pais has noted,[43] one sensed a lack of intimacy between the two, and surely this must have been very hard on Elsa, whose nature was warm and loving.

As time went on, the distance between the two grew greater. Once Einstein remarked to Nathan, "Marriage is the unsuccessful attempt to make something lasting out of an incident."[44] Shortly before his own death, Einstein's lifelong friend Michele Besso died. Einstein wrote in a very moving letter to Besso's son and sister: "What I most admired in him as a human being is the fact that he managed to live for many years not only in peace but also in lasting harmony with a woman—an undertaking in which I twice failed rather disgracefully."[45]

A few days after his wife's death, Einstein was again at work at Fine Hall. "Now more than ever," he told Banesh Hoffmann, one of his assistants and later his biographer, "I need to work."[46] Infeld went to see him at that time and wrote in 1940: "He looked tired, his complexion was more sallow than before." But in spite of his grief there was work to be done. "We discussed a serious difficulty in our scientific problem as though nothing had happened. Einstein worked with equal intensity during his wife's illness as later, after she died. There is no force which can stop Einstein's work as long as he is alive."[47]

5

The Scientist and the Institute

rinceton is a madhouse: its solipsistic luminaries shining in separate and helpless desolation. Einstein is completely cuckoo. . . ." This assessment of the Institute for Advanced Study was made by thirty-year-old Robert Oppenheimer in a letter to his younger brother in January 1935. The future director of the institute went on to say, "I could be of absolutely no use at such a place. . . ." Clearly, a change in Oppenheimer's thinking took place in the intervening dozen years, but his comments about Einstein and his colleagues cannot entirely be dismissed as mere "youthful cockiness."[1] In his tactless way, he accurately conveyed a sense of how Einstein's later work was viewed by a great number of younger physicists, who, like Oppenheimer, had little patience either with the elder physicist's critical approach to the revolutionary discoveries in quantum mechanics of the preceding decade, or with his long and patient search for a unified field theory. Furthermore, Oppenheimer's observation that the institute scholars had little contact with each other—a superficial and snap judgment made on the basis of less than a day in Princeton—was essentially correct in Einstein's case.

It is generally assumed that Einstein was the first appointment to the institute; however, the honor actually belongs to Oswald Veblen, nephew of the famous economist and social theorist Thorstein Veblen. Woodrow Wilson had brought the young mathematician to Princeton in 1905 to serve as one of the original preceptors. He was made a full professor in 1910 and was instrumental in developing Princeton's first-rate mathematics department over the succeeding two decades.

He became one of Flexner's earliest and most influential advisers and played an important role in the decision to begin operations of the institute with the School of Mathematics and to restrict the institute to postdoctoral scholars. By the late thirties, however, relations between Flexner and Veblen had deteriorated over issues of faculty power and the future development of the institute.

In the summer of 1932, Flexner sandwiched a visit to Paris between his stops in Oxford and Berlin. There he met with the distinguished French mathematician Jacques Hadamard who recommended that he appoint Hermann Weyl. Weyl had an unusually broad range of interests in mathematics, mathematical physics, philosophy, art, and literature, and had done very significant work in many fields of mathematics. He believed that the problems of science could not be separated from the problems of philosophy, and that mathematics was a creative activity, just like music, art, and literature. He once said, "My work has always tried to unite the true with the beautiful; and when I had to choose one or the other, I usually chose the beautiful." In 1930 Weyl had been appointed to Göttingen as successor to the great German mathematician David Hilbert. When Flexner invited Weyl to the institute in 1932, Weyl declined because of his commitment to Göttingen. Although his Jewish wife did not wish to emigrate, Weyl, who was not Jewish, refused to remain in Hitler's Germany, and he joined the institute faculty in January 1934.[2]

Veblen's contributions to the early success of the institute were not confined to the advice and guidance he gave Flexner; he was also instrumental in luring James Alexander and John von Neumann, the final two original faculty members, away from Princeton University. Alexander, one of Veblen's most gifted students at Princeton, was a distinguished topologist who had once run for mayor of Princeton on the Communist Party ticket. A man of independent wealth, Alexander refused to accept a salary for his teaching.

Von Neumann, born in 1903, was the youngest faculty member, and like Weyl he had been a student of Hilberts. He was a Hungarian Jew and had first come to Princeton University as a visiting professor in 1929; the next year he was made a full professor. While still a young man, von Neumann established the mathematical foundations of quantum mechanics. In later years he worked on the Manhattan Project and served on the Atomic Energy Commission, but he is best known for his contributions to the development of computers. Of the original institute faculty members, he was the most productive during his period of association with the institute because the great achievements of the older men had largely been accomplished by the time of their appointments.

Once he had assembled a faculty, Flexner realized that the success of the institute depended upon healthy relations with Princeton University. Ordinarily, this would have been an almost insurmountable task because three of the five faculty members had been lured away from Princeton's mathematics department. Flexner, however, had been careful to ask permission from the Princeton administration before offering positions to Alexander, von Neumann, and Veblen. More than forty years later Harold W. Dodds, who became President of Princeton in the fall of 1933, stated that he never forgave Luther Eisenhart, the Dean of the Graduate School, for letting Veblen go, but aside from this, he and Flexner quickly developed a close working relationship to the mutual benefit of both institutions.

Although the university lost its three leading mathematicians, it had been more than compensated by the presence of Einstein, Weyl, and numerous other distinguished European and American scholars at the institute. From 1933 to 1939 the mathematicians of the university and the institute shared office space in Fine Hall (where the official language was "broken English"), and they cooperated on numerous joint ventures including the publication of the quarterly journal, *The Annals of Mathematics*. Fine Hall in the 1930s housed some of the finest mathematicians and physicists ever assembled under one roof.

The close working relations with Princeton University enabled Flexner's scholars to enjoy the full privileges of Princeton's outstanding library as well as a multitude of less tangible cultural advantages. In return, more students and faculty members have been invited to the institute as temporary members from Princeton University than from any other institution.

The only element of life in Berlin that Einstein generally missed after 1933 was the intimate and regular association with the greatest German and European scientists. There, he had been a regular at the weekly lectures, seminars, and colloquia, and he relished the sessions with Planck, von Laue, and many younger physicists. His fellow professors at the institute were mathematicians, and only Weyl had worked for a time in the area of relativity. The absence of colleagues engaged in research in his field in conjunction with language problems in his early years in Princeton and his growing differences with the proponents of the prevailing quantum theory, served to isolate him scientifically. As a result, Einstein's circle of friends in Princeton consisted, in the main, of current and former assistants. His contact with other outstanding physicists from Princeton University and elsewhere was more formal, less regular, and often led merely to another futile attempt by supporters of quantum theory to convert the "old relic." It is important to remember that even his harshest critics held his earlier work in relativity and quantum theory in the highest esteem but, by the 1930s they had come to believe that he was wasting his time on the unified field theory and, in the process, denying the world of science his unique genius. As early as 1921, at a time when he was feeling the pressures of fame and various nonscientific commitments, he had confided to a friend, "Discovery in the grand manner is for young people anyway, and, hence, for me a thing of the past."[3]

The discoveries of twentieth-century physics rank among the greatest intellectual achievements in man's history. Einstein, of course, is best known for his work in relativity theory, which deals with the macrocosm—the laws governing the universe. His fundamental contributions to the other great system of modern physics—the quantum theory, which studies the microcosm, the invisible universe of atoms, and their components—must not be forgotten when discussing his objections to later developments in the quantum theory.

Einstein was convinced there could only be one fundamental law that unified the forces of nature. His work in relativity theory had demonstrated the relationship between mass, energy, and gravitation, and in his search for a unified field theory he sought to discover the relationship between gravitation and electromagnetism and, he believed, the quantum theory of atomic phenomenon would emerge from his theory. Most physicists felt that his basic assumptions for the unified field theory were not sufficiently convincing. (In contrast, the assumptions upon which he had based his general theory of relativity were convincing.) Einstein blamed his failure to devise a successful unified field theory on the lack of adequate mathematical tools available to him at the time. In his last revision of his unified field theory, he developed equations which connected gravitational fields with electromagnetic fields. Further mathematical work was necessary before he could derive conclusions from the equations that could be tested by experiment.

Unlike some of his critics, who were dogmatic in their support of quantum mechanics, Einstein never claimed that his approach was the only way; he simply felt he had chosen the most promising path, and he did not conceal his uncertainties. What he did not doubt was that the relationship he sought did exist and could ultimately be discovered. In one of his last conversations with Otto Nathan he indicated that in his heart he felt he was right, but he could not yet prove it.[4]

Einstein's 1905 paper on the photoelectric effect, for which he won the 1921 Nobel Prize in physics, had been, after Max Planck's pioneering work in 1900, the most important early contribution to quantum theory. By 1925–1926, when an extraordinary series of major discoveries in quantum theory followed in rapid succession, Einstein became more critical of the direction of modern physics.

For five hundred years Western scientists have known that the observer affects that which he is attempting to observe, but they believed there were ways of correcting this influence. In 1926 the young German physicist Werner Heisenberg formulated his "uncertainty principle," which makes the assertion that there is no way to correct this influence. According to the "uncertainty principle," one can measure the velocity of a particle (for instance, an electron), or one can measure its position, but not both at the same time, and one cannot measure specific individual particles, but only an aggregation of identical particles by a series of repeated measurements to achieve a predicted position or velocity.

At first Einstein objected to Heisenberg's theory because the probablistic nature of the uncertainty principle violated his deep philosophic faith in causality and prompted him to say on more than one occasion, *"Gott wurfelt nicht"* (God does not play dice); by this he meant that the behavior of subatomic particles is not left to chance. If he had to surrender causality, he once told Max Born, he would rather be a shoemaker or an employee in a gambling casino. He resisted the uncertainty principle until the 1930 Solvay Conference (a gathering of the leading physicists of the world), when the great Danish physicist Niels Bohr dramatically demonstrated that Einstein's own general relativity theory disproved the idealized experiment Einstein had brought forth in support of his contention. Thereafter Einstein accepted the uncertainty principle as a correct statement about what happens, although he remained convinced that physical theory based fundamentally on the concept of probability would ultimately prove to be unacceptable.[5]

Einstein believed that the physical world exists independently of man and man's observations of it, and for the rest of his life he maintained that while quantum theory was a useful preliminary version of a more fundamental theory, it was incomplete and offered "no useful point of departure for future development."[6] His gut feeling was that the complete theory should not be based on probability because even though the scientist cannot observe the phenomena, a theory should describe a reality, not a probability.

Most physicists accepted the tenets of quantum theory, but a few of the older generation, notably Planck, von Laue, Erwin Schröedinger, and Einstein, remained skeptical. For thirty years Einstein and Bohr carried on their friendly but intense debate over the basic issues of quantum theory. Bohr had a permanent appointment to the institute, and he spent parts of 1937, 1948, and 1954 in Princeton, where the debate continued. Einstein took the position that the theory contradicted his view of reality, and the frustrated Bohr replied, in essence, that, if that were the case, then Einstein's theory of reality was simply too limited. The two old warriors had the deepest respect for each other as men and as thinkers, but they never were able to change the other's view. By the late 1940s Einstein probably no longer enjoyed the discussions because there was no real common ground for debate: their fundamental premises were simply irreconcilable.

Einstein told physicist Otto Stern, "I have thought a hundred times as much about the quantum problems as I have about general relativity theory."[7] Abraham Pais has described him as the "loyal opposition" whose penetrating criticisms and questions presented extremely valuable challenges to the supporters of the theory. Pais has expressed his conviction that in his later years Einstein "lost his touch of physics" and became "enamored of the power of mathematics."[8] By this time, debates with the quantum theorists had become rather distasteful to him because he felt that the defenders of the theory were no longer listening to what he had to say, but were more interested in converting the heretic than in exchanging ideas. He developed a kind of "resigned bitterness," and to one physicist who attempted to convince him of a new approach he repeated his famous statement that he did not believe God played dice with the universe, and then added, "But maybe I've earned the right to make my mistakes."[9] Despite the unpopularity of his approach to quantum theory, and his inability to complete his unified field theory, Einstein never felt he was wasting his time. Science is a process of trial and error and, as he was fond of remarking, the only sure way to avoid making mistakes is to have no ideas. He once scrawled the following verse on a page of calculations by one of his assistants:

Nicht schwer ist's Neues auszusagen	(It's easy to say something new
Wenn jeden Blüdsinn man will wagen.	If all sense one will eschew,
Doch seltner füget sich dabei	But hardly is it ever found
Dass Neues auch Vernünftig sei.[10]	That the new is also sound.)

Throughout his life science remained Einstein's first love, and the passion with which he sought to unravel the mysteries of the universe remained undiminished even after his physical faculties began to decline. He was always curious about everything, forever engrossed in some problem and eager to discuss these questions with colleagues. Whatever he was involved in, he was thinking about science. Valentine Bargmann, who worked with Einstein from 1938 to 1943, remembers that once Einstein had been to a benefit dinner in New York and the next day he said to Bargmann, "You know, yesterday, when I was sitting at the dinner, I was thinking about the following problem . . ."[11]

He possessed extraordinary powers of concentration, and when he worked, seated in his study with a writing block on his knees, gazing out the window upon the garden, the expression on his face was relaxed and dreamy. His work provided him with an escape from the realm of the "merely personal" into an objective and timeless universe. Absorbed in thought, Einstein could become absentminded. Once in Berlin he frightened Margot when he did not emerge from his bath after more than an hour. Finally she knocked upon the door, called his name, and aroused him from his reverie. Sitting in the tub all that time he had been working on some problem and, he confessed to her, "I thought I was sitting at my desk."[12]

Einstein scorned the popular notion that he was the greatest scientist. He liked to say that God had given him a mulelike stubbornness to stick with a difficult problem and the intuitive powers to conceptualize complex hypothetical situations in his mind. For Valentine and Sonja Bargmann he once inscribed the following ditty in a book of essays about his science and philosophy:

> *Eines sieht man klar darin*   (One can clearly see herein
> *Was vermag der Eigensinn.*[13]   Just what stubbornness can win.)

His consuming passion was the search for universally valid laws of nature. He sought to make a picture of the universe that was clear and beautiful; he was not interested merely in solving problems, no matter how seductive a specific one might be. His approach to scientific work was that of an artist, and his pleasure was derived from the act of comprehending the perfect order of the physical world, not in the possibilities for practical application which a scientific discovery might open up. He was convinced that a scientist who persisted in the attempt to identify and solve the most important and fundamental questions even in the face of discouraging results contributed more than one who found solutions to relatively easy problems, even if the labors of the former only advanced knowledge slightly or were able only to demonstrate the magnitude of the problem. Scientific greatness, he was fond of saying, was less a matter of intelligence than character, whereby the scientist refuses to compromise or accept incomplete answers and persists in grappling with the most basic and difficult questions. The impudent Swabian attributed his success to the formula: Success $= X+Y+Z$ where $X=$work, $Y=$play, and $Z=$keep your mouth shut.[14]

Abraham Pais, who was a young physicist at the institute in the period after the Second World War, often found himself in disagreement with Einstein, but he had the highest respect, reverence even, for the man and his accomplishments, and he has said that Einstein "had a touch of perfection." Pais believed that Einstein was intellectually fearless to ask the most profound questions free from inhibiting preconceptions and previously accepted beliefs. He was free, Pais says, to follow his intuition, to follow his own line of thought regardless of the attitudes of others. Once a question had gotten hold of him, however, he was not free to ignore it, "and that's part of his greatness," Pais believes.[15] Once captivated by a question, he would persist with it for years and years. He grappled with the problem of general relativity for more than a decade before successfully formulating the theory which is acclaimed as his greatest work, and although he was to be denied similar success in his search for a unified field theory, he worked at the problem for almost four decades undeterred by criticism or failure.

Throughout the years, Einstein had relatively few followers; no students took their doctorate under him, and he was the founder of no school of thought. He was not a team player—a horse for a single harness is how he once described himself. Nevertheless, especially in his Princeton years, he did not work alone. He always had one or two assistants or co-workers who generally were recruited more for their mathematical skills than their knowledge of physics. When Ernst Straus and Einstein first met to discuss working together, the young mathematician confessed unhappily, "I know absolutely no relativity theory." Einstein replied, "That doesn't matter. I know relativity theory. You can read up on the necessary part."[16]

As a young man Einstein had chosen a career in physics rather than mathematics because of his inability to "scent" out the most fundamental problems in mathematics. Sometimes in later years he would disparage his mathematical abilities, but, Professor Bargmann believes, Einstein underestimated his knowledge. Bargmann notes that Einstein was not especially skilled in formal manipulations and, although this is not yet mathematics, most great mathematicians are extremely skilled manipulators. He did have difficulties doing calculations and preferred that his assistants attend to those tasks. Once he greeted a new and awestricken assistant, Bruria Kaufman, with some equations which had been tormenting him for two or three weeks. Within a half-day she discovered that a factor of 2 was missing and, in disbelief, went to one of his former assistants to see if it was possible for the great man to have made such a mistake. She learned it was. "So I got used to the fact that I could correct him." Another time she quoted some known theorems to him which struck him as very beautiful, and which, he was convinced, she had invented.[17] According to Ernst Straus, Einstein's problems with calculations were due not to sloppiness but to an inability to accustom himself to routine. "When I look at one thing, I forget the other," Straus quotes him, "and thus I cannot form a picture in my mind of the whole calculation."[18]

By the time he settled in Princeton, he had long been the most famous scientist alive, and as he was thirty to forty years older than most of his assistants, they invariably approached their first meeting with trepidation. Einstein genuinely desired to be on equal footing with his colleagues and assistants and he had the rare ability to dissolve the tension and quickly put younger workers at ease. John

Kemeny was a young graduate student in 1948 when he went to work for Einstein, and he recalls how Einstein put away his calculations and, despite Kemeny's protestations, insisted that the younger man describe his own work. Kemeny was touched by Einstein's interest, although it was in a field with which Einstein had no familiarity.

In Princeton he followed a work routine that rarely varied, except during summer vacations or illness. His assistants usually called on him at about 10:00 A.M. and they would slowly walk to the institute, discussing a wide range of topics such as the state of the world, general questions of physics, or a specific problem relating to their work. At the institute they compared notes and discussed the results of the previous day's work. Then they began to talk about conclusions which might be drawn from this work. Next they turned to the more difficult task of deciding how they should proceed, which computations to work on and how to go about the task. They worked together until lunchtime, and then, depending upon the weather, Einstein either walked home or rode in the institute bus. In the afternoon he worked alone in his study at home for several hours.

Collaboration with Einstein was intense, yet, Bargmann notes, "There was always a wonderful calmness and serenity about him."[19] He encouraged criticism from his co-workers and loved a good argument. When he worked, he was relaxed, patient and, from time to time, he would break the routine with a small

Peter Bergmann, Ernst Straus (1922–1983), Banesh Hoffmann, and Valentine Bargmann at the symposium "Working with Einstein" at the Institute for Advanced Study, March 7, 1979. Those fortunate to be in attendance were treated to a moving, informative, and altogether lovely experience. (Courtesy of Margot Einstein)

joke followed by an explosion of laughter—and then, back to work. Kemeny recalls that his face usually had a look of deep concentrated thought, but that on occasion a mischievous smile would appear.

Some of Einstein's assistants did not speak German fluently, and with them business was conducted in English. When he was puzzled by a problem, he would often unconsciously lapse into German, and this sometimes led him to a solution. Banesh Hoffmann relates that when he, Infeld, and Einstein were stumped, Einstein would say, "I will a little tink." Then, "He would pace up and down and walk around in circles, all the time twirling a lock of his long gray hair around his forefinger." His face showed no strain, and he gave the impression of being in another universe. Hoffmann and Infeld would remain silent. Finally Einstein would relax and describe his solution, which, Hoffmann recounts, almost always seemed to work. "The solution sometimes was so simple we could have kicked ourselves. . . . But that magic was performed invisibly in the recesses of Einstein's mind, by a process that we could not fathom. From this point of view the whole thing was completely frustrating." Hoffmann has confessed that on occasion he, too, has twirled his hair around his forefinger in the hope that he might be visited by inspiration, but it was in vain.[20]

While he and his assistants were investigating a theory, Bargmann has written, Einstein was "quite enthusiastic, and his attitude was not perturbed by occasional doubts which might occur to him or to us, his assistants. If the doubts, however, persisted then he would become his own severest critic, who would not tolerate any appreciable defect of the theory.

"If he convinced himself that the theory did not live up to his high standards, he would drop it without regrets." Invariably, the following morning he would have a new idea and the rejected theory would be a thing of the past.[21]

Unsuccessful work is an occupational hazard for any thinker, and Einstein certainly endured his fair share during his thirty-five-year search for the unified field theory. A great deal of his time was spent exploring theories and approaches to theories that proved to be unfruitful. Sometimes months and years of work had to be discarded. Even when his assistants felt despair, Einstein remained optimistic, adopting the attitude that they had still learned something in the process. Banesh Hoffmann recalls how at such times he would remark, "The world has waited this long, another few months won't make much difference."[22] Once at a seminar he was discussing his latest attempt to formulate the unified field theory when a student asked him about a previous approach which had by this time been discarded. Einstein laughed loudly and answered, "*Dieser Schweiss war umsonst vergossen* [Well, this sweat was in vain]."[23]

Those who worked with Einstein were devoted to him. One of his assistants described him as a father figure to whom he could take his problems and ask for advice. Einstein was always eager to be of help to his younger fellow workers; on one occasion, this willingness made him a best-selling author. In 1937, while he was working with Leopold Infeld, the latter's grant at the institute ended and, despite Einstein's efforts, the grant was not renewed. "My fame begins outside

Princeton," he remarked to Infeld. "My word counts for little in Fine Hall."[24] At this same time, Flexner had also vetoed Bertrand Russell's appointment to the institute despite support from Einstein, Weyl, and Veblen.

Infeld had been unable to secure another appointment in America and was faced with the dread prospect of returning to Poland. In desperation he conceived the idea that he and Einstein write a book describing for the nonscientist the advances of modern physics. He fully realized that a book for the general reader by Einstein would sell briskly and, in the interim, he could live for the next year on his portion of the advance money.

They continued their scientific collaboration, and once a week they devoted their time to the book, which was titled *The Evolution of Physics*. Infeld did the writing, but only after thorough consultation with Einstein. Einstein believed that there were remarkably few fundamental ideas at the base of modern physics and that these could be expressed without the use of complicated formulas. His purpose was to trace the logical (and historical) development of these basic ideas in a book that the intelligent nonscientific high school student could understand. After a brief survey of the development of physics from the time of Galileo and Newton until the end of the nineteenth century, *The Evolution of Physics* explains the rise of field theory, the discovery of special and general relativity, and the development of the quantum theory. After forty-five years it remains an excellent general introduction to the fundamentals of relativity and quantum theories.

The book was an immediate success. It reached the best-seller lists in the spring of 1938, and eventually was translated into several languages. The only discordant note came from Germany, where Nazi scientists continued their assault on Einstein and his theories. Einstein responded to these attacks with an allegorical poem about a lark and a dung beetle:

Die Lerche trillert am sonnigen Tag,	(The lark trills on a sunny day.
Mistkäfer es nicht leiden mag.	Dung beetle listens with dismay.
Dein Sing-Sang ist ganz	"Your singsong is a rotten jest,"
* unbegründet,*	He proclaims with swollen chest.
Er mit geschwellter Brust verkündet.	
"Nur Männer wie ich sind zu	"I'll only greet those men who keep
* begrussen,*	Their feet on the ground without a
Hab'stets den Boden unter den	peep,
* Füssen,*	And what I cannot understand,
Und was ich nicht begreifen kann,	Is nonsense—I'm the cleverest man!"
Ist blöd—ich bin der klügste Mann!"	
Die Lerchen trällern ihr Liedchen	Skylarks warble their songs in May,
* im Mai,*	Ignoring what the beetles say,
Der Mistkäfer ist ihnen einerlei,	"If the song disturbs your slumber,
"Stört ihm Gesang in dumpfer Ruh'	Plug your ears and you'll grow
So stopf' er sich die Ohren zu."[25]	number.")

By 1939, when the institute moved to its own campus on the grounds of the former Olden Farm, a mile and a half southwest of the center of town, Flexner's vision had proved sound, and the care with which he had organized the community of scholars had been amply rewarded. The location in Princeton and the exceptionally friendly relations with Princeton University guaranteed first-class working and living conditions for the scholars. Office space in Fine Hall, unlimited access to the university's library, generous assistance from President Dodds in the opening of the new School of Humanistic Studies and the School of Economics and Politics, and the friendly collaboration between the university and institute mathematicians had contributed immeasurably to the institute's early success and stability. Flexner and Dodds worked especially well together, and the director expended a great deal of effort to insure that relations remained healthy. This arrangement had been particularly beneficial from a financial point of view because it had spared the institute the necessity of constructing either an office building or a library during its experimental years, which happened to coincide with the worst years of the depression.

Einstein's acceptance of an appointment in 1932 had assured the institute's prestige with both scholars and the public, and Hitler's seizure of power in Central Europe had turned some of the most gifted European scholars into refugees, a number of whom became members or professors. From the very beginning the institute enjoyed an international flavor (in addition to Einstein, von Neumann, and Weyl, six of the twenty-three members in 1933–1934 were from abroad) which both promoted international intellectual cooperation and enhanced the international life of the town of Princeton itself.

To ensure that the institute projected an image of excellence from the outset, Flexner had selected mathematicians who had already established their reputations. Einstein, Veblen, and Weyl had passed their fiftieth birthdays and, as is common with mathematicians and physicists, they had passed their prime. Flexner, despite all his talk about freedom from the pressures of a timetable, eventually became upset that some members on the faculty were producing little or nothing original, and in his autobiography he advised that future vacancies be filled by younger men of great promise but lesser renown who had not yet completed their most creative and productive years. Einstein, of course, was well aware of his ornamental value to Flexner's institute, as the following story attests.

Every spring there is a dance for the members of the institute, and on the morning of the dance in Flexner's final year as director, Einstein said to Valentine Bargmann, "I'll see you tonight." When Bargmann indicated surprise that Einstein would be attending such a social function, he replied, "Of course I'm going—I'm taking this very seriously because that's what Mr. Flexner bought me for." The inevitable roar of laughter followed.[26]

The factors that had coalesced to insure the institute's early success nearly tore it apart in the late 1930s over the issue of faculty power and relations with the aging and increasingly autocratic Abraham Flexner. Originally Flexner had conceived of the institute as a haven for scholars in which the director and his staff would relieve the faculty of routine bureaucratic chores which interfere with the scholars' research. He did intend to consult with the faculty on a regular basis on matters of educational policy and academic appointments. In the beginning he tried to involve the faculty in discussions about the direction and future development of the institute. These plans were largely vetoed by Mr. Bamberger, a self-made businessman who had little formal education. He had the highest respect for education, as his endowment of the institute eloquently testifies, but as is often the case with men of affairs, he did not believe that professors were sufficiently flexible to understand what was best for the institute as a whole. He had unqualified faith in Flexner's vision and abilities, and he did not wish to jeopardize his investment in the early years by permitting the faculty to interfere with the director's work. In time, as difficulties developed between the director and certain faculty members, particularly Veblen, Flexner abandoned any pretext of consulting the faculty on important decisions and appointments.[27] When the faculty attempted to participate in the running of the institute, Flexner's judgment abandoned him as he labeled them "intriguers"[28] who were unable to profit from complete freedom from practical concerns.

In the mid-thirties, the faculty made a formal request to the director for representation on the board of trustees of the institute. Flexner rejected the proposal in such a way that the faculty never knew if the issue had been raised before the board. For the next few years relations between director and faculty grew increasingly strained. Finally, toward the end of 1937, the dispute came to a head over the issues of the seventy-five-year-old Flexner's successor, the role of the faculty in academic appointments, and the faculty's concern that Princeton University was exercising an increasingly unhealthy influence in purely institute matters.

On November 3, 1937, Einstein addressed a long letter to Samuel Leidesdorf, treasurer of the institute's board of trustees and one of the financial advisers to Louis Bamberger, who had introduced Flexner to Bamberger in 1930. Leidesdorf, had also assisted Einstein on several personal financial matters. The letter, Einstein wrote, was prompted by the fear that a growing number of "small matters" might lead to a situation that could jeopardize the autonomy and development of the institute. The first item of concern was the growing influence of the university on issues which were internal concerns of the institute. At a recent faculty meeting Professor Alexander had made a formal statement to the effect that "a young mathematician was denied admission to the Institute, in a discreet manner, because being colored Princeton University would have objected to him." Flexner did not question the facts, but denied any knowledge of this incident. Could this not, both Alexander and Einstein wondered, mean that other "undesirables," for instance, Jews, might be limited or excluded? Einstein added that he had learned on "good authority" that a high-ranking administrator at the university had recently told a group of friends, "There are too many Jews [at the institute]."

Einstein was also deeply concerned about the choice of a new director. For some time it had been generally understood that Frank Aydelotte, president of Swarthmore and trustee of the institute since its inception, would be selected. Aydelotte's prospective appointment met with the approval of Einstein and most senior faculty members, but President Dodds was openly hostile to the choice, and Flexner had given signs that he no longer favored Aydelotte. Because of Flexner's autocratic attitude, Einstein was worried that the final decision would be made without the participation of the faculty and that the influence of the university would be brought to bear upon the institute in such a subtle but decisive manner that even the trustees would be unaware of the interference.[29] Einstein and Leidesdorf met in New York to discuss this letter.

After discussions with Alexander, Veblen, David Mitrany of the School of Economics and Politics, and E. A. Lowe from the School of Humanistic Studies, Einstein sent Leidesdorf a second letter on December 16, 1937, in which he reiterated that the basic grievance of the faculty was the lack of a voice in the affairs of the institute. Although there were two faculty members serving on the board (Veblen and Winfield Riefler) they did not represent the faculty because they had been appointed by Flexner "for reasons of his own without any consultation with us." (As an aside, Einstein added that it was "peculiar" that none of the Jewish professors had been appointed.) The only possible solution would be for the faculty to choose its own representatives and invest them with "formal authority to represent our views to the board." The letter concludes with a request that Leidesdorf initiate appropriate action with the board.[30] There is no evidence of a reply from Leidesdorf to this second letter, and apparently no action was taken.

By the end of 1938 Flexner's behavior so infuriated the faculty that it felt compelled to confront the director. One of Flexner's pet projects had been the creation of the School of Economics and Politics. He believed it could make a significant contribution to ending the depression through the establishment of better contact between scholars and practicing economists. Flexner wished to invite professional economists to the institute in order to give them the same chance as philosophers and theoreticians to study their problems without academic or business pressures to produce results. The mathematicians were highly skeptical of such a plan. Skepticism gave way to open rebellion when Flexner appointed Walter Stewart and Robert Warren to the School of Economics and Politics at the beginning of the 1938–1939 year without consulting two of the three professors of that school. Neither appointee was a distinguished scholar; their experience had been with the Federal Reserve Bank; they had not taught for several years, and without Ph.D.s they would have been unqualified to teach on the faculty of a graduate school. Nevertheless, Flexner brought them in at the maximum salary. Einstein felt especially strongly that in the selection of new faculty members it was essential that the highest standards be maintained. When discussing a proposed appointment he wanted to know if the candidate's work had actually changed his field. Was his work original and significant?

This latest action by Flexner revived faculty fears that they would be bypassed in the choice of the director. On February 14, 1939, Einstein sent yet another letter to Leidesdorf, marked "private and confidential." Evidence indicated that it was more and more likely that Flexner intended to impose one of two men as his successor. Neither would be acceptable to Einstein and his colleagues, and although Flexner had promised to take no action without the concurrence of the faculty, Einstein remained wary: ". . . all our experience suggests that we need to be extremely cautious, as until now all important decisions concerning the Institute have been prepared with the greatest secrecy, after the method of the 'fait accompli.'" If either of the two men were chosen, he warned, the faculty would revolt, "even at the risk of an open scandal."[31] Once again, nothing came of this letter, and in the light of a statement contained in a letter to his friend Dr. Bucky, a decade later, in which Einstein characterized Leidesdorf as a man who does not like to expose himself and who disliked Einstein because of certain public statements, it is probable that Leidesdorf did not sympathize with the faculty.[32]

In March 1939 the faculty met and passed a resolution which again asked Flexner to bring before the trustees the faculty request to be consulted on the appointments of the director and faculty. The resolution, dated March 15, was signed by Einstein, Marston Morse (mathematician), and Hetty Goldman (School of Humanistic Studies). Within the next ten days Flexner met with Einstein and Morse, but they remained unsatisfied, as he neither agreed nor refused to act upon the resolution. Accordingly, on March 26, Einstein felt impelled to inform Aydelotte of the faculty grievance with Flexner's evasive behavior. Aydelotte was in a very uncomfortable position, because he already knew that he had been designated to succeed Flexner, but was not in a position to inform Einstein. Furthermore, if he acted upon the faculty's request to open the selection process, he would, in all likelihood, succeed only in removing himself from contention.

Throughout the spring and summer the battle raged on bitterly but discreetly. Finally, in early August Flexner admitted that he could no longer coexist with his faculty and tendered his resignation effective October 9, at which time the institute would be occupying its new offices at Fuld Hall. At the end of August he wrote to Frank Aydelotte: "Don't, for your own sake and that of the Institute," he warned, "underestimate that you are dealing with intriguers. I freely confess that I was a baby in their hands."[33] He then retired to write his memoirs in which he recommended that his successor make no changes in the institute for at least ten years. Since he remained a member of the board, it was inevitable that he and Aydelotte would eventually clash over institute policy.

In October 1939, peace returned to the institute. After the tumult of the preceding years, Aydelotte immediately exerted a calming influence; his openness and willingness to consult with the faculty proved to be ideal. Furthermore, he knew how to leave the faculty alone. The move to Fuld Hall meant that the director was no longer isolated from his scholars (Flexner's office had always been at 20 Nassau Street, not in Fine Hall), and this daily contact proved to be immensely helpful. With the move to its own campus, the university's excessive influence was terminated, and, in fact, under Aydelotte, in large part because of Dodds's antipathy toward the new director, relations with the university were decidedly cool.

What is to be made of Einstein's role in this rebellion? He loathed faculty politics and harbored no personal ambitions, yet he was a leading figure in the revolt. Part of the problem stemmed from the lack of communication between the faculty and Flexner, Bamberger and the trustees. Flexner's tactless actions, combined with Bamberger's behind-the-scenes opposition to requests for increased faculty power, created a serious crisis, which caused Flexner to take a more autocratic stance to protect what he viewed as *his* creation. Einstein had been particularly attracted by the promise of freedom of research unhampered by administrative details. As Flexner grew more tyrannical, the fine line between freedom from detail and the scholars' quite natural desire to help shape the destiny of this scholars' paradise became blurred until Flexner came to perceive the faculty as meddling intriguers while the faculty feared Flexner had become a dictator. Flexner was no villain. He had performed a great service, but his tragedy lay in his failure to recognize when it was time for him to retire with grace.

Einstein, Frank Aydelotte, Director of the Institute for Advanced Study, 1939– 1947, Oswald Veblen, and Marston Morse, both mathematicians who were on the original faculty. Picture taken at Fuld Hall, ca. 1940. (Courtesy of the Institute for Advanced Study)

Four critical and independent factors coalesced between 1930 and 1935 to insure the success of the institute. Foremost, naturally, was Flexner's original idea. Einstein's decision to join gave the institute an air of quality and integrity and insured it the approval of scholars and the public. The third factor was the emergence of Hitler. The influx of refugee scholars to America, and especially to the internationally oriented institute, quickly closed the gap that had existed between institutions of higher education and research in America and Europe.

Finally, the association with Princeton University permitted the institute to experiment in its early years without spending large sums of money on buildings and a library. Despite the divisive conclusion of Flexner's tenure as director, the institute, by 1939, was established as one of the leading research centers in the world.

6

Refugees

instein's arrival in the United States in 1933 was a profound symbolic event for world Jewry. That the most celebrated living genius could be hounded from his home because of his Jewish heritage dramatized the plight of the Jews in Germany, and the leaders of American Jewry wasted no time in soliciting his support for their activities. Einstein naturally was eager to accommodate them in any way he could, but he was hindered by a number of factors in addition to his natural inclination to privacy and solitude. As a newcomer, he was reluctant to become involved in American politics for fear that his activities might be regarded as presumptuous and be used to prevent other European Jews from receiving asylum. He also feared that the Nazis would exploit his pronouncements to justify a new round of terror against Jews still under their control. As he was soon to discover, American Jews lacked cohesion, and many even failed to appreciate either the danger of Nazism or their responsibility to assist Hitler's victims. Finally, Einstein realized that effective propaganda in the United States against Hitler must not come from exclusively Jewish sources. Jewish attacks against Hitler would be dismissed by non-Jews as typical of "wailing Jews."

In certain respects the behavior of the Jews of America paralleled the behavior of the German Jews in the period after the First World War. Einstein had noted the schism between the older immigrants—primarily from Germany—who were eager to continue the process of assimilation into mainstream American society, and the more recent immigrants from Russia and Poland who had originally been poor, badly educated, and inclined to socialism. His sympathy then, as always, was for the outcasts of Eastern Europe. He was openly contemptuous of "those of our fellow Jews who are flabby as jellyfish"[1] who were afraid of large Jewish immigration because of the danger of increased anti-Semitism, who refused to believe the atrocity stories coming out of Germany, and who felt no sense of communal responsibility for Jewish victims of tyranny. At the end of the decade, for instance, a small but influential number of American Jews opposed liberalization of the immigration laws because of the perennial fear that this might aggravate domestic anti-Semitism. Like the German Jews who were reluctant to leave Germany after 1933, many American Jews refused to believe that Hitler could long survive. American Jewish disunity provided the Roosevelt administration with a convenient excuse not to challenge Hitler on this issue or to stir up the wrath of the restrictionists who opposed any further immigration (especially of Jews) into the United States. The government intervened only when Nazi brutalities involved American citizens. Secretary of State Cordell Hull and other officials comforted themselves with the belief that the worst Nazi excesses were over after March 1933, and a great many both in and out of government saw the Nazis as a positive force. After all, they reasoned, had not Hitler rid Germany of the threat posed by socialism and communism?[2]

A small incident in February 1934 illustrates the extraordinary affection American Jews felt for Einstein. In that month the Maurice Schwartz Yiddish Art Theater presented *Yoshe Kalb* at Princeton's McCarter Theater. After the performance, the actors repaired to the dressing room; there was "a sudden hush" and then the entire cast returned to the stage to catch a glimpse of Einstein, who had come backstage to pay his compliments to the players. A few words of Yiddish were exchanged, and a university undergraduate who witnessed the scene later wrote: "The reverence shown [him] was overwhelming."[3]

Upon his arrival in Princeton, Einstein was deluged with requests for his support and invitations to fund-raising dinners by various Jewish organizations, whose goals were often in conflict. In the early years Einstein frequently relied upon the advice of Rabbi Stephen S. Wise. Throughout the twenties and early thirties Wise was highly critical of Weizmann's leadership. After 1935 Wise and the American Zionists mended their differences with Weizmann in an effort to present a united front against Hitler. Wise was a radical democrat who supported every humanitarian cause. He was a celebrated orator, and like Einstein, a lover of Spinoza. The two men became good friends, and Wise, along with Otto Nathan, who was also a close friend of Wise, kept Einstein abreast of the latest developments in the Jewish crisis. Wise also frequently sought Einstein's participation in or support for various activities, but he was careful not to alienate Einstein by excessive demands upon his time and energy. Einstein often turned to Wise for protection from overzealous individuals and organizations.

From late 1933 until the onset of his wife's fatal illness, Einstein attended several fund-raising dinners, at which, invariably, he was the guest of honor. On one occasion in 1935 he attended a dinner to raise money for the children of German refugees. The following day he was quoted in the *New York Times* as having declared that any regime that made such a gathering necessary condemns itself. Another dinner that year was for the benefit of non-Jewish refugees from Hitler: socialists, pacifists, individuals with some Jewish blood, and those who refused to live under Nazi tyranny. The causes were extremely important to him, although he loathed these undemocratic $50- to $500-a-plate dinners, filled with bejeweled women and big shots making speeches. Einstein was always the center of attention, and he hated this form of idolatry. He felt that everyone involved had better things to do, and his weak stomach and restricted diet made the "rubber chicken" banquets unbearable.

Otto Nathan recalls a dinner in Einstein's honor at the Newark Armory early in 1934. After a series of laudatory speeches by politicians and Jewish leaders, the guest of honor was invited to make the final speech. Einstein stood up and said he had nothing to say, sat down, and refused to yield to the pleas of the chairman. Although the crowd was disappointed, apparently no one took offense. On the ride home he explained to Nathan, "I just couldn't stand it anymore."[4] By 1936 he had begun to refuse almost every invitation of this kind, and in response to one such appeal he composed the following ditty:

Taeglich wird man dran erinnert	(Alas, one is reminded daily
Dass hier endlos wird gedinnert	That endless dining goes on gaily
Ehre oder Geld zu spenden	So fools might make a large donation.
Dass es schier ist zum verenden.	What a needless aggravation!
Bleib fuer dich und friss dich satt	Gorge yourself voraciously,
Ganz allein, fern von der Stadt,	All alone, sagaciously.
Wer sich solches leisten kann	Whoever knows how to do this
Gluecklich ist ein solcher Mann.[5]	Has found the path to mortal bliss.)

The Einstein-Wise correspondence, from the years 1933–1936, reveals the state of helplessness of the Jews against Hitler. These letters are filled with ideas for economic boycotts, the need to assist not only Jews but also Social Democrats, Communists, and pacifists. On June 30, 1934, Hitler purged the leadership of the Sturmabteilung (SA), the brawling Nazi street army known as the Brown Shirts. Ernst Roehm, leader of the SA, was murdered along with more than one hundred other "enemies." Einstein drew fresh hope that Hitler's "insane and desperate act" signaled the end of the Nazis. Nine days later Wise, reflecting the opinions of Jewish leaders, expressed the hope that Hitler would not survive the winter, ". . . one can hardly think any longer in the term of years for the continuance of Hitlerism."[6] Roehm had been in the process of attempting to transform the SA into an army which he hoped would absorb the German army, whose officers he characterized as "old fogeys." It was his dream to turn the new Nazi regime into a military dictatorship—an idea that was anathema to Hitler. Einstein and Wise could not have known at the time that Roehm's murder had been ordered by Hitler to prevent this and to secure the backing of the Prussian generals who were alarmed by Roehm's behavior.[7] Contrary to the hopes of Einstein and Wise, the smooth dispatch of this powerful rival demonstrated Hitler's absolute power. After the June 30 *putsch,* some Jews returned to Germany because they believed

Einstein at a banquet, ca. 1934. After Elsa's death he refused to attend these affairs, citing poor health. Generally his health was fine, but the mere thought of these dinners made him feel ill. (Courtesy of Margot Einstein)

that Hitler had purged the criminal element of the Nazis and that he would now govern Germany by law, not terror.

This fatal illusion would be shattered a year later with the announcement on September 15, 1935, of the Nuremberg Laws, which completed the disfranchisement of the Jews. The Reich Citizenship Law deprived the Jews of German citizenship, and the law for the Protection of German Blood and German Honor prohibited marriage or sexual relations between Jews and those of "German or kindred blood." Before the issuance of the Nuremberg Laws, non-Zionists viewed emigration as "a" solution to the Nazi persecutions, while the Zionists believed it was "the" solution. After September 1935, almost all German Jews realized their choice was to emigrate or perish, and yet, surprisingly, between 1934 and 1937 emigration from Germany never exceeded 25,000. Some of this was due to old age or lack of money, but primarily it was caused by an inability to secure visas for immigration into some other country.

Einstein believed it essential that American non-Jewish public opinion be brought to bear against the Nazis, and he suggested that a boycott sponsored by the American Federation of Labor against Germany would be more effective than a Jewish boycott. On the infrequent occasions that he did mix in American politics in the mid-thirties, he invariably urged the United States to end its policy of isolationism and join the League of Nations. He was against a preventive war to stop Nazism, but he believed it essential that Europe present a united armed front to convince Germany of the futility of aggression. In August 1935 he described his former pacifist views as "intellectual resistance" which was insufficient against Hitler, and he gloomily predicted war within two or three years. Attempts to inspire anti-Nazi actions in America failed because of the prevailing mood of isolationism, an inability to believe Hitler could be as evil as the "hysterical" Jews were claiming, latent anti-Semitism in American society, and the depression-inspired fear that immigrants would take scarce jobs away from American workers. This concern had led President Herbert Hoover to revive a statute which prohibited the entry of aliens who might become a public charge. The State Department took full advantage of the vague phrasing to reject visa applications of those who might *possibly*, rather than *probably*, become a public charge.

American anti-Semitism, which assumed the guise of social discrimination rather than the crude violence of the German and Russian pogroms, was a legacy of the frontiersman's suspicion of unfamiliar cultural ways, the tradition of isolationism, which resulted in an attitude of hostility toward foreigners, and religious bigotry. Academic anti-Semitism in America was especially acute in the 1920s and 1930s. Restrictive quotas on Jews were common, and Jews searching for a teaching position frequently encountered discrimination. In addition to outright discrimination, there existed throughout American society a general insensitivity to the plight of the European Jews. In 1936 Einstein refused to participate in the celebration of the Harvard tercentenary. Years later he explained that his absence was due to "the fact that representatives of German Universities had been invited, although it was generally known that they were in full cooperation with Hitler's acts of persecution against Jews and Liberals and against cultural freedom in general."[8] In September 1937 the Roosevelt administration sent an envoy to the Nuremburg Nazi Party festival despite the protest of America's Ambassador William Dodd. The administration, although strongly opposed to Nazi methods, maintained formal relations until after Hitler's *Kristallnacht* pogroms in November 1938.

Throughout the late 1930s, Einstein refrained from public involvement in political matters as much as possible. After Hitler entered Austria in March 1938, Otto Nathan was so upset that he went to the *New York Times* to see if they would print a message from Einstein. Then he went to Princeton and spent the day futilely urging Einstein to make such a statement. Einstein refused and, instead, composed a private letter to Felix Frankfurter. Nothing came of this overture.[9]

During this period, Einstein devoted a considerable amount of energy and time to the procurement of affidavits so that refugees could secure visas to enter the United States or another haven. To appreciate the hopelessness of the task and the daily heartbreak that Hitler's victims lived with during the years of the Third Reich, the situation in Europe and Palestine must be examined.

The betrayal of Czechoslovakia at Munich, and Hitler's invasion of Poland on September 1, 1939, meant that more than half of the world's 16 million Jews were under the power of Hitler or Stalin. Most of the Jews who were able to escape from the Nazis hoped for sanctuary in Western Europe (especially France or Great Britain), the United States, or Palestine. In the late thirties a cruel series of events shattered these desperate dreams.

With the appearance of Hitler and the 1924 American immigration law, Palestine assumed a significance unimagined at the time the Balfour Declaration was issued in 1917. In 1918 there were fewer than 60,000 Jews in Palestine; in 1935, while 6,000 Jews entered the United States, 62,000 entered Palestine, and by the end of the decade there were 475,000 Jews in Zion. These developments and the disastrous relations among Arabs, Jews, and the British had transformed Palestine into a battleground.

The roots of the conflict between Arab and Jew in Palestine are to be found in the three historic destinies (British, Jewish, and Arab) that collided in Palestine during and immediately after the First World War. The British were involved in an effort to defeat the Axis powers and to preserve their empire. The Middle East, especially the Palestine-Suez region, was the crossroad of Europe, Asia, and Africa. The Suez Canal was an indispensable link with Great Britain's Asian colonies, particularly India and the oil fields in Iraq and Arabia.

When the disintegrating Ottoman Empire, which had ruled the Middle East for four centuries, joined the Axis powers, the British took steps to prevent the German-Turkish forces from capturing either the oil fields or the canal. They adroitly recognized and exploited the resurgence in Arab nationalism which had begun in the final decades of the nineteenth century. On October 24, 1915, Sir Henry McMahon, the British High Commissioner in Egypt, gave Sharif Hussein of Mecca a written pledge that Great Britain would support and uphold Arab independence in the region that roughly comprises Syria, Iraq, Palestine, and the Arabian peninsula, and promised to recognize an Arab caliph if one were proclaimed. With this assurance, Hussein's army, led by his son Faisal, whose adviser was the enigmatic T. E. Lawrence, revolted against Turkish rule in June 1916. The British forces under General Edmund Allenby united with Faisal's troops to conquer Palestine and then Damascus, and by December 1917 the Turks and Germans had been expelled from this critical region.

Even before Allenby completed his work, the Balfour Declaration proclaiming British support for the creation of a Jewish homeland in Palestine was issued. The British motives are not entirely clear, but it is certain that in November 1917 their real concern was in furthering the war effort, and the endorsement of the Zionist call for a national home for the Jewish people was an element of the war strategy. By endorsing colonizing rights for Zionists, they assured themselves of an active and important role in Palestinian politics. David Lloyd George and Balfour had great admiration for the Jewish people and believed that Christians had wronged them for two millennia. The Balfour Declaration, they believed, represented a step toward redressing that wrong. The Arabs saw things very differently. A European nation had granted another largely European group the right to settle in a non-European territory without consultation or concern for the aspirations of the native majority.[10] The McMahon letter and the Balfour Declaration appear to be incompatible, but in fact they are not a product of British duplicity but of a highly compartmentalized bureaucracy frantically seeking ways to defeat the enemy.

After the Balfour Declaration had been issued, Hussein became extremely nervous, and to reassure their ally the British pledged in January 1918 that Jewish settlements would not be allowed to interfere with the political and economic freedom of the Arab population. Hussein then promised to offer sanctuary "to a humanitarian and judicious settlement of Jews in Palestine." In 1919 Weizmann, Lawrence, and Faisal met in London, and after Weizmann assured the Arab leader that the Jews were interested not in a state governed by Jews but in developing the country as much as possible without damaging Arab interests, Faisal signed an agreement of cooperation with Zionism under the condition that Great Britain fulfill its pledges of Arab independence. Thus in 1919 Arab-Jewish cooperation appeared to be possible.

Events soon destroyed that dream. Anticipating the collapse of Turkish rule in the Middle East, the French and British in 1916 concluded the secret Sykes-Picot Agreement in which France claimed Syria and Lebanon while England received Iraq and Palestine. At the Versailles Treaty negotiations in 1919, the French pressed their case and forced the British to go back on their promise to support Arab independence. In Arab eyes Syria, Lebanon, and Palestine were one country, and when France was awarded a mandate in Syria and Lebanon while the British controlled Iraq and Palestine, the Arabs felt they had been cheated.

Nineteen twenty is known to the Arabs as the year of the catastrophe. Arab independence had been betrayed; the moderate Faisal, installed as king of Syria, was driven into exile in July by the hated French; European imperialists, who had exploited the Arabs for centuries, were again the dominant force in the region, and (in the view of the Arabs) this time they were using Palestine as a dumping ground for their unwanted Jews. Arab nationalism became united in opposition to the Western powers, and violence erupted in Syria, Iraq, and Palestine.

Starting on April 4, four days of riots against the Jews broke out in Palestine over the issue of Jewish immigration. Ironically, most of the victims of the violence were Orthodox Jews who were unsympathetic to Zionism because they believed Jews should not return to Zion until the advent of the messianic age which signifies the perfection of the world. After their betrayal, the Arabs identified Zionism with Western imperialism and assumed the attitude that any Jewish immigration represented an invasion by the colonial powers. The Zionists, who had not devised any Arab policy by 1917 and understood neither the extent of Arab national yearning nor Arab hatred of the West, responded by seeking protection from the British occupying forces. British officials feared Arab hostility and were openly anti-Semitic, so that in 1919–1920 tensions between the British administration, the Jews, and the Arabs were high. At no time did the Arabs or the Jews of Palestine make a serious effort to cooperate and seek understanding. The Zionists were further mistaken in their assessment of Arab opposition: they interpreted the riots as artificially fomented by irresponsible Arab landowners, and they optimistically expected to pacify the Arab peasants by the economic benefits to be gained from the colonization of the land, while at the same time quietly bribing the disgruntled Arab leaders. The Arabs were concerned not about an improvement in their standard of living but with the fear that one day the Jews would become masters of their country. Furthermore, the Palestinian Arabs were resentful of the fact that Jewish wages were significantly higher than Arab wages.

Riots again erupted in Tel Aviv–Jaffa on May 1, 1921, while Einstein was in America. Lord Herbert Samuel, the British High Commissioner in Palestine, himself a Jew, temporarily suspended Jewish immigration in an effort to cool Arab passions. The Arabs were not appeased, and the alarmed Zionists lost faith in the British commitment to the Balfour Declaration. In response, they began the illegal importation of arms and organized the Haganah, a secret, illegal Jewish army. They also began for the first time to work toward the goal of achieving a Jewish majority in Palestine. Samuel's sincere efforts to bring Arabs and Jews together in a constitutional government failed to gain Arab cooperation, and after 1923 Palestine was governed by the high commissioner who consulted with the executive and administrative councils, so that the mandate became a government by bureaucracy unchecked by popularly elected representatives of Arabs or Jews, who were separately developing their own political institutions. In essence there were three national governments functioning in isolation. Cooperation between Arab and Jew was almost nonexistent.

From 1921 to 1929 a tense peace reigned. Because of a serious economic depression in Palestine in 1926–1927, Jewish emigration exceeded immigration. But by 1928 the Zionists made a dramatic recovery. While immigration was on the increase and more and more of the desert was being reclaimed, the Arab leadership, under the Mufti of Jerusalem, was warning the masses of the threat to the Arab holy places posed by Judaism. In August 1929 tension developed when a Jewish partition to separate men and women was erected at the Wailing Wall. The Arabs began to demonstrate loudly and burn books. One Jew was killed in a brawl. Three days later his funeral became a massive Jewish demonstration. On August 23 the Arabs inaugurated a series of bloody riots and massacres of Jews which began in Jerusalem and spread throughout Palestine. Arab police joined the attacks, and, although the Mufti was later acquitted of charges of instigating the violence, his yearlong campaign against the alleged Jewish threat to Muslim holy places in Jerusalem had clearly exacerbated the dangerous situation.

The shock of the riots led the British to reevaluate their policy. British officials were disgusted with the Zionists, who were always demanding something from them; they were frightened by the growing hostility of the Muslim world, especially in India, and they did not wish to jeopardize their oil and communications interests because of a handful of Jews. The Arab ringleaders in the riots were sentenced to death, but in 1930 the British Foreign Office issued a White Paper, known as the Passfield Paper, which curtailed Jewish immigration. After anguished outcries from the Zionists the paper was slightly modified, but Weizmann was not reelected President of the World Zionist Organization at the 1931 Zionist Congress because of his close ties with the British and the mounting desire by the more nationalistic Zionists for a Jewish majority in Palestine.

As a result of the riots, the British became disenchanted with the Balfour Declaration; the Arabs learned that violence was their only means of achieving their desired ends; and the Zionists, realizing that they could no longer rely upon Britain's good will, began to arm themselves in earnest so that they might insure large-scale immigration which would give them a majority in Palestine and lead to the achievement of political sovereignty.

The riots of 1929 profoundly disturbed Einstein. He was furious that the British authorities had been unable to protect the Jewish victims and issued a public statement to the *Manchester Guardian*. He was contemptuous of the barbarity of the rioters, yet at the same time he joined with War Resisters International in calling for amnesty for the condemned Arab rioters because he felt that the right-wing Jewish youth shared the blame. Publicly and privately he appealed to Arabs and Jews to find a way to settle their differences and put an end to the almost total lack of contact between the two communities. He felt the two cultures could complement each other, and he suggested that Jewish children should learn Arabic.

The political solution Einstein envisioned was similar to the proposals of Brit Shalom (Covenant of Peace), a small group of Zionist intellectuals and pacifists who wanted to see Palestine as "a state of two nations."[11] The binational solution, endorsed by Weizmann in 1930, appealed to cultural Zionists but was rejected by those who saw in Zionism a political solution to the diaspora. Most Zionists believed Palestine belonged to the Jews and that the Arabs were blocking progress. When Brit Shalom failed to gain support among the Jews, the Arabs rejected it as an insincere diplomatic maneuver, and put forth their own demands for an Arab majority and an Arab state with a small Jewish minority. Brit Shalom disbanded after 1933.

The Zionists did not understand the nature and extent of Arab hostility, and by 1930 almost all attempts to reach a modus vivendi had been abandoned. The Zionist view of the Arab world had been largely shaped by nineteenth-century Western European values. To them, the holy land was the place where the Jews enjoyed a unique historical privilege and obligation to rebuild a Jewish homeland. The backward native population, centuries behind the civilized West, was nearly invisible. The Zionists made the fatal mistake of all advanced societies in assuming that the disruption of the native culture would be atoned for by the blessings of civilization which they would bring to the region in the fulfillment of their aspirations. They remained tragically unaware that the native Palestinians were not interested in the uplifting blessings of Western civilization. Einstein also underestimated the depth of Arab alienation, labeling the differences in outlook "more psychological than real."[12] He thought that good will and honesty could reconcile the two sides, but he realized it was essential that Jewish reconstruction of Palestine be made to serve the real needs and interests of the Arab population. The British retreat in 1930 taught him that the Jews had been mistaken in relying upon the British to establish satisfactory relations with the Arabs. The achievement of peaceful coexistence was strictly a problem for Jews and Arabs.

The growing "blind nationalism" of the Palestinian Zionists after 1930 worried Einstein greatly. All his life he had fought the narrow nationalism of the European countries which had created so much suffering and, despite his abiding commitment to the creation of a peaceful homeland in Palestine to secure for the Jews a national identity, he found Jewish nationalism as hateful as German or French nationalism. In a letter to Weizmann in November 1929, he registered his disgust with Jewish nationalists and his conviction that reliance upon the British in lieu of discovering a method of peaceful coexistence with the Arabs would be fatal to Zionist hopes:

> Should we be unable to find a way to honest cooperation and honest pacts with the Arabs, then we have learned absolutely nothing during our 2,000 years of suffering, and deserve all that will come to us. Above all, in my opinion, we must avoid leaning too much on the English. If we fail to reach real cooperation with the leading Arabs, we will be dropped by the English, not perhaps formally but *de facto*. And they will, with their traditional "religious eye-opening," claim themselves innocent of our *débâcle*, and not raise a finger.[13]

Weizmann, however, remained convinced that the British would stand by the Zionists.

In the first decade of the mandate, Arab opposition had focused upon the issue of independence; after 1932 the issue became self-preservation. The Arabs opposed all further Jewish immigration and transfer of land to the Zionists. Taking his cue from the 1929 riots and subsequent retreat from Zionism by the mandate, the Mufti carefully orchestrated a series of Arab strikes in April 1936, which degenerated into riots against both Jews and the mandate forces. By the middle of the following year, Nazi propagandists were exploiting the Palestinian situation in an effort to gain Arab support and weaken the British position in the Middle East.

The British reacted by reducing Jewish immigration by 80 percent in 1937, and then appointing another investigating body, known as the Peel Commission, to determine the future course of the mandate. The report they issued in 1937 was the most thorough and carefully researched of the many reports made during the years of British rule in Palestine. The commission concluded that "there is no common ground between [Arab and Jew]," that the mandate was unworkable, and that a binational government of Jews and Arabs would be impossible. It recommended a partition of Palestine, giving the Jews 20 percent of the land.[14] The Zionists were deeply split within their own ranks. Some demanded all of Palestine while others like Magnes and Einstein continued to resist the idea of a Jewish state. Weizmann and David Ben-Gurion, leader of the Labor Zionists and bitter rival to Weizmann, and the 1937 Zionist Congress endorsed the idea of partition, but with radical qualifications, particularly over the size of the proposed Jewish state. The Arabs rejected anything less than Arab independence and statehood, and by the fall of 1937 they had resumed hostilities. In March 1938 the British set a quota of 3,000 immigrants for the next six months. By that summer, the Jewish terrorist organization, the Irgun, was openly retaliating against the Arabs.

On April 17, 1938, in a speech entitled "Our Debt to Zionism," delivered in New York, Einstein spoke of the Jewish tradition of humaneness, which continued to unite beleaguered Jews. He noted that the Zionist work in Palestine deserved much of the credit for reviving a sense of community and self-respect among all Jews. He warned his fellow Jews against the tendency to "narrow nationalism" in response to Arab violence, and then offered his own controversial attitude on the issue of partition, which, in essence, was to remain his position until 1947:

> I should much rather see reasonable agreement with the Arabs on the basis of living together in peace than the creation of a Jewish state. Apart from practical consideration, my awareness of the essential nature of Judaism resists the idea of a Jewish state with borders, an army, and a measure of temporal power no matter how modest. I am afraid of the inner damage Judaism will sustain—especially from the development of a narrow nationalism within our own ranks, against which we have already had to fight strongly, even without a Jewish state. We are no longer the Jews of the Maccabee period. A return to a nation in the political sense of the word would be equivalent to turning away from the spiritualization of our community which we owe to the genius of our prophets. If external necessity should after all compel us to assume this burden, let us bear it with tact and patience.[15]

On another occasion he defended Jewish nationalism as a movement "whose aim is not power but dignity and health."[16]

The hardening of Zionist political demands and the racial hatred of Arab and Jew had prompted him to speak out. At the heart of his political philosophy was his uncompromising conviction that the fate of man must be the central concern of any political action, that human and spiritual considerations take priority over purely practical politics, and that lasting political security and justice can be assured only when the spiritualization of the community is afforded the highest priority. Einstein was a stubborn idealist, but he was not dogmatic. If external necessity makes binational government impossible, then, he warned, we must bear the "burden" of statehood "with tact and patience," not with aggressive nationalism.

The speech provoked strong reactions. American Zionists like Wise and Brandeis, who opposed partition, applauded loudly. Weizmann, who had read a garbled account of the speech, angrily fired off a 2,000-word letter to Einstein to clarify the official Zionist position and to register displeasure over Einstein's characteristic outspokenness. Einstein replied in tones that barely concealed anger and disappointment. He denied that the speech was either a breach of faith with Zionism or a compromise with its opponents. "I am suffering no less than any one of us in these bitter times the Jews have to live through," he wrote, "and I feel my ties with the common fate during every hour of my life."[17] The extent of his anger can be gauged by another letter he wrote to an American Jew in July in which he accused Weizmann of being influenced by people with money or political clout, and not someone like himself.[18] The two men had the highest personal respect for each other and both were devoted to the cause of Zionism, but they were often critical of the other's political views. Einstein felt Weizmann, whom he once called "the chosen one of the chosen people,"[19] was inclined to practice *realpolitik,* while Weizmann thought Einstein's politics were impractical and utopian. Although he was always prepared to exploit Einstein's fame, he did not welcome the physicist's outspoken idealism.

The most heartening response to Einstein's endorsement of binationalism came from F. I. Shatara, President of the Arab National League in New York. Four days after the speech, Shatara wrote to Einstein requesting a meeting because he believed that Einstein's Zionism was palatable to Arab nationalism. The two men met in Princeton and formed a high opinion of the other's character. Einstein believed that an attempt should be made to bring together influential and responsible representatives from the Arab and Jewish side for the purpose of devising a solution to the Palestinian problem which would avoid the division of the country. If a meeting ever was arranged, it bore no fruitful results because of the disastrous turn of events in Europe and Palestine and the lack of political influence of moderates like Einstein. However, the contact established between Shatara and Einstein belies the Zionist position that no Arab moderates existed and that reasonable dialogue was no longer possible.

In November 1938, as the reign of terror against the Jews under Nazi rule intensified, the British yielded to Arab violence and abandoned the idea of partition. In March and April 1938 the Nazis had passed laws denying the Jewish religious communities their legal status and requiring all Jews to report their personal property. Late in May large numbers of Jews were arrested and most were shipped to Dachau. Then, on the night of November 9–10, in retaliation for the assassination of Ernst vom Rath, a secretary at the German Embassy in Paris, by a distraught seventeen-year-old Polish Jew whose parents had just been expelled from Germany, Nazi hooligans embarked on a well-rehearsed assault upon the 350,000 Jews still in Germany. This was the infamous *Kristallnacht* (Night of the Glass) so named because of the widespread smashing of display windows in Jewish-owned stores. As a result of this reversion to medieval terrorism, nearly one hundred Jews were murdered and approximately 30,000 Jewish men (many of whom were chosen because they were wealthy) were arrested and sent to concentration camps. Jewish businesses, property, and synagogues were looted, demolished, and burned, and the Jews were then subjected to a collective fine of one billion marks to pay for the damage. The only Nazis who were punished were the rapists, whose acts violated the Nazi racial laws.

For months after the *Kristallnacht,* suicides accounted for more than half the Jewish burials in Germany. Although the British and American governments were staggered by the depredations against the Jews, they did not change their immigration policies. On November 22, 1938, 10,000 Jewish children from Germany were denied entrance to Palestine. Although they were subsequently received by England, the Zionists felt betrayed. Weizmann, his faith in England badly shaken, noted sadly that the Jews now "had got the courage of desperation."[20]

If 1920 was the year of the catastrophe to the Arabs, to the Jews it was 1939, because in that year official British policy, wavering since 1929, turned decisively away from the support of the Balfour Declaration at the very moment the Jews of Europe needed a real, not merely symbolic, place of refuge. On March 15, 1939, Hitler entered Prague and annexed Bohemia and Moravia. That same day, the British privately informed Arab and Jewish leaders of His Majesty's government's new Palestinian policy. The shift of policy, embodied in the 1939 White Paper, which was released publicly two months later, set a limit on Jewish immigration to 15,000 a year for five years and after that, unless the Arabs consented, it prohibited further immigration. The avowed purpose of the White Paper was to move Palestine toward independence in ten years with a permanent Arab majority. Its real purpose was to protect the British position in the Middle East in preparation for the now inevitable war, and one pretext employed by the British (and also by the United States) to justify the limitation upon immigration was the fear that Nazi agents disguised as Jewish refugees might enter the country, although none ever did. Just when the fate of the Jews trapped under Hitler's rule became desperate, Great Britain, for military purposes, closed the most important escape route, and made no serious effort to find alternative sanctuaries for the Jews remaining in Europe.

The White Paper was a disaster. The Zionists rejected it at once. The Arabs were equally displeased because they demanded an immediate cessation of the

Jewish "invasion." Both sides turned increasingly to terrorism against each other and against the mandate, so that, throughout the war, the British were under fire in Palestine, and the authority of the mandate was practically destroyed. Weizmann's moderating influence was discredited and the Jews turned to smuggling weapons and immigrants into Palestine. After 1939 the Zionists abandoned attempts to have binational parity accepted as official policy; they were now committed, at least unofficially, to the creation of a Jewish state. When war came, David Ben-Gurion summed up the plight of the Zionists: "We shall fight the war as if there were no White Paper, and the White Paper as if there were no war."[21]

The United States and Great Britain absorbed more refugees than any country except Palestine, yet the performance of the two great democracies in the rescue of Hitler's victims is one of the most shameful episodes in their histories. Anti-Semitism, bureaucratic paranoia, and the legitimate demands of the war effort effectively scuttled all serious relief efforts until it was too late.

In Britain, anti-Semitism, although free of the virulence found in Germany, was a social factor especially strong in the Foreign Office and the military. The English were forever worrying that anti-Semitism would increase if more Jews entered the country, and when the war broke out they interred German-Jewish refugees living in England as enemy aliens.

They also worried that Hitler might drive hundreds of thousands of Jews out of the Reich in an effort to force the Allies to feed and shelter them—or, worse, to embarrass them if they failed to do so. After the war began, few Jews were admitted to England because of the unfounded fear of enemy agents. The excuse that the population could ill afford to absorb more than one or two thousand Jews rings hollow when considered in the light of preparations in 1940 to receive 300,000 Dutch and Belgian refugees on short notice. In the final analysis, the saving of Jewish lives was not a primary war aim that would contribute to a victory over Hitler.

In America, the shameful story is even less excusable. The size of the United States, its tradition as a haven for the oppressed, and its nonparticipation during the first twenty-seven months of the war made it the most practical place of refuge. If as much effort had been put into the rescue of Jews as was expended in preventing their entry, thousands upon thousands of lives would have been saved. During this period, however, the United States was, in the words of Chaim Weizmann, "violently neutral," and mention of the Jewish tragedy frequently was branded warmongering.[22] The primary means of preventing Jewish immigration in the Hitler years was the 1924 immigration law, which was an undisguised attempt to put an end to the tremendous influx of poor immigrants from Southern, Central, and Eastern Europe who had entered America in massive numbers during the early part of this century. These immigrants were mostly Catholic, Greek Orthodox, and Jewish, and they tended to cluster in cities and retain language and cultural barriers to assimilation. The extent of the success of the 1924 law can be gauged by the fact that immigration had fallen from an average of 900,000 per year during the period 1900–1915 to 154,000 in 1929. Whereas 70 percent of the prewar figure had come from Central and Eastern Europe, more than half of the 1929 figure hailed from England and Ireland. The 1924 immigration law set quotas upon each nationality and made no distinction between refugees and immigrants. This enabled the State Department, which sympathized with the policy of the British Foreign Office, to treat all refugees as potential and undesirable immigrants without regard for mitigating circumstances. Restrictionist anti-Semitism, near-paranoia about possible saboteurs and spies entering disguised as Jews, and lack of Jewish unity in fighting the bureaucracy were the primary reasons for the dismal record of saving refugees.

President Roosevelt enjoyed enormous support from the American Jewish community. Several of his most trusted advisers were Jews, and in anti-Roosevelt circles, his administration was sometimes referred to as the "Jew Deal." There is no question that Roosevelt personally sympathized with the plight of the Jews and desired to help them, but he was a consummate politician who understood the extent of restrictionist hostility to the refugees. Since he needed the support of the restrictionists for his war preparations, he was unwilling to antagonize them over what was perceived to be a side issue. Thus, during the crisis years he followed the path of statesmanship: He opted for rhetoric and delegated the actual work to the State Department, which was free to pursue its own course of obstruction. Instead of offering temporary shelter to the refugees in the United States, Roosevelt proposed utterly impractical, gigantic resettlement schemes in Africa and Latin America. One student of the refugee crisis has written of Roosevelt's behavior: "He fell easily into the role of elder statesman poised above the battle."[23]

Breckenridge Long was the State Department's man in charge of administering the immigration laws. He was a trustee of Princeton University and a Midwestern patrician who served as ambassador to Italy from 1933 to 1936, and in 1938 lobbied in Washington for Franco. He was an isolationist, willing to accommodate Berlin when necessary, a sophisticated anti-Communist, an anti-Semite, and a self-righteous paranoid who interpreted criticism of his work as a personal affront. Even before he joined the State Department in 1939, the restrictionist forces had been so successful in blocking rescue attempts that the German quota for 1932–1938 was not filled. Symptomatic of the restrictionist attitude was a call by the American Veterans of Foreign Wars in 1938 for a ban on all immigration. In March 1939 another avenue of escape was closed when the United States suspended further issuance of visitors' visas unless the applicant could guarantee his return to his native land.

From 1939 to 1943 Long almost single-handedly blocked Jewish immigration. Justifying his actions by exploiting the spy hysteria, he interpreted the 1924 law with merciless rigidity and invented numerous legal ploys to delay processing papers for those who were lucky enough to qualify for a visa. On June 26, 1940, Long wrote in a departmental memo: "We can delay and effectively stop for a temporary period of indefinite length the number of immigrants into the United

States. We could do this by simply advising our consuls to put every obstacle in the way and to resort to various administrative devices which would postpone and postpone the granting of the visas."[24] One of Long's tricks was the invocation (or failure to revoke) Section 7(C) of the 1924 immigration law which required the applicant to furnish a police certificate of good character for the preceding five years "if available." The police in most cases were, of course, the Gestapo.

In 1938–1939 a committee whose membership included Otto Nathan and the daughter of Rabbi Wise (Einstein was an inactive member) managed to have special legislation introduced into Congress to permit the admission of 20,000 Central European children to the United States outside of the yearly quota. Known as the Wagner-Rogers Bill, it was supported by Eleanor Roosevelt and most religious groups, but was denounced by patriotic groups like the Daughters of the American Revolution, the Veterans of Foreign Wars, and the American Legion. After President Roosevelt, guided by State Department advice, had written on the bill "File, no action," it was killed in committee by one of Long's allies. More than forty years later, memory of the story was "heartbreaking" for Nathan.[25] Long, however, viewed sympathy for the refugee children as "an enormous psychosis."[26] At this time, Congress was prepared to admit British children outside the quota system.

Nazism, the Palestinian civil war, and British and American obfuscation combined to seal the fate of 6 million Jews and countless non-Jews who were trapped inside Hitler's German Empire. Almost from the moment of his arrival in Princeton, Einstein was deluged with desperate requests for assistance from friends and strangers trapped in Europe. If an applicant could produce an affidavit from a relative already settled in America who pledged to assume financial responsibility for his kin, then immigration was much more likely. The vast majority of the refugees could make no such claim and their only hope lay in securing an affidavit from someone of means who was willing to insure that the immigrants would never burden the bulging welfare and unemployment rolls.

The Einstein Archives overflow with letters from refugees, and Einstein did everything in his power to help them. He wrote affidavits for so many, despite his own limited resources, that by the late thirties his signature on an affidavit no longer carried much weight with the authorities. For others, he wrote letters to relatives, if they had any, or to wealthy nonrelatives who were willing to sponsor strangers. There were various committees assisting in this rescue work, and Einstein had several wealthy friends who helped to the limits of their resources. It was a tedious chore to fill out the necessary forms to satisfy the red tape of the bureaucracy, and Einstein sometimes described his desk, covered with legal forms, as a "lawyer's office." In the fall of 1938 he explained his plight to his friend Michele Besso, who was living in Switzerland and frantically doing what he could to help refugees escape Europe: "I cannot give any more affidavits and would endanger those that are still pending if I were to give more. The resources of the few, more or less well-to-do people I know are also already strained to the utmost. The pressure on us from the poor people over there is such that one almost despairs, faced as one is with the magnitude of misery and the few possibilities of supplying help. . . . [I]t will be extremely difficult if these people don't have any relatives here, because affidavits from relatives are considered first, and this implies more and more that all others are excluded."[27] When he was unable to do anything for someone, he would write him and offer comfort. After Einstein's death one stranger who had begged for help wrote to the estate that Einstein's letters to him and his family had helped to sustain their morale and faith in humanity.

By the summer of 1941, Long's policies, callously and efficiently implemented by most of the American consuls in Europe, had succeeded in closing off the United States to all but a few refugees. In June Long managed to push a law through Congress that permitted the consuls to deny visas to anyone they felt would "endanger the public safety of the United States."[28] At the same time the "close relatives" edict made it almost impossible for anyone without relatives in the States to enter America. Because of the imaginative steps taken to complicate the visa procedure, it now took about six months to process each application. The screening procedure required a biographical statement, two financial statements, and supporting letters of reference from two United States citizens. The applicant and the affiants were then investigated for security clearance. After the outbreak of war, the State Department required signers of affidavits to come to Washington to face the interrogation of what Nathan has described as the "most unfriendly committee I ever saw,"[29] which asked such questions as "For whom did you vote in the last election?"

The application was then screened by an interdepartmental committee with representatives from the State Department, Justice, the FBI, Military Intelligence, and the Office of Naval Intelligence. If the application managed to pass this bureaucratic maze, the consuls in Europe still had the authority to deny the visa and, in an effort to gain the favor of their superiors, often did just that. In 1939 and 1940 the combined German-Austrian quota was 27,370, and in both years it was filled. In 1941, with America still neutral, less than half of the legally possible visas were issued; in 1942 the figure fell to 17.8 percent. The State Department, in fact, managed, between 1933 and 1943, to leave unfilled more than 400,000 places within the quota for countries which were under Nazi domination.[30] Although the United States was not as endangered as Great Britain, its screening procedure was more rigid. President Roosevelt, preoccupied with war preparations, relied upon State Department briefings, and consequently did not realize there was a conspiracy afoot to exclude refugees.

In the summer of 1941 Nathan visited Einstein's retreat at Saranac Lake. He was so upset by the State Department's efforts to prevent Jewish immigration he convinced Einstein that they must do something. Einstein was very skeptical that their efforts would be fruitful, but he agreed to accompany Nathan to a nearby lake where Stephen Wise was vacationing. The three men composed a letter to Eleanor

Roosevelt dated July 26, 1941, in the hopes that she could stir her husband's conscience. The letter read:

> A policy is now being pursued in the State Department which makes it all but impossible to give refuge in America to many worthy persons who are the victims of Fascist cruelty in Europe. Of course, this is not openly avowed by those responsible for it. The method which is being used, however, is to make immigration impossible by erecting a wall of bureaucratic measures alleged to be necessary to protect America against subversive, dangerous elements.

Einstein urged the First Lady to investigate the charges and if she agreed with his allegations, to bring it "to the attention of your heavily burdened husband in order that it may be remedied."[31] Mrs. Roosevelt replied that she would show the letter to the President, but Einstein was no more successful in changing the policy than she had been.

Late in 1943, Secretary of the Treasury Henry Morgenthau was informed by Stephen Wise of the State Department's policy, and he immediately launched an investigation into the situation. The result was a report for Roosevelt which originally bore the title "Report to the Secretary on the Acquiesence of this

Einstein and Rabbi Stephen S. Wise, probably in the mid-1940s. (Courtesy of Margot Einstein)

Government in the Murder of the Jews." Roosevelt, profoundly shaken, ordered the creation of the War Refugee Board in January 1944 to be administered by the Treasury Department. Despite its disgracefully late appearance, the WRB was able to alleviate some of the suffering of those who had escaped the Nazi gas chambers. It also demonstrated how much more could have been done if the Roosevelt administration, from the start, had been passionately committed to saving lives.

In the end—to the eternal shame of Great Britain and the United States—the petty bureaucratic bickerings cost thousands of lives. However, the grim truth is that no amount of dedication on the part of the Western democracies could have saved most of the victims of the Holocaust. Only the Nazi leaders could have prevented the death of millions.

7

"Against Necessity No One Can Fight and Win"

L ong before Hitler's tanks roared into Poland, where they were met by the Polish cavalry on September 1, 1939, events of the thirties, which the poet W. H. Auden branded the "low, dishonest decade," had assured the advent of a second European war in one generation. Although no one at the time could possibly have imagined the horrors of Hitler's "final solution" of the Jewish problem, the image of Hitler ruling much or all of Europe was unbearable to the refugees from European fascism. In December 1938, while the Western democracies continued the halfhearted struggle to summon the resolve to oppose German expansionism, a remarkable discovery in a Berlin laboratory raised the possibility that the awesomely rebuilt German war machine might be delivered a new ultimate weapon—an atomic bomb.

Popular mythology holds that Einstein was the "father" of the atom bomb. This mistaken belief is based on two separate but mutually reinforcing pieces of evidence: his 1905 discovery of the relationship between energy and matter ($E = mc^2$) and the letter he signed (but almost certainly did not compose) in August 1939 warning President Roosevelt that recent discoveries in Nazi Germany brought the construction of an atomic bomb within the realm of possibility. Einstein did indeed make the 1905 discovery, and he did sign the 1939 letter but, as will be shown, neither fact qualified him as the father of atomic weapons.

Even before Einstein's discovery of $E = mc^2$, Ernest Rutherford, the great British experimental physicist, had predicted in 1904 that if artificial disintegration of the atom were possible, then an enormous amount of energy would be released. As late as 1937, the year of his death, Rutherford believed that such a process would be impractical because the energy required to disintegrate an atom would be greater than the energy released from the reaction. Throughout the twenties and thirties, Einstein shared Rutherford's skepticism. In 1921, on a visit to Prague, a young man had attempted to show Einstein his plans to produce a nuclear weapon based on Einstein's formula. Philipp Frank, who witnessed the encounter, reports that Einstein curtly dismissed the would-be inventor, saying, "You haven't lost anything if I don't discuss your work with you in detail. Its foolishness is evident at first glance. You cannot learn any more from a longer discussion."[1] As late as 1935 he is reported to have told a press conference in Pittsburgh that the likelihood of transforming matter into energy "is something like shooting birds in the dark in a country where there are only a few birds."[2]

In the twenties and thirties man's knowledge of the atom increased dramatically. In 1932 the Englishman James Chadwick discovered the neutron. Then in 1934 Enrico Fermi in Italy and Frédéric Joliot-Curie in France independently produced disintegrations of heavy atoms, but neither scientist recognized that he had split the atom. The critical step occurred in December 1938 in Berlin, where Otto Hahn and Fritz Strassmann, working at the Kaiser Wilhelm Institute, split heavy uranium with a neutron bombardment. Hahn and Strassmann identified one of the large fragments as barium, an element whose mass is somewhat greater than half the mass of uranium, but they were unable to interpret their findings. They did, however, send the results of their work to a colleague in Sweden, the Austrian physicist Lise Meitner, who being half-Jewish had fled Germany immediately after the Anschluss in March 1938. With her nephew, Otto Frisch, a colleague of Niels Bohr, she correctly surmised that the uranium atom had been split into two approximately equal parts, that Hahn and Strassmann had achieved atomic fission. In the process a very small amount of the mass of the heavy uranium had been lost, and an enormous amount of energy had been released. Bohr, who was on his way to the United States, was immediately notified of these startling developments, and at a scientific meeting in January 1939 he created a furor with his announcement of the successful splitting of the atom. The experiments were repeated and verified by a number of scientists within hours of Bohr's talk, and the excitement generated by the news was so intense that during the fateful year of 1939 more than one hundred papers on nuclear fission were published.

By mid-March, the Hungarian physicist Leo Szilard, Fermi, and others had established that in the process of nuclear fission, along with the release of energy, extra neutrons were emitted which might be used to split more atoms, thereby producing a controlled chain reaction which meant that, in theory, the release of atomic power could be sustained at a controllable rate. Even with this major advance, the scientists involved were far from feeling confident that this could be accomplished.

Before continuing with the remarkable events of 1939, it is time to inter the notion that Einstein's work in 1905 had paved the way for the bomb, and—as some have charged—he ought to have foreseen the consequences of his work, suppressed the discovery, and thereby averted the nightmares of the nuclear age. $E = mc^2$ tells us that there is a fundamental relationship between mass and energy; it provides a theoretical explanation for the release of energy in the process of fission. It does not predict fission or the accomplishment of a chain reaction for a very simple reason: fission requires neutrons and neutrons were unknown until 1932. Even if Einstein had known about the existence of neutrons and the possibility of a chain reaction, it would have been impossible to suppress the relationship between energy and mass. In February 1955 Einstein answered a correspondent who suggested that he ought to have been more prescient in 1905:

> . . . . it would have been ridiculous to attempt to conceal the particular conclusion resulting from the Special Theory of Relativity. Once the theory existed, the conclusion also existed and could not have remained concealed for any length of time. As for the theory itself, it owes its existence to the efforts to discover the properties of the "luminiferous ether"! There was never even the slightest indication of any potential technological application.[3]

The problem, therefore, is not that Einstein made a beautiful discovery which later produced a most terrible invention, but that man's ethical and social qualities have been unable to utilize the fruit of science in a humane manner.

It should also be noted that the construction of atomic weapons did not depend on Einstein's formula. Even if he had not made the 1905 discovery, the production of atomic bombs would have been possible once experimental physicists discovered the way to split uranium. Einstein's equation provides a theoretical explanation for the process, but the process could have been discovered without the theoretical explanation.[4]

In mid-March 1939, while Szilard and his colleague Walter Zinn of Columbia University were putting the finishing touches on the report of their discovery that a controlled chain reaction was possible, Hitler entered Prague. Fermi, Szilard, and several other scientists involved in nuclear research were refugees from fascism, and fearing that German scientists were making similar advances, they turned their attention to two crucial questions: Should scientists voluntarily impose secrecy upon the developments in nuclear physics, and should the United States government be made aware of the possibility of creating nuclear weapons? On the first question, the émigré scholars were far more inclined to support censorship because of their experience with German and Italian fascism, while American scientists still did not sense approaching disaster. The issue was scuttled when Joliot-Curie published an article in France in April. With the notable exception of Szilard, most scientists were relieved not to be forced to adopt the odious task of self-censorship. In April the scientists attempted to open communication with the navy, but on July 10, a spokesman informed Szilard that the navy had no further interest in following developments in nuclear physics at that time. By this time the governments of both Great Britain and Germany had been alerted to these developments.

Szilard emerges as the central force in the strange drama of the summer of 1939. He had worked with Einstein in Berlin in the late twenties and together they had taken out a patent on a refrigerator in 1930. In 1939, he was an alien in the

United States with no official position; he had performed his work that spring at Columbia as a temporary guest. Eugene Wigner of Princeton University, another Hungarian physicist, describes Szilard as "a very gregarious person [who] had the flair to get in touch with important people."[5] Noting that Germany had stopped selling uranium ore from Czechoslovakia, Szilard and Wigner became concerned that Germany might begin buying large quantities of uranium ore from the Belgian Congo, and they decided to alert the Belgian government. Wigner remembered that Einstein knew the Queen Mother of Belgium, and they decided to seek Einstein's assistance.

Einstein was passing the summer peacefully at a remote spot on Long Island, where he was able to sail daily. He monitored the deteriorating international situation and especially the plight of European Jewry very closely, but as he wrote to Queen Elizabeth later that summer, "except for the newspapers and the countless letters, I would hardly be aware that I live in a time when human inadequacy and cruelty are achieving frightful proportions."[6] When Szilard and Wigner called to ask if they might see him, he had no inkling of the purpose of their visit.

On or about July 15, 1939, the two Hungarian physicists drove to Long Island with an address for Einstein that proved to be incorrect. They became lost and almost abandoned the search when they came upon a small boy who directed them to Einstein's cabin. When they told Einstein about the possibility of a chain reaction, he expressed surprise but quickly grasped the scientific and political implications of the discovery, and the three men began searching for the best course of action. Possibly due to the navy's lack of interest, Szilard argued against involving the U.S. government because, he insisted, it would create a lot of red tape. Einstein was equally reluctant to write to the Queen Mother and suggested instead that he write to a member of the Belgian cabinet whom he knew, but he agreed with Wigner's contention that it was improper to write a foreign government without first warning the State Department. Apparently they also discussed the possibility of approaching the U.S. government about the question of financing further research. By the end of this first meeting, they had tentatively agreed that Einstein should draft a letter to the Belgian government which they would forward to the State Department, and if no objections were raised, they would send it on to Belgium.

Szilard realized that Columbia could not continue to support the growing research without outside assistance, and at about the time of his visit to Einstein he spoke to a friend in the financial world, who put him in touch with Alexander Sachs, a well-known economist and banker, who was a friend and informal adviser to President Roosevelt. Sachs suggested that the letter be addressed directly to the President and volunteered to deliver it personally. On the basis of one meeting with Sachs, Szilard decided that he could be trusted, and in a letter to Einstein dated July 19, he recommended they follow Sachs's advice. Enclosed in that letter was a suggested draft for the letter Einstein was to write.

Some time before the end of July Szilard visited Einstein a second time. As Wigner was in California, he was accompanied by yet another Hungarian physi-

Einstein and Valentine Bargmann on Long Island, summer 1939. (Courtesy of Valentine Bargmann)

cist, Edward Teller, who was later to be known as the "father" of the hydrogen bomb. Einstein dictated another draft for the letter in German to Teller, which served as the basis for the English version composed by Szilard, probably under the guidance of Sachs. Einstein signed the letter on August 2, and it was then entrusted to Sachs. By signing the letter, Einstein put his seal upon its contents, but several hands had shaped it, and Szilard, using Einstein's dictated draft as a basis, had actually written it.

On September 1, 1939, Hitler invaded Poland and for the next several weeks Roosevelt was busy with the revision of the neutrality laws. By the time Sachs delivered Einstein's letter on October 11, almost two months had elapsed. He never explained why he had failed to deliver it in August while Europe was still at peace.

The letter alerted the President to the fact that recent discoveries indicated "that it may become possible to set up nuclear chain reactions in a large mass of uranium, by which vast amounts of power and large quantities of new radium-like elements would be generated. Now it appears almost certain that this could be achieved in the immediate future."

> This new phenomenon [the letter continued] would also lead to the construction of bombs, and it is conceivable—though much less certain—that extremely powerful bombs of a new type may thus be constructed. A single bomb of this type, carried by boat or exploded in a port, might very well destroy the whole port together with some of the surrounding territory. However, such bombs might very well prove to be too heavy for transportation by air.[7]

On behalf of his colleagues Einstein requested that the American government establish contact with the scientists working on nuclear physics, and that it help subsidize research and the procurement of uranium. He concluded by warning that the Germans had stopped the sale of Czechoslovakian uranium. He speculated that this might be due to the fact that C. F. von Weizsäcker, son of the German Under secretary of State, worked at the Kaiser Wilhelm Institute, "where some of the American work on uranium is now being repeated."[8] At that time, Einstein and Szilard could not have known that since September 1938 the elder von Weizsäcker had been involved in resistance to Hitler, and the younger von Weizsäcker's early illusions about the Nazis—he and Teller had known each other in 1933–1934—had, by 1939, been lost.

Roosevelt received the letter on October 11, and acted immediately, taking steps to create a three-man Advisory Committee on Uranium which was ordered to report its findings to him as soon as possible. The committee, chaired by Lyman J. Briggs, chief of the Bureau of Standards, met with Szilard, Wigner, and Teller on October 21, 1939; Einstein did not attend. The Briggs committee report to the President on November 1, 1939, urged a thorough investigation of nuclear physics and the coordination of work being done at the various universities. President Roosevelt filed the report "for reference," and nothing further was heard from the White House for more than two months.

At this point Briggs asked Sachs for ideas to give new impetus to the government's role in nuclear research. Sachs visited Einstein in February 1940 and, after further meetings, Einstein wrote a second letter regarding atomic energy on March 7, 1940. This letter, although addressed to Sachs, was designed to rekindle Roosevelt's interest in uranium research. "Since the outbreak of the war," Einstein wrote, "interest in uranium has intensified in Germany." The letter then turns to the delicate issue of censorship, a subject repugnant to all scientists, particularly Einstein: "Dr. Szilard has shown me a manuscript . . . in which he describes in detail a method for setting up a chain reaction in uranium. The papers will appear in print unless they are held up, and the question arises whether something ought to be done to withhold publication." After the resumption of war in Europe in April 1940, voluntary censorship practices, in effect since the preceding September, were tightened.

Sachs took Einstein's second letter to Roosevelt on March 15, 1940, and on April 5 the President ordered the Advisory Committee on Uranium to be enlarged. For the next year and a half American governmental participation in uranium research remained limited, because prospects for atomic weapons available for the war were not promising. Furthermore, Americans hoped to remain neutral. In October 1941 British scientists showed Vannevar Bush, the Chairman of the National Defense Research Committee, a report that stated that prospects for the development of atomic weapons for use in the war were now much more favorable. It was this information, not Einstein's two letters, which inspired the United States government to make a full commitment to the development of atomic weapons by the creation of the Manhattan Project on December 6, 1941.[9]

Otto Nathan was Einstein's close personal friend and staunchest political ally for two decades. As an editor of *Einstein on Peace,* he and co-editor Heinz Norden have written that signing the letter to Roosevelt, and the subsequent bombing of two Japanese cities, constituted "the most tragic experience in his life."[10] In the final decade of his life this tragedy weighed heavily upon his heart. Yet, as he knew, under the circumstances created by Hitler's megalomania, he had had no choice but to act as he did. The consolation of knowing he had done what he had to do saved him from despair and fueled his uncompromising efforts to help make the world safe from nuclear suicide. Twenty-five hundred years ago, Aeschylus placed these words in the mouth of the Titan Prometheus, chained to a desolate rock in the Caucasus by Zeus for the crime of giving pitiful humanity the knowledge of fire:

> So I must bear, as lightly as I can,
> the destiny that fate has given me;
> for I know well against necessity,
> against its strength, no one can fight and win.[11]

8

A Private Life

O n October 1, 1940, Einstein, his daughter Margot, and secretary Helen Dukas took the oath of American citizenship in time to cast their first vote a month later for the reelection of President Roosevelt. At the ceremony in Trenton, a larger than usual contingent of newsmen and photographers lined the walls of the crowded courtroom. A policy of no picture taking did not prevent the cameramen, or "light monkeys" *(Lichtaffen)* as Einstein dubbed them, from photographing Einstein and scores of others taking the oath. After the ceremony he quipped to the reporters that he would even renounce his beloved sailboat if such an action were "a part of my citizenship." His daughter and secretary then explained to the eager scribes that "when he goes out in the boat he becomes oblivious to everything else in the world."[1]

Citizenship, for Einstein, was largely a symbolic matter. He was grateful for the safety he and thousands of other refugees from Hitler had found in America, and he felt it was important to assume the formal responsibilities of American citizenship. Nonetheless, as he had said in 1933, his citizenship was a "strange affair," because, as an internationalist, his primary allegiance was to humanity rather than to any individual nation. In 1945, as the Allies were discovering the extent of the slaughter of the Jews by the Nazis, Einstein wrote to one correspondent, "I am not, incidentally, a German, but a Jew by nationality."[2]

With the decline of civilization in Europe, Einstein had become estranged from the world of his youth. He was too old and disinclined to put down new roots in America, where, emotionally, he remained a stranger. He loved the American ideal of democracy, which permitted the individual to dissent from the values of society, and he found Americans to be open, friendly, and helpful. He had been contemptuous of bourgeois values in Switzerland and Germany, and it is hardly surprising that he was critical of the materialism in America.

What he and the majority of refugee intellectuals found most distasteful about American society was the undercurrent of anti-intellectualism which pervades so many aspects of American political, religious, social, and even educational life. In a business-oriented society a premium is placed upon decisive action and pragmatic thinking which yields quick and exploitable results. Knowledge and science are often valued only when they contribute tangibly to progress, whereas contemplation and deliberation are viewed as unproductive, with the result that throughout American history the intellectual has been viewed with suspicion or antipathy. On one occasion Einstein noted contemptuously that a new garter is more prized than a new philosophic idea. He especially disliked the dominance of businessmen in American universities.

In spite of his often sharp criticisms of politics and culture, Einstein genuinely enjoyed his quiet private life in Princeton. It did not take long for Princetonians to become accustomed to their famous neighbor, whom they generally treated as just another resident. By 1937 Einstein could write that he enjoyed "that solitude which only life among people with an utterly different past and attitude toward life can afford."[3] Because of age and personal inclination he never fully adjusted to the faster, younger, and louder society he encountered. Although he soon became fluent in English, he was only really comfortable when speaking German. While his wife was alive he had led a modest social life, but that ended, for the most part, with her death. He had never enjoyed socializing and, at his age, he saw no reason to suffer something he disliked.

The small circle of friends in Princeton and New York City was composed primarily of other Europeans, most of whom were German-speaking. In Princeton, in addition to his colleagues at the institute, there were intellectuals like Paul Oppenheim, a philosopher of science, the historian Erich Kahler, the novelist Hermann Broch, and Erwin Panofsky, the art historian at the institute. There were younger scientific colleagues like Valentine Bargmann, a few near neighbors and, of course, the Buckys in New York. These relationships were very informal, almost familylike. His privacy was scrupulously respected, and, as one neighbor said, "None of us ever went to him unless it was with some reason. But whenever that happened we were always beautifully received."[4]

Thomas Mann lived in Princeton from 1938 to 1941 but, except for a shared hatred of the Nazis, the two famous refugees had little in common. The patrician Mann disliked Princeton and described the lectures he delivered at Princeton University as two years of jokes. He lived in an imposing red-brick fortress on Library Place, just a block away from Einstein's first Princeton home. An undergraduate of the time describes the reception a group of Christmas carolers received from the two men in December 1938. At Mercer Street, "[Einstein] came out in shirt sleeves [and no socks]. His housekeeper came out and put a coat over his shoulders. He stood listening until we were done, then shook each of our hands. . . . [T]hat same night we sang outside the rented abode of Thomas Mann, a grand place with high French doors facing the street. Through cracks in the curtains we could see elegant guests moving about. No one came out, though some peeked out. The contrast impressed me."[5]

While the State Department and the restrictionists fought to keep refugees out of America, the majority of Americans received the victims of European fascism in a generally friendly and helpful manner. In many quarters of American and British society, however, there was great admiration for Hitler's economic and social triumphs. The reports of Nazi murders and atrocities against the Jews and the Left were frequently dismissed as Zionist exaggeration or propaganda. Even after the outbreak of war, a sense of false security prevailed in America, and refugees like Einstein, who clearly understood Hitler's intentions, were viewed as troublemakers trying to plunge the United States into another European war. Many of the patriotic groups who had assailed Einstein's pacifism a decade earlier now branded calls for intervention as warmongering.

In October 1937 Hans Albert Einstein came to America to find work and a place of refuge from the Nazis. He remained in Princeton until January 1938 when he returned to Switzerland. He came back to the United States in June 1938 with his family, and after a brief visit with his father, settled in South Carolina. Later he moved to the West Coast, and from 1947 to 1971 he was a professor of hydraulic engineering at the University of California at Berkeley. Although Einstein had continued to visit his sons in Zurich after the separation from Mileva and had often entertained them in Berlin, relations between Hans Albert and his father remained strained, and the younger Einstein often manifested antagonism toward his father. In America, Hans rarely visited his father and did not disguise his resentment over the divorce and subsequent marriage to Elsa.

In 1938 Mussolini began to ape Hitler's policy against the Jews, and the wife and children of Robert Einstein, Albert's cousin, were brutally murdered. Robert escaped only because he was away at the time, but when he returned, he took his own life. This prompted Einstein to write a carefully worded letter to his sister, Maja, who was living in a suburb of Florence with her husband, Paul Winteler, son of Einstein's admired teacher in Aarau, suggesting that she pay him a visit in America. While her husband joined his family in Switzerland, she entered America in 1939. At first the war and, later, illness prevented her return to her husband and Italy. Ever since their childhood Albert and Maja had been very close, and she, probably more than any other person, understood his detached and solitary nature. One friend retains the vision of "these two old people sitting together with their bushy hair, in complete agreement, understanding and love."[6]

In many respects Maja was very similar to her brother. She was a kind and sensitive person with a keen sense of humor, extremely intelligent, but painfully shy. She had a quiet nature and gave the impression of calmness of spirit but, her niece recalls, she could be temperamental. With close friends, however, she became outgoing. Because of her brother's fame, it took her a long time to accept that people loved her for her own qualities and not merely because she was Einstein's sister. She was knowledgeable in mathematics and was the only

Maja Einstein-Winteler, ca. 1940. Photo by Lotte Neustein, Dr. Bucky's assistant. (Courtesy of Margot Einstein)

Margot Einstein with one of her works. (Courtesy of Margot Einstein)

member of the household with whom Einstein could, and did, discuss mathematics and physics. Even in the last year or two of her life, when she was bedridden and impaired in speech, Einstein would explain mathematical problems to her. She and her husband "Paulie" had no children but their Italian home had many cats. Margot Einstein has said that she had a "heart of gold" for the Italian peasant. Maja never mastered English, but Italian women living in Princeton would visit with her to speak Italian.

Einstein's surviving daughter, Margot, is an artist. Small, frail, often in poor health, she is a wonderful sculptress. Although not Einstein's blood daughter, she is, through her mother, a cousin of Einstein's, and there is a distinct family resemblance—especially in her gentle, compassionate eyes. Blessed with a poetic and sensitive nature, she, like her father, is a lover of nature and animals. She always kept parakeets and cats, and her special pleasure in later years has been to feed the birds of Princeton in winter: cardinals, mockingbirds, purple finches. In her shy and modest way, she is a latter-day Saint Francis. Einstein loved this kindred poetic spirit and said of her, "When Margot speaks, you see flowers growing."[7] For years at a time she suffered serious illnesses, yet her spiritual strength is enormous. In the early days of Nazism, she nursed her dying sister in Paris. Two years later, she cared for her mother in her last months. After 1946, when her beloved Aunt Maja's health deteriorated, she again became nurse and companion.

The third woman of the household was Helen Dukas, whose original role of secretary-housekeeper increased substantially after Elsa Einstein's death in 1936. To her fell the task of running the house and shielding the professor from the public. The thankless job of watchdog often put her in contention with the newsmen who always seemed to be hovering nearby. The family had an unlisted telephone number, but somehow the press managed to discover it, and she was forever harassed by reporters and photographers who, she has said, "were my natural enemies." As Einstein's intermediary with the public she was expected to answer all manner of questions, including queries about the meaning of his scientific work. Einstein devised the following explanation for her to give when asked to explain relativity: An hour sitting with a pretty girl on a park bench passes like a minute, but a minute sitting on a hot stove seems like an hour.

After Einstein's death Helen Dukas became co-trustee of the trust that owned all of Einstein's writings and papers. Scientists and students of Einstein's life and work are forever in her debt because she is largely responsible for the preservation and ordering of Einstein's writings, his massive correspondence, and miscellaneous papers.

Another important member of the family was Chico, the wirehaired terrier Margot liberated from the Buckys, whose cook used to beat him. In the early 1940s Dr. Bucky had a serious operation and Chico, a high-strung dog, barked too much for the convalescent. Margot happily agreed to take him to Princeton on a temporary basis. Chico loved life there and became a permanent fixture in the Einstein house in the 1940s. He was an intelligent dog and, sympathizing with his master's plight, he used to try to bite the mailman because he brought too many letters.

Margot was the zoologist of the family, but Einstein loved animals, and there are several amusing stories about Einstein and animals. Ernst Straus records that when it rained, Tiger, the family tomcat, would become miserable, and Einstein would tell the poor creature apologetically, "I know what's wrong, my dear, but I really don't know how to turn it off."[8] Once Margot returned from a visit to the Panofskys', where she had just met their dog, Moses, a large, long-haired creature. As she concluded describing the beast, she said that he had so much fur that one could not distinguish his front end from his rear. To this Einstein responded, "The main thing is that *he* knows."[9]

In the summers the family would vacation near water in New England, Long Island, or, during the war years, at Saranac Lake in the Adirondacks where Einstein could indulge in his favorite sport of sailing, away from the muggy New Jersey weather and pesky newspaper reporters. Sailing, "the sport which demands the least energy,"[10] was Einstein's great passion, and he found in America many

Einstein, Helen Dukas, and Chico, in Princeton in the late 1940s. (Photo by Abraham Mandelstam. Courtesy of Margot Einstein)

beautiful places to sail his battered little boat *Tinef,* which roughly translates into English as "worthless." He was like a child in the way he enjoyed the sport and once told Helen Dukas, who was prone to seasickness, "I could really live on a boat." He was not interested in racing or long trips; instead he could happily lose himself in thought and dreams while the wind carried him along, or he could view sailing as an exercise in practical physics, challenging him to harness the winds in his sails. Alone or in company, at night under a full moon, or under the midday sun, sailing gave him a feeling of freedom. He loved it when the sea was calm and quiet, and he could sit in *Tinef* thinking or listening to the gentle waves endlessly lapping against the side of the boat. He was just as happy when it was rough and he could feel the power of the elements upon his small craft. Eva Kayser describes one time when she sailed on Long Island Sound with Einstein: "It was a rough sea; I'd rather have bitten off my tongue than to say, 'Look, this is a little bit rough, let's turn around.' He was sailing away, bending down under the boom, and I said, 'I bet this is one of the few things in this world under which you bend.' He laughed and said 'Yes.' Finally he said, 'Well, maybe we'd better turn back,' and enthusiastically I said 'Yes!' "[11]

Margot Einstein has recalled: "Going on the boat meant to him that he was together with the elements. And when one was with him on the boat you felt him as an element. He had something so natural and strong in him because he was himself a piece of nature. . . . He sailed like Odysseus."[12] Odysseus, however, knew how to swim; Einstein did not. His wife and family constantly worried about him because of his stubborn refusal to carry safety rings or an emergency motor. He despised machines, and, his daughter believes, he would have preferred drowning to permitting a motor aboard his craft.

In the summer of 1944 an accident occurred which could have cost Einstein his life. He had been sailing with friends in choppy water when he hit a rock; the boat quickly filled with water and capsized. Fortunately the water was warm and a motorboat was not too far away. Einstein was caught in the sail and was underwater for quite a while until he could disentangle his leg from a rope with his other leg. Writing to the Buckys a few days later, he described his "sailing adventure," noting that neither he nor his three companions thought to use the life preservers. Throughout the entire ordeal, his pipe never left his hand.

When he was a child, his father had read Heine and Schiller aloud to the family at night. In later years Einstein loved to read aloud in the evenings to Maja, Margot, and, in the summer, to any guests who might be visiting. At these sessions Einstein was always the reader, and he spoke in a very low voice. Among his favorites were Herodotus, *The Golden Bough,* and selections from Freud, works that reflect his interest in *Aberglauben* (superstition).

He had a special reason for reading Freud. His younger son, Eduard, suffered from schizophrenia and for most of his adult life was confined to a home in Switzerland. Only four years old when his parents separated, he had been an extremely sensitive child. For Einstein, leaving his sons had been the most painful experience of his life, and his son's later illness compounded his grief. His interest

Einstein with his younger son Eduard Einstein in Switzerland, summer 1933. This was the last time he saw Eduard. (Courtesy of Margot Einstein)

in Freud stemmed to a significant degree from his concern for Tetel and a desire to gain a clearer understanding of the dark spaces of the mind (although in 1927 he declined to undergo psychoanalysis "because I should like very much to remain in the darkness of not having been analyzed").[13] For the same reason, Einstein always took an interest in the unbalanced people who tried to see him in Berlin and Princeton. In a soft and reassuring voice he would gently explain that they must see a doctor. His quiet manner generally had a calming and positive effect upon them.

Einstein thought Freud was a fascinating writer and a great social philosopher. He respected him as one of the outstanding individuals of his age and as a great teacher, yet he was never fully able to believe in Freudian theory. He suspected that if one underwent analysis long enough one would begin to dream the Freudian way. He also felt Freud was too fanatic in his emphasis upon sex in his analysis, which, as a result, discounted or ignored other important factors. Margot suggested to him: "You cannot judge Freud because you are too healthy."[14]

Freud and Einstein met at least twice in Berlin and had the highest mutual personal regard. In his diary on December 6, 1931, Einstein wrote: "I do not believe in him, but I love very much his concise style and his original, although rather extravagant, mind. . . ." Freud felt that Einstein had even less understanding of psychology than he (Freud) had of mathematics. In 1929 he attributed Einstein's greatness to "his freedom from countless human foibles. . . ." He added: "In praising my style and skill in presentation, Einstein merely proves how well-meaning a man he is. He would like to give me credit for the content of my writings. But lacking the necessary understanding, he praises at least my style. . . ." In 1936, on Freud's eightieth birthday, Einstein had been pleased to admit to him that he had heard of a few cases which had demonstrated the validity of Freud's theories: ". . . it is always a blessing when a great and beautiful conception is proven to be in harmony with reality."[15] Freud drolly replied:

> . . . I always knew that you "admired" me only out of politeness and believed very little of any of my doctrines, although I have often asked myself what indeed there is to be admired in them if they are not true, i.e., if they do not contain a large measure of truth. By the way, don't you think that I should have been better treated if my doctrines had contained a greater percentage of error and craziness? You are so much younger than I am that I may hope to count you among my "followers" by the time you reach my age. Since I shall not know of it then I am anticipating now the gratification of it.[16]

Alas, for Freud, it never quite came to pass.

In literature, Einstein's tastes were generally classical in nature. He loved Shakespeare's poetic form and wonderful feeling for characterization. Don Quixote was rich in fantasy and full of beautiful characters and stories. He often identified himself in a lighthearted way with the ill-fated knight, and sometimes when Margot was ill as a child he would entertain her by reading from it because it was cheerful, healthy, and full of humor. Tolstoy and Dostoevsky were special favorites. Shortly after completing the general relativity theory, he told Alexander Moszkowski, who wrote the first biography of Einstein in 1920, that Dostoevsky "gives me more than any scientist. . . . It is the moral impression," he told

Moszkowski, "the feeling of elevation, that takes hold of me when the work of art is presented. . . ."[17] A decade later he told an interviewer that Dostoevsky's "aim is to present us with the mystery of spiritual existence and to do so clearly and without comment."[18] He loved the great novels of Tolstoy, *War and Peace, Anna Karenina,* and *Resurrection,* and he also was delighted by the simple truth and wisdom of Tolstoy's peasant folktales and fables. His favorite short story was "How Much Earth Does Man Need?"—the delightful moral tale of a man who is given the opportunity by the devil to own all the land he can circumambulate in a single day. In the end, he perishes from his own greed and shortsightedness, thus providing Tolstoy with the answer to the question in the story's title: about six feet, or enough for a grave. He admired Tolstoy's moral leadership, and in 1935 declared: "He remains in many ways the foremost prophet of our time . . . there is no one today with Tolstoi's deep insight and moral force."[19] (At that time he admitted great respect for Gandhi, but expressed reservations about aspects of his social program.) He was critical of Tolstoy's fanatic emphasis on sexual abstinence.

From childhood on he had revered Schiller, Heine and, with certain reservations, Goethe. He felt that Goethe was one of the cleverest and wisest men of all time and a "unique poet." He did not enjoy Goethe's prose, and his reason is revealing of his own character: "I feel in him a certain condescending attitude toward the reader, a certain lack of humble devotion which, especially in great men, has such a comforting effect."[20] Also of interest is his dismissal of romanticism: "[It] seems to me a kind of illegitimate excuse to achieve in the easiest possible way a deeper appreciation of art. . . ."[21]

Except for the aforementioned works, he generally preferred "books of universal content," especially philosophy. In addition to Spinoza he enjoyed reading Schopenhauer, Hume, and Mach, and to a lesser degree, Plato, Aristotle, and Kant. Einstein actually did not spend much time reading literature in his later years. His scientific work and the demands upon his time made by manuscripts and political tracts prevented it. Nevertheless, the great poets of the ages were his spiritual family. In 1932 he declared, "Although I am a typical loner in daily life, my consciousness of belonging to the invisible community of those who strive for truth, beauty and justice has preserved me from feeling isolated."[22]

His greatest pleasure in life came from music, especially from playing the violin, and when he settled in Princeton he was delighted to discover that the town afforded him ample opportunities to indulge this love.

Einstein's violin is as celebrated as his crown of white hair. As a young boy he had flirted with the idea of becoming a professional musician before science claimed him. Often in later years he said that if he had not been a scientist he would have become a musician. Whether playing his violin, improvising on the piano, or attending a concert, he found in music "the highest possible degree of happiness."[23] Music provided the ideal antidote to the strain produced by endless calculations, and an inner solace from the sorrows of the external world. "Music does not *influence* research work," he wrote in 1928, "but both are nourished by the same source of longing, and they complement one another in the release they offer."[24] He loved music for its purity, clarity, simplicity, and balance; Mozart was his ideal. "[A]s always," he wrote the Queen Mother of Belgium in 1936, "the springtime sun brings forth new life, and we may rejoice because of this new life and contribute to its unfolding; and Mozart remains as beautiful and tender as he always was and always will be. There is, after all, something eternal that lies beyond reach of the hand of fate and of all human delusions."[25]

In addition to Mozart he loved the older masters like Bach, Vivaldi, and Corelli. Of the nineteenth-century composers only Schubert appealed to him strongly. He had a very strong preference for the classical structure of music, and the exaggerated emotion of the nineteenth-century romantics was too "sugary" for his taste. Although he loved some of the earlier works of Beethoven, he found the later Beethoven "too dramatic and too personal." He detested Wagner. "I admire Wagner's inventiveness, but I see his lack of architectural structure as decadence. Moreover, to me his musical personality is indescribably offensive so that for the most part I can listen to him only with disgust."[26] He felt that nineteenth- and twentieth-century music did not possess enough formal structure.

In describing his own approach to music, he wrote in answer to a music questionnaire in 1939: "In music I do not look for logic. I am quite intuitive on the whole and know no theories. I never like a work if I cannot intuitively grasp its inner unity (architecture)."[27] Beethoven, he felt, had "created" his music, while Mozart's music was so pure and perfect "that one felt he had merely 'found' it—that it had always existed as part of the inner beauty of the Universe, waiting to be revealed."[28] The music of Mozart was spontaneous, effortlessly written, and free from passion.

Professional musicians as well as amateurs loved to make music with him, although opinions vary as to the level of his violin-playing ability. Anton Reiser tells how one Berlin music critic, unaware of Einstein's fame as a scientist, wrote of one of his performances in the early 1920s: "Einstein's playing is excellent, but he does not deserve his world fame; there are many other violinists just as good."[29] Some people who knew him only as an older man do not speak as favorably of his playing. Clearly, he was not a professional—he did not have the time to practice— but he was a good amateur filled with a deep love and intuitive understanding of music, whose pleasure was infectious. When he played with professionals he preferred to play more slowly. Several musicians have agreed that what he lacked in technique he compensated for with "marvelous phrasing and feeling."[30] In 1959 one of his Belgian partners wrote Margot Einstein: "Einstein's playing of Mozart was unique. Without being a virtuoso and perhaps because of that, he reproduced the depth and the tragic of Mozart's genius so naturally with his violin. . . ."[31] Einstein, who considered himself to be a scratcher on the violin, especially as he grew older, wrote this little poem for a musical friend in 1939:

Wenn man auch recht eifrig geigt,	(Just because one loves to fiddle,
Ist es doch nicht angezeigt	It's still not right to try to diddle
Andern etwas vorzumachen	About your skills to other folks
Denn dies waere rein zum Lachen.	Or you'll become the butt of jokes.

Der Dilettant hat ja sein recht,	Still, the dilettante has the right
Und spielte er auch noch so schlecht;	To scratch and scrape all through the
Doch soll es andre nicht verdriessen	night;
So muss er brav die Fenster	But so his neighbors do not mutter
schliessen.[32]	He must kindly close the shutter.)

He was happy to play music on almost any occasion. Once a week for several years before and during the war, he played sonatas with his scientific assistant Valentine Bargmann accompanying on the piano. Before 1939 Einstein was a member of an informal chamber quartet with Mrs. Barbara L. Rahm as first violinist, Alfred Hopkins as violist, Einstein as second violinist, and various guest cellists. Einstein refused to take the first violin part, and the only disagreements the group had with him concerned tempo. "Facetious jokes were made about Einstein's counting ability," Mrs. Rahm has written. "They were not true. He had a good sense of rhythm. However, I remember one evening when we had difficulty with a Beethoven adagio movement marked in $12/8$ rhythm and usually counted in 4. I said that we should take it very slowly and count 12. Professor Einstein looked abashed and said, quite innocently, 'Oh, I don't think I can count 12.' There were guests that night and I think it afforded them some quiet amusement."

By coincidence, the birthdays of Alfred Hopkins and Mr. Rahm were also on March 14, and for about three years the group celebrated with dinner and music. When the war came, they broke up, but the happy memories of musical evenings with "that remarkable man" remained vivid even after forty years.[33]

Robert and Gaby Casadesus, celebrated French pianists, lived in Princeton during the war years and occasionally played with Einstein. In January 1941, Einstein, accompanied by Mme. Casadesus, gave a violin recital at the Present Day Club in Princeton. This rare public appearance by Einstein the musician was for the benefit of the American Friends Service Committee, whose Princeton chapter was making clothes for refugee children in England. Also on the program was a children's play written by a local teacher and performed by her pupils. Einstein, anticipating a young audience, had chosen simple compositions. To his surprise the audience was composed almost entirely of adults and reporters who had come to see him perform. Mme. Casadesus recalls that as they began their first selection, "Sonata No. 4 in E minor" by Mozart, "We had so many people taking [photographic] shots that at first I thought he would stop playing, but, fortunately, he did not. He went through playing very well and he was not disturbed. . . ." His second and third numbers were entitled "Old Indian Song" and "Russian Dance," both written by his friend Frieda Bucky. As an encore he performed a minuetto by Bach. Mme. Casadesus believes that he played "very, very well," adding, "Don't forget to say he was a true musician. Naturally he did not have the time to practice, so maybe he would not be able to do things that were difficult in technique, but anyway, he played very well."[34]

As he grew older he found the "scratching" sounds he made on the violin increasingly displeasing. His reflexes were slowing down, a fate common to aging violinists, and around 1947 or 1948 he abandoned the violin for the "easier" piano.

Einstein at the piano, ca. 1934. Photo by Sylvia Salmi. (Courtesy of Margot Einstein)

Margot Einstein remembers that once during a concert at the house, when he made a mistake playing a piece by Mozart, he exclaimed, "Mozart wrote such nonsense here."[35]

After retiring his violin, he continued to improvise on the piano in the downstairs drawing room. To relax from his calculations he played melodies of his own invention. Once at the Buckys' home in New York Eva Kayser heard him playing the piano and she quietly entered the back of the room and sat down to listen. "Somehow he became conscious of another person being present," she remembers. "He looked up, saw me, and stopped immediately. I said, 'I'm very sorry, please continue.' But he wouldn't; he wasn't angry, just embarrassed . . . playing was something personal."[36] His improvisations possessed an air of lightness of feeling like Mozart, Vivaldi, or Haydn. His playing was never loud and was free from inner struggle or passion. He played with serenity, creating an atmosphere of harmony whose spirit was in a higher sphere, above the concerns of daily life. It was an expression of his soul and his mind. Whether he was thinking, or lost in dreams, he was freed momentarily from worldly fate and was inexpressibly happy.

9

Hitler's War

hree weeks after Einstein signed the letter warning President Roosevelt about nuclear fission, Germany and the Soviet Union concluded the infamous Nonaggression Pact, which opened the way for Hitler's unopposed invasion of Poland on September 1, 1939. Within four weeks Warsaw fell and the Second World War entered an eerie holding period known as the "phony war," which lasted until Hitler invaded Denmark and Norway on April 9, 1940. During the autumn of 1939, with German might focused on Poland, the French and British forces outnumbered German troops on the Western Front by more than four to one. Defeatism in the Allied high command prevented an attack which might have crushed Germany before Hitler could bring his war machine into high gear.

Throughout the war years Einstein kept a low public profile, reasoning that his voice could contribute little to the defeat of Hitler. He continued to urge American intervention and, as always, he maintained that future peace could be guaranteed only by a strong supranational world government. In his private correspondence he was less circumspect. When a young pacifist from Missouri wrote to him for advice about refusing to bear arms, Einstein responded in July 1941: "Sound pacifism tries to prevent wars through a world order based on power, not through a purely passive attitude toward international problems. Unsound, irresponsible pacifism contributed in large measure to the defeat of France. . . ."[1]

From September 1939 until the end of 1942 Western civilization faced extinction. The defiant heroism of the British after the fall of France, Holland, and Belgium in June 1940 and Hitler's self-defeating war plans are responsible for the survival of Western European liberty. Hitler's erratic assault on Great Britain, his suicidal decision to invade Russia in the summer of 1941, repeating Napoleon's 1812 blunder, and his declaration of war against the United States in deference to his Japanese allies insured his eventual defeat.

The invasion of Russia marked the beginning of the end of Hitler's mad vision, although for a full year it appeared that his reckless audacity would be rewarded with victories in both East and West. Immediately following the invasion, Winston Churchill, for a quarter-century one of England's leading anti-Bolsheviks, proposed a joint Soviet-British alliance against Hitler. Thus was born the Grand Alliance which would soon welcome the United States into its ranks. From the beginning, the Grand Alliance was an uneasy marriage of convenience based on mutual need, not mutual trust. Ever since 1917 Great Britain and the United States had been vehemently opposed to the Soviet regime because they viewed the Bolshevik revolution as an attack upon the existing world order, dominated by their capitalist and imperialist economies. Generally forgotten by the Western world is that early in 1919 the Allied powers of the First World War, including the United States, invaded the Soviet Union. Alarmed by temporary Communist successes in Berlin, Munich, and Budapest, they sent troops to seize Russia's Arctic ports, provided assistance to the counterrevolutionary White Army, established a blockade on food shipments to Soviet Russia, and moved to establish an anti-Communist buffer zone in Eastern Europe. In the 1920s and 1930s aggressive Russian communism was perceived by the British and Americans to threaten their world leadership and, until 1936 or 1937, was viewed as a greater danger than Nazism.

The First World War, the depression, and the failure of France, Britain, and the United States to prevent Hitler's rearmament in the period 1933–1936 made a second war inevitable. Efforts to appease Hitler and turn his attentions to the east provoked Stalin to protect his interests by concluding the Nonaggression Pact with Hitler. Stalin, whose greatest fear was a German invasion of Russia, hoped that the takeover of Poland would cause England and France to honor their commitments and that Hitler's resources would be diverted to the west by a long and costly war. While Hitler overran Poland, France, and the Low Countries, Stalin moved his western boundary farther to the west as he swallowed the Baltic States and portions of Poland, Rumania, Finland, and the Balkans.

Hitler launched the invasion of the Soviet Union on June 22, 1941, and for the next three years the Russian people bore the brunt of the fighting for the Allies. In the early weeks of the war against Russia, it appeared that the Germans were on the verge of a victory more remarkable than the conquest of France. The shock of Hitler's betrayal plunged Stalin into a state of nervous collapse for several days. The Germans reached the outskirts of Moscow in the autumn, and in October Stalin fled the city, leaving the government in disarray. Providential rains at this juncture slowed the Nazi advance and early in December the regrouped Russians launched a successful counteroffensive. By this time over 2 million Soviet soldiers had been captured and 40 percent of the population (approximately 60 million souls) was out of Stalin's control. As a consequence of the victory at Moscow,

Stalin, the murderous despot, became transformed into the great national leader of a heroic people who were leading the fight against fascism. The barbarous treatment of Russian war prisoners made for excellent propaganda. Forgotten were the Soviet's foul deeds of the 1930s.

The reversal at Moscow coincided with America's entry into the war, and in consequence of these stirring events, large segments of American popular opinion soon began to view the Russian war effort as a "moral crusade" against fascism.[2] Churchill sought to keep a sense of distance from Stalin, but Roosevelt supported the Soviet Union enthusiastically because, even though he had no illusions about the nature of Stalin's regime, he believed it was essential to preserve big-power unity to avoid future wars. Ignoring the fact that Russia was more feared than Germany by the states between the two powers of Eastern and Central Europe, and ignoring Stalin's behavior from 1939 to 1941, the American mass media adopted a strong and uncritically pro-Soviet attitude. *Life* magazine, published by Henry Luce, a once and future staunch anti-Communist, solemnly proclaimed in a March 29, 1943, issue devoted entirely to the Soviet Union, that the Soviet secret police were a "national police similar to the FBI."[3] Socialists and pacifists, on the other hand, generally maintained a more critical view of the Soviet Union.

For some time after the reversal at Moscow and the entry of the United States into the war, the Allied cause remained precarious. In the summer of 1942, despite his losses the previous winter, Hitler still appeared to be unstoppable. In south Russia crucial oil supplies were in jeopardy, while in Africa Erwin Rommel was master. Finally, in the autumn of 1942, after three years of German conquests, the tide began to turn. In late October the British Eighth Army, led by General Bernard Montgomery, defeated Field Marshal Rommel at El Alamein, and in mid-November the Russians launched the counteroffensive at Stalingrad which, by February 2, 1943, had decimated the German forces.

Einstein was very active in Russian War Relief, and during the worst of the fighting at Stalingrad, just a week before the great counteroffensive was launched, the Jewish Council for Russian War Relief held a testimonial dinner in Einstein's honor, which his customary plea of poor health excused him from attending. By telephone hookup he delivered a most interesting speech in praise of the Soviet struggle against fascism, which reflects the sentiments of the time. Einstein asserted that in the period before the war the Soviet Union had labored "more honestly and unequivocally to promote international security than any of the other great powers." This statement, a product of the emotional climate, reflects the attitude of many liberal intellectuals who had been alienated by the failure of capitalism and the appeasement of the fascists by the Western democracies in the 1930s. After 1933 Stalin, in an effort to strengthen Russia against attack, became a vocal exponent of peace, joined the foundering League of Nations at the time of German and Japanese withdrawal, issued a constitution in 1936 which, on paper, was the most democratic in the world, and supported the Loyalist cause in Spain. The "unfortunate" Nonaggression Pact, Einstein's speech continues, was forced on Russia by the attempts of the Western powers to turn Hitler eastward at Munich.

"Severe coercion" exists in Soviet society, Einstein conceded in his speech, but he chose to gloss over these "difficult matters" that evening and proceeded to praise the unity and sacrifices of the Russian people. Under the Soviets, he pointed out, the intellectual opportunities of the average person had grown magnificently, and "the equality of all national and cultural groups is not merely nominal but is actually practiced." It is true that the traditional tsarist pogroms had been abolished by the October Revolution and that in the twenties and early thirties Soviet Jews were secure. By the mid-1930s, however, Stalin had instituted a policy of forcibly assimilating Soviet Jews.

The conclusion of the speech contained the real message from Einstein: The defeat of Hitler is imperative and, had it not been for Russia, "the German bloodhounds" would probably have already conquered Europe; therefore, out of respect for the sacrifices of the Russian people in addition to our dictates of self-preservation we must support Russia in this hour.[4] In later years, remarks of this kind were used against Einstein to brand him a dupe of Moscow. The charge was baseless; to Einstein in October 1942 any ally in the fight to defeat Hitler and save civilization and the Jews of Europe merited enthusiastic support.

During the bleakest hours of the summer, Einstein was asked by a correspondent to write President Roosevelt to protest Nazi-Vichy war crimes. In an uncharacteristically vitriolic outburst written on September 3, he refused because he felt it would produce nothing more than "lame and half-hearted lip-service." Furthermore, he charged, the American government was quietly helping Franco. It had an official representative in Vichy France and did not recognize the French government-in-exile. Finland was "treated with kid-gloves" and the American government had made "no really serious effort to assist Russia in her dire need." He rejected official explanations of this policy and added:

> . . . it is a government controlled to a large degree by financiers the mentality of whom is near to the fascist frame of mind. If Hitler were not a lunatic he could easily have avoided the hostility of the Western powers. That he *is* a lunatic is the sole advantage in the present sinister picture of the world.
> . . . I don't like to mention those things, especially as one who is grateful having sought and found refuge and protection in this country.[5]

While it was true that Finland was allied with the Germans, Einstein was unfair to that unhappy nation. The Soviet Union attacked Finland on November 30, 1939, because the Finns had refused to accede to Soviet demands for "territorial readjustment." After June 1941 the heroic Finns, who, incidentally, were the only First World War Allies to repay American loans, found themselves forced into the Nazi camp as their only hope for survival.

The accusation that the United States had failed to provide adequate assistance to Russia referred to the controversy over the "second front" in Western Europe which Stalin had called for repeatedly. Stalin used the second front issue masterfully, censuring his Allies for their "betrayal" of the millions of Russian war dead and, in the process, obscuring the stigma of his pact with Hitler and his inept leadership before and during the invasion in 1941. In May 1942 Roosevelt promised an invasion of Western Europe, but Churchill quickly vetoed the idea because he realized that the burden would fall primarily on British troops, and he desperately wanted to keep down British casualties. Instead, he convinced Roosevelt to concentrate on the invasion of North Africa planned for 1943. Stalin felt betrayed by the Anglo-American policy of attempting to defeat Hitler by means of technology rather than manpower. Finally, Einstein's assertion that the American government was controlled by fascist-minded financiers is better understood in light of the government's refusal to acknowledge the reports of the Holocaust.

Rumors of atrocities against the Jews began leaking to Western Europe late in 1941. In December 1941 and again in January 1942 Thomas Mann, speaking over the BBC, made public the first unconfirmed reports of mass killings. In August 1942 the Polish government-in-exile informed the United States government of the atrocities against the Jews imprisoned in Poland, and by the autumn there was proof that Hitler's "final solution" was a reality.

Both the British and the American authorities refused to believe the reports, and even after confirmation was received, they dragged their bureaucratic feet. The State Department, under the guidance of Breckenridge Long, chose to suppress evidence of the "final solution." In September 1942 the administration dismissed the idea that the Nazis were following a well-organized program of mass extermination, and Roosevelt, coached by the State Department, claimed that the deported Jews were being used to build fortifications on the Soviet frontier. From February to April 1943 Long actually falsified cables and misinformed Treasury Secretary Morgenthau about the mass murders, and until 1944 the State Department recognized only a "refugee problem" while continuing to suppress all information on the death camps.

In December 1942 the British began to use the atrocity stories in their propaganda reports, but they made no change in their immigration policy in Palestine. In April 1943 representatives of the American and British governments met in Bermuda to discuss the refugee situation. The conference, a thinly veiled attempt to justify British and American policy toward the refugee tragedy, had been given what one student of the subject has labeled a "mandate for inaction."[6] The prevailing attitude of the participants was that nothing short of Allied victory could solve the problem, and when it was proposed that the Allies try to negotiate with Hitler in an effort to save the rest of the Jews in Central Europe, the British demurred because they were afraid Hitler might consent to release millions of "useless people" that he would otherwise be forced to take care of. Their cold-blooded logic was unassailable: As long as Hitler had millions of Jews on his hands, he had to feed them or expend valuable resources to exterminate them. Either way, the Allied war effort stood to benefit.

Through his contacts with Jewish leaders, Einstein was as well informed as anyone could be about the tragedy in Europe. Nothing in his life caused him greater anguish. To his old friend, the psychiatrist Otto Juliusburger, a fellow Jew from Berlin living in New York, Einstein wrote in the summer of 1942: "Due to their wretched traditions the Germans are such a badly messed-up people that it will be very difficult to remedy the situation by sensible, not to speak of humane, means. I keep hoping that at the end of the war, with God's benevolent help, they will largely kill each other off."[7] By the end of September when the tide began to turn against the Nazi war machine Einstein was able to write to Juliusburger: "I believe that we can now at last hope to see the day when the unspeakable wrong may be somewhat expiated. But all the misery, all the desperation, all the senseless annihilations of human lives—nothing can make up for that."[8]

Einstein's deterministic outlook taught him that men act as they do because they lack free will and, therefore, sin does not exist. One of Einstein's neighbors once remarked that Einstein was too great a man to bear grudges against others, but after a pause, he added, "except Hitler."[9] Nevertheless, Einstein held the German people responsible for electing Hitler and acquiesing in his unutterable crimes. The Germans, he wrote in a tribute "To the Heroes of the Warsaw Ghetto," "deliberately used the humanity of others to make preparation for their last and most grievous crime against humanity." In his heart he could find no forgiveness for such calculated "moral degradation."[10]

After the war, Einstein supported measures to restore Germany to the community of nations so as to avoid a repetition of the Versailles Treaty. He approved of efforts to rebuild the German economy and to resume normal political and diplomatic relations. However, he believed that it was essential to disarm Germany permanently, and he was outspoken in his opposition to the rearmament of West Germany during the most dangerous days of the Cold War[11] because, in addition to his lasting distrust of German militarism, he feared that German rearmament would be viewed by the Soviet Union as a provocative act.

Personally, he could not bring himself to forgive the Germans for the crimes of the Nazis and he rejected all reconciliatory efforts. In 1951 President Theodor Heuss of the Federal Republic of Germany (West Germany) invited Einstein to join the Peace Section of the old Prussian order *Pour le mérite*. Einstein had been a member prior to 1933 but, in accordance with his postwar refusal to be associated publicly with any German organization he declined Heuss's invitation. "Because of the mass murder which the Germans inflicted upon the Jewish people," he explained, "it is evident that a self-respecting Jew could not possibly wish to be associated in any way with any official German institution."[12]

Rabbi Leo Baeck had been the leader of the Berlin Jewish community. When Hitler came to power, Baeck, an old man, refused to abandon his people and was imprisoned in the so-called model concentration camp at Theresienstadt, where German Jews over sixty-five and injured Jewish veterans of the First World War were incarcerated. Purely by accident Baeck was not sent to one of the extermination facilities, and he, along with 2,500 elderly people there, survived the war. His spiritual courage in the face of annihilation set a heroic example for his fellow prisoners, and he will always be honored as one of the heroes of the Holocaust.

On Einstein's seventy-fifth birthday Baeck wrote to thank Einstein for being Einstein: "In days when the question of the existence of morality seemed to find only the answer 'no,'" Baeck wrote, "or when the very concept of humanity remained in doubt, I was privileged to think of you, and feelings of peace and affirmation came over me. How many a day have you stood before me in my mind and spoken to me."[13]

Throughout his life, scientific work remained Einstein's best defense against the crimes and follies of mankind. In the late thirties and early war years, he was assisted by two young refugee physicists, Peter Bergmann and Valentine Bargmann, affectionately referred to as "the Berg and the Barg" by Helen Dukas. While the unified field theory continued to evade his unrelenting efforts, working conditions at the institute improved markedly after 1939 because of the open and conciliatory direction of Frank Aydelotte. The new director had for many years been the President of Swarthmore College, and, earlier, a professor of English. His intellectual abilities were not of the same caliber as those of his faculty, but his academic and administrative experience in conjunction with an ability to reconcile conflicting views and a willingness to listen to his scholars soon healed the wounds created by Flexner's unhappy administration. Aydelotte agreed to hold regular meetings with the faculty at the beginning and end of each term, and he understood how to leave his scholars alone. Einstein was genuinely fond of Aydelotte and, referring to the director's lack of scholarly pretensions, he once joked in a friendly way that the most important quality for a director of the institute is that he be "a little stupid" so that he did not interfere with the work of the faculty.

The first two years of Aydelotte's tenure were probably the smoothest and most harmonious in its often turbulent history. Then the institute went into cold storage as almost all its professors engaged in some form of war work, much to the chagrin of Abraham Flexner, who believed they should give the institute their full time in war as in peace. He was even more deeply disturbed that all the mathematicians except Einstein and Hermann Weyl spent time away from Princeton.

Einstein's first opportunity to contribute to the war effort came shortly after Pearl Harbor at a time when the United States had just begun to organize its atomic research on a large-scale basis. Dr. Vannevar Bush, Director of the Office of Scientific Research and Development, asked him to work on one of the many problems relating to the formidable task of separating the extremely rare uranium-235 isotopes from uranium-238. Bush was a conservative, abrasive engineer, a business consultant and pragmatist who disliked the New Deal but enjoyed political power. In deference to the military's exaggerated faith in absolute secrecy, he had imposed a policy of compartmentalization which ensured that no scientific worker would be permitted access to any more information than was deemed necessary. Bush contacted Einstein through Aydelotte's office at the institute, and the work was considered to be so secret that Einstein submitted the manuscript in his own handwriting without having someone else type it. In a covering letter to Bush, Aydelotte wrote that Einstein was eager to help in any way that he could but, when it became clear that Einstein would need to be given more information for his work to be of any value, Bush balked, and Einstein's contact with the atomic bomb project was terminated. In an extraordinary letter to Aydelotte dated December 30, 1941, Bush explained his refusal:

> The reason that I am not going further is that I am not at all sure that if I place Einstein in entire contact with his subject he would not discuss it in a way that it should not be discussed, and with this doubt in my mind I do not feel that I ought to take him into confidence on the subject to the extent of showing just where this thing fits into the defense picture, and what the military aspects of the matter might be. If I were to explain more than I already have, I feel sure that the rest of the story would immediately follow. I wish very much that I could place the whole thing before him and take him fully into confidence, but this is utterly impossible in view of the attitude of people here in Washington who have studied into his whole history.[14]

Bush later testified that he had been unaware of Einstein's 1939 letter to Roosevelt and, insofar as the pressures on Bush and all other bureaucrats were exceedingly great in December 1941, the possibilities for confusion were enormous. Nevertheless, the refusal to grant a security clearance for work on the atomic bomb project to the man whose letter to the President had initiated the government's involvement in the effort to develop a nuclear weapon is nothing less than bizarre and—prior to the recent declassification of the FBI files on Einstein—inexplicable.

A number of questions remain unanswered but, according to the files, Einstein was apparently recommended by the Office of Scientific Research for clearance "in connection with the limited field of study for which his services were needed." The navy gave its assent, but the army, in a letter dated July 26, 1940, and signed by General George Strong, refused to give Einstein clearance. The letter from General Strong is not among the released documents and is only referred to in an FBI character check on Einstein in reference to a relative of his who had applied to enter the United States on a visa.[15]

The FBI files do contain a letter from Brigadier General Sherman Miles, Acting Assistant Chief of Staff of the Army, to J. Edgar Hoover, Director of the FBI, dated July 30, 1940. General Miles refers to a letter he had written Hoover four days earlier regarding other scientists being considered for security clearances, and then requested information regarding "the activities and sentiments" of Einstein and Alexander Sachs. Hoover's reply on August 15, 1940, contained a photocopy of the lengthy memorandum prepared by the Woman Patriot Corporation in 1932 with the note that the "reliability of the information contained in this memorandum is not known." He then listed a number of activities in which Einstein had engaged between 1932 and 1939, including participation in various pacifist organizations, an antifascist group, and several that supported Loyalist Spain. Included in this was an anonymous report that Einstein had stated that "he felt ashamed that the democratic nations had failed to support the Loyalist Government of Spain." Hoover also noted that Einstein was "reported" to be a member of an anti-Nazi organization.[16]

Apparently Einstein's pacifism and support of antifascist groups were sufficient to render him unfit for a security clearance, although in 1943 Bush invited Einstein to become a consultant to the Office of Strategic Research and Development. In any event, he had no further contact with the Manhattan Project, and because of Bush's secrecy, Einstein may have been unaware of the nature of the work he had performed in December 1941.

Apropos secret scientific work, in the summer of 1942 the FBI received an anonymous, undated letter which claimed that the secret report of an organization called the "Music Boys" dated November 1, 1938, from the Biltimore [sic] Hotel, New York, should be investigated. According to the tipster, Rabbi Stephen S. Wise had presided at the meeting where Louis Lipsky, a prominent Zionist, had stated that: "Einstein is experimenting with a ray which will help us to destroy armed opposition—aircraft, tanks and armored cars. He hopes that with it a dozen men could defeat 500. Through it 5% could rule a nation." There is no evidence that the FBI took this report seriously.[17]

In June 1943 the navy's Bureau of Ordnance hired Einstein on a part-time basis to do some work which dealt with the theory of explosions. This area of research did not require the kind of top-secret security clearance necessary for working on the Manhattan Project and, furthermore, the navy's interest in Einstein was enhanced by the obvious publicity and propaganda value of his famous name.

Although eager to help the war effort in any way he could, he was distinctly uncomfortable in this line of work. "I am also in loose contact with the navy as a theoretical expert," he wrote in September 1943 to Juliusburger, "and I hope the war will be over before my activity in this respect will produce tangible consequences. Endeavors where so many people have a say are, strangely enough, always ugly. Old Goethe was indeed correct with his statement that individuality is still the most enjoyable thing in this life on earth. But even that is rare."[18]

Late in 1943 Einstein was presented with another opportunity to help the war effort. An organization known as the Books and Authors War Bond Committee was collecting original manuscripts to be auctioned off for war bonds. The committee wanted the manuscript to the original special relativity paper of 1905, but as Einstein explained to one of his correspondents, it no longer existed. "My first manuscript about relativity was not burned by the Nazis. I myself threw it into the waste-basket after it was printed, judging it was good for nothing. At that time I knew nothing of the snobbery of this human world."[19] In its place he offered his most recent paper, "Bivector Fields," written in collaboration with Valentine Bargmann. The committee gratefully accepted this offer and then, "with some hesitation," they suggested that Einstein might copy out the 1905 paper in longhand. Julian Boyd, the librarian at Princeton University (later the editor of the monumental Jefferson Papers), who acted as intermediary, apologetically conveyed the suggestion to Einstein who "very graciously said that when others were doing so much for the war, this was the least he could do. He found it extremely difficult to understand how a manuscript by him could be expected to realize any real sum in war bonds."[20]

Despite this reservation, he complied at once, conscripting Helen Dukas to read to him the published version. As Banesh Hoffmann has written: "It makes a piquant picture: Einstein taking dictation from his secretary." Once he interrupted to ask of a certain passage, "Did I say that?" To Helen Dukas's affirmative reply he added, "I could have said it much more simply."[21] Boyd gave the finished product to an émigré who was an expert bookbinder and who made a "superb" slipcover for it. In February 1944 the two manuscripts together fetched $11.5 million in Kansas City, and were immediately donated to the Library of Congress. When informed of the anticipated purchase price of the two manuscripts, Einstein shook his head and said to Boyd, "The economists will have to revise their theories of value."[22]

Another Princetonian, George Cook, was attached to the Office of Naval Intelligence during the war. He was once ordered to interview Einstein to obtain information about a woman who had been Einstein's secretary briefly in California ten years earlier. Cook writes:

> I was told that the woman was being investigated to determine her dependability to be entrusted with "classified matter" (confidential and secret information) as a prospective yeoman (clerk, secretary) in the Naval Intelligence service. I made the appointment

Einstein and Leo Szilard, Saranac Lake, September 1945. (Courtesy of Gertrud W. Szilard)

and interviewed Dr. Einstein at his residence where, after considerable probing, I was able to verify to my satisfaction that the applicant was in his opinion a loyal American of complete integrity who was a qualified secretary, but, he said, "Not for Naval Intelligence." When I asked "Why?" he replied, "Because she is not intelligent." And that is, verbatim, the way my report was submitted—whether she got the position, or not, I never learned.[23]

Einstein carefully followed the newspaper and nightly radio war reports. After Stalingrad, Hitler's war machine began to break apart, as the Allies piled up victories in North Africa, Italy, and on the Atlantic Ocean in 1943, while conducting devastating day and night air raids over Germany. Early in June 1944 Rome fell and two days later, on D-Day, the Allies returned to Western Europe for the first time since the evacuation at Dunkirk in 1940. Finally, on May 8, 1945, Germany surrendered.

Meanwhile, in the Pacific, Japan doggedly fought on. In March the British had driven Japanese forces from the Asian mainland but, despite the inevitability of defeat, the imperial forces refused to submit to Allied demands of unconditional surrender and the war continued through the summer. In Washington, some experts forecast that it might take an additional two years to defeat Japan.

Then on August 6, 1945, Hiroshima was destroyed.

Three days later Nagasaki was annihilated.

On August 6 Einstein was resting at Saranac Lake after lunch.

> It was in the afternoon [Helen Dukas recalled] and I was lying down listening to the news, and I remember very well they only brought it as the second [news item]. They reported something else about the war, and then said a new kind of bomb has been dropped on Japan. And then I knew what it was because I knew about the Szilard thing in a vague way. . . . As Professor Einstein came down to tea, I told him, and he said, "Oh, Weh" [Alas, oh, my God] and that's that.[24]

The day Einstein died, Leo Szilard spoke of his friend and colleague on American television. At one point he related the following incident:

> When I visited Einstein at Princeton shortly after the bomb was dropped at Hiroshima and Nagasaki, our conversation turned back six years to the visit on Long Island when we discussed the letter he might write to the President. "You see now," Einstein said to me, "that the ancient Chinese were right. It is not possible to foresee the results of what you do. The only wise thing to do is to take no action—to take absolutely no action."[25]

10

"Music of the Spheres"

T he defeat of Hitler removed the primary cause of Einstein's generally low profile in the preceding dozen years. The destruction of Hiroshima and Nagasaki and the dawning of the age of nuclear warfare propelled him again into the forefront of public debate, a position he did not relish but one which he felt morally obliged to assume. Thus in the final decade of his life, Einstein, still cherishing his privacy, assumed an aggressively active role in the movement to control nuclear weapons and abolish war.

The year 1945 marks a dramatic shift in Einstein's place in American society. Before turning to this poorly understood aspect of his life, it is important to examine the social, political, and ethical values which shaped Einstein's answer to the problem faced by all responsible individuals: How should I behave in the world of man?

Einstein was a scientist, and it is with his approach to the practice of science that we shall begin. Next, we shall examine his attitude toward religion and his reconciliation of the apparently irreconcilable claims of religion and modern science. This leads to his appraisal of the relationship between religion and morality and finally to the social and political values which grew out of his ethical outlook.

A successful scientific theory must agree with the experimental facts and must make the fewest assumptions to explain those facts, while enjoying the widest range of applicability. Einstein's approach to scientific theory has been described as "esthetic." The qualities he sought in a theory were "naturalness," "inner perfection," and "logical simplicity." "A theory is the more impressive," Einstein wrote in his autobiography, "the greater the simplicity of its premises, the more different kinds of things it relates, and the more extended its area of applicability."[1]

The closer a theory comes to experience, the greater the confidence we may place in the theory; but as the depth of his knowledge increases, the scientist is forced to surrender this advantage of "closeness to experience" in the "quest for logical simplicity and uniformity in the foundations of physical theory."[2] This was true of the theory of relativity of which Einstein wrote: "The initial hypotheses become steadily more abstract and remote from experience. On the other hand, it gets nearer to the grand aim of all science, which is to cover the greatest possible number of empirical facts by logical deduction from the smallest possible number of hypotheses or axioms. Meanwhile, the train of thought leading from the axioms to the empirical facts or verifiable concepts gets steadily longer and more subtle."[3]

Physical theories which interpret and order the given sense experiences are man-made inventions of logical thought; that is to say, the ordering of the "chaotic diversity"[4] of sense experience and the derivation of natural laws from physical events are works of reason. The aim of science is to create a rational expression of the connection between seemingly unrelated sense experiences, but one who scorns (or lacks) the power of intuition will never rise above the ranks of journeyman calculator. Einstein possessed an extraordinary intuition and imagination in matters of science, and these powers played a central role in his scientific work. A word of caution is in order. Einstein's reliance upon his imagination should not be misconstrued. He did not indulge in wild speculation; in fact, he only resorted to his intuitive resources when no other approach was available. He did not guess if he could resolve a problem in a logical way. However, he was unwilling to limit the working of his mind to cold logic—there had to be a place for leaps of imagination. There were other scientists whose mathematical abilities surpassed his, but few who possessed his intuitive ability to sense the way things had to be. When he did employ nonrational powers in the construction of a proposition or theory, later he would always employ logic to achieve the necessary connection between fact and theory which would bring theory into harmony with experience. In this context, Ernst Straus quoted him as saying, "When we are working at something, we come down from our high logical horse and sniff around with our nose on the ground. Then we obliterate our traces in order to become more godlike."[5]

As a twelve-year-old studying his "Holy Geometry booklet" Einstein had been awed by the discovery that man, through his ability to reason, is capable of making order out of apparent mystery and chaos. As an adult Einstein developed a kind of religious faith which took "the form of a rapturous amazement at the harmony of natural law, which reveals an intelligence of such superiority that, compared with it, all the systematic thinking and acting of human beings is an utterly insignificant reflection."[6] No matter how successful the scientist is in comprehending the incomprehensible, there comes a point when man's intellect must yield to wonder.

In 1952 Maurice Solovine wrote to express concern over Einstein's willingness to reserve a place in rational science for nonrational wonder. Einstein replied:

> You find it remarkable that the comprehensibility of the world (insofar as we are justified to speak of such a comprehensibility) seems to me a wonder or eternal secret.

Now, *a priori*, one should, after all, expect a chaotic world that is in no way graspable through thinking. One could (even *should*) expect that the world turns out to be lawful only insofar as we make an ordering intervention. It would be a kind of ordering like putting into alphabetic order the words of a language. On the other hand, the kind of order which, for example, was created through [the discovery of] Newton's theory of gravitation is of a quite different character. Even if the axioms of the theory are put forward by human agents, the success of such an enterprise does suppose a high degree of order in the objective world, which one had no justification whatever to expect *a priori*. Here lies the sense of "wonder" which increases ever more with the development of our knowledge.

And here lies the weak point for the positivists and the professional atheists, who are feeling happy through the consciousness of having successfully made the world not only god-free, but even "wonder-free." The nice thing is that we must be content with the acknowledgment of the "wonder," without there being a legitimate way beyond it. I feel I must add this explicitly, so you wouldn't think that I—weakened by age—have become a victim of the clergy.[7]

In light of his great scientific discoveries between 1905 and 1916, he came to understand that his belief in the rational order of the natural world was a kind of religious faith which served as the foundation of his scientific work. As he wrote in 1929, physical theory seeks to know not only how nature works,

> but also to reach as far as possible the perhaps utopian and seemingly arrogant aim of knowing why Nature is *thus and not otherwise*. Here lies the highest satisfaction of a scientific person. . . . [O]ne experiences, so to speak, that God Himself could not have arranged these connections in any other way than that which factually exists, any more than it would be in His power to make the number 4 into a prime number. This is the promethean element of the scientific experience. . . . Here has always been for me the particular magic of scientific considerations; that is, as it were, the religious basis of scientific effort.[8]

The theory of relativity, with its revolutionary claims, assumed mystical proportions in the mind of the public and prompted, especially in America, a great deal of concern about Einstein's religious beliefs. In 1929 Cardinal O'Connell of Boston charged that relativity "cloaked the ghastly apparition of atheism" and "befogged speculation, producing universal doubt about God and Creation." The cardinal's attack prompted a New York rabbi to cable Einstein: "Do you believe in God?" Einstein replied: "I believe in Spinoza's God who reveals Himself in the orderly harmony of what exists, not in a God who concerns Himself with fates and actions of human beings." Upon receipt of Einstein's response, the rabbi declared: "Einstein's theory if carried out to its logical conclusion would bring to mankind a scientific formula for monotheism."[9] The following year, after the appearance of an essay in which he described his "cosmic religious feelings" one leading American cleric suggested that the "s" should be deleted from "cosmic." The clergyman had been offended by Einstein's criticisms of traditional religion, particularly with his rejection of the notion of a personal God.

Einstein was a strict determinist who believed that for every action there necessarily exists a cause, and in line with Spinoza, he maintained: "Our actions should be based on the ever-present awareness that human beings in their thinking, feeling and acting are not free but are just as causally bound as the stars in their motions."[10] From the point of view of the determinist it is impossible to subscribe to the idea that God has a moral design or purpose for the world, as is taught by Judaism and Christianity. To assume that God wishes to bring about a state of affairs that does not yet exist is to assume that at present God lacks something. This, Spinoza asserts, is impossible and absurd because God, who is identical with nature, and must necessarily act according to eternal and necessary laws, cannot, in his infiniteness, lack anything. Thus, Spinoza continues, miracles, if they existed, would demonstrate God's impotence, not his power, because they would prove the existence of some power not constrained—as He is—by necessity. Einstein believed that since man's actions are determined by necessity, he cannot, strictly speaking, be held responsible for them, and that the idea of a rewarding and punishing God is näive anthropomorphism. Furthermore, he argues:

> [I]f this being is omnipotent, then every occurrence, including every human action, every human thought, and every human feeling and aspiration is also His work; how is it possible to think of holding men responsible for their deeds and thoughts before such an almighty Being? In giving out punishments and rewards He would to a certain extent be passing judgment on Himself. How can this be combined with the goodness and righteousness ascribed to him?[11]

Although on occasion he bluntly dismissed the idea of a personal God as "childish" and a form of superstition, he was careful to emphasize that "mere unbelief in a personal God in itself is no philosophy at all."[12] Despite his serious differences with the doctrines of Judaism and Christianity he was no more comfortable with freethinking than he was with superstition.

Einstein believed it was a fatal mistake of the ethical religions, in an effort to educate and indoctrinate their followers, to have tied their moral and ethical precepts to epics and myths which, although beautiful from a poetic point of view, are not essential to the truth of the moral teachings. In modern times belief in the truth of the moral codes had been undermined by the scientific repudiation of the myths and epics, so that when representatives of religion dogmatically defended the validity of the creation myth, for instance, the result was a weakening of the credibility of all aspects of religion.

Einstein had mixed feelings about the Bible, whose contents he described as "in part beautiful, in part wicked." It had been written by men and there was no reason to believe everything it said. "[I]t is an interesting monument to past times . . ." he wrote in 1943, but "[t]o take it as eternal truth seems to me also superstition which would have vanished a long time ago would its conservation not be in the interest of the privileged classes."[13] In many of the Psalms of David and in certain of the Prophets he recognized the beginnings of "cosmic religious feeling," and although he rejected what he called the "Hebrew Myths," the ethical teachings of the Bible had exercised a decisive influence upon his moral values.

Einstein's distrust of all authority is reflected in his attitude toward organized churches. He believed they had originally been established by "movements whose driving force was the purification of morality, but degenerated later on."[14] They had become interested in the accumulation and preservation of political and economic power, and they maintained their sway over the masses through a combination of superstition, fear, and "divinely sanctioned" dogma. On more than one occasion, Einstein expressed his contempt for the rigid priestly mentality that fought the theories of Copernicus and Darwin. "Churches are and have always been greedy for power," he wrote in 1945, "and have worked in company with other powerful political groups, mostly groups with reactionary tendencies working to keep the people in ignorance and to exploit them. . . . In the present time all reactionary groups, religious and secular, are fascist-minded and working against the economic liberation of the people."[15] The harshness of this assertion must be viewed in the context of 1945 when, as a Jew, he was especially bitter about the silence of Pope Pius XII to the Nazi murders of the Jews. In general, Einstein only criticized the actions of the representatives of organized religion when they strayed from their own territory into the realms of science or reactionary politics.

Einstein, unlike Bertrand Russell, Freud, or Shaw, refused to fight against dogma, superstition, and the belief in a personal God taught by the organized religions. He did express his own convictions when queried, but he did not feel that he or anyone else had the right to determine what other people should believe and, furthermore, it seemed to him that belief in a personal God was better than atheism. Instead of fighting the churches in a war of propaganda, he expected that in time many of the superstitions and myths would be rendered harmless by the gradual education and enlightenment of the general public. Time and truth were more effective, less destructive, weapons than propaganda.

Despite his thoughtful responses to questions about his religious beliefs, his ideas about religion were constantly misinterpreted. The tendency of the press to ferret out information about Einstein and then to present it in a simplistic and sensationalized manner made it very difficult to refute these mistaken notions. In 1940 he wrote a paper on "Science and Religion" for a Symposium on Science, Philosophy, and Religion sponsored by the Jewish Theological Seminary. When his remarks were made public without his knowledge or permission Einstein found himself under attack for his supposed atheistic views.

In the paper he attempted to define the legitimate role of both science and religion, what their limitations were, and how, through the proper understanding of the role of each, they actually served to strengthen each other. In the course of his analysis, he repeated his scientific objections to the concept of a personal God and called upon religious teachers to abandon the fight with science over this issue:

In their struggle for the ethical good, teachers of religion must have the stature to give up the doctrine of a personal God, that is, give up that source of fear and hope which in the past placed such vast power in the hands of priests. In their labors they will have to avail themselves of those forces which are capable of cultivating the Good, the True, and the Beautiful in humanity itself. This is, to be sure, a more difficult but an incomparably more worthy task. After religious teachers accomplish the refining process indicated they will surely recognize with joy that true religion has been ennobled and made more profound by scientific knowledge.[16]

Einstein's message was, simply, that at a time in which men too often perceive the choice as between superstition and atheism, the teachers of religion ought to lead the way to a higher path, one that draws upon the teachings of both science and religion. Nowhere does he advise men to become atheists or to renounce faith in the wonder of life.

Einstein had expected the scientists, philosophers, and theologians attending the symposium to discuss the merits of his ideas, and the press attacks against his statement in several emotional articles and editorials were an unpleasant surprise. *Time* magazine complained that "Einstein's message was the only false note of the entire conference. . . ."[17] Although the press was generally negative, the majority of the letters Einstein received were favorable. A few, however, were vicious. One evangelist labeled the statement a "mark of ingratitude" to the United States. Another defender of the faith wrote: "In the last ten years nothing has been so calculated to make people think that Hitler had some reason to expel the Jews from Germany as your statement."[18] Many who wrote to support him were freethinkers and atheists who were overjoyed by the prospect of counting Einstein among their number. With a touch of annoyance and sadness, he assessed the response to his statement:

> I was barked at by numerous dogs who are earning their food guarding ignorance and superstition for the benefit of those who profit from it. Then there were the fanatical atheists whose intolerance is of the same kind as the intolerance of the religious fanatics and comes from the same source. They are like slaves who are still feeling the weight of their chains which they have thrown off after hard struggle. They are creatures who—in their grudge against the traditional "opium for the people"—cannot hear the music of the spheres. The wonder of nature does not become smaller because one cannot measure it by the standards of human morale and human aims.[19]

"My religious feeling," he had written in 1927, "consists in a humble admiration for the infinitely superior spirit manifesting itself in the little of reality that we are able to recognize with our weak and frail reason."[20] Nature was Einstein's God—not the spirit gods of primal religions, but the immanent God of Spinoza who had affirmed that God is Nature, Nature is God *(Deus Sive Natura)*. Einstein described himself as a "deeply religious nonbeliever," adding on one occasion, "This is a somewhat new kind of religion."[21] His "cosmic religion" had neither church, nor Bible, nor dogma, and it appealed to the sort of person who wished to escape the "merely personal" and experience the universe as "a single significant whole." The cosmic religious feeling is the "strongest and noblest motive" for the artist and the scientist.

> Only those who realize the immense efforts [he wrote in the 1930 essay on cosmic religion] and, above all, the devotion without which pioneer work in theoretical science cannot be achieved are able to grasp the strength of the emotion out of which alone such work, remote as it is from the immediate realities of life, can issue. . . . Only one who has devoted his life to [scientific research] can have a vivid realization of what has inspired these men [scientists like Newton and Kepler] and given them the strength to remain true to their purpose in spite of countless failures. It is cosmic religious feeling that gives a man such strength.[22]

Einstein did not believe that modern science discredited religion; rather, he maintained that religion, properly understood, and science, properly utilized, served to strengthen each other. The conflict occurs only when representatives of religion assert the absolute truth of the Bible even when it contravenes scientific fact; or when scientists and philosophers attempt to devise an ethical code based upon rationalism, as in utilitarianism. Einstein held that science produces objective knowledge of "what is," but it cannot tell "what should be." Religion treats the subjective questions of the individual's relation to nature and the ethical values and goals of both individual and society. Science encourages people to think in terms of cause and effect and thereby undermines superstition and dogmatic assertions, but it does not subvert the moral teachings of traditional religions. In fact, by purging religion of superstition and anthropomorphism, science has freed religion from the necessity of enforcing its ethical teachings by means of fear (of a rewarding and punishing God). "[S]cience without religion is lame," he once wrote, "religion without science is blind."[23] The conflict between faith and knowledge dissolves when one is careful to distinguish the true role of science from the purpose of religion. Simply put, as Einstein wrote to a minister in 1953, "If you understand under religion a confidence in certain moral values and humility concerning our understanding of things outside the human sphere, knowledge is obviously not in conflict with religion."[24] The real enemy of true religion is the spirit of ruthless competition which poisons economic and political life by destroying feelings of fraternity and cooperation.

One consequence of the rejection of the belief in a personal God is that morality becomes a problem for men and not God. Judaism, which believes in man's moral and spiritual maturation, teaches that man is free to choose whether or not he will obey God's commandments. Belief in free will in ethical affairs is so critical that Jewish theologians have preferred to limit God's freedom in order to preserve man's freedom. Einstein, like Spinoza, maintained that man's ethical behavior was every bit as determined as the motion of celestial objects, but he was no gloomy fatalist. He thought that man's actions were governed both by "external compulsion" and "inner necessity," and in support of this belief he quoted Schopenhauer's aphorism, "A man can do what he wants, but not want what he wants." This means that a man has desires which determine his actions (and which he often mistakenly designates as "free will"), but these desires (or "inner necessity") are determined by an external cause. Even the desire to create a more just society belongs to the factors which partake of causality.

Despite Einstein's belief that man's behavior is determined, he still maintained that man must conduct his moral life as if he were free. Philosophically, a criminal is not responsible for his crime but, in reality, society has the right and the obligation to protect itself from his antisocial behavior. When Michele Besso informed Einstein of his conversion to Catholicism, Einstein replied: "I agree with your remark concerning loving one's enemies as far as actions are concerned. But, for me, the intellectual basis is confidence in unrestricted causality. 'I cannot hate him since he must act as he does.' Thus, for me, it's Spinoza rather than the

Prophets. That's why I can't accept 'sin.' "[25] A causal understanding of the way things happen leads to a more sympathetic attitude toward men and to a lowering of feelings of hatred; it is a source of consolation in the face of tragedy because one realizes that events could not have turned out otherwise; it liberates one from fear, hatred, and bitterness; and it teaches genuine humility which prevents man from taking himself too seriously.

For Einstein, morality is the foundation upon which all human values are built, and its "highest attainment" occurs "when a man can put himself in the skin of another person and know all of that person's suffering and all of that person's joy."[26] It was in the realm of ethical relations that Einstein felt most deeply his Jewish heritage. For the Jew life is a moral task involving a never-ending quest for the perfect society. Man cannot be God, but he must strive to become Godlike in his moral attributes. The moral code of the Hebrews remains fresh after more than three millennia because it is based upon the principle that life is holy. A central precept of Jewish ethics is the commandment: "Love thy neighbor as thyself." In the Talmud an alternate rendering of the Golden Rule is given by Hillel: "That which is hateful unto thee do not do unto thy neighbor." In a healthy society this sympathetic outlook becomes a powerful tradition and succeeding generations are educated according to this precept as a matter of course.

In a famous essay, "The World as I See It," written in 1930, Einstein described himself as a "lone traveler," who had a "pronounced lack of need for direct contact with other human beings and human communities." The individual, particularly one such as Einstein, thinks, feels, and labors in solitude. The need for distance from others teaches the "limits of mutual understanding and consonance with other people," and enables one to achieve an "inner equilibrium" independent of the opinions and judgments of others.[27] The individual's dignity, welfare, and opportunity to develop his inborn talents are fostered by a society in which men do their duty to their fellow men out of love rather than fear of punishment or desire for reward. This naturally implies the toleration and encouragement of differences among individuals and groups.

Just as society owes each of its members the right to develop his own character, so the individual must recognize his responsibility to serve the community because man is both a solitary and a social being, and it is impossible to imagine him outside the bounds of a society which provides him with food, clothing, and shelter. Even the most resolutely self-reliant souls are indebted to society for language, modes of thought, medicine, art, and science. As Einstein phrased it, "My inner and outer life are based on the labors of other men, living and dead and . . . I must exert myself in order to give in the same measure as I have received and am still receiving."[28]

Einstein's view of the role of the individual in society was shaped by the moral teachings of Judaism. He characterized the essence of Judaism as "an affirmative attitude to the life of all creation." "The life of the individual," he wrote, "only has meaning in so far as it aids in making the life of every living thing nobler and more beautiful. Life is sacred, that is to say, it is the supreme value, to which all other values are subordinate."[29] The Judaic sanctification of life is the source of the indestructible sense of community which has enabled the Jewish people to survive thousands of years of political impotence and persecution.

Einstein's social, political, and economic views were an expression of his ethical outlook. He was a democrat, a socialist, and a champion of individual and intellectual freedom and responsibilities. The ideal of democracy, that every man be respected as an individual but none idolized, had, in his youth, inspired him to become a citizen of Switzerland. He opposed all forms of tyranny because they are based on force, which, he wrote, "always attracts men of low morality . . ."[30] Nevertheless, he acknowledged that for society to achieve its objectives, it is necessary that one person, chosen by the people, lead without coercion and bear responsibility for the workings of government. In this respect he preferred the American system to the parliamentarian system of the Weimer Republic (recall he was writing in 1930), because the American President was granted sufficient time and authority to exercise his responsibilities. Einstein was, however, careful to point out that democratic institutions do not automatically solve problems, but they do offer "a useful framework for their solution."[31] Ultimately, the success of democracy depends on the political and moral qualities of the citizenry.

Einstein was a committed socialist. "[I]t is no mere chance," he writes of the traditional Jewish belief in the solidarity of all human beings, "that the demands of Socialism were for the most part first raised by Jews."[32] His views are succinctly presented in an essay written in 1949 entitled "Why Socialism?"[33] He believed that socialism is a "social-ethical" philosophy whose purpose is "to overcome and advance beyond the predatory phase of human development," which has been characterized by conquest, subjugation, and exploitation. Man's intellectual qualities make it possible for him to evolve to a higher plane of living so that "human beings are *not* condemned, because of their biological constitution, to annihilate each other or to be at the mercy of a cruel, self-inflicted fate."

Einstein believed that capitalism cannot protect the worker from unemployment and that it is vulnerable to severe cycles of economic depression. Capitalism exerts a corrupting influence on political parties which have become dependent upon the financial support of private concerns at the expense of public interest. The most pernicious consequence of capitalism, Einstein felt, was the stimulation of egotistical drives provoked by competition against others. In the educational system, students learn to worship "acquisitive success" and to view achievement in terms of preparation for a successful future career rather than in terms of love for productive work and creative inquiry. The social drives of students trained by this system are often stifled and the individual develops into an insecure, lonely, and selfish figure. Einstein maintained that a healthy democratic political system with a socialist economy could help to foster in society and in the schools the values of service and responsibility to one's fellow men so necessary for the full development of the individual and the flourishing of society.

Einstein's own formal education had, except for the year at Aarau in 1895–1896, been an unhappy ordeal for the sensitive and exceptional youth. In German schools, discipline, memorization, and conformity poisoned the atmosphere and alienated Einstein from his teachers. At the ETH, Einstein's independent spirit and lack of respect for the often pompous professors resulted in ostracism from academic circles after graduation. His greatest learning experiences had come outside the classroom, where, alone or in the company of one or two friends, he procured for himself a first-rate education in the fundamentals of physics.

The memory of his school experiences never left him, and throughout his life he advocated educational reforms designed to instill positive values and to foster creative learning by emphasizing cooperation and respect for others. He abhorred the coercion, arbitrary discipline, and destructive competition among young students that the German school system fostered. Independence of thought and insatiable curiosity were the qualities most responsible for his development as both a scientist and a human being, and these were the qualities he believed must be nurtured in the young. Late in his life he wrote to a Brooklyn minister:

> The most important human endeavor is the striving for morality in our actions. Our inner balance and even our very existence depend on it. Only morality in our actions can give beauty and dignity to life.
> To make this a living force and bring it to clear consciousness is perhaps the foremost task of education.[34]

Einstein believed that the purpose of education must be to prepare the child to develop, to the fullness of his God-given potential, the human qualities that best serve the welfare of the community to which he belongs. Each individual is born with a unique potential that must be nourished by healthy training in early life. The German system, he believed, stunted the development of independent personalities. Basing the teacher's authority on fear and coercion destroys individuality, self-confidence, and the inquiring spirit of the young and produces weak and submissive characters. The teacher, to be worthy of the respect of his students, must love his subject and be able to bring it to life in a way that captures their imagination, by presenting the material in a manner that arouses curiosity with the result that the student's work brings him joy and stimulation.

He criticized American schools for standardization and mechanization of teaching and the unhealthy competition among students. He felt that teachers should be given more leeway in designing their courses and that less reliance should be placed upon standardized textbooks because this sort of mechanized teaching operates like a factory assembly line and results in conformity and mediocrity. Competition encourages egoism and aggression, warps the character, and undermines creativity. In 1952 he wrote: ". . : by emotional heritage, man is a cross-breed of a beast of prey and a social being. To insure his survival education must strive to develop the social side of his nature and to tame his egotistical drives directed towards mutual destruction of individuals and groups. At the same time, it is important for the common good to foster individuality: for only the individual can produce the new ideas which the community needs for its continuous improvement, needs, indeed, to avoid sterility and petrification."[35]

Einstein believed that education should be made to relate to, and be a part of, real life, with an increased appeal to the senses—in nature, if possible. As an example, mathematical relationships—dimensions, angles, and trigonometric functions—would be much more rapidly understood if the student is shown how to measure a field which is compared to another, or if he is instructed to measure the height of a building and then to compare the length of its shadow to the height of the sun at various hours of the day. This would ground mathematics in the real world and give it tangible meaning for the student.

Einstein felt strongly that the study of history should focus on the development of civilization, with special emphasis on those individuals who have exercised independence of character and judgment in the service of humanity. Instead, history has been taught as a parade of warriors, tyrants, and national chauvinists. The spirit of international solidarity and cooperation, not the spirit of aggressive nationalism and militarism, should be impressed upon the young. The study of history should begin with the humanistic tradition of the Greeks, whose "achievement of harmony and beauty in the human relationships"[36] remains unsurpassed.

In addition to intellectual training, Einstein believed that every student should learn a useful trade such as carpentry or plumbing because, after all, "Prometheus did not begin his education of mankind with astronomy, but by teaching the properties of fire and its practical uses."[37]

Even though physics requires highly specialized knowledge, Einstein opposed specialized education for the young because it produces a "useful machine but not a harmoniously developed personality."[38] Education should provide a solid foundation from which the individual can, at a later time, develop a specific vocation. What is truly important is not the mastery of facts and techniques but the ability to think and work independently. It is this independence that protects the individual from narrowness of outlook. An interesting example of Einstein's attitude toward memorization occurred on his 1921 visit to the United States. While in Boston he was given a questionnaire developed by the inventor Thomas A. Edison who believed that education should be directed toward learning relevant facts and that a college education was of no value to practical people. The questionnaire was designed to demonstrate that most college graduates were unable to answer practical questions. When Einstein read: "What is the speed of sound?" he answered, "I don't know. I don't burden my memory with such facts that I can easily find in any textbook." Einstein was of the opinion that it is "not so very important for a person to learn facts." For that he does not really need a college. He can learn them from books. The value of an education in a liberal arts college is not the learning of many facts but the training of the mind to think something that cannot be learned from textbooks."[39]

Einstein believed he was put on this earth to be a scientist, and that he best served society by his scientific work. It was his joy and his refuge, yet more important even than science was the welfare of man. "Only a life lived for others," he once said, "is a life worthwhile."[40] He described the goal of ease and comfort as the "ideal of a pigsty,"[41] and he was contemptuous of popular notions of success

Einstein walking on Mercer Street to the institute, ca. 1950. The "good life."
(Courtesy of Margot Einstein)

which honored those who take more from life than they put in. Margot Einstein recalls advice he gave his daughters on the eve of his departure for Japan in 1922: "Children, use for yourself little, but give others much."[42]

In his actions, whether private or public, he saw himself as a servant—to his fellow man, to truth. He was guided by universal moral principles which are the basis of the great world religions, and he was guided by these principles in all matters, whether great or small. Recall these words written in his last week: "In matters concerning truth and justice there can be no distinction between big problems and small; for the general principles which determine the conduct of men are indivisible. Whoever is careless with the truth in small matters cannot be trusted in important affairs."[43] Einstein was careful to emphasize, however, that "moral conduct does not mean merely a stern command to renounce some of the desired joys of life, but rather a sociable interest in a happier lot for all men."[44]

There is an old rabbinic saying: "The world exists by reason of three things: truth, justice, and peace." This is the foundation of freedom. The goal of God's law is justice, and the high-minded citizen must defend truth, justice, and peace from all attempts to subvert them. To evade this responsibility is to become an accomplice to the perpetration of evil. Jewish history has been the saga of great empires trying to destroy the nation and spirit of Israel. The justification for this unprecedented persecution has always been that the Jews refused to accept the laws of the land and chose instead to follow their own laws. In rejecting the notion that "the king [the state] can do no wrong," the Jew has become the rebel of history. When the king's law conflicted with God's law, the Jew became an outlaw. Nearly 3,000 years ago a group of rebels, the Prophets, arose within the ranks of the Jews to challenge the evils of the social order. For these "spokesmen of God" morality was the most essential teaching of Judaism. Without fear they condemned Jew and non-Jew for acts of injustice, violence, and the oppression of the weak and defenseless. Every age in history has had need of the prophetic voice. In the twentieth century, one such voice belonged to Einstein.

Two years before he settled in Princeton, a disciple of Tolstoy asked him to describe his attitude toward "the Good." Einstein replied:

> It is almost impossible to define "good" (in its ethical sense) conceptually. What is done out of love for living creatures, that, to my mind, is "good." Enjoying the joy of others and suffering with them, these are the best guides for man. I always notice that first I sense what is good and only afterward try to account for it. The arguments, however, are usually not worth much. But, after all, it's very much the same in art, and isn't it an art to lead a good life?[45]

11

"Ticket of Admission"

Maybe . . . it would be more prudent to die soon," Einstein wrote on September 6, 1944, to Otto Juliusburger, "so as not to be disappointed again, as in the years between 1918 and 1939."[1] At the time he was afraid that the Western powers, in their efforts to save "holy capitalism" from the threat of Russia, would again permit Germany to become strong. Less than twelve months later an unprepared world was hurtled into the atomic age. The technological advances in warfare in the two world wars, and the creation of the atomic bomb, the most sophisticated technological advance of all, had permanently threatened man's very survival.

In the days and months that followed the dropping of the first atomic bombs, Einstein emerged from his self-imposed wartime silence to become one of the leading voices in the fight to secure lasting peace and security from the threat of any future war. In the final years of his life he persistently advocated the creation of a world government vested with adequate powers to police the world and settle disputes between nation-states peacefully in an international court and to deprive individual nations of all arms. He was at the forefront of the campaign waged by atomic scientists to educate the public and the leaders of the world about the implications of nuclear energy and the absolute necessity of not developing nuclear weapons. As the Cold War intensified he steadfastly opposed the policies of the United States government with regard to Russia, especially the rising tide of militarism and hysterical anticommunism which poisoned the mood of the country in the late 1940s. To appreciate Einstein's postwar political activities and ideas, it is necessary to review the wartime relations between the United States and the

Soviet Union, the decision to use the atomic bomb on Japan, and the factors that determined the course of the Cold War.

By the summer of 1943 two sensitive issues had severely strained Soviet–Anglo-American relations: the question of a second front in Western Europe and the fate of Eastern Europe after the war. In the winter of 1941–1942 Roosevelt refused to discuss the Russian proposal that Eastern European postwar boundaries revert to those in existence in June 1941 because of the United States commitment to the principle of self-determination and its refusal to honor secret accords. By 1943 Roosevelt realized that the only way to keep Russia from controlling Eastern Europe would be for the Allies to reach Eastern Europe first, or else to be willing to risk a direct confrontation with Soviet forces. Then, at the Teheran Conference in November 1943, Churchill, in an attempt to blunt Stalin's pressure for a second front, proposed moving the boundaries of Poland westward, conceding Eastern Poland to the Soviet Union. Stalin could hardly have hoped for such an offer, and for the rest of the war he exploited the issue of Allied unity to extort further concessions from his Alliance partners. At the Yalta Conference in February 1945 Stalin agreed to endorse the vague Allied promise that the nations of Europe would enjoy self-determination. Amid all the fine-sounding rhetoric about self-determination, Roosevelt failed to prepare the American public for the inevitable Soviet takeover of Eastern Europe. Americans, despite their own sphere of influence in Latin America, reacted angrily when it became apparent that Stalin intended to establish his sphere of influence in Eastern Europe. They interpreted this as a renewal of the feared Communist world revolution rather than as a reflection of Stalin's desire to make Russia secure from future invasions from the West. Before long America's former ally replaced Hitler as the world's greatest villain.

During the war, Roosevelt's highest priority had been to win Stalin's cooperation in the postwar period, a cooperation based not upon dreams of an ideal world order but upon the realities of power. He did not believe that a totalitarian domestic policy necessarily leads to a totalitarian foreign policy committed to the subversion of the existing world order.[2] The dictates of propaganda may have required a Marxist-Leninist rhetoric, but reality demanded that the Soviet Union behave like the great power it was and, above all else, Stalin was a realist who feared worldwide upheaval more than did his capitalistic Allies. Roosevelt believed that the demands of great nationhood required of Stalin a traditional foreign policy based upon balance of power and spheres of influence. Following this reasoning, he realized it would be pointless to oppose Russian influence in Eastern Europe. Instead, he chose to work to win Stalin's trust and cooperation in setting up the postwar world order, while, at the same time, attempting to limit the extent of Stalin's penetration into Europe. It is tantalizing to speculate about the fruits of this policy. Unfortunately it was a program which, in large measure, existed in Roosevelt's mind and depended on his imagination, savvy, and personal charm. It was without support in the State Department.

Following the display of harmony at the Yalta Conference, relations between Stalin and Roosevelt began to deteriorate because of Stalin's attempts to impose his will on Eastern Europe and Poland. Then, on April 12, 1945, just three weeks before the capitulation of Germany, Roosevelt died, leaving as successor the inexperienced and overwhelmed former Senator from Missouri, Harry S. Truman. The Vice President had been completely excluded from the process of shaping postwar foreign policy so that Roosevelt's death created a vacuum just as American scientists were assembling the first atomic bombs.

In his early days in office Truman relied heavily for advice upon the State Department, Churchill, and Averell Harriman, Ambassador to Moscow. These men did not share the late President's inclination to pursue a flexible approach toward Stalin. They viewed Soviet aims in a more sinister light than Roosevelt and found in Truman a sympathetic ear. Truman knew nothing of Roosevelt's efforts to ensure Stalin's postwar cooperation. In the tradition of Woodrow Wilson, the new President despised balance of power and spheres-of-influence politics; he had no patience for subtleties and tended to see issues in black and white. Truman judged the Soviet quest for security to be a smokescreen to hide their expansionist goals. He believed that the Russians had taken advantage of American generosity over Lend Lease and that they had broken their solemn commitment to permit Eastern Europe self-determination. He and his advisers failed to understand the importance of Poland to Soviet security and, in the pursuit of a course of "messianic liberalism"[3] they made Soviet actions in Poland a test case by which to gauge Soviet behavior. After Truman learned of the existence of the atomic bomb, he jumped to the conclusion that its mere possession would be sufficient to convince Stalin to cooperate with American objectives in Eastern Europe. Where Roosevelt had employed charm, compromise, and flexibility, Truman simply showed force. He was tactless and unsophisticated in his determination to assert his authority, and the Russians correctly surmised that Truman's tough talk indicated an abandonment of Roosevelt's policy of conciliation.

In the tense three-month period extending from Roosevelt's death to the final meeting of the Big Three at Potsdam in mid-July, relations between the Soviet Union and the United States eroded steadily. Truman and his advisers became convinced that Russia was committed to world revolution and unlimited Soviet expansion in pursuit of world dominance. This alarmist view, reinforced by numerous incidents in Germany, Poland, Trieste, and Eastern Europe, ignored Stalin's record as an adherent to traditional power politics, and overlooked the dreadful state of prostration of the Soviet Union in 1945. Even if Stalin had desired world conquest, it would have been impossible. Working from the assumption that Russia posed an immediate military threat, the United States increasingly chose to abandon diplomacy and to apply threat and force. Truman and his advisers felt certain that possession of the atomic bomb assured the success of this approach.

Truman first learned the details of the Manhattan Project from Secretary of War Henry Stimson almost two weeks after assuming the presidency. Neither as a Senator nor as Vice President had he been aware of this awesome undertaking. Stimson had informed Truman of the research on a superweapon on the day of Roosevelt's death. On April 25 Stimson and General Leslie Groves, the head of the Manhattan Project, told the President that the atomic bomb, if used properly, could provide the United States with the opportunity to shape the postwar peace. James F. Byrnes, the good-old-boy South Carolina politician, whom Truman had tabbed Secretary of State-designate, put the matter less delicately than Stimson had; the bomb, Byrnes boasted, might conceivably enable us to "dictate our own terms" at war's end.

Truman's position was not enviable. Propelled unprepared into the White House, he then discovered that a superweapon that had cost billions of dollars and incredible amounts of human resources and time in the previous four years was poised to end the terrible war. It had long been the assumption of his advisers and, naturally, it became his unchallenged opinion that, if available, the weapon should be used to advance the war effort. Even the dominant figure of Roosevelt may have found it difficult to arrest the momentum behind the project. For the overwhelmed Truman, such an action was most unlikely.

Several months before the capitulation of Germany, the Americans had learned that Germany would be unable to produce an atomic weapon, and that the war in Europe would be over before the American bomb was ready. By May 1945 it also was clear that the Japanese could not win the war in Asia, but it was by no means certain that they could be defeated quickly. The Anglo-American policy of "unconditional surrender" helped stimulate the beleaguered Japanese to continue fighting until they received assurances they would be permitted to retain their imperial institutions.

As work on the Manhattan Project approached completion, many scientists began to worry about the lack of contact with the policymakers regarding the future use of atomic weapons and energy. Leo Szilard and others had always resented the military's obsession with compartmentalization and security. After learning in late 1944 that the German bomb project was not a threat, they began to worry about what the United States government might do to other countries. To Szilard, Einstein, and the majority of refugee scientists, the justification for a crash program to develop atomic weapons had been the very real danger that Hitler's scientists were developing the dread weapon. With the collapse of Germany, the necessity and the moral justification for development and use of the atomic bomb had been removed. By and large, the refugee scientists did not share the prevailing attitudes of the American public toward the Japanese, nor the official antipathy to America's ally, the Soviet Union.

The first attempt to approach the political leaders by a scientist was taken by the Danish physicist Niels Bohr, in the spring of 1944. Bohr had escaped in dramatic fashion from Nazi-occupied Denmark in October 1943. The great scientist was immediately given privileges to visit all the plants in the bomb project and he spent several weeks in Los Alamos from December 1943 to January 1944. At that time he discussed his fears with many scientists, especially with Robert Oppenheimer, the director of the project. Bohr believed the advent of the bomb demanded a radical change in foreign relations and the necessary first step would have to be an offer by the Americans and British to share control of atomic weapons with the Soviet Union. The alternative, he knew, would be a disastrous arms race.[4]

In the spring of 1944 Bohr met with Churchill and later with Roosevelt to urge that the Russians be invited to join postwar atomic energy planning before the end of the war and the completion of the bomb; he did not advocate sharing the secrets of the bomb at this point. He hoped this would demonstrate to the Soviets that no Anglo-American alliance was being formed against them. While there could be no guarantee that this would produce the desired Soviet cooperation, he was certain that without this policy no cooperation would be possible.

Bohr's meeting with Churchill in May 1944 was an unqualified failure. The Prime Minister was determined to preserve and extend Great Britain's economic and military power. Viewing the bomb as a powerful bargaining instrument in postwar negotiations with Russia, he thought it would be madness to surrender such an advantage. Churchill rejected Bohr's contention that the existence of the bomb would revolutionize international relations, and he took an instant personal dislike to the great physicist. When he met with Roosevelt in September, he convinced the President to disregard Bohr's proposal. In order to prevent him from leaking secrets to Russia, Churchill argued that they place Bohr under surveillance because "he is very near the edge of mortal crimes."[5]

Einstein, although not involved in the Manhattan Project, was certainly aware that intensive nuclear research was being conducted by the government. Numerous top scientists, including many of his friends and colleagues, had disappeared; the volatile Szilard had been silent; and the publication of articles on nuclear energy in scientific journals had ceased. In December 1944, after several conversations with his old friend Otto Stern, a part-time consultant to the Metallurgical Laboratory in Chicago, Einstein wrote Bohr to express his concern that politicians did not appreciate the destructive potential of atomic weapons. He proposed the "radical step" of engaging influential scientists who would be able to gain a hearing with political leaders and pressure them to take the initiative in internationalizing military power in order to avoid an arms race. Bohr, sobered by his recent encounters with Churchill and Roosevelt, recognized the futility of such a plan. He dissuaded Einstein because, he reasoned, while the war continued such considerations remained the province of the authorities, and private citizens lacked sufficient information to act safely. Einstein agreed to drop the plan.

In March 1945 Szilard, long frustrated by his role in the Manhattan Project with its rigid military policies of secrecy and compartmentalization, and like Bohr and Einstein deeply worried about the lack of contact between scientists and policymakers, drafted a document which prophetically described the dangers of an arms race. Although security regulations prevented him from revealing the nature of his concern, he again prevailed upon Einstein to write him a letter of introduction to President Roosevelt to discuss his ideas. Einstein's letter, dated March 25, 1945, was found in Roosevelt's office after his death on April 12. Truman referred it to James F. Byrnes, then still a private citizen. On May 28 Byrnes met with

Szilard and two other scientists, and as had been the case a year earlier when Bohr met Churchill, the politician developed an immediate dislike for the scientist and was ill-disposed to consider his ideas, particularly Szilard's proposal that certain scientists meet with cabinet members to discuss atomic energy. Byrnes made an equally unfavorable impression upon his visitors, who were chagrined to discover that he was unaware that atomic energy had potential for peaceful uses. Szilard later recalled that the future Secretary of State believed the atomic bomb would provide the means to "render the Russians more manageable in Europe." After reading Szilard's memorandum, Byrnes blithely informed his visitors that there could be no danger of an arms race because General Groves had assured him that Russia possessed no uranium![6] Three days later, Byrnes, as a member of the War Department's Interim Committee on Atomic Weapons,[7] voted to recommend to Truman that the bomb be used against Japan without prior warning.

General Groves was not a member of the Interim Committee but, as the government's choice to head the project, he had unique access to both the politicians and the scientists. He used his position to dominate the proceedings of the committee on May 31 and June 1 when the decision to use the bomb was reached. On May 31 the Interim Committee met with its scientific advisory panel which was composed of Robert Oppenheimer, Enrico Fermi, Ernest O. Lawrence, and Arthur H. Compton. With the exception of Fermi, these scientists had been primarily administrators. Their perspectives were different because of their work with General Groves and other nonscientific members of the Manhattan Project and they clearly did not represent the views of those scientists who were opposed to using the weapon. The topic for discussion was not whether to use the bomb, but how to use it; that it would be used if ready was a foregone conclusion. The committee briefly considered the effect of the bomb on the Japanese, but they did not seriously explore the dangers of radiation. The possibility of negotiating a surrender with the Japanese before dropping the bomb was not discussed and the scientists were given no information regarding the imminent collapse of the Japanese navy and air force, nor were they told that since spring a growing Japanese peace movement had been seeking ways to end the war.[8]

During a break for lunch, Byrnes asked the scientists about the feasibility of a demonstration of the bomb on a barren island or desert to be witnessed by representatives of the Japanese government with the ultimatum that they surrender or face the prospect of atomic destruction. Capping an informal ten-minute discussion, Oppenheimer, who was prone to refer to the bomb as "the gadget," expressed his fear that no demonstration could be sufficiently impressive, that the bomb might be a dud which would cause a loss of face and almost certainly inspire the Japanese to stiffen their resistance; this of course would lead to an uproar in Congress. The suggestion that a warning be given to the target city was also rejected when someone speculated that the Japanese might move American prisoners there. By the end of the day it was generally agreed that the Americans ought to employ the bomb without any prior warning on a Japanese city that housed military installations. The following day a recommendation that the

Russians be informed prior to dropping the bomb in the hopes of gaining their cooperation in the postwar control of nuclear energy was vetoed by Byrnes, who had been persuaded by General Groves that United States technology and its uranium monopoly assured that it would take the Soviet Union twenty years to build an atomic bomb. The Interim Committee adjourned without discussing the long-range implications of atomic energy or outlining the approach the United States ought to follow to secure the peaceful international control of atomic weapons. They had discharged their duties faithfully, but without consideration for long-term consequences.[9]

In the two months before the bombing of Hiroshima, there were other desperate efforts by scientists to dissuade Truman and the policymakers from dropping the bomb on Japan. In June the physicist James Franck, Szilard, and five other scientists from Chicago wrote Secretary Stimson to urge that representatives of all the member states of the United Nations be invited to witness a harmless demonstration of the new weapon. The Franck Report, as this prophetic statement has come to be called, warned against the illusion that an arms race could be avoided by attempts to control the raw materials and to keep secret the underlying scientific principles of the bomb. The scientists urged the policymakers to weigh short-term benefits against the terrible costs of a postwar arms race, which they realized would begin at once if no agreement on arms control were achieved immediately after the initial use of the bomb. Its use would seriously undermine America's moral leadership, whereas refusal to use it would have been an impressive bargaining chip in the efforts to outlaw its use. In an appeal to the pragmatism of the policymakers, the report noted that from a purely practical point of view, the best interests of the United States still would be served by nonemployment of the weapon. If an arms race was to be started, the best chance to gain the biggest possible headstart lay in keeping secret the very existence of the bomb. The scientists knew that the only real secret was the fact that it could be manufactured. Once that was known, any nation with first-rate scientists and the willingness to commit manpower and resources to such a project would eventually be capable of reproducing the work of the Manhattan Project without need of espionage. The basic scientific laws were known to all experts in the field and no amount of secrecy could controvert this.[10] Tragically, the American policymakers never fathomed this elementary scientific truth.

James Franck had submitted an earlier memorandum to Secretary of Commerce Henry A. Wallace on April 21, 1945, which had lamented that the efforts then under way to create the United Nations were already obsolete. "[W]e hear about plans to control industries, etc., in the aggressor states," Franck wrote, "but we know in our hearts that all these plans are obsolete, because the future war has an entirely different and a thousand times more sinister aspect than the war which is fought now."[11] A last-minute petition organized by Szilard and signed by more than sixty scientists called on President Truman not to use the bomb against Japan without adequate warning and before it had been given a reasonable opportunity to surrender. The petition reached Washington on July 17, 1945, the day after the first successful test at Alamogordo, New Mexico. Truman by then was at Potsdam and the irreversible decision to use the bomb as soon as possible had already been taken.

The Potsdam Conference with Churchill, Stalin, and Truman was already under way when Truman learned of the success of the test blast. The news transformed him into a confident, at times arrogant and cocksure negotiator, no longer in awe of Stalin, and it caused a complete reversal of American aims. Before July 17, Truman's primary goal had been to ensure that Stalin would honor his commitment to enter the Japanese war on August 8, but with the news from New Mexico the American delegation decided that it no longer needed Soviet assistance to defeat Japan. Now the new weapon would do the job, and if used

Niels Bohr, James Franck, Einstein, and Isidor I. Rabi in Princeton, October 1954. Franck and Einstein were awarded honorary degrees from the Technion Israel Institute of Technology. Bohr was spending a term visiting the Institute for Advanced Study. Rabi, a leading experimental physicist, was a professor at Columbia University. (Courtesy of AIP Niels Bohr Library)

before the Soviets declared war on Japan, it would also exclude Russia from the spoils of war, in particular the occupation of Manchuria.

Urged by Churchill to use the atomic bomb as a diplomatic lever against Stalin, Truman abandoned efforts to induce a compromise surrender which would guarantee the status of the Emperor. On July 24, Truman casually informed the Soviet leader that the United States had developed "a new weapon"; he did not elaborate. The poker-faced Stalin remarked only that he hoped the United States would use it to advance the war effort. He did not betray any curiosity and to this day it is not entirely certain whether or not he appreciated the significance of Truman's information. Two days later, Great Britain, the United States, and China issued a final call for unconditional Japanese surrender; the Soviets, technically neutral, were not invited to sign.

While still at Potsdam, President Truman noted in his diary that the atomic bomb would be used by August 10 on a military, not civilian, target after a warning to surrender had been issued.[12] In the end, however, two civilian centers with military installations were chosen. The light emitted from the bombs which destroyed Hiroshima and Nagasaki was so bright that it could have been seen from another planet.

After nearly four decades, the haunting question persists: Why did the United States employ nuclear weapons on two Japanese cities in August 1945? A host of related questions follow. Why were the efforts of Bohr, Szilard, Franck, and many other scientists unavailing? What role ought the scientist to play in the political process which determines the application of his scientific discoveries and technological advances? What role ought ethical considerations to play in political decisions? Can man afford to ignore moral questions in the pursuit of political expedience? Most disturbing of all is the question which was not asked by the pragmatic policymakers: How could we justify use of this most terrible of weapons before we had charted a policy for peaceful and military uses of nuclear energy?

These are questions which have evaded satisfactory explanation because the answers lie in the hearts of men now dead, men who did not fully understand their motivations and deeds even at the time. The attempt here will be only to provide essential background and the most plausible ideas which have been advanced through the years, in an effort to shed as much light as possible on the forces and events which shaped the public activities of Einstein in his final decade.

In the summer of 1945, with Hitler dead, the war-weary American public not unnaturally was eager for peace. This fact assumed a significant role in the deliberations of Truman and his advisers. By this time only the Japanese army and the question of the status of the Emperor remained formidable obstacles to peace; the Japanese navy and air force were in ruins. The United States had long since cracked the Japanese code and by mid-July it was known that the Japanese were attempting to sue for peace. Before the successful testing of the atomic bomb, the Americans had been planning an autumn invasion of Japan but, based on the extraordinarily fierce resistance encountered at Okinawa, casualty figures were projected to be several hundred thousand. Within the American government, there was much disagreement concerning the best course to take to gain an early victory. The Joint Chiefs of Staff felt that Japan could be forced to surrender without the need to use the bomb or to launch the scheduled autumn invasion because it was felt that the Japanese could not long survive a naval blockade and a continuation of conventional bombing.[13] Secretary Stimson and Undersecretary of State Joseph Grew urged Truman to permit the Emperor to retain his imperial office, but Byrnes and the Joint Chiefs, fearful that this would be interpreted as American weakness and would inspire the Japanese to fight on, prevailed upon Truman to demand unconditional surrender. It has never been satisfactorily explained why, after the atomic bombings, the United States abandoned this demand and permitted surrender conditioned upon the retention of the Emperor.

Another factor that unfortunately must be considered was the prevailing attitude in America toward the Japanese people. The sneak attack on Pearl Harbor was in Roosevelt's words, a "day of infamy" and Emperor Hirohito became a wartime symbol of depravity. Whereas the European refugee scientists perceived Hitler as the greatest enemy, most Americans hated the Asian foe with equal fervor. A letter written by Truman on August 11, 1945, referred to Pearl Harbor and the killing of U.S. prisoners of war and went on to say: "The only language they seem to understand is the one that we have been using to bombard them. When you have to deal with a beast you have to treat him as a beast."[14] It is hardly surprising that in such an atmosphere emotion may have played tricks on political judgment.

Truman's decision to use the bomb against Japan was shaped by a number of forces which were largely beyond his control. He and his advisers believed that it was legitimate to use this new weapon, and he never questioned the inherited assumption that if it was ready for use during the war, it would be used. Unlike Einstein, Szilard, and other refugee scientists, Truman saw no difference between Germany, which was thought to be building a similar weapon, and Japan, which was not involved in any such undertaking. In other words, he did not share the refugee physicists' belief that this was a defensive weapon. Of all the alternatives for ending the war quickly, unconditionally, and with the smallest loss of American life, the atomic bomb appeared the most promising. A great deal of thought went into the search for a quick victory; precious little was devoted to the postwar implications of nuclear arms. By 1945, policymakers were more or less inured to the killing of civilians in such exercises as the fire bombing of Tokyo, and they preferred the sacrifice of Japanese civilians to American soldiers.

The deteriorating relations between the Soviet Union and the United States also played a significant role in the decision process. Truman, relying heavily upon the advice of Roosevelt's more hawkish advisers, believed the bomb was just the right tool to force Stalin to cooperate with American postwar plans, especially in Eastern Europe. To accomplish this, they believed, nothing less than a combat demonstration would be sufficiently impressive. Unfortunately, the United States never evolved a clear strategy for utilizing the weapon as a bargaining instrument, and when the Soviets refused to be intimidated, this strategy collapsed.

The self-perpetuating nature of a $2 billion bureaucratic enterprise cannot be underestimated. During a bitter war being fought on two fronts, Congress had authorized vast sums of money without knowledge of the activities of the Manhattan Project. Roosevelt and his advisers were extremely nervous about the political consequences of failure, and they knew that only success could protect the political and military leadership from attack and congressional investigation.[15]

Finally, due consideration must be paid to the advice Truman received from the leaders of the Manhattan Project, especially from General Groves and Robert Oppenheimer via the Interim Committee. Because of the highly sensitive nature of the Manhattan Project and the technical complexity of the problem of developing an atomic bomb, Groves was able to control and manipulate information coming from the project. Groves was a blunt, hard-nosed career army man who was enormously proud of the new weapon. He had no doubt that it ought to be employed and that it was the ideal means to convince the Russians to cooperate with American postwar plans. Unfortunately, Groves also harbored the wild notion that the United States could control the entire world supply of uranium, and that it would take the Soviet Union at least twenty years to duplicate America's achievement. He actually spent millions of dollars of the resources allocated to the Manhattan Project in an effort to corner the uranium market. He used his unique position to frustrate the efforts of dissidents like Szilard, and he dominated the critical meetings of the Interim Committee.

Robert Oppenheimer, as director of the Manhattan Project, was the most influential scientist, and while he certainly did not subscribe to Groves's pipe-dreams, he failed utterly to challenge the delusions which played such a pivotal role in the decision to bomb Hiroshima and Nagasaki. Oppenheimer is a mysterious and tragic figure whose motivations can only be guessed at. Association with several Communists and Communist-supported causes in the prewar years coupled with damaging lies told to army security agents had compromised Oppenheimer. His security clearance was withheld until General Groves demanded that it be granted. This placed Oppenheimer in Groves's debt, and it is impossible to know how much this influenced his performance in the decision process. What is known is that he did not openly challenge Groves's misconceptions, and he did not champion the concerned scientists who advocated careful long-range planning before inaugurating the atomic age. When his moment to speak arrived, Oppenheimer carefully confined himself to the subject of the best way to use the new weapon. As an adviser to the Interim Committee, he opposed the Franck Report's proposal to give the Japanese a demonstration, and he failed to press for a serious study of the long-range consequences of atomic weapons and warfare from the point of view of the scientific expert. Perhaps Oppenheimer was irresponsible or perhaps he was a victim of the irresistible allure of the scientific and technical challenge of man's attempt to harness atomic energy. Certainly, in the context of a world at peace, it would have been a thrilling challenge to discover peaceful uses for atomic energy. In war, however, it became a nasty but necessary job. There is something chilling about the response of Oppenheimer and other scientists to this seemingly thankless job. The scale of the project, the thrill of discovery under such pressure and, ultimately, the remarkable success of the invention, obscured the ugly reality of the purpose of their work. While Oppenheimer and others rejoiced over their successful development of the "technically sweet" invention they eerily labeled "the gadget,"[16] they forgot the gadget's purpose was to destroy life. Later, Oppenheimer came to appreciate that in enjoying the work on the bomb, physicists had "sinned," but at the time he savored the new feeling of power; the Greeks would have called it hubris.[17] Frank Oppenheimer, Robert's younger brother, who also worked as a physicist on the Manhattan Project, has stated that the general first reaction to the news that Hiroshima had been destroyed was a sense of relief that the bomb had not been a dud; only then did he and his brother experience a sense of revulsion. Before then they had never really thought about the human target. In the month following the destruction of Hiroshima and Nagasaki, Oppenheimer on several occasions wistfully expressed his hope that atomic energy could become a force for good.[18]

The decision to bomb Hiroshima was reached by pragmatic men of politics and the military (the scientists really had very little input) who were guided by emotion, wishful thinking, misinformation, and a belief that short-range advantages could somehow be parlayed into long-term blessings for America and the world. It was an evil act, but malevolence probably was not a factor in the deliberations of the Truman administration. The men who understood the awesome potential for destruction and the long-range political crisis atomic energy would provoke had effectively been silenced. Men like Bohr, Szilard, and Franck were ignored or ridiculed when they attempted to get their message across to the policymakers. In the minds of the politicians, the scientist's job was to build the gadget and keep his mouth shut.

Today, many historians believe that the bombings were unnecessary and did not affect the timing of the Japanese surrender as decisively as the Russian declaration of war on August 8 and the Allied willingness to permit the survival of the imperial institutions. The Japanese surrender on August 10 came only after the government had received assurances that the throne would be preserved. This has lead Martin Sherwin to conclude that "*neither* bomb may have been necessary; and certainly . . . the second one [on Nagasaki] was not."[19]

The question still remains: Why did the Truman administration rush to use the bomb without adequate planning for a future in which the possibility for nuclear annihilation had become an inescapable reality? As relations with the Soviet Union deteriorated in the last months of the war, the makers of United States policy deluded themselves into believing that the Soviets would renounce geographical, political, and ideological ambitions to secure neutralization of atomic weapons. There is no evidence that serious consideration at the highest levels was given to the possibility that Russia would not cooperate in this scenario. After Japan's surrender and the Soviet refusal to be intimidated, the American nuclear policy unraveled in confusion as Truman and Byrnes chased the next chimera— secrecy and monopoly. In part, because Truman and his advisers had refused to permit the opening of channels of communication between scientists and policy- makers, the administration concluded that its best defense lay in tightening security to keep the secret of the bomb from Russia. The scientists, of course, knew that this was a futile exercise and that any effort to do so would needlessly exacerbate relations with Russia and intensify the dangers of an unrestricted arms race.

We now have discussed at some length the historic and political factors which led to the bombing of Hiroshima and Nagasaki. Whether or not the atomic bomb was used for the reasons stated by the American policymakers, and whether or not its use achieved their political and military objectives, the critical question to Einstein and to the unborn victims of the atomic age was, and remains: Can man afford to ignore moral considerations in the pursuit of political expedience? Perhaps the question should read: Under what circumstances can man justifiably ignore moral considerations in the pursuit of political expedience? In the case at hand—the atomic bombing of two Japanese cities—one must ask: How many American soldiers must be saved in order to justify not only the human tragedy at Hiroshima and Nagasaki but also the uncontrollable arms race which threatens man's humanity as surely as it threatens his survival?

Einstein never wavered in his conviction that use of atomic weapons on Japan was morally unjustifiable. His pacifism was based upon the commandment "Thou shalt not kill." The only time in his life he qualified this belief was during the Hitler years, and then only as a matter of self-preservation: Hitler's murderous practices must be terminated. Einstein's letter to Roosevelt in 1939 was provoked by the terrifying likelihood that Hitler might soon have access to atomic weapons, and it was a matter of self-defense for the democracies to thwart the madman's quest for world domination. Although Einstein never forgave the German people for their acquiescence to the Nazi slaughter of Jews, he would never have endorsed the use of atomic bombs on Germany once it became known that the German atomic bomb project had failed. The bomb was a defensive weapon and no amount of German barbarity could justify American barbarity when the danger of a similar German bomb was removed. In an interview given a year after the bombing of Hiroshima and Nagasaki, Einstein reportedly told a British journalist that he believed that Roosevelt would not have used the atomic bomb, which, Einstein charged, had been used to end the war in the Pacific before the Soviet Union became involved.[20]

Three months earlier, America had concluded its "moral crusade" against Hitler. Now, use of a revolutionary weapon upon densely populated civilian centers without warning and without a clearly formulated policy of international control revealed that the United States had, in Einstein's words, adopted the "degradingly low ethical standards of the enemy."[21] The standards of the next war, he predicted, would be degraded by our own actions. America had rejected the credo of the nineteenth-century Nihilists which had become the fundamental belief of the Nazis (and Stalin) that "everything is permitted." It would be outrageous to accuse the men who decided to bomb Hiroshima and Nagasaki of such criminality. It would be almost as wicked to absolve them of their utter failure to consider the moral ramifications—both in the immediate act and for the future—of their decision and their failure to ask the question: "What is permitted?" The ancient Greeks knew well that he who tries to play God is destroyed by his own folly.

At the climax of the magnificent prologue to the "poem" the "Legend of the Grand Inquisitor" in Dostoevsky's *The Brothers Karamazov* (possibly Einstein's favorite work of literature), Ivan, the rationalist, tells his saintly younger brother that "if the sufferings of children go to make up the sum of sufferings which is necessary for the purchase of truth [and future harmony on earth], then I say beforehand that the entire truth is not worth such a price. . . . I don't want harmony. I don't want it, out of the love I bear to mankind. . . . [T]oo high a price has been placed on harmony. We cannot afford to pay so much for admission. And therefore I hasten to return my ticket of admission. . . . It is not God that I do not accept, Alyosha. I merely most respectfully return him the ticket."

When Alyosha replies softly that this is rebellion, Ivan answers, "I'm sorry to hear you say that. . . . One can't go on living in a state of rebellion, and I want to live. Tell me frankly, I appeal to you—answer me: imagine that it is you yourself who are erecting the edifice of human destiny with the aim of making men happy in the end, of giving them peace and contentment at last, but that to do that it is absolutely necessary, and indeed quite inevitable, to torture to death only one tiny creature, the little girl who beat her breast with her little fist, and to found the edifice on her unavenged tears—would you consent to be the architect on those conditions? Tell me and do not lie!"

"No, I wouldn't," Alyosha said softly.[22]

12

"Between Anarchy and Tyranny"

George Santayana's warning that "those who cannot remember the past are condemned to repeat it" has been given a tragic twist by the history of the twentieth century. In the thirties, Western leaders, in an attempt to avoid a repeat of the First World War horrors, adopted a policy of appeasement toward Hitler, whose avowed goal was to undermine the international order. After the Second World War, American policy was dominated by the belief that Stalin was another Hitler, that he sought to overthrow the world order and consequently that diplomacy, negotiation, and compromise were appeasement. Any criticism of this politics of force would be discredited by the image of Munich. In the obsession to avoid the errors of the past, the American foreign policy establishment failed to evaluate the present in its own context, and entered the nuclear era preoccupied with mastering the lessons of the age that had vanished at Hiroshima.

The great tragedy of the postwar era is that responsible statesmen failed utterly to recognize that the release of atomic energy marked the dawning of a new age. Instead, they seized upon the bomb as an ultraweapon with which they could compel Russia to acquiesce in American policies or face the consequences.

Churchill had prevailed first upon Roosevelt and later upon Truman to keep the bomb's existence a secret from Stalin because he hoped to use it as a counterbalance to Soviet power in Europe. General Groves's assertion that it would take the Russians twenty years to build their own bomb had contributed to the Interim Committee[1] decision to reject a proposal to inform Stalin before the bomb was used in combat. When Truman told the Soviet leader at Potsdam that America possessed a new superweapon, he avoided specifics. On August 9, the day Nagasaki was bombed, President Truman, in an address to the American people, proclaimed that the United States would keep the "secret" as trustees to protect the U.S. and the world from total destruction. Truman had been advised that the only secret was that the bomb existed and that it worked, but he and Byrnes did not understand atomic energy. For the first year of the atomic age, they deferred to General Groves, who, according to future Secretary of State Dean Acheson, in early 1946, was running American atomic policy.[2]

In truth, no one was running the policy because, except for the decision to use the bomb, no policy existed. The first discussion on international control of atomic energy took place in September, and it would be three months before the Truman administration formulated any kind of program. At a cabinet meeting in mid-September, the retiring Secretary of War, Henry Stimson, advocated a direct approach to the Soviet Union whereby America would offer to share nuclear knowledge and pledge cooperation in future research. He did not advocate sharing the design and technology of the bomb. Stimson conceded it was a gamble, but he realized that monopoly was not sustainable and that it was imperative that a firm basis for Soviet-American cooperation be established before that date. Only Henry Wallace supported Stimson and, after the meeting, someone leaked to the press that Wallace wanted to give the secret to the Russians. This false story stirred up a storm in Congress which thereupon demanded absolute secrecy. Early in October Truman announced that the "secret" would not be shared. During this period, 73 percent of the American public supported the government's policy, while only 14 percent believed that it should be entrusted to the United Nations. The policymakers who favored atomic monopoly referred to themselves as "realists."

The bombings of Hiroshima and Nagasaki immediately thrust Einstein into the public eye as the discoverer of the principle behind the release of atomic energy. On the day after the destruction of Nagasaki, the government released its official account of the Manhattan Project—*Atomic Energy for Military Purposes*—written by Princeton physicist Professor Henry DeWolf Smyth, which credited Einstein's letter to President Roosevelt in August 1939 with initiating government participation in nuclear research. A consequence of the Smyth Report, which plagued Einstein the rest of his life, was that many people mistakenly assumed that the atomic bomb and the devastation of Hiroshima and Nagasaki were somehow his fault.

Einstein remained secluded at Saranac Lake until the end of September. During this period he was in frequent contact with Szilard and other colleagues who shared his revulsion that the new weapon had been employed against a defeated enemy. In addition to moral repugnance he, like Szilard and Franck, sadly realized that America had squandered its unique historical opportunity to establish a postwar order which could ensure lasting peace. Had representatives from other nations been invited to Alamogordo to witness the first test, he reasoned, subsequent American "renunciation of this weapon as too terrible to use would have carried great weight in negotiations and would have convinced the other nations of our sincerity in asking for their cooperation in developing these newly unleashed powers for good and peaceful purposes."[3]

Ever since the First World War, Einstein had been convinced that international anarchy could be prevented only by a world organization which possessed a monopoly over military power. In his opinion, the advent of the atomic age accelerated the urgency of this necessarily radical change in world politics. From the beginning of the atomic age, he emphasized that the development of nuclear weapons did not create a new problem so much as it intensified the need to abolish war. Measures to regulate atomic energy were insufficient; the real cause of war was the continued existence of competing sovereign nations. Einstein repeated time and again that the only solution was the creation of a supranational world government in which member nations abandoned their sovereignty in possessing arms. In early September he warned an educator who had invited him to a conference on the implications of atomic energy that "[a]s long as nations demand unrestricted sovereignty we shall undoubtedly be faced with still bigger wars, fought with bigger and technologically more advanced weapons."[4]

The November 1945 issue of the *Atlantic Monthly* contained Einstein's first public statement about atomic weapons in an article entitled "Atomic War or Peace,"[5] which was based upon an interview Einstein had given to Raymond Gram Swing, a radio commentator whose weekly reports on atomic energy had earned high praise from atomic scientists. Einstein told Swing that the United States should immediately announce its readiness to give the secret of the bomb to a world government with jurisdiction over all military matters. He did not think it wise to give the secret to either the Soviet Union or to the United Nations as currently constituted. It is interesting to note that in this early statement he spoke of a "secret," whereas later on he would dispute the idea that a secret existed. The change is one of nuance rather than substance; he knew there was no scientific secret to be kept from other countries, and he obviously referred to the specific technology of the weapon constructed at Los Alamos. Since the laws of physics were known, it was only a matter of time before the related technological problems would be solved by other nations.

Shortly after the end of the war in the Far East, and long before the Truman administration had formulated any policy regarding international control of atomic energy, the War Department drew up the May-Johnson Bill, which would have given to the military full control over all uses of atomic energy, peaceful as well as military. The proposed law would have made the administrator of the atomic energy agency independent of both the President and the Congress. It would have placed all nuclear research under the same rigid security measures which the civilian scientists of the Manhattan Project had found so inhibiting. The unmistakable message the bill sent to the rest of the world was that America was preparing to dominate world politics by means of nuclear arms.

Concerned scientists, already disturbed by the destruction of the two Japanese cities and the absence of any coherent international policy in Washington, were galvanized to action by the May-Johnson Bill. In the fall of 1945, many veterans of the Manhattan Project formed the Federation of Atomic Scientists to lobby against May-Johnson and in favor of a sane national nuclear policy. Scientists like Szilard had been silenced immediately after Hiroshima and Nagasaki because they had been given the erroneous impression that the United States and the Soviet Union had made a secret agreement.[6] The federation members descended on Washington to provide the men in power with a crash course in the realities of atomic energy. In their unaccustomed role as political lobbyists, they were generally perceived as "woolly-headed,"[7] naïve, and alarmist. Szilard's spontaneous, disorganized style and his habit of asserting that chances of avoiding nuclear war with the Soviet Union were between 5 and 10 percent, if not typical, were certainly noted by the pragmatists who did not welcome meddlesome intellectuals attempting to dictate policy.

Their efforts were instrumental in the defeat of the May-Johnson Bill and in the eventual creation of a civilian-controlled Atomic Energy Commission, but it was a success that was not to be repeated in the early years of the Cold War.

As relations between the United States and the Soviet Union worsened and prospects for eventual nuclear war became more real, Einstein intensified his political activities, despite his realistic assessment of the remote hopes for success. He knew that as long as weapons were permissible, there might be wars, and the only hope for lasting world peace lay in the creation of a supranational world authority[8] endowed with adequate powers to guarantee the abolition of war through universal disarmament. The only responsibilities of the world authority would be to effect and maintain worldwide disarmament and to mediate and arbitrate conflicts which threatened world peace or fell outside local jurisdiction.

Einstein believed that the creation of the United Nations by the victorious Allied forces in 1945 represented a timid first step. Because its charter had been drawn up before the bombing of Hiroshima, the United Nations was, as a product of the preatomic age, designed to secure peace in a world which had ceased to exist on August 6, 1945. The U.N. was constructed in a manner which prevented it from living up to its purpose. Its decisions were not binding, and it had no power to enforce the execution of its decrees. The U.N. Charter failed to confront the issue of nationalism, and member nations were permitted to retain their own sovereignty and military forces. The inherent weakness of the United Nations was best illustrated by the Security Council veto which enabled any one of the great powers to veto a council decision. All five great powers—the United States, the Soviet Union, Great Britain, China, and France—had insisted upon the veto power as a guarantee that they could not be forced into a war against their will. The effectiveness of the new organization was, from the outset, made hostage to the continued cooperation of the five nations. Einstein recognized that peace could not be achieved by such gradualist, piecemeal steps; it required "a decisive, radical step. . . ." Otto Nathan recalls Einstein saying that you cannot cut the tail of a dog in many small pieces, you must cut it by one stroke; in other words, you need to take a radical step.[9]

The "radical" proposals Einstein supported after 1945 were variations of the same ideas he had been advocating since 1914, albeit revised to reflect the lessons learned from the growth of Nazism, the development of the atomic bomb, and the existing structure of the United Nations which, he felt, could be a useful frame upon which to graft the more far-reaching powers necessary to guarantee an end to war. The essential points in his program were: (1) the member nations must yield to the supranational government their sovereign power to be armed; (2) the new world government would possess an international military force, with a monopoly over military power, composed of individuals from all member nations integrated into a single force which would derive its power from international law subscribed to by the members as interpreted by a world court (similar to the United States Supreme Court), whose decisions must be binding; and (3) the military branch of the world government must be able to enforce these decisions. He believed that in time, perhaps over the course of several centuries, national boundaries would dissolve. In the current state of "anarchy" in international relations, each sovereign state is concerned only with its own security. But, Einstein hoped, in a world of international law, Russia's security would be every bit as important to America as its own.[10]

Einstein felt it was essential that the world government restrict its activities to matters dealing with world security. It should not be allowed to interfere in the internal political, economic, social, and cultural affairs of the member states unless, as in Nazi Germany, a minority was oppressing the majority. Some control over world economic matters might be necessary to avoid an international crisis, but the individual states ought to be free to choose their own economic system. Representatives to the General Assembly of the world government—the legislative branch of the government—should be popularly elected by the citizens of each region; they should not be political appointees of the individual states. This would lead, he hoped, to "more statesmen and fewer diplomats,"[11] working to eliminate war. Finally, world government, free from the dangers of competitive sovereign states, would abolish scientific and military secrecy, and permit scientists to work without restrictions and government meddling, and rid the world of a dangerous source of distrust.

Einstein's ideas regarding the nature of a world authority which would effectively deal with the abolition of war and the control of weapons reflect clearly his views on democracy, socialism, pacifism, and internationalism. Renunciation of national sovereignty is a natural approach to the solution of the problem of nationalistic wars for someone who is a pacifist-internationalist. His advocacy of the control of weapons and the economics of war by the world authority represents a form of supranational socialism. Care should be taken not to confuse this very limited form of socialist control with the far more sweeping call for the implementation of worldwide socialism in all societies. This latter ideal appealed to Einstein as a socialist, but he carefully avoided including this idea in his world government proposals. With two exceptions, he explicitly stated that the individual states should be permitted to practice their own form of economics; the exceptions related to the economics of war and the need for some control over world economic matters to avoid an international economic crisis, such as the

Great Depression. Finally, his call for the popular election of the representatives to the world government, a proposal which would have been especially difficult to implement, is an expression of his faith in democracy and the judgment of the public.

Immediately after the war Einstein proposed that Great Britain, the United States, and the Soviet Union should draft a constitution of the world government to embody these elementary and essential proposals; then they should commit all their military resources to that new body and invite the other nations throughout the world to join. He also proposed that Russia, since it was not in possession of the technological secrets of the atomic bomb, should draw up the first draft upon which the three great powers could base their discussions. He felt this would reassure the Russians of the good intentions of the Western democracies. At no time did he advocate giving the technology of the bomb to Russia, although he realized that soon they would discover it themselves.

America, with its temporary monopoly of the bomb, was in a unique position to use it in a benevolent fashion as leverage toward world government and effective nuclear disarmament. Einstein believed that since there was no defense against the atomic bomb, no amount of increased military strength could protect the American people, and that an arms race would leave the United States vulnerable to attack, therefore, possession of the bomb actually weakened American security. Dismissing the notion that a nation can work to prevent war while simultaneously preparing for it, he repeatedly urged American leaders to relax their inflexible stance against Russia, to abandon competition and to begin to seek means whereby cooperation might be restored among the former Allies. The United States and Russia must be willing to give their arms to the world government, to submit to mutual arms control, including inspections, and to abide by the decisions of the world government. He supported universal, not piecemeal, disarmament, and he never advocated that America disarm unilaterally. The real goal was not the outlawing of individual weapons, but the abolition of all war.

Einstein realized that he and those who supported the creation of a world authority were working against almost insuperable odds. He understood that the attempt to integrate societies with alien cultures, languages, and traditions that were accustomed to resolving international differences by warfare was an unpromising task. He also knew that opening the closed Soviet society to the jurisdiction of a world authority would require something of a political miracle, but to the frequent criticism that his ideas were hopeless dreams, he responded testily, "If the idea of world government is not realistic then there is only *one* realistic view of our future: wholesale destruction of man by man."[12]

In retrospect, it is clear that world government as envisioned by Einstein could never have been implemented in the existing environment. The critical preliminary stages of the Cold War had come to pass before the hot wars in Europe and Asia had been concluded. Whatever slim chances for cooperation had survived the war were quickly dashed as the Cold War soured international relations. Furthermore, it is inconceivable that either the Soviets or the Americans would ever have surrendered to a world authority the sovereign right to possess military forces. What was achievable in 1945 might have been a modus vivendi with Stalin which could have led to greater trust and cooperation between the champions of capitalism and communism.

On May 8, 1945, the day Germany surrendered, a large crowd of citizens of Moscow spontaneously assembled outside the U.S. embassy to pay heartfelt honor to their American Allies. This genuine expression of goodwill did not influence either Soviet or American leaders; instead, in the nine-month period from May 1945 to February 1946 the Grand Alliance of the war years collapsed and the irreversible steps that brought on the Cold War were taken. Exhausted Russia had lost 16 million soldiers and civilians in the war, whereas the Allied forces had suffered fewer than one million military casualties.[13] Stalin's immediate concerns were with security and recovery, and in his mind this could only be accomplished by a period of isolation in which to rebuild industry and agriculture while maintaining the illusion of enormous power. Secrecy was critical because, above all else, Stalin feared a revelation of Russian weakness (apparently he was less concerned about exposure of his police state). He disguised Russia's weakness by bluff, pretending the bomb did not scare him, and he exploited Western ignorance of the regime in a multitude of ways. Stalin's tactics caused American policymakers to exaggerate Soviet strength, which led directly to an escalation of the arms race in the decade following the war. The Cold War can be seen, one student of the period has written, as "a history of mutually reinforcing misconceptions."[14]

Except in Poland, which Stalin viewed as essential to Soviet security, the Soviet dictator had not imposed Communist regimes throughout Eastern Europe by the fall of 1945. Elections in Hungary and Czechoslovakia had produced non-Communist governments, and Bulgaria's government had seemed to be relatively fair in the opinion of various Western observers. Nevertheless, Truman, with his monopoly on atomic weapons, took a hard line against the Soviets. He abruptly cut off Lend Lease, whittled down German reparations suggested at Yalta, and ignored a request from Moscow for a reconstruction loan to rebuild the shattered Russian economy.

In addition to the confrontation over the fate of Eastern Europe, a second source of conflict between the great powers developed immediately after the collapse of the Nazis regarding the future of Germany. Stalin genuinely feared the rearming of Germany and believed a weak Germany would insure a strong Russia. Three days after V-E Day, Truman had clumsily revealed his plans to terminate Lend Lease at an early date. In response, to help Russian reconstruction, Stalin began to dismantle German industry in the Soviet zone and transport it to the east. Britain and America, as Einstein had feared, viewed Germany as a buffer to Russian communism.

Einstein believed that Germany should be permanently disarmed so that his former countrymen could never again cause another global war. He was convinced that world peace was not possible while the Germans possessed an army. Militarism was too deeply ingrained in the consciousness of the people. Hitler's rise could not simply be blamed on the Versailles Treaty because militarism had warped the German outlook since the time of Frederick the Great in the eighteenth century and had been solidified under Bismarck a century later. There could be no such thing as education through experience because the Germans always managed to rationalize their failures with irrational explanations—such as the notorious "stab in the back" theory of 1918 which blamed their defeat on the Jews, pacifists, and socialists. To an American woman who was about to join her husband in Berlin after the war Einstein warned, "You will find them affable, intelligent, and they will seem to agree with you, but you must not believe a one of them."[15]

It was essential, Einstein believed, to place Germany under the administration of a supranational government. The control of industry should be removed from the "war lords"; natural resources should also come under the authority of the world government. This, Einstein felt, was a policy of "utmost security" against further aggression, not revenge. It was necessary, he maintained, to limit the external freedom of the Germans so that their "inner freedom can take root again."[16] Instead, as the Cold War intensified, the Western democracies used Germany as a shield against the Soviet Union, just as they had done after 1918. In 1950, after the Korean War started, West Germany was rearmed.

The postwar situation was additionally exacerbated by the rise of the Italian and French Communist parties in those war-ravaged countries at a time when reaction to the New Deal was settling in in the United States. After September 1945, Republican anti-New Dealers, alarmed by the swing to socialism in Great Britain, launched violent attacks against Truman's foreign policy and began to charge that there were Communists in academic circles. Hysteria tends to fuel itself, and it was not long before the early postwar optimism turned sullen. Communist rhetoric, reflecting an ideology committed to the overthrow of capitalism, in conjunction with the growing popularity of Western European Communist parties, convinced Washington that Moscow had embarked upon a new program of expansion. Fearful that the Russians might steal their nuclear secrets, the Americans, despite their monopoly of the bomb, actually felt more insecure than ever. The bomb scared its possessors more than it intimidated their enemies.

By the beginning of 1946 the American domestic economy was hobbled by strikes, inflation, and unemployment. On February 9, 1946, Stalin delivered a rare public speech in which he stressed the incompatibility of communism and capitalism and blamed the Second World War upon the uneven rate of development of the capitalist countries. Secretary Wallace interpreted the speech as a "friendly challenge" to capitalism to prove that the American system could escape the cycle of frequent depressions. Most other Americans agreed with *Time* magazine that Stalin's speech was a "warlike pronouncement."[17] That same month Russian troops entered Manchuria and Iran and the Soviet Union used its veto power in the

United Nations Security Council for the first time on the question of Anglo-French forces in Syria and Lebanon. Then, on February 16, 1946, the Canadian spy case broke, and the United States was forced to admit that some atomic secrets had been stolen. This development, renewing fears of an international Communist conspiracy, was especially alarming to Americans who began to see danger lurking everywhere.

The Truman administration responded with its "get tough" policy, which was announced by Secretary of State Byrnes on February 28, 1946. A week later, with Truman in the audience, Churchill delivered his famous Iron Curtain speech in Fulton, Missouri. This reorientation of United States policy to a strategy of "negotiation from strength" reflected its leaders' frustration with and fear of Soviet policies. They believed that Russia had a well-rehearsed master plan which could be countered only by force. Diplomacy and negotiation, the tactics of Roosevelt, were now branded "appeasement."

To win popular and congressional support to rebuild the military, establish a program of universal military training, and strengthen foreign aid, the administration felt it necessary to dramatize the perceived crisis, with the consequence that Stalin became equated with Hitler.[18] This simplistic analysis was no less dangerous than the tendency of Western leftists to view Stalin as a friend because, in equating Stalin with the erratic Nazi whose historical vision often led to impetuous risks with disastrous consequences, American leaders blinded themselves to the fact that the Soviet leader was not a fanatic idealist, but a crafty and cautious diplomat who, in the words of one biographer, was a "hard-working dictator."[19] The vision of Stalin as Hitler ignored the fact that Russia was incapable of large-scale aggression so soon after the war, that Soviet paranoia, not aggressive ideology, dictated their actions in Eastern Europe and other bordering areas, and that Stalin's fears of the West were as misinformed as the growing American hysteria toward the Soviet Union.

The administration's simplistic and apocalyptic statements succeeded in whipping up support for the new policy, but at the cost of discrediting rational analysis and criticism. During the spring and summer of 1946, American actions, supposedly a response to Soviet aggression, confirmed the Communist theory that conflict with capitalist countries was inevitable. On July 1, 1946, the United States conducted an atomic test blast on Bikini Island in the Pacific. Not unexpectedly, this led to an immediate acceleration of the Soviet efforts to acquire nuclear arms and to institute a new round of propaganda against American motives. In August the United States resorted to "gunboat diplomacy" in the Mediterranean to thwart a Soviet bid for the Dardanelles. Steps were being taken to create a strong West Germany to block Russian movement into Western Europe, and in some circles there was talk of waging a "preventive war" to force the Russians out of Europe. Secretary Byrnes was the highest public official to advocate such measures, and when he left office early in 1947 he complained bitterly that the Russians "don't scare." Against this backdrop, the first serious efforts to achieve international control of the military uses of nuclear power were being played out at the United Nations.

The first official approach to the Soviet Union regarding international control of atomic weapons did not take place until November 1945 despite knowledge that Soviet espionage had uncovered the existence and general outline of the Manhattan Project.[20] Late in December the U.S. and the U.S.S.R. tentatively agreed to establish a United Nations Atomic Energy Commission. The Soviets wanted it under control of the Security Council, where they held veto power, whereas the Americans sought to place it under the U.S.-controlled General Assembly.

Early in 1946 the United States advanced the Acheson-Lilienthal plan which was essentially drawn from a proposal for atomic energy control composed by Robert Oppenheimer. The Oppenheimer program would have placed the military uses of atomic energy under the jurisdiction of an international agency with the authority to regulate the mining, refining, and utilization of the world's supply of atomic raw materials. After fissionable materials had been denatured by the international authority, and could no longer be utilized for the manufacture of nuclear weapons, individual nations would be free to develop the peaceful uses of atomic energy. Oppenheimer's plan, which emphasized the benefits of international cooperation, was amended by the Acheson-Lilienthal Committee to include transitional stages for the American surrender of its monopoly and provisions for punishment of violators. The transition stages would serve to freeze American nuclear superiority for an indefinite time.

Truman made the unfortunate appointment of Bernard Baruch as chief American negotiator at the United Nations. He was a self-made millionaire with a history of self-promotion which had endeared him to the public, the press, and Congress. His appointment dismayed the atomic scientists because Baruch was ignorant of the technical aspects of atomic energy and inexperienced in diplomacy. By early 1946, the American military establishment, having come to view the atomic bomb as the foundation of the national security of the United States, warned Baruch that unless he achieved a foolproof plan for total disarmament (in particular, of conventional Soviet ground forces), the international control of atomic weapons would infringe upon America's best interests. Accordingly Baruch, in cahoots with General Groves, revised the Acheson-Lilienthal proposals in a way that assured Soviet rejection of the plan. Baruch insisted on an initial international raw materials survey, the abolition of the Security Council veto (a desirable, but irrelevant side issue which had the effect of waving a red flag at the Soviets), and the protection of the national economy against "interference" by international authority. Baruch clearly conveyed the attitude that international control would be on American terms or not at all. After studying the Baruch plan, Einstein refused to endorse it because he viewed it as a composite of interim measures which did not go far enough, and he also felt it was unfair to the Soviets that the United States retain its monopoly throughout the transition period.

On June 14, 1946, Baruch formally presented the American proposals to the United Nations, and five days later Soviet Ambassador Andrei Gromyko responded by calling for a ban on all atomic weapons, including a renunciation by the United States of its present monopoly. The Soviet plan had no serious provision for inspection procedures; the Soviets claimed that national inspection would be sufficient, and they subsequently labeled inspection proposals "capitalist espionage." Gromyko also insisted that the Security Council veto was nonnegotiable.

The Soviets opted for a strategy of delay until they could develop their own weapons and bargain from parity. Negotiations eventually broke down in the autumn, but from the start this attempt to achieve international control of the military uses of atomic energy was stillborn because the Americans had never privately approached the Soviets for the purpose of devising a mutually acceptable plan. Instead, the unilateral proposal, coupled with Baruch's attitude that control would be on American terms or not at all, facilitated Soviet rejection. The major substantive stumbling block was over the issue of inspection. Stalin simply would not permit an international presence on Soviet soil. In the final analysis, both sides deserve the blame for failure to achieve early international control of atomic energy. Success would have been possible only in an atmosphere of mutual trust, confidence, and understanding. Instead, both remained mired in their own nationalist ideology and self-interest, and neither side ever demonstrated the ability to rise above traditional power politics to view the harnessing of atomic energy as a unique historical crisis which demanded statesmanship and vision rather than propaganda and militaristic posings.[21]

As the early attempts by Einstein and his fellow scientists to educate world leaders and their constituents met with growing resistance occasioned by the deterioration of Soviet-American relations, Einstein became ever more deeply concerned about the future. He maintained that mankind did not enjoy the luxury of time; survival demanded an immediate decisive act. He felt the need to educate world leaders was so compelling that he became involved with several groups whose purpose was to provide information on the crisis of global security. His sense of urgency overcame his aversion to working with groups and committees but, nevertheless, he entered the struggle aware that frustration was the likely outcome.

From May 1946 until the end of 1948 he served as Chairman of the Emergency Committee of Atomic Scientists, which was founded as a nonprofit organization to raise funds for the purpose of educating the general public about nuclear energy. Offices were set up in New York, Chicago, and in Princeton, where Einstein worked closely with the executive secretary. The work for the Emergency Committee took precedence over all other nonscientific work. As the official chairman of the committee, Einstein played a significant role in determining policy, but Leo Szilard actually directed the workings of the committee.[22] Fund-raising letters were sent out over Einstein's name. A fund-raising conference was held in Princeton on November 17, 1946, and Einstein's address that day was carried over national radio.

From the outset, the FBI files reveal a deep concern with the activities and motives of the Emergency Committee. In June 1946 the Newark office of the FBI took steps to determine whether the committee was "communistically infiltrated and dominated and whether or not Albert Einstein was the actual force behind the organization or whether his name was being used as a respectable front for other persons."[23] The fact that Einstein was in the vanguard of the movement for world government while the Communist Party was waging a bitter fight against it apparently did not impress those who felt that Einstein was a dupe of Moscow.

Copies of all public statements and fund-raising letters of the Emergency Committee were collected, and after the conference in Princeton in November 1946, the army "Weekly Intelligence Summary #95" for the period December 6–13, 1946, published an article on the committee which described Einstein as the leader and chief spokesman, "who in the past has been used by various Communist Front organizations as a 'big name' 'innocent' sponsor." The report repeated all

Harold C. Urey, Einstein, and Leo Szilard, Princeton, ca. 1946–1948. Einstein was chairman of the Emergency Committee of Atomic Scientists, Urey was vice-chairman and Szilard was the driving force. (Courtesy of Margot Einstein)

the old familiar derogatory allegations concerning his participation in pacifist, antifascist, and Soviet-friendship organizations since 1932. These groups were described as "Communist controlled and Communist Front organizations." The FBI noted that this information came from "a completely reliable source" and was "probably true."[24]

A campaign launched by the Emergency Committee in February 1947 to raise $1 million triggered another investigation by the FBI. The fund-raising letter sent out over Einstein's signature warned that the revolutionary force of atomic energy could not be fitted into "the outmoded concept of narrow nationalism," and that control of atomic energy required "the aroused understanding and insistence of the peoples of the world." Accordingly, the letter continued,

> We scientists recognize our inescapable responsibility to acquaint our fellow citizens with the simple facts of atomic energy and its implications for society. In this lies our only security and our only hope: we believe that an informed citizenry will act for life and not for death.
> We need $1,000,000 for this great educational task. Sustained by faith in man's ability to control his destiny through the exercise of reason, we have pledged all our strength and our knowledge to this work.[25]

On February 14, 1947, according to FBI files, the *Times Herald* (Washington) carried an article headlined "Scientists Seek Funds to Reveal Atom Secrets." The article alleged that the Emergency Committee intended to use the funds, in the words of the FBI report, "to finance efforts to divulge information concerning atomic energy, which the American government was trying to keep secret as a safeguard against international trouble. . . ."[26] Because of the FBI's role in guarding atomic energy secrets, it was proposed that someone from the bureau's Atomic Energy Section discuss the activities of the Emergency Committee of Atomic Scientists with a member of the Atomic Energy Commission. It was further proposed that a member of the AEC acquainted with Einstein be directed to meet personally with the physicist to "ascertain . . . just how far his Committee intended to go in divulging information concerning atomic energy, in order that some opinion might be reached as to whether or not these activities by the Committee violated deeper provisions of the Atomic Energy Act."[27] Cooler, better-informed heads prevailed at the AEC, and in a meeting with an FBI agent on March 7, 1947, the AEC showed no interest in interviewing Einstein because, it was explained to the agent, Einstein had had no close contact with the Manhattan Project.[28]

The FBI continued to monitor the activities of both Einstein and the Emergency Committee, which it referred to as a group of "aged scientists." In March 1947 the FBI reported that the committee had donated $5,000 to the Committee for Foreign Correspondence, which, in the previous year, had sent over 10,000 pamphlets on the international control of atomic energy to scientists in sixty nations, including individual scientists and scientific societies in the Soviet Union.[29]

By June 1947 disagreements among committee members had developed over whether or not to push for total disarmament. The good intentions of the Emergency Committee often were translated into watered-down resolutions. Einstein tried to reconcile conflicting points of view within the committee, but without much success. As always, Einstein found that the consensus of the group was less bold and far-reaching than his own thinking.

As the Cold War settled in, the atomic scientists, as political neophytes, found themselves increasingly excluded from further opportunities to participate in the formation of nuclear policy. After the successful campaign to defeat the May-Johnson Bill, the scientists exerted less and less influence on the decision makers. Even Oppenheimer, the scientist with the greatest access to the politicians, was largely shut out. As chairman of the General Advisory Committee to the Atomic Energy Commission beginning in 1947, his role was to provide advice on technical, not political, questions. His 1949 opposition for technical and moral reasons to the decision to develop the hydrogen bomb would play a major role in the loss of his security clearance in December 1953. Already, by the summer of 1946, his increasingly critical attitude toward the "air atomic policy" being devised by the Pentagon caused General Groves to permit Oppenheimer to observe the Bikini Island tests, but not to evaluate them. His one meeting with Truman had so unnerved the President that he ordered Vannevar Bush never to bring that "crybaby scientist" to the White House again.[30]

The events of the war, and particularly the development of nuclear weapons, brought about the participation of scientists in the public arena on a large scale. Einstein was a rarity among prewar scientists because of his active role in political matters since 1914. He believed that it was impossible to study physics unless there was some order in the world of men and, Otto Nathan remembers, he said a great scientist is "one who cares about other things."[31] Questions of war and justice are concerns of everyone, and the responsible citizen cannot escape the dictates of his conscience to act in concert with the highest ethical values.

With each passing year Einstein's participation and political sophistication increased despite a thorough distaste for politics and politicians, and a belief that the possession of power was "boring."[32] Part of his problem with the nature of politics is that it is a science of endless variables, and one can never know the results of one's actions in advance. In 1933 Einstein had written to the Dutch astronomer W. de Sitter: "The physiologist [Jacques] Loeb once said to me in conversation that political leaders must all really be pathological because a normal person would not be able to bear so tremendous a responsibility while being so little able to foresee the consequences of his decisions and acts." A few years later (1937) he composed the following aphorism: "Politics is a pendulum whose swings between anarchy and tyranny are fueled by perennially rejuvenated illusions."[33]

The entry of the atomic scientists into active, almost frenetic, participation in the political sphere was forced upon them by the realization that the atomic age

posed new and catastrophic dangers for an unprepared world, and by the awareness that the men in power were unable to appreciate the fateful implications of this
new age. The scientists were frightened men and women who realized that politics
as usual would spell irreversible disaster for those who possessed the weapons and
for those who did not. The purpose of the Franck Report, of Szilard's memoranda
and petition, of the Federation of Atomic Scientists and the Emergency Committee
of Atomic Scientists was to provide a crash course for the policymakers and the
public alike in the realities of nuclear energy.

The men in power believed atomic weapons represented an extraordinary
advance in the technology of war. Churchill, Truman, Byrnes, and Groves
thought the new weapons could assure the achievement of their policy objectives.
Because they did not comprehend the science involved, and because they ignored
the expert advice of those who *did* understand the scientific and technological
issues of nuclear power, they concluded that America could retain a monopoly for
years to come if only the system were made secure from the threat of espionage.
They did not understand that the atomic bomb would be useless in a game of
political bluff or "brinksmanship." They had no appreciation of the long-range
implications of atomic energy; they saw only immediate short-term benefits.

The historian Richard Hofstadter suggests that the divorce of intellect and
power in contemporary society is largely the result of the enormous growth of
specialization in the last century.[34] In the relatively unspecialized society of the
Founding Fathers, men like Jefferson and Franklin were respected members of
both the scientific and political communities. The creators of our political institutions could not have foreseen that the advent of technology would give rise to a
society in which an expert in one field would be a novice in other areas.

At the dawn of the atomic age the political and military experts, charged with
the responsibility to determine America's nuclear policy, viewed the atomic
scientists as novices in political and military matters who should be essentially
excluded from the political decision-making process. Even Oppenheimer, the
atomic scientist most respected by the politicians and military men, was generally
kept out of the political side of the deliberations. The prevailing viewpoint of the
politicians was that scientists like Szilard, Franck and, later on, Einstein, had not
thought out the nonscientific issues as thoroughly or with the experience, perspective, or responsibility of the political and military leaders. Lacking the full picture
of the war effort, it was felt, they could not adequately evaluate the issues
involved. Szilard, attempting to explain why the Americans had miscalculated in
estimating when the Soviet Union would succeed in developing its first atomic
bomb, later wrote of the political experts: "If you are an expert, you believe you
are in possession of the truth, and since you know so much, you are unwilling to
make allowances for unforeseen developments."[35]

In the final analysis, the miscalculations could be attributed not only to the lack
of dialogue between scientists and politicians but also to the failure of the
politicians to listen to the technical advice they were given. Had they understood
the message of the atomic scientists, how could they have followed General

Groves's advice to keep the phantom "secret" of the bomb while attempting to corner the world's supply of uranium? Unfortunately, the technical advice of the scientific experts was heeded only insofar as it fitted the goals and preconceptions of the policymakers. Scientific facts at variance with these intentions were selectively edited from reports to the men at the top whose decisions in 1945 shaped the course of postwar history.

The attitude of the men of power toward these contentious scientists is clearly revealed in a report written for Secretary of State George Marshall by William T. Golden, an aide to Lewis Strauss, who was an original member of the Atomic Energy Commission. Golden visited Princeton on June 6, 1947, as a representative of the State Department. Einstein had requested the interview because he felt it was essential to try to rekindle negotiations with the Soviet Union. Golden reported that Einstein "spoke with deep feeling but with almost childlike hope for salvation and without appearing to have thought through the details of his solution. The field of international politics is clearly not his métier." At the meeting Einstein admitted the difficulty of realizing his proposals, but stressed that every effort should be made, "no matter how remote the chance," because otherwise "all will be lost."

Einstein denounced the rising spirit of American militarism, likening it to the Germans under the Kaiser, and he pointed out the futility of "Pax Americana," maintaining that it was the "certain precursor of war and grief. There can be no lasting enforced peace. The benevolent despot becomes a tyrant or a weakling; either way his structure crumbles." Golden concluded his report with this appraisal of Einstein's political understanding:

Professor Einstein's manner was warm and completely informal. He seemed to speak from emotion rather than from reasoned conclusions and it was surprising, though perhaps it should not have been, that, out of his métier of mathematics, he seemed naïve in the field of international politics and mass human relations. The man who popularized the concept of a fourth dimension could think in only two of them in considerations of World Government.[36]

Einstein realized that politicians and statesmen regarded him as a cross between a well-meaning fool and a meddling nuisance. When colleagues, abashed by his outspoken criticisms of American policy, countered by asking him how he would act as Secretary of State, he laughed. "They would fire me in half an hour."[37]

Golden's report cleverly dismissed, not Einstein's beloved person, but the validity of Einstein's thinking outside of science. Since he was clearly supposed to be "out of his métier," it followed naturally that his ideas were based on emotion rather than reasoned analysis, that he was naïve in international politics and mass human relations and, Golden concluded with self-satisfaction, his ideas concerning a world authority were two-dimensional.

Nowhere in the report is there any analysis of Einstein's ideas, nor does Golden refute his observations. Instead, one is left to conclude that Einstein's ideas are naïve because they ran counter to State Department policy. In this case, one must wonder, what role is there for the exercise of democratic dissent if such criticisms are dismissed as naïve because they disagree with prevailing wisdom?

A careful reading of the forces which brought about the Cold War and determined its course in the decade following the end of the Second World War supports the judgment that Einstein's ideas were, by and large, far from naïve, that, taken as a whole, they were remarkably prescient. By no means is it claimed that all his ideas were correct. What is maintained is that his ideas were derived from an ethical foundation which placed the welfare of man and life on earth ahead of more secular concerns such as advancing the cause of one nation, group, or individual at the expense of those who oppose or interfere. It is further asserted that Einstein was a conscientious private citizen who was extremely well informed on pertinent political, social, and technical issues, and that his ideas were based upon careful, rational analysis of issues and information available to the nonexpert. He never pretended to be an expert in international affairs or in mass human relations. In fact, in 1952, when he declined the offer of the presidency of Israel, he wrote that having devoted his life to objective matters, he lacked "both the natural aptitude and the experience to deal properly with people. . . ."[38]

Nevertheless, when the nonexpert ideas of Einstein, and many other scientists who were less well known to the public and the politicians, are compared with the assumptions of the experts, one must wonder which group was most vulnerable to the charge of naïveté in the appreciation of the implications of atomic weapons in the period 1945–1947. Was the Franck Report with its prediction of an uncontrolled arms race naïve? Was General Groves (the man who most influenced Secretary Stimson and President Truman to use atomic weapons against Japan) wise to believe that he could corner the world's supply of uranium and thereby prevent the Soviet Union from developing nuclear weapons for upward of twenty years? The contention here is not that the scientists ought to have run American nuclear and foreign policy in the dawning atomic age, but that the so-called political experts ought to have possessed the flexibility and wisdom to admit their own limitations in understanding this new phenomenon, to have shaped their policy on the basis of sound scientific advice on the technical aspects of atomic energy, and to have given careful consideration to the ideas of the scientists concerning the political, social, and moral implications of these developments in an imperfect world.

The attitude toward Einstein is revealing of the chasm separating the scientists and the policymakers. The tragedy is not that one individual, Einstein, was misunderstood, but that the democratic process had been so weakened that those in power were incapable of identifying and utilizing the best possible advice at a time when nuclear weapons could have been controlled. Why were politicians and scientists unable to collaborate at the dawn of the nuclear age?

The example of Einstein, while hardly definitive, is instructive. In choosing a career in science, he had fled from the I and WE in favor of the IT. The scientist works with problems which, at least in theory, are capable of objective resolution. He seeks an understanding of natural phenomena whose behavior has been determined by a power greater than man. Scientists, Einstein included, have traditionally found it exceedingly difficult to apply scientific principles to the complex political and social problems of human society. The scientist is trained to examine a new theory with an acutely critical eye. This quality has traditionally made it very difficult for the scientist to take a strong stand on political questions where justice is rarely on one side. Usually, therefore, the scientist has found it easier to remain aloof from political struggles.[39] Isaiah Berlin, who has written about Einstein with perception and sympathy, states, "Perhaps [Einstein's] very gifts as a scientist led him to schematise, to oversimplify practical problems, including complex political and cultural ones, which allow of no clear-cut solutions. . . ." Berlin speculates that "there may exist a certain difference between the gifts of scientists and humanists."[40]

After 1947 Einstein experienced a growing sense of frustration occasioned by the ineffectualness of groups and individuals attempting to influence the course of the Cold War in a constructive way. To Ernst Straus Einstein spoke of having to divide his time between politics and his equations but, he continued, "to me our equations are far more important. For politics are only a matter of present concern. A mathematical equation stands forever."[41] On another occasion Straus reports that Einstein told him that there are no good ideas in politics. The ideas are all obvious, and the problem is to get people to act on them. Straus goes on to say that Einstein never tired of examining a scientific idea from every conceivable angle, whereas, with political ideas, he felt that the idea was clear, the problem was to state it effectively. "I think that the constant preoccupation that marked his scientific work," says Straus, "simply did not happen in his political thought."[42]

Otto Nathan disagrees sharply with Straus's assessment of Einstein's political thought. It is true, Nathan says, that Einstein was obsessed by science, that even on his deathbed he continued to search for a unified field theory. Nevertheless, he devoted a remarkable amount of time to political issues, particularly after 1945. Nathan's contention that Einstein thought very deeply about political issues, that he weighed the issues and questions with the utmost care, is borne out by Einstein's writings and by the passage of time which, again and again, has testified to the inherent soundness of Einstein's position.[43]

The comments of Berlin, Straus, and Nathan suggest something further in the comparison of political and scientific ways of thinking and problem-solving. Politics is a field of endless variables where the truth, or justice, of the matter may not reside on one side. Negotiation and compromise are necessary to resolve a problem. The scientist, on the other hand, searches for understanding of an objective truth which Leibnitz described as a "preestablished harmony." The scientist cannot negotiate a theory; nor can he compromise with a rival in order to arrive at a greater understanding of the truth. Einstein said of theoretical physics that it "demands the highest possible standard of rigorous precision in the description of relations. . . ." The theorist attempts to describe "the most simple events which can be brought within the domain of our experience . . . with . . . subtle accuracy and logical perfection. . . ."

The scientist must labor over a problem with no guarantee he will ever discover the truth. "The longing to behold this preestablished harmony," Einstein writes, "is the source of the inexhaustible patience and perseverance" required to persist in a problem without allowing oneself to "be diverted to more grateful and more easily attained ends. The state of mind which enables a man to do work of this kind. . .is akin to that of the religious worshiper or the lover; the daily effort comes from no deliberate intention or program, but straight from the heart."[44]

These comments by Einstein, which were made in 1918 in honor of Max Planck, provide a revealing explanation for Einstein's forty-year search for a unified field theory. Careful study of this speech, in conjunction with the foregoing comments on politics and science, also provides an important clue to Einstein's political ideas and actions. In the day-to-day politics of debate, negotiation, compromise, and the implementation of decisions whose consequences cannot be foreseen, Einstein was an outsider, as he himself freely admitted.

However, there is another realm of human affairs—the ethical behavior of individuals and groups, which, for want of a better name, may be referred to as moral politics. Just as Einstein's proposed world authority was to be concerned only with the most critical issues of war and peace and not with the details of governing each of the member states, moral politics is concerned only with the most fundamental philosophical and ethical questions of society and mankind. The regulation of all other affairs between individuals and states is the domain of the politics of compromise. In moral politics, there are certain truths which must not be compromised. Foremost is the commandment not to kill. The second truth is that each individual enjoys the God-given right to develop his powers to the fullness of his potential.

Clearly, Einstein's efforts to abolish war are an example of moral politics. The practitioner of moral politics must approach the truth with the same reverence, persistence, and rigorous precision as the scientific theorist. The truth in moral politics, like scientific truth, cannot be arrived at by compromise. If killing is wrong then mass killing is wrong, and it cannot be justified. Thus, in the case of nuclear warfare, the question is: What steps must be taken to prevent nuclear suicide? This is the approach Einstein took. It was not naïve or unworldly. It was, in truth, the only possible sane approach. The strategy of the worldly-wise politicians—to seek to use nuclear weapons to achieve temporary and illusory advantages against perceived enemies—was not sane. The naïve presupposition that nuclear superiority in an unstable and frequently anarchic world can achieve security without risking full-scale nuclear war was a product of the muddled thinking of practitioners of the politics of compromise and expediency in the context of the growing Cold War paranoia which shaped American foreign policy after 1945. Illustrative of this thinking is a 1948 State Department critique of a paper urging use of the bomb in the event of war, which stated that questions of policy "should be answered not so much on the basis of humanitarian principles as from a practical weighing of the long-run advantage to this country."[45]

Einstein, as a representative of the thinking of moral politics, said we must deal with first things first. If we fail to control nuclear weapons, then the time will come when they will annihilate life on earth, and political cleverness will be helpless to save the planet, and all short- and long-term advantages accrued by nuclear war or nuclear blackmail will be meaningless. To control nuclear weapons, man must cease immediately to use these weapons as bargaining chips and tools of partisan politics. All mankind must be saved, or all will perish. To arrive at this understanding, one need not possess the intellect of Einstein but, like Einstein, one must possess a reverence for all life, the persistence to achieve the abolition of war whatever the difficulties, and one must be guided by a rigorous demand for truth in moral politics which is akin to the rigor required of the scientist.

13

The Road Toward General Annihilation

B y 1947 relations between the United States and the Soviet Union were so poisoned by threat and propaganda that every act by one side was interpreted by the other side to be part of some coherent master plan. In January 1947, the predecessor of the CIA, the Central Intelligence Group (CIG), reported several examples of Soviet behavior which appeared to signal a more conciliatory attitude. The Soviets had made concessions on Trieste, reduced the occupation forces in Eastern Europe, relaxed their stance on the Security Council veto, and expressed a willingness to begin drafting peace treaties for Germany and Austria. Instead of exploring the possibility that these gestures might lead to a thaw in Soviet-American relations, Washington interpreted them as devious moves designed to advance Stalin's plans for world domination. To meet this perceived threat, the United States embarked on a program that it announced to be defensive, but which actually resulted in an enormous expansion of America's political, military, and economic role in the world.[1]

The anti–New Deal Republican Eightieth Congress had been elected in November 1946 to cut government spending and income taxes, and it was not in a mood to vote enormous increases in the defense budget. To convince Congress of the urgency of the moment, Truman needed to dramatize the crisis in Europe. Late in February the British provided the issue when they informed the administration that they could no longer afford to give military aid to Greece, where a Communist-led guerrilla movement threatened to topple the pro-Western Greek regime.

The guerrillas were supplied by Yugoslavia, Albania, and Bulgaria, but Stalin, conscious that Greece was within the Western sphere of influence, had actually directed the Greek Communists to refrain from violence.[2] This was the first but certainly not the last time a civil war involving Communist guerrillas would be interpreted by Washington as proof of Soviet expansionism. On March 12, Truman addressed Congress on the Greek crisis. The central theme of the speech was the struggle between communism and democracy. The policy he proclaimed, known as the Truman Doctrine, warned that the United States would "support free people who are resisting attempted subjugation by armed minorities or by outside pressures."[3] The Truman Doctrine speech achieved its desired effect as an aroused and worried Congress soon voted large increases in foreign aid and the military budget. In response to Truman's speech, Walter Lippmann noted that intervention to maintain the balance of power is justified and necessary, but that indiscriminate intervention in support of unstable client regimes is wasteful and dangerous.[4]

The Truman Doctrine signaled an abandonment of diplomacy. Ever since the time of de Tocqueville, Europeans have noted a characteristic American impatience to achieve a desired goal, be it riches or power. Consequently, there has been a pronounced tendency to focus on present advantages without adequate consideration of future ramifications of an action. Stalin exploited this tendency in his dealings with the Truman administration, which lacked the patience, understanding, and flexibility necessary to resolve problems without recourse to threats and force.[5] Toughness and superior American technology appeared to promise quick advantage against the foe, whereas compromise, concession, and efforts to improve Soviet-American understanding could, the administration reasoned, only be interpreted by the Soviets and domestic critics as weakness.

The delusion of power blinded the American leaders to the precariousness of their thinking. Richard Barnet, a student of Soviet-American relations, has noted: "[T]hose with power easily convince themselves that they do not need to understand their adversaries. Those without power know they cannot afford not to understand."[6] In the fall of 1945 Lippmann warned that America's newly acquired world power must not be misjudged, and thereby misused, as had so recently been the case in Germany and Japan. America must learn how to measure its power and how to appreciate the possibilities it offers within the context of its limitations:

> Nothing is easier . . . [he wrote] than to dissipate influence by exerting it for trivial or private ends, or to forget that power is not given once and forever but that it has to be replenished continually by the effort which created it in the first place. The wisdom which may make great powers beneficent can be found only with humility, and also the good manners and courtesy of the soul which alone can make great power acceptable to others.
>
> Great as it is, American power is limited. Within its limits, it will be greater or less depending on the ends for which it is used.[7]

This advice was ignored by a Washington committed to a course of Wilsonian idealism and hard-nosed *realpolitik* to defend the free world and, not incidentally, to extend American political and economic influence. From the moment they learned that the Manhattan Project had succeeded in producing an atomic bomb, Byrnes, Groves, and Truman regarded it as the ultimate diplomatic weapon which emboldened them to impose demands on the Soviet Union which, ordinarily, they would not have advanced. By 1947, those who sought to understand the Soviet point of view were forced to defend themselves against charges that they were defending the enemy. At this time, Soviet propaganda was very effective in linking "peace" with Soviet foreign policy, and Truman, fearing that "wishful thinking" would weaken America, began to equate "peace" with "appeaser," "dupe," or "subversive." He was so successful in pushing the notion that preparing for war is the best way to peace that by the early 1950s any organization with peace in its title was suspected of Communist ties.[8] More than three decades later, it has become axiomatic on both sides of the Cold War that peace can best be achieved through preparation for war.

Einstein's efforts to abolish war and his unwillingness to play the Cold War propaganda game earned him a reputation of Russian sympathizer. To some, he was merely a dupe; to the more rabid anti-Communists, his activity was considered dangerously close to subversion. The FBI files contain numerous allegations of Einstein's association with Communist Party front organizations, including a report from the Office of Naval Intelligence dated February 10, 1948, entitled "Subversive Trends of Current Interest," which stated that Einstein was one of the backers of a plan to recruit 1,000 prominent Americans to call for the abolition of the House Committee on Un-American Activities. The report characterized Einstein as "one of the chief proponents of the Soviet inspired propaganda of fear." Other reports gathered by the FBI in this period assert that Einstein was not a Communist, but a well-meaning dupe who had been deceived and exploited by Communists playing upon his hatred of Nazism and fascism.[9]

It is true that the American Communist Party did use some organizations which Einstein supported. The actual influence of the Communists, and the extent of their infiltration was, however, grossly exaggerated by the distemper of the times. Furthermore, the myth that Einstein lent his name indiscriminately to any liberal-sounding movement is refuted by a careful study of the Einstein Archives, which provide numerous instances of Einstein's refusal to accede to requests for his support.

The real problem with the question of front groups was that as American politics became more reactionary and more rabidly anti-Communist in the late 1940s, almost any organization critical of the status quo came under suspicion. This, naturally, provided the Communist Party with an easy opportunity to exploit genuine reform movements—notably peace and civil rights organizations—for its own purposes. It is a fact of political life that when reactionary groups deny all peaceful and legal channels of reform and redress of grievances, unscrupulous extremist elements will always be found waiting in the wings to exploit the situation.

In the late 1940s Einstein refused to view the Soviet Union as the fount of all evil, and he attempted to establish a healthier dialogue with Soviet intellectuals. He had behaved in a similar manner in Germany during and after the First World War, and had been similarly reviled by the political Right.

Einstein never had any firsthand contact with Russia. He turned down several invitations in the twenties and early thirties to visit the Soviet Union because of the suppression of individual freedom and his awareness that the regime would exploit his visit for their propaganda. In September 1946 the FBI received a report that Einstein had been offered Soviet citizenship. Allegedly Einstein had written to Stalin that he could not do so until he was told why Jewish scientists and intellectuals were not better treated. The State Department naturally deduced from this report that the Soviets wanted atomic scientists. Unless documentation is forthcoming, the story must be viewed with skepticism because this was a time when a lot of nonsense regarding the atomic bomb, atomic scientists, and Einstein himself was in the air.[10] The FBI certainly took the story seriously, for a month later, when Einstein, Helen Dukas, and four friends innocently took a brief vacation at the home of friends in Cumberland, Maryland, the Baltimore division of the FBI recorded their whereabouts and monitored the area newspapers, including that of the local high school.[11]

Einstein believed in a democratic socialist economy which gave full measure of protection to the rights and needs of the individual and, at first, he viewed the Russian Revolution with sympathy and optimism until the brutal means employed by the regime to limit individual freedom became known. However, even after 1945, he never considered the Soviets to be the main threat to world peace. Prior to 1945, Einstein's first concern had been the defeat of Hitler, and afterward his greatest concern was the abolition of war and the international control of atomic weapons; Soviet actions were always viewed within the context of these two critical issues. During the Second World War, when the support of the Soviet Union had been essential, he rationalized the internal policies of repression and erroneously asserted that Russian Jews were being treated fairly when, in fact, since the prewar period the Russians had followed a policy of forcibly assimilating Jews. After 1945 when the overriding issue for Einstein was the need for an effective world government, he felt it was essential that the United States and the Soviet Union discover a way to cooperate. As a result, in the years 1945–1947 Einstein played down the significance of Stalin's responsibility for the Cold War impasse, and he continued to search for a means of securing Soviet cooperation in international relations long after the Cold War had become institutionalized.

Shortly after the war ended Einstein wrote a statement for a conference that never convened in which he was highly critical of American policy against Russia. "Who is the potential enemy that serves as a target of all these maneuvers?" he asked. "Who creates such fear among the American people that they should be obliged to accept permanent military bondage? The answer is that it is the same Russia which, so far, has been the leader in the search for international security and the most loyal supporter of the League of Nations."[12] When Russia made clear its unwavering opposition to world government, Einstein, although disappointed, blamed Russian xenophobia on the treatment the Soviet Union had received from the Western powers ever since 1917—the support by the West of the Soviet regime's enemies, political and economic boycotts, appeasement in the face of fascist aggression in the thirties, and the ill-fated attempt at Munich to turn Hitler's expansion to the East. Russian isolationism was as logical as it was unfortunate, but, Einstein believed, postwar Russian expansion into Eastern Europe was for reasons of security rather than world conquest. In a letter written in 1953 he dismissed his correspondent's contention that there was a danger the Communists would overthrow the American government and then added: "Eastern Europe would never have become a prey to Russia if the Western powers would have prevented German aggressive fascism under Hitler which grave mistake made it necessary afterwards to beg Russia for help."[13]

By the end of 1947, in response to Russia's refusal to cooperate, he began to advocate that plans for a world government proceed without the Russians. He was careful to emphasize that extreme care should be taken to gain their confidence by permitting them observers at every session of the organization and operation of the world government, and no secrets should be withheld from them. He hoped that this would impress upon the Soviet leaders the futility of aggression so that, in time, Russia would wish to become a full member of the world government.

Privately, Einstein was already highly critical of much of what was happening in the Soviet Union, but he refrained from making his criticisms public for fear of adding to the prevailing warlike atmosphere. In addition to impatience with Russia's attitude to world government, Einstein discovered on several occasions in 1947 and 1948 that fair dealings with Stalin's Russia were next to impossible.

From May until December 1947 Einstein became peripherally involved in the attempts to rescue the Swedish hero of the Holocaust, Raoul Wallenberg, who had disappeared from Budapest in January 1945 while in the "protective" custody of Russian soldiers. In early 1944 the U.S. War Refugee Board asked the neutral Swedish government to assist in the efforts to save the remnants of Hungarian Jewry, which by then was the last large surviving Jewish population under Nazi control. The Nazis, led by Adolf Eichmann, were feverishly attempting to eradicate the 500,000 surviving Jews before the Russians reached Budapest. Wallenberg, the thirty-two-year-old son of a wealthy Swedish banking family, arrived in Budapest on July 9, 1944, and for the next six months waged a one-man war against the Nazis' "final solution." He had been given full diplomatic accreditation as third secretary of the Swedish legation in Budapest. By January 1945 he had distributed at least 20,000 Swedish passports to Jews and had managed to shelter 13,000 Jews in "safe" houses he had rented, over which flew the Swedish flag. Defying the Nazis, he literally pulled people out of the death marches and distributed Swedish papers to Jews already imprisoned in the deportation trains and then demanded their release.

Wallenberg, financed primarily by American funds, had been trained as an architect in the United States and in the months he spent in Budapest he had drawn up plans for a rehabilitation program for postwar Budapest. Russian troops entered the city on December 24, 1944, but did not defeat the Germans until February 14, 1945. On January 17, apparently on a mission to secure Russian help to quash Nazi-instigated terrorist gangs, Wallenberg disappeared behind Russian lines. For four decades his fate has remained a mystery. At first the Russians admitted that he had been under their protection but by 1947 they denied this and put out the story that he had been killed in street fighting in Budapest. The contradictory stories, fueled over the years by vague reports of a Swedish prisoner in Russia, convinced his family and friends that he is still alive. They have speculated that the Russians, already at odds with the United States over Eastern Europe's future, took him for a spy. His capitalist background, charmed life under Nazi rule, endless supply of money, and rehabilitation plans which certainly conflicted with Russian plans for Budapest's future, undoubtedly made him suspect in Russian eyes. Despite the fact that he enjoyed diplomatic immunity, the Swedish government passed up several opportunities through the years to confront the Soviet Union on this issue.[14]

In May 1947 journalist Dorothy Thompson wrote Einstein to acquaint him with the case and solicit his assistance in the efforts to free Wallenberg. Her letter documents the prevailing view that Einstein was a Russian sympathizer. She wrote: "Your long friendship and wish for cooperation with the Soviet Union, may now stand you in good stead in performing an act of signal justice."[15] Einstein declined to act at that time because he did not know any Russian official and he felt that any action he might take would adversely affect the situation.

A week later he received another request for assistance from Wallenberg's half-brother, Guy von Dardel, who was a physics student at Cornell University. Einstein replied on June 6 that until he could find a realistic way to be of help, it was important to avoid any action which might be harmful to Wallenberg. Speculating that the Russians were living in a "perpetual persecution complex" which caused them to suspect all foreigners of espionage, Einstein concluded that the only reasonable approach would be to open personal channels in an informal way to bring the situation to the attention of influential Russians. As he did not know any, Einstein could only renew his offer to help if the proper occasion came along.

Von Dardel responded on June 9 with a request, repeated on October 20, that Einstein write a brief personal letter to Stalin. Late in October Einstein consented to write Stalin, and von Dardel on November 8 suggested the wording, which Einstein subsequently used verbatim. In addition, von Dardel requested that Einstein support efforts to nominate Wallenberg for the Nobel Peace Prize, which he also agreed to do, although he noted that he was only permitted to nominate in the categories of physics and chemistry. The letter to Stalin, dated November 17, 1947 read:

Dear Mr. Stalin:

As an old Jew I appeal to you to do everything possible to find and send back to his country the Swede Raoul Wallenberg, who was one of the very few who, during the bad years of Nazi persecution on his own accord and risking his own life, worked to rescue thousands of my unhappy Jewish people.[16]

Einstein sent the letter to the chargé d'affairs at the Soviet Embassy in Washington so as to prevent it from falling into the hands of the American press. He explained to the chargé that he was acting for reasons of conscience, and not out of political considerations. A month later, the embassy reported that Stalin had received the letter and that a search failed to produce "any positive results."[17] In a final letter to von Dardel on December 22, Einstein noted, "It is clear that the remarks [of the chargé d'affairs] refer to investigations which allegedly have been made before."[18]

Einstein's failure to help secure Raoul Wallenberg's release from the Soviet Union would not be surprising under ordinary circumstances. However, by the time of this incident a period of extreme brutalization, even by Stalin's standards, was under way. Stalin's immediate postwar foreign policy included a significant demobilization of Soviet forces. But after two years of escalating Cold War tensions he embarked on a heavy-handed program of military build-up designed to counter the growing threat of nuclear war and to consolidate his empire. Soviet society was more isolated from external observation at the end of the war until Stalin's death in 1953 than at any other time in its history. The period of recovery from the war was a bleak time for the Russian people, not only because of the accelerated process of rebuilding but because of the dark impulses tormenting Stalin's psyche. Solzhenitsyn has written that the Soviet army was thrice betrayed; first on the battlefield, second when the millions of captured soldiers were abandoned to starve in Nazi prison camps, and finally when the repatriated prisoners of war were shipped en masse to gulags. At the same time Stalin was pardoning war deserters. Solzhenitsyn asks: "[Did Stalin] simply conclude that cowards represented no danger to his rule and that only the bold were dangerous?"[19]

In 1946 Stalin began a series of cultural purges whose chief targets were Western intellectuals and artists like Picasso, Sartre, and Einstein. Sometimes Soviet interference in science has been heavy-handed, most notably in the notorious genetics fraud by T. D. Lysenko, who claimed that environment and not heredity determines the development of the individual. Generally speaking, Soviet political interference has been more sophisticated than the Nazi attempts to achieve racial purity in science. Because of the practical value of physics and mathematics, theories like Einstein's work in relativity have been denounced in philosophical journals while the scientists have been left alone to pursue researches which made significant contributions to Russia's drive for modernization.

In *Materialism and Empiriocriticism* written in 1908, Lenin had charged that those who taught there could be more than three dimensions were theologians masquerading as scientists.[20] Since that time relativity theory had been suspect among some Bolshevik ideologues for its links to Western idealist philosophy. Beginning in 1946, relativity was condemned as "cosmopolitan," and followers of Einstein in the Soviet Union were attacked for their worship of foreign models and a lack of reverence for Russia's culture and achievements. Abstract theory was labeled "formalism," which is a preoccupation with theoretical problems that have no relation to life.

Einstein's persistent advocacy of world government and universal disarmament eventually provoked an attack by four Soviet scientists. In the October 1947 issue of the magazine *United Nations World* Einstein asserted that the traditional view of national sovereignty must be modified and that a popularly elected General Assembly, not the veto-shackled Security Council, should be the dominant force in a world authority. On November 26, 1947, four Soviet physicists and chemists responded with an article entitled "Dr. Einstein's Mistaken Notions"[21] which praised his character but charged that in advocating world government he was the unwitting tool of the capitalists who were using world government as a pretext to extend their imperialistic designs. This dogmatic response, Einstein noted with regret, reflected an unwillingness to put aside propaganda for the sake of securing an answer to the question of world peace. It almost certainly represented the more or less official view of Einstein held by Moscow at the end of 1947.

In 1948 rumors were rife of preventive war against Russia while America still enjoyed its atomic monopoly and Soviet-American relations lurched from one crisis to the next. Because of the irresponsible talk emanating from Washington, Einstein felt that America constituted a greater menace to world peace than even the Soviets. As America moved toward a permanent war economy and a major build-up of aviation power, Walter Lippmann wrote in January 1948: "We shall be repeating the supreme error of powerful states— which is to think that power is a substitute for diplomacy, and that absolute power gives absolute security."[22]

Stalin began to consolidate his empire in February 1948 by instituting a crackdown on the non-Communist elements in liberal Czechoslovakia, a move which strengthened Washington's fears that Stalin had embarked on a policy of world conquest. Secretary of Defense James Forrestal and Air Force Secretary Stuart Symington spoke privately of preventive war, using atomic bombs against the Soviet Union. Fearing Russia was about to make a move in Germany and in other parts of Europe, Truman acted with haste to frighten Congress and the public into support of four key administration programs: the Marshall Plan, a return of the draft, an expanded aviation budget, and a universal military training program.

The call for universal military training was widely supported. Einstein vehemently opposed it because he believed that it inculcated a spirit of militarism, that it would lead to an acceleration of the arms race, and that it corrupted the democratic spirit of the youth with authoritarian discipline. In peacetime a regular army composed largely of technicians was, he felt, all that was necessary.[23]

Einstein's opposition to the militarization of American society should not be interpreted to mean that he opposed every activity of the military in society; rather, it was the "basic pattern" that he found to be so dangerous. Instead of responding to all problems with military answers, he maintained that political leaders ought to be guided by the question: "What can we do in the prevailing situation to bring about peaceful coexistence among all nations?" The conquest of mutual fear and distrust was more important in the long run than institutions like courts of justice and police.[24] The democratic ideal, George Kennan has written, is to increase enlightened social attitudes through education and social progress, not to make war to achieve democracy's purposes. War ought to be a last resort to defend and protect the democratic state from external danger.[25]

Einstein strongly supported the intent of the Marshall Plan to help achieve the economic recovery of Western Europe, but he felt that it was a program which ought to be sponsored by the United Nations to avoid giving the Russians the feeling that it was aimed against them.[26] Stalin, in fact, did view the plan as an attempt to turn Western Europe into an armed anti-Soviet camp. In response, he increased the pace of sovietization in Eastern Europe.

Matters came to a head in June 1948 when the Soviets began the Berlin blockade in a desperate attempt to thwart secret Anglo-American efforts to create a state of West Germany. Throughout the summer there was nervous talk of war in both Moscow and Washington. Army Secretary Kenneth Royall undoubtedly expressed a popular military attitude when he complained to the President: "[W]e have been spending 98 percent of all the money for atomic energy for weapons. . . . Now if we aren't going to use them, that doesn't make any sense."[27] The dramatic Berlin airlift defeated the blockade, which Stalin finally lifted in 1949. The American leadership, still oblivious of postwar Soviet economic weakness, assumed that only Stalin's fear of the atomic bomb had prevented him from making war during the Berlin crisis.

Shortly after the imposition of the Berlin blockade, Einstein and Otto Nathan were invited to attend a World Congress of Intellectuals to be convened in Wroclaw, Poland, in August 1948. The preceding fall, at the suggestion of Leo Szilard, the Emergency Committee of Atomic Scientists had attempted to arrange such a gathering in Jamaica. Einstein's support for the Jamaica conference was so strong that he stated that he would be willing to attend if boat transportation could be provided for him. Ultimately the plan was abandoned after the State Department indicated a total lack of interest and the Soviets claimed that their scientists "did not wish to participate."[28] Although Einstein was unable to attend the Wroclaw conference, he and Nathan carefully prepared a statement describing the role of the intellectual in achieving lasting world peace through the creation of a supranational world government. As it turned out, the conference was carefully stage-managed by the Soviet and Polish Communists. Nathan was told to delete passages in Einstein's message referring to world government. When he refused, the conference leaders, without consulting Nathan and during his momentary absence from the meeting, arranged to have read to the conference a letter Einstein had written two months earlier to the organizing committee of the conference, claiming that this was Einstein's message. Einstein immediately released the text of the suppressed message to the *New York Times* to set the record straight.

This incident was particularly disturbing to Einstein. As a longtime champion of international intellectual cooperation, he believed that voices of reason from intellectuals of the hostile countries could serve to sustain a healthy exchange of ideas which might eventually promote improved understanding among the peoples and leaders of the respective nations. The exchanges with the intellectuals from the Communist countries disabused Einstein of this cherished belief, at least as long as Cold War tensions remained at fever pitch.

Shortly before the Wroclaw incident Einstein assured one correspondent that he was "not blind to the serious weaknesses of the Russian system of government and I would not like to live under such government. But it has, on the other side, great merits and it is difficult to decide whether it would have been possible for the Russians to survive by following softer methods."[29] After the Wroclaw conference his private comments about life in the Soviet Union became somewhat less guarded. Soviet scientists and intellectuals were "humiliated" and Russian society conveyed a depressing impression of a "complete lack of objectivity, moderation, and ease."[30]

For the rest of his life Einstein remained privately critical of Soviet society, but he refrained from joining in the chorus of American Cold War critics of Stalin's system because, as he wrote to the great American socialist Norman Thomas in 1954, American criticism, however well intentioned, was futile. In the letter to Thomas, Einstein summarized his postwar attitude toward Soviet society:

> Russia is, in a very clear sense, a "politically underdeveloped country," about like Europe at the time of the Renaissance and a bit later. Murder, with and without legal accounterments, has become a commonplace means of daily politics. The citizen enjoys no rights and no security against arbitrary interference from the power of the state. Science and art have become wards of those who govern. All this is certainly abominable to the taste of modern civilization. But I believe that it is the problem of the Russian people to make changes there. We cannot advance a progressive development by threatening Russia from the outside. Similarly, our well-intentioned criticism cannot help because it will not come to the ears of the Russians.[31]

By the summer of 1948 political dialogue in the United States was not very healthy either. The Czech crisis followed by the Berlin blockade had coalesced domestic anti-Communist sentiments, and critics of American policies were increasingly under attack from Red baiters. Einstein was so disgusted with Truman's reckless handling of foreign policy that he vigorously supported the quixotic, third-party presidential candidacy of Henry Wallace in 1948. In a speech in September 1946 Wallace urged the government to recognize the reality of Stalin's spheres of influence, advised Great Britain to give up its "imperialistic" policies which seemed to be no more justified than Russian activities in Eastern

Europe, warned of the folly of the "get tough" policy, and also criticized Russian attempts to spread communism. Einstein warmly endorsed Wallace's position, but Truman, sending a clear message of toughness to Russia, fired Wallace on September 20, 1946.

In the 1948 campaign Wallace condemned the anti-Communist mania which was sweeping the country. He declared his opposition to the militarization of society, and he called for an opening of negotiations with the Soviet Union to end the Cold War. He supported such advanced social programs as federal health insurance, the protection of women's rights in the economy, and racial desegregation. Wallace, however, was not a good politician and, in addition to his failure to develop support from liberals and labor, he was unable to disprove Truman's charge that the Progressive Party was a Communist front. Truman was aided by a statement of the secretary of the American Communist Party that Wallace was Roosevelt's heir. Wallace's disappointing showing at the polls marked the nadir of American liberal politics in the postwar era. A few months after the election, in a letter to Henry Wallace concerning his opposition to the creation of NATO (it "is a horror in my eyes"), Einstein described the prevailing attitude in American politics as "imperialistic and half-fascistic."[32]

In an article published in November 1947 Einstein expressed his disillusionment with the events of the preceding two and a half years. "The atomic scientists . . ." he wrote, "have become convinced that they cannot arouse the American people to the truths of the atomic era by logic alone. There must be added the power of deep emotion which is a basic ingredient of religion."[33] Unfortunately, the Cold War propagandists' skillful manipulation of the public fear of Soviet plans for world conquest had proven far more successful than the attempts to outlaw atomic weapons and war, so that by the end of 1948 it was apparent that the Cold War had settled in for a long siege. Any chance for an effective supranational government with control over atomic energy had been missed and the events of 1948—the Berlin blockade, the Communist takeover of Czechoslovakia, the purge trials in Hungary, the Stalin-Tito rift, the Communist gains in China, the war between Arabs and Jews in the new state of Israel and the depressing ineffectualness of the United Nations—had overwhelmed Einstein and many of the atomic scientists and peace activists then associated with him.

Late in 1948 the Emergency Committee of Atomic Scientists suspended its activity. In addition to the developments of the Cold War, several factors conspired to doom it. The provision in its nonprofit charter which prohibited the committee from trying to influence legislation hamstrung operations and frequently caused internal divisions over policy. It was often difficult to assemble the trustees, and when they did meet they could not agree on whether to push for partial world government or to hold out for a more total realization of the goal. In endeavors of this kind, Einstein's greatest contribution usually was his famous name and his renown as one of the preeminent moral figures of the century. Einstein was very active, on a daily basis, with the workings of the Emergency

Committee, and was in constant contact with the committee's branch office in Princeton. More than at any other time in his life he participated in the formulation and execution of policy.

The Emergency Committee remained inactive until 1951 when it was disbanded. Its assets were contributed to the *Bulletin of the Atomic Scientists,* despite the recommendation of Einstein and Szilard that they turn the money over to the American Friends Service Committee. For the rest of his life Einstein generally avoided organizational activities, preferring instead to take his stand as an individual.

Dr. Eugene Rabinowitch, editor of the *Bulletin of the Atomic Scientists,* worked closely with the Emergency Committee in its active period. He opposed disbanding the committee, believing instead that it ought to have transformed itself into a more permanent "general staff" of the scientists' movement. He felt that the committee represented a successful first step in the long process of educating the politicians and the public, and he chided those scientists who, disappointed by the lack of quick results, were unwilling to take part in the long struggle ahead.[34]

In the summer of 1949, talk of preventive war against the Soviet Union continued to fill the air. Truman and his advisers persisted in the belief that the American monopoly of the atomic bomb would last another five to fifteen years. The American public, too, had been led to believe that America still monopolized the bomb's "secret." They had been warned by the scientists that no secret existed, but the scientists were no match for the political propagandists. Then, on September 23, 1949, President Truman stunned the nation with a report that Russia had successfully detonated an atomic weapon. For the next six months policymakers in Washington were in a state of near-panic over the horrible prospect that the Soviet Union might already possess nuclear superiority.

The Soviet Union had been at work on the atom bomb for two years by the time Truman informed Stalin of the new American bomb at the Potsdam Conference. Just as Hans Bethe and other atomic scientists had predicted, it took only four years for the Soviets to duplicate the work of the Manhattan Project. By then, however, the American public, induced to believe that an actual "secret" existed, had grown so fearful of the image of the supposed Communist conspiracy, that news of the Soviet bomb confirmed their worst fears. The myth that spies, and not the passage of time, had deprived the United States of its atomic monopoly threw citizens and politicians into a state of panic which has never entirely abated.

In consequence of the security mania which began with the Manhattan Project and the misguided belief that an atomic secret could be denied the Soviets, the United States had made itself hostage to a growing obsession with potential espionage. Revelations of the 1946 Canadian spy case and the Alger Hiss scandal in 1948 intensified the efforts to purge the government of alleged traitors. Toward the end of 1948 the National Security Council listed the following groups to be watched for Soviet espionage, subversion, and sabotage: European émigrés, ethnic minorities, "intelligent people . . . who . . . have a perennial weakness for 'causes,'" and "various youth and women's organizations."[35] The assault on civil liberties in the guise of loyalty oaths and inflammatory congressional hearings was already well under way before September 1949.

On February 3, 1950, a German-born physicist who had been employed at Los Alamos, Klaus Fuchs, confessed that he had been spying for the Soviet Union since the war. This revelation reinforced the fiction that Russia owed the possession of atomic weapons solely to espionage. In the ensuing hysteria, it was forgotten that there was no real secret to begin with and that whereas the Soviets had only developed a plutonium bomb, Fuchs's work at Los Alamos had been primarily in the area of uranium enrichment. After years of misperceptions, faulty hypotheses, and frightening propaganda, it was hardly surprising that Americans had lost the ability to view their Cold War adversary with the reasoned objectivity which enlightened action would have required.[36]

For the next several years, hysterical rhetoric drowned out the few voices of reason. On February 9, 1950, the then obscure Wisconsin Senator Joseph McCarthy delivered the first of his notorious speeches claiming to have in his hand a list of the names of card-carrying Communists working in the State Department. The age of McCarthyism had begun.

Three days before the Fuchs confession, President Truman, on the basis of seven minutes of cabinet-level discussion,[37] had announced that the United States was embarking on a crash program to develop a hydrogen bomb—the "super." Even though this was peacetime and there was no declared emergency, Congress and American citizens were excluded from the decision process. The decision to escalate the arms race was a direct consequence of America's lost atomic monopoly.

As early as August 1945 Robert Oppenheimer had submitted a report to Secretary Byrnes outlining possible future developments in atomic energy, including the hydrogen bomb, a weapon whose destructive potential was thousands of times greater than the bombs dropped on Japan. Oppenheimer recommended that the terrifying nature of this weapon made international control even more imperative. Byrnes, already committed to his vision of atomic diplomacy, said no. If hydrogen bombs could be made, then the United States must be the country to make them.[38]

In 1947 Edward Teller attempted to win the support of the Emergency Committee of Atomic Scientists for his vision of the "super." When Einstein indignantly rejected his overture, Teller complained that the man who had warned Roosevelt in 1939 was guilty of inconsistency. Teller, unlike Einstein, believed the Soviets were as great a threat to world security as Hitler had been.[39]

By October 1949 research on the "super" had been so unpromising that the General Advisory Commission of Scientists headed by Oppenheimer recommended to the Atomic Energy Commission that it not embark upon a crash program to develop it. Privately, Oppenheimer expressed his belief that insufficient reflection had been given to the political implications of such a hasty decision, and he, along with many other scientists, felt a profound moral repugnance for the weapon. His rather restrained opposition led directly to his disgrace and political downfall four and a half years later during the height of McCarthyism.

Einstein, ca. 1950. Photo by Marcel Sternberger. (Courtesy of Margot Einstein)

Einstein viewed the escalation of the arms race with undisguised horror. On February 12, 1950, he appeared on a television broadcast hosted by Eleanor Roosevelt to discuss the implications of the hydrogen bomb. Reviewing the consequences of a policy which he described as "security through superior force, whatever the cost," Einstein noted that American militarization at home and abroad was proceeding at an unprecedented pace; a growing domestic police force was supervising the loyalty of its citizens; political dissenters were subjected to harassment, and the arms race between the Soviet Union and the United States has assumed "hysterical proportions." "If [efforts to build the hydrogen bomb] should prove successful," he said with deep feeling, "radioactive poisoning of the atmosphere and, hence, annihilation of all life on earth will have been brought within the range of what is technically possible. The weird aspect of this development lies in its apparently inexorable character. Each step appears as the inevitable consequence of the one that went before. And at the end, looming ever clearer, lies general annihilation."[40]

Three years earlier, Einstein had been asked what weapons would be used in the third world war. He is alleged to have replied; "I don't know. But I can tell you what they'll use in the fourth—rocks!"[41]

14

A Princeton Landmark

T he town of Princeton experienced a period of dramatic growth in the postwar period as the last great estates were broken up. Led by RCA and the Educational Testing Service, numerous large corporations began to build research centers in the outlying districts of Princeton. Construction of new schools, houses, and stores increased dramatically, and Princeton at mid-century was in the process of being transformed from a quiet university town into a burgeoning suburban center, whose population nearly doubled in two decades.

In this period, as Einstein was emerging from his self-imposed wartime silence to assume a leading role in the crusade to educate the world about atomic energy, his activities became more and more confined to Princeton for reasons of privacy and health. Despite his American citizenship, he had remained, at heart, a European. Although he had always been cognizant of the many shortcomings of American society, his sincere gratitude to his new homeland and his overriding concern for the defeat of Hitler had muted his criticism of America during the war. In the postwar era, his critical observations of America's social, political, and economic life occurred more frequently.

After the war, Einstein experienced a tinge of homesickness for the haunts of his youth. His letters to old friends like Besso, Solovine, Max Born, and Elizabeth, the Queen Mother of Belgium, are often colored by nostalgic references to the uncomplicated days before the First World War when his time had been occupied by science, the violin, and outings in the lakes and mountains of Switzerland. More than once he confessed a desire to return to Europe but, because of his health and the fuss he knew he would be subjected to, he never seriously considered making the trip. Often during these years he sought out people who could provide him with reliable information about postwar Europe.

In the spring of 1946 Senator Claude Pepper of Florida, a leading liberal who had been critical of Truman's attitude toward the Soviet Union and had interviewed Stalin in 1945, spoke at Princeton University about his recent trip to the Iron Curtain countries. Einstein attended, and afterward he invited the Senator to Mercer Street to learn more about conditions in Eastern Europe.

Senator Pepper brought with him several undergraduates and their faculty adviser who later described the meeting in Einstein's living room as a "sparring match"[1] in which the two men questioned each other at cross-purposes, Einstein eager to discuss Eastern Europe and Pepper far more interested in relativity. Eventually, Pepper prevailed and Einstein described how he had first begun to think about light when he was about sixteen years old.

In 1947 Einstein's admired colleague Max Planck died in Germany. Despite Planck's disappointing behavior at the time Einstein resigned from the Prussian Academy, Einstein's admiration for Planck as a scientist had never wavered. Planck had suffered terribly; one son had died in the First World War and his other son had been executed in 1944 after being implicated in the abortive plot to assassinate Hitler. Recalling the happy hours they had spent together discussing physics and making music in Berlin, Einstein wrote a moving letter to Frau Planck expressing his admiration for her husband and his feelings of gratitude for all that Planck had done for him. "How different, and how much better it would be for mankind," Einstein reflected, "if there were more like him. But this cannot be; it seems that fine characters in every age and continent must remain apart from the world, unable to influence events."[2]

Mileva Einstein died in Zurich in August 1948. Hers had been a hard life. She had never reconciled herself to the divorce, and her bitter feelings had strained relations between Einstein and their sons, particularly with Hans Albert. She had suffered periodic bouts of melancholy (her sister was mentally ill), and Eduard the younger son, whom Margot Einstein remembers as a very sensitive, kind, and poetic soul, suffered from schizophrenia.

Einstein's postwar feelings about Germany on the one hand, and German individuals on the other, are very revealing. He could never forgive the Germans for their crimes against the Jews. His cousin Lina Einstein was murdered at Auschwitz; Bertha Dreyfus, another cousin, perished at Theresienstadt. During the war he had compared the mentality of the Germans to "the mentality of an ordinary band of gangsters,"[3] and to the end of his life he refused to have anything whatsoever to do with the land of his birth. He maintained that the rehabilitation of Germany through "moral persuasion" was impossible. When he was invited in 1949 to rejoin the Kaiser Wilhelm Institute, renamed in Max Planck's honor, he bluntly refused. "The crime of the Germans is truly the most abominable ever to be recorded in the history of the so-called civilized nations. The conduct of the German intellectuals—seen as a group—was no better than that of the mob. And even now, there is no indication of any regret or any real desire to repair whatever little may be left to restore after the gigantic murders."[4]

Beside this unyielding attitude toward the Germans must be set an incident recounted by Ernst Straus. Some time after the war, a distinguished mathematician who had become a German citizen after the Nazi takeover of his homeland came to visit Princeton. Several professors at Princeton University and the institute circulated a letter protesting his visit. Einstein was asked to sign, but when Straus explained the issues involved, Einstein was shocked. "You mean," he asked, "they want me to sign something just to harm another human being?" With that the petition was thrown in the trash.[5]

Einstein took his responsibilities as an American citizen especially seriously, as the following story told by Judge Philip Forman testifies. Judge Forman had presided over the ceremony at which Einstein, Helen Dukas, and Margot Einstein had become citizens in 1940, and a warm friendship between the judge and Einstein had grown out of that occasion. Shortly after the war, the President had proclaimed an "I Am an American Day," a patriotic day (now forgotten) which was particularly meaningful to naturalized Americans. The judge "caught a bit of the fever" and arranged for an outdoor ceremony to induct new citizens on that day at Cadwallader Park in Trenton. Invitations were sent out to all new citizens of the previous ten years. To Forman's delight and amazement, approximately 10,000 citizens, families, and friends attended, including Einstein, his daughter, and his secretary, although they had received no special invitation. More than three decades later, Judge Forman warmly recalled that for much of the ceremony Einstein sat with a small girl on his lap.[6]

Einstein was more frequently critical of various aspects of American society in his later years than he was in the period before 1945. He felt that the most offensive aspect of life in the United States was the unjust treatment of its black citizens. The "worst disease" in American society, he once wrote, is "the treatment of the Negro. Everyone who is not used from childhood to this injustice suffers from the mere observation. Everyone who freshly learns of this state of affairs at a maturer age, feels not only the injustice, but the scorn of the principle of the Fathers who founded the United States that 'all men are created equal.' "[7]

There was a genteel strain of racism in Princeton which reflected the wealth and intellectual orientation of the town. Princeton University was known as the northernmost Southern school because of its large numbers of white Southern students. (When the Civil War broke out residents of the town forcibly evicted Southern students who had seized Nassau Hall.) Just before the First World War Paul Robeson, who was born three blocks from Princeton University's Nassau Hall, was discreetly advised to enroll at Rutgers rather than Princeton. In its September 25, 1942, issue the *Princeton Herald* agonized in an editorial over the question of admitting blacks to the university. It concluded that although blacks should be afforded the same rights and opportunities as whites, Southerners would be offended by the presence of blacks in their classes, and, in light of the university's dependence upon and responsibility to its Southern undergraduates, the *Herald* decided that integrating the university was a noble idea whose time had not yet arrived. The university remained almost totally segregated in the years Einstein lived in Princeton, and although a few black students did attend the university on the G.I. Bill after the war, substantial numbers of blacks entered it only after the civil rights movement of the mid-1960s forced the issue. When Einstein arrived in Princeton, there was a separate section in the movie theaters for blacks, shoe stores would not permit blacks to try on unpurchased shoes, and the grammar school system remained segregated until 1947. (The only high school in town had been integrated in the late 1920s.)

Every year universities and colleges from around the world invited Einstein to accept honorary degrees, which he referred to as "rolls of ostentation."[8] By the mid-1930s he had adopted a policy of declining all such offers because he was unwilling to attend the ceremonies, but in May 1946 he made an exception to this practice when he accepted an honorary degree from Lincoln University in Pennsylvania as a way to demonstrate his support for Negro education. A few months earlier he had written an article for *Pageant* magazine contrasting race prejudice with America's tradition of equality. "The more I feel an American," he wrote,

Einstein addressing students at Lincoln College, May 1946, on the occasion of receiving an honorary degree. Peace Photo. (Courtesy of Margot Einstein)

"the more this situation pains me. I can escape the feeling of complicity in it only by speaking out."[9]

In response to two major race riots in Northern cities and six lynchings in the South in 1946, he endorsed a public appeal to President Truman in September to put an end to lynching. The cure for race prejudice, he realized, would require education and enlightenment; much time and patience would be needed to undo the damage caused by traditional racist values.

At the dedication of the Wall of Fame, which honored illustrious immigrants and Negroes, at the 1940 New York World's Fair, Einstein declared:

> As for the Negroes this country still has a heavy debt to discharge for all the troubles and disabilities it has laid on the Negroe's [*sic*] shoulders; for all that his fellow-citizens have done and to some extent are still doing to him. To the Negro and his wonderful songs and choirs we owe the finest contribution in the realm of art which America has so far given to the world. And this great gift we owe, not to those whose names are engraved on this "Wall of Fame" but to children of the people, blossoming namelessly as the lilies of the field.[10]

In the late 1930s Einstein and Margot became friends of Marian Anderson, whose renditions of the Negro spirituals affected them profoundly. He also loved her versions of some of his favorite German songs, especially Schubert's "Death and the Maiden." Once when Miss Anderson gave a concert in Princeton, she was refused a room at the Nassau Inn, whereupon Einstein invited her to be his house guest. Thereafter, whenever she sang in Princeton, she would stay at Mercer Street. Margot had a parakeet named Bibo who could say, "Beautiful, oh how beautiful" and "Give me a little kiss" and once when Miss Anderson was visiting the Einsteins, she went upstairs to Margot's room to practice before her concert. She was unaware that Bibo was in his cage covered for the night, and as she began to practice, he sang "trruu, trruu, trruu . . ." Miss Anderson broke out laughing, and when she was able to regain her composure, another less vocal practice room was provided for her.[11]

Although Einstein had suffered major physical breakdowns in 1917 and 1928, and had been on a restricted diet for many years, his health was generally good, and he remained robust well past his sixtieth birthday. After the Second World War his health began to falter, and at the end of 1946 he became so weak that he expected an early death. His condition was diagnosed as acute anemia, and with a proper diet he was able to regain his lost strength and weight. For several years he had suffered recurrent attacks of upper abdominal pain accompanied by vomiting which usually lasted a couple of days. In the autumn of 1948 a surgeon, Dr. Rudolf Nissen, diagnosed a grapefruit-sized growth in the abdomen. Einstein agreed to undergo an experimental laparotomy (exploratory abdominal surgery) at the Jewish Hospital in Brooklyn in December. Dr. Nissen discovered an aneurysm in the abdominal aorta. Today surgery might correct the problem, but techniques for such an operation did not exist in 1948. Throughout his stay in the hospital he remained cheerful and invariably claimed that he felt fine. Some time in 1950 it was determined that the aneurysm was growing. Einstein and a small circle around him knew that eventually the aneurysm would burst, but Miss Dukas reported to Abraham Pais shortly after Einstein's death that he "waited for [death], calmly and smilingly."[12]

After his release from the hospital in mid-January 1949, he quietly traveled to Florida with Helen Dukas and his son Hans Albert for a month's recuperation. By the end of February he was back in Princeton, still weak, but ready to resume his work. His assistant, John Kemeny, remembers being aware that Einstein was ill, but he did not realize that it was serious. When Banesh Hoffmann, who had not seen Einstein in a decade, saw him a few months after the operation, he was shaken by the profound physical change he saw. "He looked so fragile," Hoffmann recalls. "Fragile is the word that keeps coming to me. He had lost weight and he walked with great carefulness, the way old people do sometimes, and he was definitely an old man then. Nevertheless, a year or two later he looked much his old self, although he never really came back completely from the operation so far as his general looks are concerned. . . . I would say his sense of humor and wit were still there in full measure, but the energy, the *ésprit* was not there to make it bubble out."[13]

As a concession to his doctors and Helen Dukas, Einstein did curtail his pipe smoking. When Elsa Einstein was alive she had waged a constant and generally losing battle to reform his smoking habits. After the 1948 operation, Einstein made a serious effort to reduce his tobacco intake, and there are several amusing incidents related by colleagues and friends concerning his ordeal. When he received some tobacco as a present, he would give it to his friend Erich Kahler, but then would ask to be allowed to sniff it. At work he would vainly try to limit himself to one match per day, or he might shred his assistant's cigarettes. But most of the time, as he confessed to Dr. Bucky in 1950, he was reduced to sucking on a cold pipe and, he admitted, he did feel better.[14]

Although he was forced to make concessions to his ebbing physical strength, his daily routine remained essentially undisturbed. The simple, quiet existence which he had long enjoyed in Princeton permitted him to marshal his strength for the things in life that really mattered: science, family and friends, and the pressing public issues of the age. He would take breakfast around nine o'clock, read the newspaper, usually the *New York Times,* and at about ten o'clock, weather and health permitting, he would walk to the institute, often in the company of an assistant or a friend like the mathematician Kurt Gödel. He would work for a couple of hours and then return home for lunch around one o'clock, again, if possible, on foot and in the company of colleagues. After lunch he would rest for a while and then after a cup of tea, resume work, answer mail, receive visitors, or attend to political questions. After dinner he would continue work, listen to the radio or, occasionally, receive a visitor. On Sunday afternoons he might go for a walk or take a car ride with friends. Rarely in his later years did he attend concerts, plays, movies, or lectures.

Einstein officially retired from the institute on April 15, 1945. Normally this would have been deemed a newsworthy event by the American press, but the announcement, coming as it did three days after the death of President Roosevelt, was lost in the shuffle. His retirement had no impact upon his activities at the institute, but it did open the way for the appointment of Wolfgang Pauli to the position of visiting professor of theoretical physics. At the same time Kurt Gödel, a brilliant mathematician who had been a temporary member since before the outbreak of the war, was made a permanent member. Einstein was extremely fond of both Pauli and Gödel. In 1944 the three men had met at Mercer Street on several occasions with Bertrand Russell to discuss problems in the philosophy of science. Russell later wrote that he eventually gave up in frustration because the others were philosophical idealists "and in spite of our utmost endeavours we never arrived at common premises from which to argue."[15]

The sight of Einstein and Gödel talking and walking between Mercer Street and the institute was a common one after 1940. Gödel, a very solitary, reserved logician, was one of the greatest mathematicians of the twentieth century. Gödel's proof, put forward in 1931, showed that complex logical and mathematical systems including arithmetic, must remain, in some respects, incomplete; that is to say, there exist certain propositions whose truth cannot be determined within that system. He demonstrated this by producing a true theorem, the formal proof of which led to a contradiction. Gödel distrusted common sense as a means of discovering the truth, and is reputed to have resisted becoming an American citizen for several years because he had discovered logical contradictions in the Constitution.[16]

Pauli had been at the institute in 1935–1936. As a Viennese Jew in Switzerland he was invited to the institute when war broke out. He was in Princeton from 1940 to 1945 and, aside from Einstein, was the only physicist on the faculty of the institute prior to the arrival of Robert Oppenheimer in 1947. As a young man he had made a fundamental contribution to quantum mechanics by his discovery of the Pauli exclusion principle. He was somewhat critical of Einstein's work, but at one point they did write a joint paper. He was awarded the Nobel Prize in physics in December 1945, and at the dinner given by the institute in Pauli's honor, a very happy Einstein spoke with deep affection about his personal relations with his younger colleague.

In the first year after the war the institute came back to life. John von Neumann began to organize his controversial computer project. Flexner had conceived the institute as a haven for theoretical work, and in 1945 it had neither facilities nor a tradition for experimental work. Einstein, while not especially enthusiastic about the idea, felt that if von Neumann wanted it, the institute ought to provide space and assistance. By November 1945 von Neumann, greatly assisted by his colleagues James Alexander, Marston Morse, and Oswald Veblen, had persuaded Aydelotte and the institute's trustees to locate the project at the institute. The computer project, funded by the institute, the army, the navy, and eventually the Atomic Energy Commission, commenced operations in March 1946. John Kemeny, who worked with Einstein in 1948–1949, recalls that Einstein registered a mock complaint to von Neumann that the computer, which at the time performed

Einstein and Kurt Gödel, Princeton 1954. (Photo by Richard Arens)

only numerical computations, could not help with *his* complicated mathematical problems.[17]

In the autumn of 1947 Frank Aydelotte was succeeded by Robert Oppenheimer as director of the institute. After the stormy Flexner years, Aydelotte had restored feelings of good will between the faculty and administration. Aydelotte, whose tenure as director from 1939 to 1947 had been disrupted by the war, accepted his retirement gracefully but not willingly. He felt that he still had some good years left in him and that his service had entitled him to attempt to implement some of his long-deferred ideas now that the war had ended.[18]

Oppenheimer's appointment to the institute had been engineered by trustee Lewis Strauss, who was also a member of the Atomic Energy Commission. Oppenheimer's growing commitments in Washington in the immediate postwar period had made it next to impossible to resume his prewar positions at the California Institute of Technology in Pasadena and the University of California at Berkeley. Princeton, a three-hour train ride from the nation's capital, resolved the problem of geography. The recent director of the Manhattan Project became the first director of the institute to hold, simultaneously, a faculty appointment.

Oppenheimer, as discussed earlier, is one of the great enigmatic personalities of recent American intellectual history. Blessed with a brilliant mind, an incisive, occasionally savage wit, and a keen interest and knowledge of a wide range of subjects, he inspired the fiercest sort of loyalty and devotion among his admirers. Yet there was in his makeup a fatal flaw, and his great gifts, his charm and wit, created on occasion implacable enemies. He was indeed a paradox. Usually he was extraordinarily sensitive in both human and scientific relations, yet he was capable of lapses in tact which were as avoidable as they were egregious. More than one prewar friend who had not been associated with him at Los Alamos was made to feel that his newfound fame and power had gone to his head.

During the war, original research in all fields of physics had been subordinated to the war effort, and 1947 witnessed a spate of new ideas and experiments as physicists resumed their research. As a result of his wartime work, Oppenheimer was the most celebrated American physicist and, under his direction, the orientation of the institute shifted dramatically from pure mathematics toward theoretical physics, with particular emphasis on quantum theory. He was no longer active in research, but his ability to attract younger physicists turned the institute into a "center for physics"[19] (and his ability to stimulate the younger researchers remained strong). He invited new members from all over the world and created new forms of long-term temporary appointments. However, in the process he unnecessarily antagonized the members of the School of Mathematics. Regarding Einstein's search for a unified field theory, most of the younger physicists shared Oppenheimer's critical opinion that "Einstein is a landmark, but not a beacon."[20] His criticisms of Einstein's later work were sufficiently frequent and so careless that on one occasion the faculty of the institute asked him to curb them.[21] Although the two men respected each other's abilities, differences in age and temperament precluded close relations.

Princeton, with an outstanding assemblage of mathematicians and physicists at both the institute and the university, was by this time an equal in pure research of any of the great European centers. After the institute opened an internationally flavored nursery school primarily for the children of visiting and permanent members, Einstein, ever the impudent Swabian, is reputed to have quipped that the most advanced study at the institute was taking place at the nursery school.[22]

March 14, 1949, was Einstein's seventieth birthday. While congratulatory messages poured in from all over the world, Einstein, still weak from his recent surgery, celebrated the day quietly with a few friends at home. The fuss over his birthday made him uncomfortable. When, at this time, his old friend and colleague Leopold Infeld sent him a letter discussing a scientific problem, Einstein replied, "I appreciate it that you did not send me birthday greetings. It was, anyway, as if I had attended my own funeral."[23] His dietary restrictions prohibited him from eating his birthday cake, but when asked by one of his friends if he was sorry, he answered, "No, I'm not sorry at all. I can remember distinctly how it tasted. And, you know, this is what I resent with Gandhi; he never knew how these things tasted."[24] There followed a roar of laughter. He disliked being fussed over, and in general was embarrassed by presents. He did, however, enjoy relaxing with ingenious construction puzzles and gadgets based on sound scientific principles which friends often brought him. One visitor a few years later noted that Einstein's study was littered with stacks of books, manuscripts, papers, a picture of Gandhi, and a variety of toy games which, Einstein had explained, provided a welcome tonic from his calculations.

For his seventieth birthday, his colleagues at the institute, led by Erwin Panofsky, conspired to surprise him with an FM tuner and a high-fidelity record player. Herman Goldstine, one of the younger members of John von Neumann's early computer project, was enlisted to build the apparatus in the computer project machine shop. All faculty members shared in the cost and great secrecy prevailed. On the morning of his birthday, Miss Dukas telephoned Goldstine the moment Einstein left home for his office, and he rushed over to Mercer Street to install the hi-fi system and radio antenna. (Goldstine was rewarded for his efforts with a speeding ticket on Mercer Street, which, to this day, remains one of Princeton's most notorious speed traps.) Einstein was delighted by the gift, which brought his favorite music into his home and helped to fill the gap created when he gave up playing the violin.

On March 19, more than three hundred scientists gathered in Princeton to pay tribute to Einstein's scientific achievements. S. M. Clemence, Robert Oppenheimer, I. I. Rabi, H. P. Robertson, Hermann Weyl, and Eugene Wigner discussed Einstein's contributions to science and some of the work which had been inspired by his theories. Weyl spoke about the mathematical work which had been suggested through problems of general and special relativity. Robertson, who had been at Princeton University when Einstein arrived in 1933, discussed problems of cosmology and described some of the work being done in this field in California. Wigner especially remembered the affection and admiration for Einstein felt by those assembled. "We didn't honor him so much," he recalled; "we expressed our appreciation—or at least I expressed my appreciation—for his personality, for his kindness. You know, he was a very, very famous person. He could have thrown his weight around. He never thought of that. He was kind, companionable, friendly and modest."[25]

As an indication of that modesty, Einstein was genuinely distressed by the thought that so many important people would "have a sense of obligation to come and see the old man." He felt this was a terrible imposition, particularly because he had been isolated in his scientific work since the 1930s and sometimes referred to himself deprecatingly as an "old relic." John Kemeny recalls Einstein's discomfort, which was due both to his modesty and his inability to appreciate how deeply all physicists revered him. According to Kemeny even physicists who thought that Einstein's search for a unified theory was wrong absolutely revered Einstein. "People fought over tickets like mad," Kemeny remembers. "I had nothing to do with the tickets, but people somehow thought that being Einstein's assistant I had some pull, and more big shots came to me begging for an extra ticket. They were absolutely dying to get in, and Einstein just had no sense at all about what absolute reverence there was for him."[26] Abraham Pais recalls that most in attendance were already seated when Einstein entered. There was a brief, awed hush before the audience recovered and stood to greet him with heartfelt applause.[27] After the conference, Wigner saw Einstein and expressed surprise that he was not more tired after having listened to so many lectures, especially in view of his recent operation. Einstein smiled and said, "I would be tired if I had understood them all."[28]

In later years, on very rare occasions, Einstein would hold a seminar at the institute to discuss his current work. To prevent an invasion by the press and other curious laymen, announcements of these gatherings were made by word of mouth. Abraham Pais has described these occasions as "lucid, inconclusive, and otherworldly," because, he explains, with the dramatic advances in quantum electrodynamics and the discoveries of new particles, this was a time in which "the gap between Einstein's physics and the physics of younger generations was ever widening."[29]

In 1949 a collection of essays written by physicists and philosophers titled *Albert Einstein: Philosopher-Scientist* and edited by Paul Arthur Schilpp was published. Also contained in this large volume was an essay, "Autobiographical Notes" written by Einstein in 1946. The essay is a mere forty-five pages, three-quarters of which is an excellent scientific autobiography. Although the nonscientific reader may find several sections difficult to understand, this essay provides the most revealing exposition of how Einstein thought about science. It also contains some fascinating comments about his childhood and his early interest in religion and science.

In 1950 he permitted the publication of *Out of My Later Years*, a volume of occasional essays, conference papers, and addresses written between 1933 and 1950 dealing with his religious, moral, political, and scientific values, as well as a number of pieces treating Jewish and Zionist problems. Writing to a friend at the time, Einstein confessed that he was ashamed of having said so many obvious things, but he had permitted the publication of these essays because he hoped they might have a good effect "in a time which in its sophistication is blind to the most elementary matters."[30]

In 1954 a larger, more wide-ranging collection of essays and short writings titled *Ideas and Opinions* was brought out. Sonja Bargmann, wife of Einstein's former assistant Valentine Bargmann, acted as a general editor who, in addition to participating in the selection and editing of the various essays and shorter pieces, also served as official translator. In this latter capacity she checked previous translations for errors (and, she remembers, there were some egregious mistranslations), made revisions and supplied new translations where necessary. She had often done translation work for Einstein after the war, and she has described her informal working arrangement with him as an extremely gratifying collaboration. They would review the final draft together, checking for proper word choice and idiomatic phrasing, so that her translations were always authorized.[31]

Einstein's writing was clear and succinct. Sonja Bargmann recalls that he took a genuine interest in language, and despite his difficulties with English, he had a good feeling for its nuances. His pronunciation of English was never very good, and although he occasionally mixed German words into English conversation, he could express himself with exactitude and was careful to make subtle distinctions

Sonja Bargmann, Valentine Bargmann, and Helen Dukas, ca. 1970. (Courtesy of Sonja and Valentine Bargmann)

in the meaning of English words. In 1944 he explained to Max Born that "I cannot write in English, because of the treacherous spelling. When I am reading, I only hear it and am unable to remember what the written word looks like."[32] Nevertheless, in his later years he sometimes did dictate his correspondence in English, although something important was always written first in German.

After his operation in December 1948, Einstein rarely ventured forth from Princeton. And so, the world came to Einstein. The highlight of a trip to Princeton in those years for visiting dignitaries, scientists, and artists was an interview with Einstein if one could be arranged. Among his visitors in the later years were William Faulkner (who was tongue-tied in Einstein's presence), Adlai Stevenson, and India's Prime Minister Jawaharlal Nehru, who visited Einstein's home on November 5, 1949. Einstein had long been an admirer of Gandhi and Nehru and the nonviolent methods they had practiced in winning independence from the British. Nehru had been in the United States since October 11 on a state visit and his program had been fully scheduled by the State Department. Before returning to India he had one free day, and his associate Amiya Chakravarty, an Indian scholar and longtime friend of both Albert and Margot Einstein, wrote to Einstein, the "last and the one personal visit that he will make will be to Princeton to offer to you his own and India's reverence for you."[33]

Accompanying Nehru were his sister, Madame Pandit, who was Ambassador to the United Nations, his daughter Indira Gandhi, and Amiya Chakravarty. Einstein usually received visitors alone in his study, but on special occasions he received them in the living room and invited the ladies of the house to join. For an hour and a half Einstein and Nehru spoke of peace and war and the dangerous world situation. In Gandhi's spirit, they agreed one should always avoid war if at all possible, but that in the case of Hitler, war had been unavoidable. They also discussed India's role in world affairs. Einstein had begun to think that the countries with less military power, through close cooperation, might make a significant contribution to world peace by putting pressure upon the two great powers to settle their differences peacefully in the United Nations.

On November 9, 1949, Chakravarty thanked Einstein on behalf of Nehru.

This was a memorable and happy day for us all, [he wrote] and Mr. Nehru repeatedly told us that the great expectation of his life has been fulfilled. For years he had cherished the hope of meeting you, and it seems that at last he had the privilege at a crucial stage of his own life when he feels that he stands at the cross-roads and must now take the right direction for India in a world split up by power blocs. Evidently, his conversation with you that day has strengthened his conviction that India must stand outside the two big blocs and seek rather to build up and strengthen a peoples' government which would increasingly represent the millions in East and West who do not want a global war.[34]

A few days after Nehru's visit, an azalea was delivered to 112 Mercer Street as a thank-you present. It was planted in front of the house and referred to ever after by Margot Einstein and Helen Dukas as the Nehru azalea.

On March 18, 1950, Einstein signed his last will and testament. A short while before, Otto Nathan had visited Princeton. Einstein was at the top of the stairs, and instead of offering the usual greeting, "Hello, Nathan, *wie gehts?*" he said, "Nathan, I had an excellent idea, come up, I want to discuss it."[35] Einstein had decided to use his papers, correspondence and writings, and the copyrights of his books to set up a trust for his stepdaughter and his secretary. Provisions for the care of his bedridden sister, Maja, were also made. Otto Nathan was designated sole executor of the estate, and he and Miss Dukas were named jointly to serve as

Einstein and Nehru, November 5, 1949. (Courtesy of Margot Einstein)

trustees of the literary estate. The trustees were empowered to sell any of Einstein's letters and papers in order to provide for the welfare of the women in his household. After the death of Margot Einstein and Helen Dukas, he directed that his papers be given to the Hebrew University in Jerusalem. He bequeathed his violin to his grandson, Bernhard Caesar Einstein, son of Hans Albert.

Maja Winteler-Einstein died on June 25, 1951. Throughout Einstein's life she had been his closest friend, the one person who had known him as child and man. She had suffered a stroke in 1946 which led to increasing incapacitation due to arteriosclerosis and in the last years of her life she had been bedridden and her speech impaired. Her mind remained clear and sharp, and her brother continued to read to her from Bertrand Russell, Shaw, and other favorite authors almost to the last days of her life. "But there was also much that was beautiful," he wrote to a friend of Maja's, "in those evening hours in which I read to her from the most excellent books of all peoples through the ages."[36] As much as possible she was included in the activities of the household, and at the conclusion of Nehru's visit to Einstein in 1949, the Indian Prime Minister was led upstairs to meet Maja because she had been so eager to meet him.

In Maja's last years, she suffered from a hopeless longing for her beloved Italy. Her husband, Paul Winteler, who had remained in Europe, wrote her long weekly letters in the quaint language of *Switzerdeutsch* (Swiss-German). After her death, Einstein, his face pale, drawn and tense, sat quietly on the back porch with Margot. At length, pointing to the trees and the sky, in his quiet manner, he said to her, "Look into nature *(in die Natur),* then you will understand it better. . . ."[37]

15

"Jewish Saint"

The defeat of the Germans did not end the anguish of the survivors of the Holocaust. The 100,000 Jews still in concentration camps and the 200,000 displaced persons were thoroughly traumatized, hungry, and diseased. The victorious Allies found it necessary to keep them in survivor camps that were not much more palatable to these refugees than Hitler's camps had been. Homeless and unwilling to rebuild their lives in Europe, they wanted only to emigrate to Palestine, but for this to happen it was necessary for the British to reverse the policy of the 1939 White Paper. For a number of reasons they refused, and the results were disastrous.

By 1939 Ben-Gurion had reached the conclusion that Jewish safety could be secured only through the creation of a Jewish state. The war and the Holocaust settled the issue, and by the end of 1942 the goal of statehood had been adopted as official Zionist policy. After their bitter experiences with the British, they were determined never to be compelled to leave their fate in the hands of others. Jewish terrorist activities in 1944 and Roosevelt's death in April 1945 undermined Churchill's support for a partition of Palestine. In late July 1945 the Labor Party, which had pledged support for Zionism during the campaign, took office. Ernest Bevin was installed as Foreign Minister. After a month of studying the material prepared by the Foreign Office and having familiarized himself with the British Middle Eastern policy of dominance of the region on the basis of Arab nationalism subservient to British interests, Bevin abandoned the campaign pledge. The key to the British policy remained the 1939 White Paper. In November 1945 Bevin announced his intention of implementing its program. The door to Palestine—the only hope of the remnants of European Jewry—had again been slammed shut. To the Zionists, this was a declaration of war.

In July 1945 President Truman had called for unlimited immigration into Palestine, but within a month he had become more cautious. Nevertheless, as illegal immigration increased and American citizens, politicians, and Jews clamored for immediate provision for 100,000 immigrants to Palestine, relations between Washington and London became increasingly bitter. In an effort to take the heat off his government and also to implicate the United States in the political nightmare of Palestine, Prime Minister Clement Attlee announced in December the formation of a twelve-man Anglo-American Committee of Inquiry on Palestine, one of whose members was Frank Aydelotte, Director of the Institute for Advanced Study.

As the committee assembled in Washington in January 1946, the most pressing issue was the question of Jewish immigration. The Arabs opposed any further immigration. The British, in debt to Egypt and Iraq, fearful of Soviet intentions in the Middle East and desperately trying to maintain control of their crumbling empire, did not dare to antagonize the Arabs. And the Zionists, determined to control Jewish immigration into the region, were firmly committed to the creation of a Jewish state as the only means to guarantee the future of Jewish Palestine. The United States, eager to demobilize its wartime army and obsessed with Soviet activity in Eastern Europe, was unwilling to commit troops to assist the British in the Middle East, nor was Congress in a mood to relax the rigid immigration laws to permit substantial numbers of refugees into America. President Truman was also caught between the contradictory promises of his predecessor to the Zionists and Arabs over the issue of Palestine, and with America's growing dependence on Arab oil, he felt he could not risk alienating the Arab world.

Einstein, who later in the year was to decline an invitation to resettle in Palestine for reasons of health and the desire to safeguard his privacy, appeared as a witness before the committee on January 11, 1946.

By this time the members of the Palestine Committee were annoyed at the manner in which the well-organized Zionists had presented their case, although Rabbi Stephen Wise had made a very positive impression upon even the British, who had been made to feel thoroughly uncomfortable by the steady criticism of their administration of the mandate. The day before Einstein spoke, the American Arabs overstated their case. Einstein entered the hearing room while another witness was speaking, but as soon as the heavily Zionist audience recognized him, it burst into applause. Order was quickly restored, and when Einstein's turn to speak came, Judge Hutcheson, head of the American delegation, told the crowd that they were now free to give "an appropriate welcome to Dr. Einstein." Again there was great applause. Einstein observed to a friend, "I think they ought to wait first to see what I say."

"Smiling benignly" he launched into the most "wholehearted denunciation" of Great Britain's Palestine policies the committee had heard. British colonial rule was notorious for siding with the big landowners to exploit the natives, he asserted, describing Palestine as a "small model of India." The Colonial Office was responsible for fomenting clashes between Arabs and Jews because it feared that if the two peoples united to live in peace, they would quickly discover that they had no need for British rule. The British had pursued this policy of divide and conquer by sabotaging the Balfour Declaration through restrictions on immigration and on land purchased by Jews and by tolerating the behavior of the corrupt Arab landowners who systematically incited the Arab masses against the Jewish settlers. Jewish agriculture and industry had raised the Arab standard of living and this threatened the landowners whose position depended upon the continuing poverty and ignorance of the peasantry.

Einstein labeled the committee a "smokescreen" created to give an impression of good will when, in reality, the British fully intended to impose their own policies. He proposed that Palestine be administered by an international trusteeship until it was ready for home rule, and that the great majority of European refugees be settled there immediately.

Up to this point the audience "purred contentedly" while both British and American members bristled at his blunt criticisms of the committee and British policy. Following a series of questions about the offending statements, he was asked his opinion about the form of government which he would recommend for Palestine. Einstein replied, speaking softly, that a Jewish majority in Palestine was not important, and that he had never been in favor of a Jewish state: "The state idea is not according to my heart. I cannot understand why it is needed. It is connected with many difficulties and a narrow-mindedness. I believe it is bad." He preferred that an international regime govern Palestine in such a manner that both Arab and Jew could live in harmony. The audience was stunned. Richard Crossman, the British committee member most sympathetic to the Zionist cause, later wrote: "The audience nearly jumped out of their seats."[1]

American Zionist leaders were equally surprised. Three days later Rabbi Wise wrote Einstein two carefully phrased letters thanking him for his helpful testimony—"all but your word of doubt at the end with regard to nationhood for the Jewish people." He enclosed a copy of a clarifying statement he hoped Einstein would sign to undo the damage of his endorsement of bi-nationalism. "Any reference to *bi-nationalism* at this time," Wise continued, "might be exceedingly hurtful in the hearing of a Committee which is not too friendly to us." The enclosed statement read, in part:

> As National Home I consider a territory in which the Jews should have such rights that they can integrate freely within the limits of the economic absorptive possibilities and that they can purchase land without undue encroachment on the Arab peasant population. The Jews should have the right of cultural autonomy, their language should be one of the languages of the country, and a government should exist, working under strict constitutional rules that guarantee is given to both groups that no "Majorisation" of one group by the other is possible. There must be no discriminatory laws against the interests of either group.

Einstein was willing to comply with Wise's request but preferred that his statement be given directly to the Anglo-American Committee of Inquiry, and not to the Jewish press where inevitable additional controversy would blunt any favorable influence his statement might have upon the committee. That he was not entirely satisfied with this statement is evident in his final remark to Rabbi Wise: "I believe furthermore that a solution on the basis of an honestly bi-national character is the only one we can hope for and I am firmly convinced that a rigid demand for a 'Jewish State' will have only undesirable results for us."[2]

After hearings in London, Cairo, and Palestine and visits to refugee camps in Europe, the committee members retired to Lausanne, Switzerland, to write their report which, they agreed, must be unanimous. The report was submitted to Attlee and Truman on April 20 and made public ten days later. After much debate, compromise, and sifting of the voluminous evidence, the committee reached conclusions surprisingly similar to Einstein's ideas. They recommended the repeal of the 1939 White Paper, the immediate admission of 100,000 immigrants to Palestine, the continuance of the mandate with United States assistance until a binational state could be set up under the United Nations and the institution of a campaign to improve the Arab standard of living.

The committee also recommended that the Jewish army, the Haganah, not be disbanded because such an act would insure military operations against the Jews and bring on the war that the report had sought to prevent. While Truman focused attention upon the immigration recommendation and ignored the other proposals, especially those concerning America's obligation to assist the British in the execution of the mandate, Attlee seized upon the continued existence of the Haganah as a pretext for burying the report. The committee members had hoped that implementation of their proposals would help undo the political damage the White Paper had inflicted upon Jewish moderates like Weizmann. Attlee's rebuff dashed these hopes, and the desperate Zionists armed for the struggle to evict the British and fortify themselves against their hostile neighbors by stepping up illegal immigration and acts of terror. Golda Meir summed up the attitude of the Palestinian Jews when she declared, "We kept hearing the argument 'The Arabs can create so much trouble, therefore you have to give in.' So in the end we decided, very well, *we'll* create trouble."[3] According to Nicholas Bethell, author of *The Palestine Triangle,* most Israelis believed that if Great Britain had accepted the report and, in addition, admitted something like 25,000 refugees into England, and if the United States had admitted 50,000, the maximalist demands for the immediate creation of a Jewish state would have been blunted, the moderate position would have been restored, and terrorism, which had never before enjoyed wide support, would have been crippled. This also would have defused Arab complaints that the Western democracies were dumping their Jewish problem on the Middle East.[4]

While the committee was deliberating in Lausanne, Einstein wrote to his old Berlin friend Dr. Hans Mühsam in Haifa about the Palestinian crisis: ". . . one can say what one thinks, but the facts . . . will be determined mainly by the small brain—that is, by the 'men of action.' " In a letter to Richard Crossman dated June 3, 1946, Einstein praised the attempt of the committee "to achieve justice under precarious conditions." Regarding Attlee's response, Einstein noted, "You will now agree that my remark was not quite unjustified; I mean the remark that in the eyes of the British government the Commission was looked upon only as a smokescreen."[5]

Acts of terrorism steadily mounted in 1946, culminating with the destruction of the King David Hotel on July 22, 1946, by a bomb planted by the terrorist organization, the *Irgun Zvai Leumi*, whose leader was Menachem Begin. Ninety-one Arabs, Jews, and Britons were killed, and from this time on a state of undeclared war existed. The British had never devised a constructive policy toward Arab and Jewish leadership, and now they discouraged and even frustrated attempts for Arab-Jewish cooperation, while senior British officers openly expressed anti-Semitic feelings.

Einstein's letters to Dr. Mühsam at this time document his reactions to the escalating violence and his often incisive perceptions of the root causes. He believed that, in addition to the British and the terrorists on both sides, the Jews themselves for decades had mishandled the situation. Ever since 1917 they had placed too much faith in the British and had neglected their relations with the Arabs. "Unfortunately," he wrote in January 1947;

> it has to be admitted that we attend poorly to our rights. We can't agree on a central political representation. The successful ones among us behave "centrifugally." With respect to Palestine we have advocated unreasonable and unjust demands under the influence of demagogues and other loudmouths. Our impotence is bad. If we had power it might be worse still. We imitate the stupid nationalism and racial nonsense of the *goyim* even after having gone through a school of suffering without equal.[6]

The British began to imprison the illegal immigrants on the island of Cyprus in August. Writing to Mühsam in April 1947, Einstein fumed: "If I had to give orders [in Palestine], I would leave the people in peace, but send the Arab as well as the Jewish politicos to Cyprus and incarcerate them together so that they can bicker in leisure among themselves. . . ."[7]

In the bitter winter of 1946–1947, Great Britain, still in the grips of the postwar economic crisis, reached the breaking point on the issue of Palestine. After the decision to grant independence to India, Palestine had lost some of its strategic significance for the crumbling empire. As the British became fed up with terrorism, the government decided on April 2, 1947, to rid itself of a headache by returning the mandate to the United Nations, as the successor to the old league. The United States opposed the move because of fears that the Soviet Union would veto partition. However, in May Andrei Gromyko stunned the United Nations by announcing that his country would support the partition of Palestine. Although he did not say so, the reason was that it was the easiest and quickest way to get Great Britain out of Palestine. On September 1 the United Nations Special Committee on Palestine submitted its report calling for a partition of Palestine to separate Arab and Jewish states. The recommendation was adopted by the United Nations General Assembly on November 29, 1947, over the protests of the British, who refused to cooperate. From the time of the vote until their departure from Palestine on May 14, 1948, they adopted a passive attitude and refused to intervene in the civil war which broke out after the vote by the United Nations. While the British continued to sell arms to the Arabs, the United States terminated arms shipments to the Jews because of Arab threats of an oil embargo.

From December 1947 to early April 1948 the Haganah fought a defensive war, but this strategy, combined with British assistance to the Arab Legion, gave the Palestinian Arabs a marked advantage, and early in April the Haganah turned to the offensive. On April 9, 1948, the Begin-led Irgun, at odds with the more moderate Haganah, in an independent action killed 250 Arab civilians in the village of Dir Yassin. The number of panic-stricken Arabs emigrating from Palestine swelled to 300,000 by mid-May. At the time the Arabs believed the assurances of their leaders that they would return to Palestine victorious over the Jews as soon as the British withdrew. The massive Arab exodus reinforced Jewish nationalist feeling and, for the first time, led to a widespread call for creation of a homogeneous Jewish state.

On April 12 Einstein and Leo Baeck wrote an open letter to the Jews of Palestine and the world calling for an end to the violence. In their statement, published by the *New York Times* on April 18, they recognized the legitimacy of taking a defensive stance to protect one's home, but they appealed to the Jews of America and Palestine "not to permit themselves to be driven into a mood'of despair or false heroism which eventually results in suicidal measures." They called for the establishment of a homeland for the Jews "on a peaceful and democratic basis . . . in accordance with the fundamental spiritual and moral principles inherent in the Jewish tradition and essential for Jewish hope."[8] Less than a month later, however, Einstein was forced to admit that Jewish survival in Palestine required force. "We may regret that we have to use methods which are repulsive and stupid to us . . ." he wrote to a group of Jews in Uruguay. "But to bring about better conditions in the international sphere, we must first of all maintain our existence by all means at our disposal."[9]

On May 14, 1948, the state of Israel proclaimed its independence. The first act of the provisional government was to repeal the 1939 White Paper and open Israel to unrestricted Jewish immigration. In the ensuing three and a half years 687,000 immigrants from Europe, Africa, and Asia entered the new country. At the time of independence, the Jewish terrorist forces, the Irgun, surrendered their autonomy to the Haganah. On May 14, the British hastily evacuated Palestine and the United Nations moved in to secure the partition. The Arabs, who had comprised a large majority in Palestine prior to 1948, regarded Israeli independence as the result of the "eradication of Palestine," and as the British withdrew their forces the armies of Egypt, Syria, Transjordan, Iraq, and Lebanon attacked Israeli borders, in the expectation that Palestine would prove to be a military vacuum.

Instead of uniting in the common cause of restoring Palestine to the Arab natives, the Arab heads of state fought each other for the spoils of the country. Had they been united, they probably could have captured a significant amount of Israeli territory and annulled the partition. Instead, poorly organized and jockeying for position among each other, they were rudely surprised by the military strength and spirit of the Jewish defenders. Between May 15 and June 11, when the United Nations succeeded in imposing a one-month truce, the skilled Israeli forces routed their attackers and considerably extended their borders. By the end of the year, Egypt had been driven from the Negev Desert and its forces driven to the tiny Gaza strip. At this point Egypt sued for peace. At the conclusion of the hostilities, Transjordan and Egypt consumed the remnants of the Palestinian Arab State, and by early 1949 there were 700,000 Palestinian refugees, whose fate was of little concern to the Arab leadership, except insofar as they provided an ongoing pretext to oppose the existence of Israel.

Einstein continued to support the creation of a bi-national state in Palestine until the summer of 1947. As events reached a climax, he reluctantly accepted the impossibility of such a solution. On May 30, 1948, in a tribute to the new nation, he sharply criticized the weakness of the United Nations for compelling the Jews to fight for what was rightfully theirs while allowing outside states to intervene militarily against the United Nations decision for partition. While the fighting was still raging in September, he admitted to Mühsam that bi-nationalism was no longer feasible:

> You are quite correct in what you are saying about the perfidious attitude of England and the United States with respect to us. All the Arabs are only two-penny-halfpenny hirelings, who have to risk their lives for them. It seems to me that England is taking revenge and the United States are being obliging—actually, the Jews would have been safer allies than the Arabs, who, after all, have been double-crossing the English whenever the opportunity arose. I also think that in these last years an understanding between us and the Arabs which might have led to a bi-national administration was no longer possible. But previously—from 1918 on, really—we have neglected the Arabs and again and again trusted the English. I never considered the idea of a state a good one, for economic, political, and military reasons. But now, there is no going back, and one has to fight it out. At the same time, we must realize that the "big" ones are simply playing cat and mouse with us and can ruin us any time they seriously want to.[10]

"The big ones" were the United States and the Soviet Union.

Finally, on February 24, 1949, an armistice agreement between Egypt and Israel was signed. In the ensuing months, under the gifted mediation of Dr. Ralph Bunche, the U.N. Mediator for Palestine, similar agreements were reached with each of the hostile border states. After the Egyptian agreement, Einstein, recuperating in Florida from surgery, wrote to Mühsam: "There is now general rejoicing about Israel's success. The worst Zionist baiters have forgotten the past. What has been achieved can only be admired."[11]

To the end of his life Einstein remained a strong supporter of Israel but, as always, his support frequently took the form of incisive criticism. He worried about the excessive influence of narrow orthodoxy and the specter of Jewish nationalism. He supported a provision for conscientious objectors in the Israeli military service laws in 1949. With the memory of the destitute refugees from Hitler still fresh, he maintained that the greatest moral test facing the Jews of Israel was their handling of the Palestinian Arab refugee situation and the treatment of the Palestinian minority still residing within Israel's borders. Three months before his death he wrote: "The attitude we adopt toward the Arab minority will provide the real test of our moral standards as a people."[12] On the international scene, he recognized the dangerous influence the Cold War could exert on the fragile politics of the Middle East, and he strongly supported the idea that Israel, like Nehru's India, adopt a neutral stance.

There is no way of knowing if Einstein's ideas (which were shared by a minority of Jewish intellectuals and politicians) could have contributed to an easing of tensions in the Middle East because they were never given a chance. His fears of nationalism, Israel's insensitivity to the refugee problem, and its alignment with the West in the Cold War were justified by later events. Ben-Gurion's *realpolitik* was successful in establishing and defending Israel in the short run. The price it exacted, in terms of relations with the Arabs, and the concomitant triumph of Jewish nationalism at the expense of the spiritual and ethical ideals of the Jews, was enormous. Time alone will judge whether the price of victory came too high.

The discrimination practiced by European universities against Jewish students and professors had been one important reason for Einstein's decision to join the Zionist movement in 1919. The creation of Hebrew University presented an opportunity to redress this situation and, despite his stormy relations with the university between 1927 and 1935, Einstein remained one of its most loyal supporters. In the autumn of 1954, speaking at the Nassau Inn in Princeton to a gathering assembled to raise funds for the university in Jerusalem, Einstein declared that the function of a university is to produce "a spiritual and intellectual atmosphere in which creative individuals can develop. In our [Jewish] tradition," he continued, "it is neither the ruler nor the politician, neither the soldier nor the merchant who represents the ideal. The ideal is represented by the teacher, that is to say the person who is able, through his work and his efforts, to enrich the intellectual, moral and artistic life of his people."[13]

Soon after his arrival in Princeton in 1933 he had discovered that American universities maintained a subtle form of anti-Semitic discrimination by employing a quota system to keep the number of Jews in any one class from rising above a certain fixed percentage of the entire class. In March 1935, in a letter to Supreme Court Justice Louis Brandeis, Einstein expressed a desire to found a Jewish-sponsored university in the United States because he feared that the "ever-increasing negative attitude" in America would in time "push us out from the more desirable intellectual fields unless we succeed in obtaining a certain independence." He did not feel that Yeshiva College in Manhattan satisfied the need because of its "adherence to a narrow-minded ritual education."[14] Early in 1946 a group of Jews from New York and Boston took over the operation of a rundown college of veterinary medicine in Waltham, Massachusetts, which they intended to transform into a first-rate Jewish-sponsored university. Einstein was pleased to assist them, but he refused permission to name the university after him. He had asked Otto Nathan to work with him, and it was Nathan who suggested it be named in honor of Justice Brandeis. Einstein offered his support on the condition that the board of trustees and the administration of the college remain in reliable hands and that no important step concerning the organization be taken without his approval. By August the Jewish group, under the leadership of Rabbi Israel Goldstein, had been incorporated as the Albert Einstein Foundation for Higher Learning.

It did not take long before fundamental misunderstandings developed. Goldstein, who had a "flair for press releases,"[15] set about organizing fund-raising dinners and a publicity campaign. In April 1946 Einstein complained that he was not being kept well enough informed of the activities of the foundation bearing his name. The following month he refused to attend a fund-raising dinner which he characterized as nothing but a "theatrical performance"[16] and he expressed concern that financial considerations were taking precedence over the fundamental issues of academic organization and standards. He and Nathan hoped to pattern the new university after European, not American, universities. The greatest problem with American universities, in his opinion, was that they were dominated by businessmen. The new university must be different. All academic matters must be in the hands of the faculty; admission must be open to all qualified students, and the board of trustees, composed of responsible Jews, should manage the business affairs.

By July 1946 Einstein was gravely worried by the lack of substantial progress in academic matters. He proposed the creation of a committee of independent and objective men to select an academic head who would be "the real organizer of the University."[17] This individual must be a "reliable Jew" who has had knowledge of American universities and an understanding of educational problems and scholarship. He should be experienced in organizational matters and understanding of human nature and, finally, he must be willing to work with Einstein and Otto Nathan. In addition, he recommended that a board of outstanding men and women from the academic world should be created to advise the academic head on academic and organizational matters. He expected to be consulted about the makeup of both committees.[18]

Einstein continued to solicit the support of respected and influential Jews for the university. On August 20, 1946, he wrote Brandeis's successor on the Supreme Court, Felix Frankfurter, to ask for his support and to invite him to a fund-raising dinner in November, but by September 2 he had resigned from the Albert Einstein Foundation because of two actions taken by Goldstein "behind my [Einstein's] back."[19] Einstein had learned that Goldstein had invited the Jewish historian Abraham Sachar, who later served as first president of Brandeis, to submit his name for the office of president and that Cardinal Spellman of New York had been chosen to deliver the invocation at the fund-raising dinner in

November. Sachar and Goldstein later denied that anything improper had occurred, that Goldstein had merely asked Sachar to join a committee of national sponsors. The Spellman invitation was, however, another matter. The cardinal had recently returned from a visit to Spain where he had publicly and extravagantly praised Franco. Einstein was outraged by Goldstein's insensitivity. Goldstein, realizing the damage Einstein's resignation would do to the university project, submitted his resignation in order that Einstein might continue his association with the foundation. In a letter to Dr. Mühsam, written on January 22, 1947, Einstein wrote, "Nothing came of my 'rectorship' for the Jewish-American University. As usual in most practical questions I am only a 'catalyst' for collecting money. . . ."[20]

Shortly thereafter, the project was reorganized. Otto Nathan joined the board of trustees as liaison between Einstein and the board. S. Ralph Lazrus, a New York businessman, became president of the foundation, and George Alpert, a Boston lawyer, became president of the board of trustees of the university.

It was not long before new problems arose. The other members of the board believed that it was necessary to appoint a president as soon as possible in order to facilitate the raising of funds. Einstein, Nathan, and Lazrus felt strongly that the first priority was to rebuild the veterinary school, and the first appointment ought, therefore, to be a dean to direct the rebuilding. Eventually Einstein was persuaded to yield on the issue of the presidency, and in March 1947, with the board's authorization, Einstein wrote Professor Harold Laski, a British socialist scholar who had been chairman of the British Labor Party's executive committee in 1945 and 1946, to inquire if he would be interested in becoming a candidate for the presidency of Brandeis. Laski was the most prominent of the left-wing intellectuals in the Labor Party, but he had resigned his position early in 1947 as more moderate members gained control of the party. When Laski replied that he wished to remain in England, the matter appeared to be closed.

Meanwhile, Alpert had launched a high-powered public relations campaign which sought to "create an aura of success"[21] through frequent announcements of large gifts and impressive goals, while, in reality, there was barely enough money to pay operating expenses. In addition to the loud public relations campaign, which was in itself intolerable to Einstein, little progress was being made on the important issues of academic organization. By the beginning of May, Einstein, Nathan, and Lazrus had lost all patience. On May 10, 1947, Nathan and the photographer Philippe Halsman visited Einstein. On this occasion Halsman made the justly celebrated photograph of Einstein which appears as the frontispiece of *Einstein on Peace*. At one point that afternoon, Einstein and Nathan separated themselves from Halsman, his wife, and Helen Dukas, and walked to the bottom of the garden to discuss the Brandeis situation. The decision to resign was taken at that time.

On May 21, 1947, Einstein notified the physicist James Franck that he, Nathan, and Lazrus had resigned "quietly and with true regrets" due to "deep-reaching differences of opinion concerning fundamental questions of management and organization of the university" with Alpert's group.[22] The resignation of the three men was not announced until June 21. The following day Alpert charged Nathan and Lazrus with trying to give the school a "radical, political orientation." He accused them of making overtures to a "thoroughly unacceptable choice" as president. Without naming Laski, Alpert declared: "To establish a Jewish-sponsored university and to place at its head a man utterly alien to American principles of democracy, tarred with the Communist brush, would have condemned the university to impotence from the start. I made it perfectly plain to Mr. Lazrus then and later that on the issue of Americanism I cannot compromise."[23] Nathan and Lazrus were accused of creating dissension on the board of trustees and with having usurped the board's role in the shaping of educational policies and the selection of the president.

Einstein exploded. He had tried to withdraw silently in the hope that this action would not damage Brandeis. Alpert had taken a fabricated story to the press in an attempt to cover up the real differences over academic standards, questions of organization, and Alpert's deceptive public relations campaign. Realizing that the public would side with Einstein, Alpert seized upon the Laski issue to exploit the rising American anti-Communist paranoia. He also carefully avoided mention of Einstein's name, attacking, instead, his less famous associates. The truth of the Laski affair is that Einstein had approached the British economist with the knowledge and approval of the board and that the issue had been settled by Laski's refusal.

Einstein's falling out with the Brandeis group over the issues of academic quality and university financing mirrored his dispute with Weizmann and Magnes in 1928 over the administration of Hebrew University. The disagreement with the Brandeis people, however, had been muddied by the demagogic attack by Alpert against Nathan and Lazrus, and thereafter Einstein severed all connections with Brandeis University. Even after his son-in-law, Rudolf Kayser, joined the faculty in 1951, Einstein rejected the offer of an honorary degree and refused to have anything to do with the Jewish-American university he had always desired.

The sad conclusion of this affair again demonstrated the difficulties Einstein encountered with group activities. Both Goldstein and Alpert saw his participation in terms of publicity, and they failed to respect his demand that no major action take place without his approval. They were primarily interested in raising money. Einstein's overriding concern was that Brandeis provide the highest standards of education and that it contribute to the solution of the problem of discrimination against Jewish students by most American universities. The representatives of the business interests believed that a solid financial structure would insure success. Einstein knew that only by careful planning and honest attention to the academic organization of the university could a quality institution be created. Academic freedom from interference by nonacademic (i.e., business and political) influences was the first step to the creation of a "spiritual and intellectual atmosphere in which creative individuals can develop." He lent his name to assist such a project and not to support a publicity campaign which would lead to nothing more than another American university controlled by the same forces which had such a stifling effect upon American education. Years later, Otto Nathan remembered with sadness that it had been a "very nasty experience."[24]

In the postwar period, anti-Semitic barriers in universities and professional schools began to diminish. Nevertheless, it remained a serious problem which was aggravated by the crisis in Palestine and the attitude of the American clergy. The response by American Jews to this phenomenon disturbed Einstein almost as much as the situation itself. Einstein's assessment, undoubtedly colored by the recent unpleasantnesses with Alpert, is contained in a letter to Dr. Mühsam written in March 1948:

> The psychological situation of the Jews here is rather similar to the one in Germany before Hitler. The rich and successful ones try to camouflage their Jewish descent and behave like superpatriots. The others are hardly in touch with the *goyim* socially speaking, but live privately among themselves. The separation is even more pronounced than it ever was anywhere in Western Europe, including Germany. The ties among the Jews are restricted to charity, but it is surprising how much is being done in that respect, much more than in Europe.[25]

Despite his age and the demands upon his time from a myriad of other commitments and interests, Einstein always found time to assist in Jewish charity work. On a number of occasions he delivered an address over national radio at the inception of the annual fund-raising campaign of the United Jewish Appeal. In Princeton, during and after the war, he served as honorary co-chairman of the local chapter of the UJA. His position was largely symbolic, but he was eager to help his neighbors in any way possible, and he was always prepared to sign letters of invitation to the regular meetings, suggest the names of possible contributors, and on occasion make personal appeals to reluctant donors.

Every spring there were two fund-raising meetings in Princeton. One was a small gathering of about twenty people held in a private home for the larger donors; the other was a general meeting for all other donors held at the Nassau Inn. A guest speaker assigned by the central office of the UJA attended this meeting which usually attracted 150–200 people. Einstein's name was a great drawing card, and he always delivered a short speech encouraging everyone to do his duty. His fellow workers devised a trick whereby the more reluctant participants were encouraged to write out a check payable to Einstein, who then would endorse it over to the UJA. In this manner, the donor had Einstein's autograph on the back of the canceled check, and the UJA picked up an extra gift.

Einstein's labors for the local UJA, more symbolic than substantive, had a powerful effect upon his co-workers who were drawn closer together by a sense of pride at being associated with him. To them and to Jews throughout the world, he was *the Great Jew:* the embodiment of the ideals of Judaism—a man who combined the greatest intellectual accomplishments with a strong sense of social responsibility to his fellow Jews and to all mankind. In later years, with characteristic self-mockery, Einstein sometimes referred to himself as a "Jewish Saint."

He laughed not only at himself but also at the foibles of his fellow Jews. He derived especial pleasure from Jewish jokes. By chance, Professor Pais once told him one, and, Pais has related, "He looked as if he were a fifteen-year-old. He looked like a naughty, mischievous schoolboy." Thereafter, if he heard a funny Jewish joke, Pais would "hold it in reserve" for Einstein.[26] Einstein once repeated the following joke to a correspondent: A grocer had delivered an old and inedible goose to a customer. She confronted him the next time saying, "You are dishonest." He responded, "But among the dishonest I'm still the most honest."[27]

On November 9, 1952, Einstein's old friend Chaim Weizmann died, and this triggered one of the most unusual political gestures in modern times. Weizmann had been made Israel's first President in May 1948, at which time Einstein had written: "I read with great satisfaction that the Palestinian Jewry has appointed you to head the new state and thus has made amends at least partly for their ungrateful attitude toward you and your tremendous service."[28] As it turned out, Einstein was wrong in assuming that Weizmann was being returned to a position of power. Prime Minister David Ben-Gurion was unable to share power, especially with his longtime rival in the Zionist movement. He had installed Weizmann in the presidency because, as the latter resentfully soon discovered, the office was symbolic. Ben-Gurion, who had not asked Weizmann to sign the Declaration of Independence (ostensibly because he was out of the country at the time) compounded the insult by refusing to invite Weizmann to the cabinet meetings and ignoring the unhappy President's request for their minutes. Weizmann, like Einstein, wanted Israel to remain among the nonaligned nations. He was critical of Ben-Gurion's ties to NATO and the Western democracies and of the rising Jewish nationalism among the younger generation. Abba Eban has written of Weizmann's last years of semiexile within the Israeli government: "[H]e chafed at his inability to impress the new society with his own vision of intellectual integrity, aesthetic refinement, and manifest dedication to peace."[29]

Shortly after Weizmann's death, the editor of the Tel Aviv newspaper *Maariv* launched a campaign to have Einstein appointed to succeed Weizmann, and Ben-Gurion decided to inquire whether Einstein would accept the position. This was done in great secrecy but, as always, the press learned that something was afoot, and the Einstein household was first informed by a newsman rather than by the Ambassador of Israel. Miss Dukas describes the events of November 17 and 18, 1952:

> First there was a little thing in the *New York Times* that we just laughed about, because you know these newspaper stories. Then I got all these phone calls from the United Press and the *Times*. They said, "Did you hear the newspaper stories? We have a report out of Tel Aviv that Professor Einstein is really being offered [the presidency]." I could say in good faith, "No, I don't know anything about it. This is just a newspaper story."
> Well, it was in the evening, and we had our good friend David Mitrany in for supper, and, suddenly a telegram came from Abba Eban, who was the Israeli Ambassa-

dor in Washington. The telegram asked if his representative could see Einstein the next day—he had an important message from his government! If it hadn't been for those phone calls, I would not have known what he meant.

Professor Einstein said, "I cannot do that, and why should that man come all that way when I only have to say no." I think I had the idea: "Let's try to find him." I called Washington and Eban was there and Professor Einstein told him, "I am not the person for that and I cannot possibly do it." Then Abba Eban said, quite rightly, "I cannot tell my government you phoned me and said no. I have to go through the motions and present the offer officially." I took the phone over again and said to Eban: "I have gotten these phone calls, now I know why. What shall I do when they phone?" He said, "Just tell them nothing. Refer them to the embassy."

And then we started to make little jokes—"Who will we appoint minister?"—but that evening Professor Einstein said no, he didn't want to joke about it. He said, "That's not easy for me. These people are very near to my heart." It moved him.

The next day Abba Eban's deputy, David Goitein, came with his wife. Professor Einstein had already written out his letter stating why he declined, and I remember how Mr. Goitein said, "Well, I have been a lawyer all my life but I never got a rebuttal yet before I have stated my case." It was very nice. Then Mr. Goitein said, "We are a funny people. We want the best!"[30]

In his letter to Einstein, Abba Eban assured him that "complete facility and freedom to pursue your great scientific work would be afforded. . . . I am anxious

Abba Eban, Einstein, unidentified man, Moshe Sharett, ca. 1950, at a New York dinner in honor of Chaim Weizmann. Sharett was later briefly Prime Minister of Israel. Photo by A. F. Sozio. (Courtesy of Margot Einstein)

for you to feel that the Prime Minister's question embodies the deepest respect which the Jewish people can repose in any of its sons."

Einstein's prepared reply, dated November 18, 1952, said in part:

> I am deeply moved by the offer from our State of Israel, and at once saddened and ashamed that I cannot accept it. All my life I have dealt with objective matters, hence I lack both the natural aptitude and the experience to deal properly with people and to exercise official functions. For these reasons alone I should be unsuited to fulfill the duties of that high office, even if advancing age was not making increasing inroads on my strength.
>
> I am the more distressed over these circumstances because my relationship to the Jewish people has become my strongest human bond, ever since I became fully aware of our precarious situation among the nations of the world.

In a letter to the editor of *Maariv* he advanced this additional reason for his inability to accept the offer: "I also gave thought to the difficult situation that could arise if the government or the parliament made decisions which might create a conflict with my conscience; for the fact that one has no actual influence on the course of events does not relieve one of moral responsibility."[31]

Special honors had ceased to mean much to a man who had long ago grown weary of homage and notoriety, but because of his ties with the Jewish people and their tragic destiny in this century, Einstein was deeply moved by the unorthodox gesture. There was, of course, never any doubt that he would decline, because, as Otto Nathan has said, he would have been "utterly misplaced."[32] He was too old and ill to move; his ability to work on the unified field theory would have been severely impaired; he would have been required to attend all sorts of state functions and formal events, and, as he told his daughter, "If I would be President, sometimes I would have to say to the Israeli people things they would not like to hear."[33] He preferred to spare both Israel and himself such an uncomfortable eventuality. Prime Minister Ben-Gurion, aware of Einstein's unpredictable political independence, at one point asked Yitzak Navon, then his personal secretary and later President of Israel himself: "Tell me what to do if he says yes! I've had to offer the post to him because it's impossible not to. But if he accepts, we are in for trouble."[34]

A week later, Einstein wrote his good friend, the Austrian artist Josef Scharl: "I was deeply touched by the offer from my Israeli brothers. But I declined at once with really sincere regret. It is quite true that many a rebel has in the end become a figure of respectability, even a big shot [*Bonze*]; but I cannot bring myself to do so. We shall have to be satisfied, as before, at fuming at the brethren here at home."[35]

16

Enemy of America

T he period of American politics dominated by the figure of Senator Joseph McCarthy began in earnest in February 1950. A few critical dates will help to explain why Einstein became such a favorite target of the anti-Communists in the early 1950s:

- September 23, 1949: President Truman announced that the Soviet Union had ended the American monopoly of nuclear weapons by testing a plutonium bomb similar to the one dropped on Nagasaki.
- January 31, 1950: President Truman announced that the United States, in order to reestablish its lost nuclear superiority, would launch a crash program to develop a hydrogen bomb.
- February 1, 1950: Einstein, Thomas Mann, Linus Pauling, and thirteen others protested the punishment given to several defense lawyers of leaders of the Communist Party in the first of the Smith Act trials for alleged conspiracy to overthrow the government by force and violence. They warned that such actions against legal defenders of political and racial minorities and labor organizations might destroy the constitutional guarantee of a fair trial and adequate legal counsel.[1]
- February 3, 1950: Klaus Fuchs confessed to espionage.
- February 9, 1950: Senator McCarthy delivered his first celebrated anti-Communist speech claiming to have a list of card-carrying Communists working in the State Department.
- February 12, 1950: Einstein, on national television, warned against the development of the hydrogen bomb and predicted that an uncontrolled arms race would lead to general annihilation.

Recently declassified FBI documents provide additional dates of interest concerning Einstein in this turbulent fortnight in early February.

- February 10, 1950: The Phoenix office of the FBI reported that an informant (whose name has been deleted by FBI censors), inspired by the trial of Alger Hiss, recalled evidence which "might be used for the denaturalization and deportation of Einstein as an undesirable alien." The charge was that in the 1930s Einstein was a "personal courier from Communist Party headquarters" who conveyed important messages throughout the United States.[2]
- February 13, 1950: The day after Einstein's television address, J. Edgar Hoover, Director of the FBI, requested a summary of information on Einstein contained in bureau files.
- February 15, 1950: Hoover received the report, which is remarkable for its hostile tone and willingness to repeat any promising accusation, no matter how unsubstantiated. The report merits careful study.

It opens with a correct statement of Einstein's date of birth, and then claims that in December 1947 Einstein said: "I came to America because of the great, great freedom which I heard existed in this country. I made a mistake in selecting America as a land of freedom, a mistake I cannot repair in the balance of my life." No source for this quotation is provided. The report proceeds to note his scientific eminence, his 1905 discovery of the relationship between mass and energy, and his 1939 letter to President Roosevelt. It then states that he was given an opportunity to go to Russia, but did not. Two days earlier, the FBI had learned from the Atomic Energy Commission that Einstein had never been investigated for work on the Manhattan Project and that the AEC had never requested the FBI to investigate him. According to this report, Einstein was a professor of mathematics at the "Institute for Advanced Studies at Princeton University."

The report notes that Einstein belonged to at least thirty-three organizations which had been cited by the Attorney General, the House Committee on Un-American Activities or the California House Committee on Un-American Activities, and that he was affiliated with approximately fifty miscellaneous organizations which have not been cited by these three watchdogs. Einstein is characterized as a pacifist and a "liberal thinker."

Under the heading of "Expressions of Ideological Sympathies" the following appears:

> Einstein has made public statements lauding the scientific achievements of Russia and has indicated that it is the only country in which equality was not an empty phrase. He has opposed militarism and universal military training in the United States and has espoused world government. In 1948, he indicated to the Polish ambassador that the United States was no longer a free country and that his activities were carefully scrutinized. He was a sponsor of a committee to defend the rights of the 12 Communist leaders. On February 12, 1950, by transcription over NBC network, Einstein advocated barring all violence among nations to preclude "general annihilation" of mankind.

The next section of this report, labeled "Contacts and Associates" was entirely blacked out prior to release by the FBI. There is an arrow from the last three lines of this section drawn to the lower right-hand corner of the page, and the following note, almost certainly written by J. Edgar Hoover: "We should develop this. I have seen somewhere Einstein was the one who requested Fuchs [*sic*] assignment to him in England. What about this?" A second comment by the same hand on this page read: "Also I recently saw a statement to effect that a member of his family was in Russia. I think it stated it was his son."[3] Scenting a coup, the FBI was, for the next five years, hot on Einstein's trail, following up almost any derogatory tip, no matter how bizarre.

The charge that Albert Einstein, Jr. (there was no such person) was in the Soviet Union had been made in April 1949. The source of the story alleged that approximately five years earlier, Einstein and his wife had been in Pasadena, and that they were greatly concerned because their son was in the Soviet Union, and that therefore, all their actions were influenced by this. Mrs. Einstein was reportedly "scared to death" that the son might be held as hostage to force Einstein to perform some particular action. On March 10, 1950, D. M. Ladd reported to Hoover that this story was not true. Nevertheless, despite the errors in chronology and name, this sensational accusation continued to receive mention in later reports on Einstein.[4]

Whether by coincidence, or in response to Einstein's public statements in February 1950, a rash of leads reached the bureau during the next few months. The first pertained to a report in the "Times Herald" (although no location is given, it is almost certainly located in Washington, D.C.) and the *Cleveland Plain Dealer* of February 6, 1950, that the father of Klaus Fuchs had stated that when his son was interned in Canada as an enemy alien during the war, Einstein, who did not know he was a Communist, intervened to win his release, and that Einstein considered Fuchs's knowledge of nuclear energy valuable to the war effort. Helen Dukas, speaking for Einstein, denied any knowledge of this story. For the next several months, the investigation into Einstein's relations with the confessed spy continued, although no corroboration of the charge was forthcoming. Finally, in May 1950, FBI agents interviewed Fuchs in prison. He told them he had never met Einstein, that he did not know of any activity of Einstein's on his behalf, and he knew of no espionage activities engaged in by Einstein.[5] There is no record that the FBI realized that Einstein could not have recruited Fuchs for the Manhattan Project because he was not a participant in it.

By this time, two new sensational reports of Einstein's involvement in Soviet espionage dating back to the 1920s and 1930s in Berlin had been received by the government. On February 25, 1950, a German woman named Emma Rabbeis informed the State Department that she could provide "very positive statements" regarding Einstein's political activities in Berlin. She claimed that she possessed "most exact information about the particulars of a woman with whom Einstein collaborated internationally." The letter, written in German, was forwarded to the FBI, which sent it and a translation to the director of army intelligence on April 5. A counterintelligence agent interviewed her on June 22, and on July 31 Hoover received the report which concluded that the story of this Berlin dressmaker was hearsay. As proof that Einstein was a Communist, she stated that Einstein once had refused to stand during the playing of the German national anthem, and she alleged that Einstein had fathered the illegitimate child of the daughter of one of her clients who was a Communist. The agent also learned that recently Rabbeis had developed a mathematical formula for winning the Berlin lottery and had sent it to Einstein for his opinion. Einstein had not replied.[6]

A cover letter to the report on Emma Rabbeis brought to Hoover's attention for the first time that "information which emanated from former well placed K.P.D. members regarding Einstein's past activities is presently being checked and the European Command will forward a detailed report." This second charge of espionage in Berlin had been received by army intelligence prior to March 13, 1950. It was alleged that from 1929 to 1931 Einstein's chief secretary had been a Communist agent and his office had been used as a "drop" for telegraph messages from agents of the Commintern.[7]

The initial report by army intelligence on this matter was sent to Hoover on September 8, 1950, and on October 23 he replied suggesting that the unnamed secretary might be Helen Dukas. Hoover requested that the European command conduct an investigation to verify this, and that it provide more detailed information concerning the use of Einstein's office as a drop. Hoover also requested that "the information include, if possible, legal evidence and the identity of the informants who can testify to the information furnished if the need arose in connection with any action taken against Dr. Einstein and his secretary by the United States Government. It is pointed out in this connection that the Immigration and Naturalization Service is presently considering an investigation of Dr. Einstein for possible revocation of his citizenship."[8] We shall return to this remarkable development shortly.

A report from army intelligence to the FBI dated January 25, 1951, described the investigation "regarding the alleged cooperation of [Albert Einstein] in Germany with Communist and/or Soviet organizations engaged in conspirative activities during the period prior to 1933." According to the source, whose identity was apparently withheld even from the FBI, between at least 1929 and 1931, Soviet agents, operating primarily out of the Far East, had sent doubly encoded cable messages to Einstein's authorized international cable address. Because he received so much international cable traffic, it was felt that his office "would provide a relatively innocuous cover for conspirative communication." Einstein's chief secretary, whose identity was unknown to the source, was a Communist agent who had "close personal relationships, probably of an intimate nature, with an international Apparat functionary." She would intercept the messages and transmit them to a courier who would pick them up at the office.

The source doubted that Einstein knew the true nature of the setup, but speculated that he must have had some knowledge that his address was being used for other purposes. As proof of this, the informer stated that in the summer of 1930 the chief secretary left for an extended vacation without making arrangements to intercept the cables before they were given to Einstein. When she returned several weeks later, she turned over all the cables which had accumulated, and although there were "no unpleasant repercussions," the superiors were annoyed by the delay because there were important activities afoot in the Far East during this period. The source reasoned that if Einstein had received cables from the Far East which made no sense to him, he would have made inquiries of his office workers and complained to the postal authorities about the unauthorized use of his cable address. Since the address was used for another year, the source concluded that Einstein must at least have continued to tolerate the setup. The report concluded with the agent's opinion that, even though the information was secondhand, it was "probably accurate."[9]

On November 2, 1951, in the course of another investigation, the FBI interviewed Helen Dukas. She voluntarily stated that she had been continuously employed as Einstein's personal secretary since 1928. Nevertheless, doubt about the identity of Einstein's chief secretary in Berlin persisted for another three years. On August 31, 1954, Einstein's old colleague, Max von Laue, was interviewed in Berlin about his knowledge of Helen Dukas. According to the agents' notes, he was cooperative but unable to provide any useful information.[10] On October 9 the Newark office recommended that it interview her directly. Permission was granted on January 30, 1955, by Hoover, with the suggestion that to avoid suspicion the agents should approach her under the pretext that they were looking for information on people who had lived in Germany.

The interview with Helen Dukas took place in Princeton on February 23, 1955. She was apparently unaware of the allegations against her and, according to the report filed afterward, she was "extremely friendly and appeared quite sincere in her answers. She did not appear to be evasive in any manner, but spoke quite freely. . . ." She told the agents that she had been Einstein's only personal secretary since 1928, that Einstein did most of his work and correspondence at home, and that Einstein's office was really more of a work and study area. She had no recollection of any contact with any of the people who had allegedly served as couriers, and she expressed no interest in politics except for Jewish affairs and her opposition to Hitler. The agents were particularly impressed by her assertion that she had been the sole employee of Einstein since 1928, which, they felt, tended to discredit the charges against Einstein and his "chief secretary." "On the basis of the information developed during the interview," they concluded in their report to Hoover on March 9, 1955, "it is not believed that additional investigation in this matter is warranted."[11]

Thus ended the five-year investigation. It seems fantastic that the allegations ever were taken seriously but, in fairness to the FBI, under the prevailing crisis atmosphere there was at least some slight justification in following up leads which were not entirely implausible. The same concession cannot so easily be extended to the investigation launched by the Immigration and Naturalization Service into the possibility of revoking the citizenship of Einstein and Dukas.

The documents in the FBI files reveal that on March 8, 1950, the Philadelphia office of the INS requested "any derogatory information" from the FBI on Einstein because it was felt that there were enough allegations of his un-American behavior to warrant an investigation. The FBI, at this point already conducting an investigation of its own, requested on June 9 that the INS clarify the purpose of its request "inasmuch as he is a citizen."[12]

In September the INS sent the FBI a memorandum dated June 14, 1950, marked "Personal and Confidential," which apparently sets out the case against Einstein at this time. The first item states that a pamphlet prepared by the House Committee on Un-American Activities on April 25, 1949, entitled "Review of the Scientific and Cultural Conference for World Peace" listed forty-nine names of "persons who have been affiliated with from eleven to twenty Communist front organizations . . ." Einstein was one of those listed. The memorandum also cited an article in a right-wing Brooklyn newspaper, "The Tablet," which "would seem to indicate that an investigation should be conducted" to determine if his actions "might justify the filing of a suit to cancel citizenship." The article lists the usual series of Spanish Loyalist causes Einstein supported in the late 1930s, and vaguely alludes to "numerous references to affiliations since naturalization with other organizations which have been officially designated as Communist or Communist-front."[13] A second memorandum, dated July 12, 1950, draws attention to Einstein's participation in the First World Congress Against War and Fascism held in Amsterdam in August 1932. It described Einstein as a "Pacifist and Communist Sympathizer."

Careful scrutiny of the substance of these charges against Einstein reveals something about the methods of the anti-Communist smear campaigns of this period. Einstein refused to attend the 1932 congress because, while he was in full agreement with the pacifist and antifascist aims of the congress, he objected that it was "entirely under Russian-Communist domination." He did send it a message condemning the Japanese invasion of Manchuria and calling for rule by international law to prevent "brute force and the unrestrained lust for profits [of the war industries]" from threatening our culture. In contrast to the reception given the Communist orators, Einstein's message was coolly received by the congress. In his absence, however, he was elected to the World Antiwar Committee, but he refused to accept the invitation because he did not wish to align himself with the Russian Communist elements which had dominated the congress. "[I]t is important for me to retain a position of political neutrality," he explained.[14]

Einstein's association with the 1949 Scientific and Cultural Conference for World Peace is similarly remote. In April 1948, alarmed by the possibility of preventive war, Einstein had proposed to Dr. Harlow Shapley, President of the National Council of the Arts, Sciences and Professions (another favorite target of the anti-Communists) that leading intellectuals launch a strong nonpartisan counterattack against the preventive war mentality. Eventually a public meeting at Carnegie Hall on June 17, 1948, attracted about 2,000 participants, and Einstein addressed the meeting by telephone hookup. The petition subsequently drafted by this undertaking contained resolutions which, from Einstein's point of view, were too watered down to be effective, and he declined to participate any further beyond an unenthusiastic agreement to sign the statement. Apparently nothing developed from this effort except that it contributed to the preparations for the Scientific and Cultural Congress for World Peace in March 1949. Einstein was one of more than five hundred sponsors, many of whom were unaware that anti-Communists had alleged that the conference was a Communist front.[15]

On November 28, 1950, the FBI sent "all pertinent data" to the INS, including a five-page summary of Einstein's life and his pro-Communist views and a two-page list of suspect organizations with which he was affiliated. A year later, on December 5, 1951, the FBI requested the results of the INS investigation of Einstein and queried if Helen Dukas had also been studied. In mid-December the INS replied that although it had received the FBI information a year earlier, nothing had been done because, due to a bureaucratic snafu, it had received no reply from the Newark FBI office to its request for clearance to begin the investigation. A search of FBI records failed to locate the INS request, but it did reveal that although a substantial amount of information had been accumulated in Einstein's file, no investigative report had ever been prepared. Hoover directed the Newark office to rectify this oversight: "Newark should afford these matters expeditious attention and submit the requested reports within 30 days. . . ."

Another exchange of letters failed to locate the INS request or an FBI response, and on February 12, 1952, Hoover wrote the Commissioner of the INS to resolve the confusion: "In order that there will be no misunderstanding in the matter [between the FBI and INS], you are informed that the [FBI] does not interpose any objection to any investigation that the [INS] may desire to conduct concerning Albert Einstein or Helen Dukas, nor has the [FBI] ever interposed any such objection."[16]

On February 23, 1952, the FBI sent a thirteen-page summary of its Einstein files to INS. Under the heading of "Indications of Einstein's Sympathy with the Communist Party in Germany," the FBI stated that Einstein's Berlin office had been used as a drop for messages from Communist agents in the Far East.[17] Thus, without any corroboration of the allegations of the unnamed source, the FBI, whether through carelessness or malice, had upgraded the story to an accepted fact. The remainder of the report contains the usual allegations and attempts to establish guilt by association. In spite of all this discussion of an INS investigation, it appears that nothing further was done.

In response to Hoover's January 10, 1952, order to prepare a comprehensive report on Einstein, the Newark office began to assemble what was called a "correlation summary" on February 25. The effort, which lasted a year, eventually came to 1,160 pages. A summary of FBI biographical data on Einstein at the inception of this investigation reveals that the efforts of the bureau in the preceding two years had been rather unimpressive. For instance: the FBI did not know the name of Einstein's first wife; Elsa Einstein "reportedly died in 1936 or 1938." None of the names of the schools Einstein attended were known, nor his employment prior to 1933. Even a cursory reading of Philipp Frank's 1947 biography would have provided the appropriate answers. Actually, an FBI agent had read

Frank in August 1951, but he had been interested in the names of Einstein's secretaries, friends, and associates, and apparently did not note other biographical information.[18]

Because of the manner in which the FBI investigations were conducted, it is very unlikely that Einstein was aware of any of the charges described above. He was, however, almost certainly aware that his activities were being monitored. Recall that the February 15, 1950, memo to Hoover notes without any sense of irony: "In 1948, [Einstein] indicated to the Polish ambassador that the United States was no longer a free country and that his activities were carefully scrutinized."[19] It was also accepted as common knowledge by the physics community in Princeton that its members were under surveillance during this period.

The earlier criticisms by politicians and government officials of Einstein's political undertakings—particularly his support of pacifist and world government movements—had, by McCarthyite standards, been mild. He was patronized by these early critics, but by and large they exhibited a measure of fair play and restraint. They had no intention of listening to his ideas, but neither had they any interest in character assassination. This relatively higher road was gradually abandoned as the less scrupulous elements of American politics commandeered control of public opinion. Beginning in the late 1940s, and certainly by 1950, dissenters had become the prey of those who had chosen the low road.

It is hardly surprising that in the oppressive atmosphere of the early months of the McCarthy period, Einstein suffered acute feelings of estrangement from his adopted home. Three weeks after the outbreak of the Korean War on June 25, 1950, he wrote to a friend in England: "I hardly ever felt as alienated from people as right now. . . . The worst is that nowhere is there anything with which one can identify. Everywhere brutality and lies."[20] In November he told a sympathetic correspondent that the United States "has gone mad and is no longer receptive to reasonable suggestions."[21] The following January, in a letter to Queen Mother Elizabeth of Belgium, he charged that "the dear Americans" had taken the place of the Germans. "The German calamity of years ago repeats itself: people acquiesce without resistance and align themselves with the forces for evil. And one stands by, powerless."[22]

Einstein held his adopted homeland responsible for much of the crisis atmosphere. He blamed the Americans for the failure to control atomic weapons and the institutionalization of the Cold War, the crash program to produce hydrogen bombs, the obsession with possible Soviet espionage and the resultant wave of anti-Communist hysteria and, finally, the Korean "police action." Since 1945, the United States had, in Einstein's words, "conducted its Russian policy as though it were convinced that fear is the greatest of all diplomatic instruments."[23] Truman's policy of "naked power" had led to increasing militarization despite the absence of an external threat and had spread anxiety and distrust throughout the world. By 1947, America's posture of toughness had squandered any hope that conciliatory behavior might induce Soviet cooperation in the postwar period. Furthermore, despite the unchallenged power of the United States, Americans had never felt more insecure. Einstein characterized the Truman program as a policy that aims for "security through superior force, whatever the cost," and likened it to Germany in the time of the Kaiser—"through many victories to final disaster."[24]

Since the investigations by the FBI were so concerned with Einstein's political values, a brief summary of his political ideas and opinions is appropriate. Einstein was a lifelong democrat. While studying at the ETH, he managed to save enough money from his very modest allowance to enable him to pay the requisite fees to qualify for Swiss citizenship. After the First World War he was an enthusiastic advocate of the democratic and socialist Weimar Republic in Germany. He had great admiration for American democracy. The Bill of Rights, he believed, was an especially important milestone in political thinking. He took the avowed ideals of democracy very seriously, and careful study of his frequent political dissent after the Second World War reveals that his criticism was founded invariably on the belief that official actions were in violation of the spirit or the letter of the intent of the Founding Fathers. Nowhere is this more apparent than with his defense of individual rights during the anti-Communist witch-hunts.

Einstein found much to admire in America's political system, but as a socialist and a champion of the welfare of the individual, he worried greatly about the dangers to democracy and to individuals posed by capitalism. In the essay "Why Socialism?"[25] written in 1949, Einstein stated that, in his opinion, the essence of the crisis of modern times concerns the dependence of the individual upon a society which he perceives not "as a protective force, but rather as a threat to his natural rights, or even to his economic existence." Einstein was convinced that the primary cause of this "evil" is the "economic anarchy of capitalist society." Man cannot change his biological constitution, nor can he reverse the growth of modern technology. Man can, however, change his cultural institutions and values.

In "Why Socialism?" Einstein briefly outlines the destabilizing effect of capitalism on politics, economics, and society. The basis of capitalism is the private ownership of the means of production. Through competition among capitalists and the developments of technology which favor the formation of ever larger units of production at the expense of smaller units, private capital tends to become concentrated in the hands of the few. This "oligarchy of private capital" acquires enormous economic and political power which exerts a corrupting influence even on a democratic political system. Political parties are financed and controlled by the capitalists, and as elected officials become increasingly beholden to these private concerns, the interests of the weak are not adequately protected. Furthermore, capitalist control of the primary sources of information—the educational system and the media—make it nearly impossible for the average citizen to become sufficiently informed to make intelligent decisions.

Because the means of production are in the hands of private individuals, the owner hires labor to produce goods which become his exclusive property. The worker's wage is not determined by the value of his product, but by his minimum needs, the capitalist's requirements for labor power, and the number of workers competing for the job. The workers are placed in the position, Einstein writes, of "striving to deprive each other of the fruits of their collective labor." There is no protection against unemployment, and each laborer is continually faced with the threat of losing his job. Technological progress, far from easing the work burden for all, has often meant greater unemployment. Furthermore, capitalism is inherently vulnerable to severe periods of economic depression.

The "worst evil of capitalism" in Einstein's opinion, was the social damage caused by competition against others which stimulates the egotistical drives of the individual so that his social drives are too often stifled. "Unknowingly prisoners of their own egotism," Einstein describes the plight of the victims of this system, "they feel insecure, lonely, and deprived of the naïve, simple, and unsophisticated enjoyment of life." In the educational system, for example, a highly competitive attitude teaches students "to worship acquisitive success as a preparation for his future career." It is essential, he believed, for man to learn that striving for power is "ugly" and "stupid"; that preoccupation with the fulfillment of personal desires eventually leads to bitter disappointment; and that competition is "success at the expense of one's fellow men" which "conceives of achievement not as derived from the love for productive and thoughtful work, but as springing from personal ambition and fear of rejection."[26]

Einstein believed that the only way to eliminate the evils of capitalism was through the establishment of a socialist society in conjunction with an educational system oriented toward social goals. The means of production would be owned by all society and would be utilized in a planned manner, adjusting production to the needs of the community. There would be gainful employment for all able workers and protection for those unable to work. The educational system would encourage the development of the innate abilities of the individual while attempting to instill in him "a sense of responsibility for his fellow men in place of the glorification of power and success in our present society."[27]

Einstein was acutely sensitive to the great dangers socialistic centralization of economic and political power posed to the rights of the individual. In particular, it was necessary to guard against an "all-powerful and overweening" bureaucracy. He conceded that in both socialist and capitalist countries control of modern technology is in few hands. However, he pointed out that, at least in theory, under socialism the technocrats are accountable to the public, whereas, under capitalism, they are accountable only to the stockholders.[28] The best defense against bureaucratic tyranny is the aggressive protection of individual liberties, and this defense, Einstein felt strongly, is one of the chief responsibilities of intellectuals.

Einstein was careful not to blame capitalism for all existing social and political ills, nor did he assert that the establishment of socialism throughout the world would, by itself, cure the problems of humanity. He also disagreed with the belief of many socialists that it was necessary for all countries to become socialist before the abolition of war would become possible. Socialist bureaucrats could be just as aggressive as other bureaucrats. Nevertheless, he was convinced that wherever a socialist administration maintained "at least halfway adequate administrative standards," the advantages of a socialist society exceeded its disadvantages.[29]

In the prevailing atmosphere in the United States, little or no distinction was made between socialism and Soviet communism, between sincere dissent from prevailing policies and subversion. As American anticommunism grew more hysterical, Einstein's socialist beliefs, his attitude toward the control of atomic weapons, his refusal to condone the prevailing view of the Soviet Union as the fount of all evil, and his popularity with the public made him an effective enemy of the reactionary politicians, and he became a favorite target of their attacks, just as he had in Germany in the 1920s. Einstein was old enough and his health poor enough that he could have retired from the fray with grace, but in these bitter times he chose to stand and fight because he believed that the ultimate success of a democracy depends on the political and moral qualities of its citizenry.

The rise of the phenomenon known as McCarthyism can be traced back to the concluding stages of the war and the early postwar period. The United States had emerged from the Second World War victorious, relatively unscathed in a devastated world, the dominant economic and military power on earth, yet badly scared. In the years between the attack on Pearl Harbor and the bombings of Hiroshima and Nagasaki, the American view of the world had been transformed in traumatic fashion.[30]

The war completed the collapse of European hegemony in international affairs, and brought to prominence the two great prewar isolationist powers, the United States and the Soviet Union. The principal lesson Americans learned from the war experience was that the world had grown too small ever to practice isolation again. The events of the thirties, the Japanese invasion of Manchuria in 1931, the Italian war in Ethiopia in 1935, Hitler's seizure of the Rhineland in 1936, the disastrous consequences of Munich in 1938 and, finally, the attack on Pearl Harbor in 1941, had taught American leaders that the goal of totalitarianism is total world dominance to be achieved by ruthless expansion. Within a matter of months after the end of the war, this perception became an axiom of the Cold War whose rigid interpretation permitted no consideration of the nature of any individual situation. Thus, the massive sovietization of Eastern Europe was assumed to be another step along the path of world conquest. No weight was given to the possibility that Stalin's actions in 1945–1946 were motivated by a drive for security from future European invasions.

If the world is too small to practice isolation safely, Truman and his advisers reasoned, and if totalitarian movements are bent on world conquest, then it follows that all global developments have a direct impact on America's interests and trouble anywhere poses a direct threat to the security of the United States. With traditional missionary zeal, American leaders self-confidently "reached for their mandate from heaven"[31] and assumed the role of world's policemen. To enforce this posture, it became necessary to maintain a state of permanent military preparedness, because in the future there would be no grace period for mobilization. The armed forces and military technology quickly assumed positions of central importance. Paradoxically, the growth of power led not to a greater sense of security, but to an increase in perceived dangers which required urgent confrontation and solution. This way of thinking, which evolved in the early years of the Cold War, required a tangible enemy to sustain its credibility. The early cold warriors were not merely cynical manipulators of foreign policy and public opinion; they were prisoners of their own alarmist vision who believed themselves to be experts on the subject. They were unable to listen to dissident domestic viewpoints or to what their adversaries actually were saying. Instead, they pursued a line of policy with a dogmatism which, they sincerely believed, characterized Soviet policy.

The Truman Cold War policy did not unfold from some well-thought-out master strategy; rather, it developed as a series of reactions to Soviet threats, some real, some imagined. By the late forties, the United States found itself trapped into a policy which had been shaped, to a significant degree, by its own misperceptions. The early postwar arrogance of the sole possessor of the atomic bomb had been replaced by fear, frustration, and intolerance. It was in this way, and not as a consequence of some conspiracy, that antidemocratic forces had begun to erode traditional American liberties.

The weakening of American democracy during the early Cold War years was due, not to some sinister conspiracy, but to human frailty, faulty judgment, fear, and lack of vigilance in the defense of human values. During the war the internment of Japanese-Americans on the West Coast and the fire bombings of Dresden and Tokyo had been justified by American policymakers with the argument that the enemy was also guilty of such actions.[32] After the war, when the policy toward the Soviet Union and the control of nuclear weapons was being formulated, the perception of an emergency situation caused the government to enter into an "adversary relationship" with the American public regarding nuclear policies and issues: suppressing evidence of the horrors of atomic weapons, telling families of Americans killed at Hiroshima that they died elsewhere and, later, fostering the myth that the atomic monopoly was lost by spies and saboteurs. These deceptions, inspired no doubt by a feeling that an undeclared state of emergency existed, have seriously undermined the relationship between the public and its elected and appointed servants. The history of policymaking has, likewise, served to reinforce antidemocratic tendencies. Dissident voices were denied positions of power. Policy was set by politicians, generals, and their hired experts who accepted unquestioningly the basic assumptions of the American Cold War position. Debate focused not on the merits and implications of that policy, but on the size of the military budget and the allocation of funds earmarked for defense. Private citizens like Einstein who challenged the basic assumptions of American foreign policy were ignored, ridiculed as naïve meddlers, or accused of Communist sympathies.

A number of historic forces have helped to shape the American national character, chief among which are the yearning for religious and political independence, the spirit of the frontiersmen, the pragmatism of the explorer, inventor, and businessman, and the democratic ideal of equality. These same forces have been responsible for one of the gravest defects of American character—the tradition of anti-intellectualism.[33] The American settler repudiated decadent European culture as he set out to conquer a world of nature and savages. In its effort to appeal to the settlers of the South and Midwest in the nineteenth century, evangelical frontier religion tended to be anti-Eastern, antiestablishment, and anti-intellectual. American education has generally aimed to serve the practical values of the businessman. Beginning with the presidency of Andrew Jackson, America has been governed, with rare exceptions, by successful politicians, businessmen, lawyers, and soldiers.

Even cherished democratic traditions have reinforced a feeling of antipathy toward the intellectual, who is viewed as an elitist. In a 1947 *New Yorker* profile written by Niccolo Tucci, Einstein was quoted as saying:

> Only a noble soul can attain true independence of judgment and exercise respect for other people's rights. . . . [I]n Plato's time, and even later, in Jefferson's time, it was still possible to reconcile democracy with a moral and intellectual aristocracy, while today democracy is based on a different principle—namely, that the other fellow is no better than I am. You will admit that this attitude doesn't altogether facilitate emulation.[34]

In the twentieth century, the problems of modernism, arising from the industrial and technological revolutions, required solutions which nonspecialists could no longer provide. The depression served as a catalyst to force a dramatic and irreversible centralization of power in the hands of the President and legions of highly trained, appointed specialists.[35] The dramatic shift occurred in the early years of the New Deal as Washington was invaded by experts who appeared to the general public to be wealthy intellectuals from the Eastern establishment. During those years, which, incidentally, coincided with Einstein's move to Princeton, there was a brief period of good will between the public and the intellectuals, because for once popular politics and the ideas of liberal-minded intellectuals coincided. This unusual harmony lasted into the war, but all the while the resentment of the more conservative, traditionally anti-intellectual forces was building. The stereotype of the Ivy League elitist helped to rally the anti-intellectual forces during and after the Roosevelt years.

After the war, conservative Republicans and Democrats, intent on restoring their eroded congressional powers, and eager to find a way back into power, revived their longstanding charges that the New Deal was full of Communists and socialists. As the Cold War intensified, the policies and rhetoric of the Truman administration served to fuel anti-Communists' fears. In an effort to win support for his "get tough" policy Truman turned the Cold War into a holy war; the "Red menace" must be confronted and dealt an absolute defeat. Critics of this posture were branded "irrational" or "disloyal." A corollary to the theory of American omnipotence was that the Russian threat was caused by subversion. It was asserted that only a loss of faith or betrayal from within could defeat the United States.

While the administration and its hard-line critics fought to impress upon the misinformed, frightened American public the purity of their anti-Communist credentials, no one in power understood that the Communist penetration into Eastern Europe and Asia was the result of the war with Germany and Japan and not the product of some sinister conspiracy. The men in power had failed to analyze and portray accurately the phenomenon of communism. The American reaction to the failure of the atomic monopoly and the "get tough" policies resembled the response of the totalitarian mind to failed policies. Instead of admitting that errors had been caused by honest miscalculation, historical circumstances, or ineptitude, failures were blamed on conspirators and scapegoats.[36] Furthermore, attributing America's problems to a Communist threat was a tacit but unconscious confession that America was unable to shape its own destiny.

The alarming developments of 1949 and 1950 in China and Korea and the revelation of espionage by Klaus Fuchs just after the Soviet Union exploded its first atomic bomb traumatized the American public into accepting the proposition that the United States had to prevail over Russia, regardless of cost. The earlier psychological dependence upon the monopoly of the atomic bomb as the surest means of securing peace had rendered Americans particularly vulnerable to panic. The belief that the Russians could only have built their bomb by espionage paved the way for the witch-hunts designed to eliminate future subversion and betrayal of nuclear secrets.

In 1951 and 1952 Washington expected that full-scale nuclear war with the Soviet Union could come at any minute. George Kennan, who served as Ambassador to Moscow in 1952, has written that the government gave the impression of preparing for war. The policymakers wanted military information and showed little interest in actions and information that might help prevent its outbreak.[37]

It was in this environment that the various investigations into the behavior of Einstein, Helen Dukas, and countless loyal, but dissident, citizens were conducted. The Einstein and Dukas investigations dragged on for five years, at times seemingly forgotten by the investigators, followed, usually after another controversial public statement by Einstein, by a sudden burst of interest in the progress of the case against them. This pace can, in part, be ascribed to the innate lethargy of any bureaucracy. But it seems that if Einstein and Dukas really had posed a genuine danger to the security of the nation, the casual manner in which the investigations dragged on constituted serious negligence by the various agencies charged with safeguarding national security. If, on the other hand, Einstein and Dukas were not a danger to society, one searches in vain for a valid justification of this violation of their constitutional rights. The conclusion that the FBI was more interested in smearing Einstein's character than in protecting national security seems inescapable. The actual FBI reports assembled in 1952 and 1953 provide unarguable proof of the absurdity of the charges against Einstein and Dukas.

The correlation summary of information contained in bureau files on Einstein, begun early in 1952 and completed a year later, is nearly 1,200 pages long. It is a tedious, repetitive collection of fact and fancy which proves little except that Einstein generally supported left of center political causes, and that the FBI was both gullible and eager to discredit the emminent intellectual. There are a number of different categories of information gathered, including references for visa affidavits, public statements by Einstein, policy statements issued by organizations with which he was allegedly affiliated, and accusations—often anonymous—of Communist or disloyal activity on his part.

Throughout the Hitler years, Einstein had signed affidavits for numerous

Einstein preparing a radio talk, late 1940s. (Courtesy of Margot Einstein)

European Jews fleeing the Nazis. Part of each investigation involved an assessment of the applicant's political beliefs and activities. Einstein vouched for several refugees whose beliefs were leftist, and the FBI duly noted each case. In a similar vein, each allegedly "subversive" organization—including civil rights, pacifist, antifascist, and world government movements, was monitored as conscientiously as overtly subversive groups. Any activity, press release, public statement, or derogatory testimony against such groups was noted, and the name of everyone affiliated with the group was recorded. The report on Einstein bulges with this sort of information. The following is an example;

> "PM" of August 17, 1943, carried an article entitled "138 Americans Ask Roosevelt to Stop Riots."
> This article stated in part that a resolution signed by 138 noted Americans had called upon President Roosevelt, "to use all wisdom to prevent a repetition of the horrors of Detroit elsewhere in our country."
> The article stated further that the signers of the resolution included Albert Einstein and others.[38]

The allegations made against Einstein ranged from explanations by former Communists of how Einstein's well-meaning innocence was manipulated by front organizations to science-fiction stories from unbalanced people. Almost every charge was investigated, although the zanier reports were usually dismissed. The charge that Einstein had invented and utilized a mind-control robot was discounted when the FBI learned that the source of the story was a former mental patient. Another story, from 1948, charged that Einstein and ten "former Nazi research brain-trusters" had secretly observed a beam of light melt a block of steel, and that from an airplane this beam could destroy entire cities. The army intelligence research and development group judged this to be impossible, but one wonders why a story linking Einstein to former Nazis could be considered for even a moment.[39]

There would be additional investigations into Einstein's activities in the final two years of his life. One such inquiry was opened because he supported efforts to commute the death sentence of Ethel and Julius Rosenberg, who had been found guilty of atomic espionage. On December 23, 1952, Einstein sent a confidential letter to the trial judge, Irving R. Kaufman, and on January 11, 1953, he sent a public appeal to President Truman urging that the death sentence be commuted because, whether guilty or innocent, the Rosenbergs, he believed, had been made victims of political passions, and he felt that proof of their guilt had not been established beyond a shadow of a doubt. Furthermore, he thought that their punishment was out of line with the crime for which they had been convicted—transmitting secrets to a Soviet agent. They had been condemned by the testimony of a prosecution witness, David Greenglass, who had admitted to having prepared the documents, a crime Einstein believed to be a more serious offense. The fact that Greenglass had saved his own life by testifying against the Rosenbergs made the sentence appear all the more unjust.[40] Judge Kaufman turned Einstein's letter over to the New York office of the FBI, and on February 4, 1953, the Newark office reopened its Einstein investigation. On April 22 they reported to Hoover that no additional information had been found.[41]

At about this time, the FBI received another crazy accusation against Einstein from someone who claimed to have worked in motion pictures from 1919 until the early 1930s. In response to a rather benign *Reader's Digest* article which described Einstein as an innocent who had sometimes been duped by radicals, the informant wrote: "But this gentle old darling, so innocent and naïve, was introduced to me as the brain that was setting up Hollywood in the Thirties for the big Communist push." The writer, a former publicity agent, claimed that he had been summoned to the Ambassador Hotel in Los Angeles by someone who spent three hours trying to persuade him to take charge of propaganda. He resisted until finally he was told: "Well, I can see that Dr. Einstein has got to take you in hand. He's the one that never fails with the big shots." As luck would have it, Einstein was busy, but the informant did get a glimpse of him in his plush suite with, the informant believed, Charlie Chaplin. The tipster refused to "play Ball" and subsequently lost a long succession of jobs because, as he later discovered, Einstein had indeed succeeded in organizing all the big studio figures, stars, writers, and directors.[42] A lengthy investigation and subsequent twenty-page report failed to corroborate the story.

Although the various reports on Einstein consumed massive amounts of time, energy, and money, they produced no reliable evidence of disloyal behavior. The question naturally arises: Why would such an effort be undertaken to assemble derogatory information on an individual such as Einstein? The inescapable conclusion is that the reactionary elements of the American government sought to smear his reputation as a means of neutralizing—or silencing—his frequent criticisms of American Cold War policy.

Why was it necessary to utilize character assassination? One interesting idea occurs in Ronald Steele's biography of Walter Lippmann.[43] Steele noted that throughout his long career in public life Lippmann enjoyed the privileges of an insider in the highest political and foreign policy circles despite his often sharp criticism on specific issues. Steele believes that this was because Lippmann always accepted the prevailing assumptions of foreign policy objectives; when he disagreed, it was with the methods chosen to implement these unquestioned assumptions. This privileged status abruptly evaporated early in 1965 when Lippmann—then seventy-five years old—broke with the Johnson administration over the escalation of the Vietnam War. Almost overnight he became a pariah to an administration that had counted him among its most respected friends. As Lippmann's attacks on the basic premises of Vietnam policy grew more strident, officials in the Johnson administration began to leak reports that poor old Walter had suddenly become senile, that his judgment had failed, that he could no longer be taken seriously.

Is this not the response of the policymakers of the Truman and Eisenhower administrations to Einstein's attacks upon the fundamental premises of postwar foreign policy? At first the response to Einstein was rather benign. Einstein was dismissed as a kindly, well-meaning innocent. But as the Cold War intensified and the phenomenon of anticommunism flourished, the attacks became more virulent, and the dupe was transformed into a dangerous agent of evil. Today we look back and wonder that it ever could have been so crude. But a disturbing question persists: Can a democracy long survive if it remains deaf to sincere dissent, or when it is incapable of distinguishing between dissent and disloyalty?

17

"Enfant Terrible"

I have become a kind of *enfant terrible* in my new homeland, due to my inability to keep silent and to swallow everything that happens there. Besides, I believe that older people who have scarcely anything to lose ought to be willing to speak out in behalf of those who are young and who are subject to much greater restraint. I like to think it may be of some help to them.

Einstein to Elizabeth, Queen Mother of Belgium
March 28, 1954

E instein believed that the Communist witch-hunts served reactionary politicians as a pretext for mounting an assault on civil liberties, for the purpose of suppressing dissent from their Cold War policy of militarization and confrontation. He viewed the constant threat of war and the attack on civil liberties as the same problem. As he had maintained for many years, the political and economic power struggle between East and West could be resolved only by the creation of a supranational world authority. Once the Cold War was under control, the alleged Communist threat would evaporate and the witch-hunters would lose their issue. In the meantime, however, it was more important than ever to defend freedom of speech and the right of political dissent. Peace could not be secured through military alliances and arms build-up, nor could trust be restored by the methods of *realpolitik*. "The greatest danger to the future of mankind," Einstein wrote to a Japanese correspondent, "lies in man's faith in unworkable methods which are falsely put forward in the name of practical politics."[1]

Although he remained sharply critical of the Russian denial of civil liberties, the political trials, and the Soviet version of truth,[2] Einstein continued to urge that steps be taken to begin to improve relations with the Soviet Union. He believed that rapprochement could take place only if both sides voluntarily renounced certain positions which were viewed as an "immediate menace" to the other side. Instead, America's "get tough" policy and the attempt to quell the spread of Communists in Asia by military intervention in Korea[3] had succeeded in uniting Asia against the West, while McCarthyism exposed the United States to the ridicule of the rest of the world, and threatened permanently to weaken American democracy.

Einstein's response to McCarthyism was the advocacy and practice of Gandhian civil disobedience. "[I]n all cases where a reasonable solution of difficulties is possible," he wrote in 1953, "I favor honest co-operation and, if this is not possible under prevailing circumstances, Gandhi's method of peaceful resistance to evil."[4]

Gandhi taught that exploitation and inequality are the essence of violence, and the use of force is evil. Man must not violate the dictates of his conscience, even if it sets him against the authority of the state. Gandhi's nonviolent resistance to evil, "the highest expression of the soul,"[5] is a quality of the heart, rather than of the mind. It converts its enemy by the power of love and moral truth, not by force. Nonviolence attacks the system, not the individuals who represent it. "Hate the sin, and not the sinner," Gandhi wrote in his autobiography. The totalitarian mind believes sin is irreversible and must be eradicated, but Gandhi taught that sin is reversible, and the sinner can be converted through love. This is only possible if the practitioner of the nonviolent method refuses to cooperate with anything which degrades human dignity while leading a life of sacrifice in the service of humanity. The nonviolent person must not fear the violence of his enemy, must purify himself of hatred, and must "act as he is directed by his inner voice."[6] Above all, he must be willing to suffer without retaliation until he converts his enemy. Only through nonviolence, Gandhi taught, can a society built upon genuine and lasting justice be created.

All his life Einstein had been a pacifist. His temporary renunciation of conscientious objection in 1933 had not been a repudiation of pacifism, but a recognition of the extreme threat of Nazism. He was unwilling to support high-sounding but not ineffectual ideals. Einstein's pacifist views were almost the same as Gandhi's, except that Einstein would resist violently any attempt on his own life or that of his people, or an attempt to deny them the basic rights of existence. Against a totalitarian enemy, passive resistance is a form of compliance with their genocidal policies.

With the outbreak of the Korean War, Einstein again saw an opportunity for conscientious objection and pacifism to play an effective role in the struggle for peace, and he supported young men who refused to serve the military against their conscience. He no longer campaigned publicly as he had in the period before 1933, but he did make his position known, and privately he strongly encouraged several pacifists. "The conscientious objector is a revolutionary," he wrote a friend of one pacifist who had been sentenced to ten years in prison for refusing military service. "In deciding to disobey the law he sacrifices his personal interests to the most important cause of working for the betterment of society."[7] To another young conscientious objector who had written a book on Gandhi, Einstein wrote in April 1953:

> There is a sphere of conflict between the written laws of one's country and the unwritten laws, the existence of which becomes manifest in what we call our conscience. In the event of conflict, the state adheres to the written law; only with great reluctance does it take into account the unwritten law of conscience. But even the state has recognized the

duty of the individual to act according to the unwritten law when commands based on national laws are in striking conflict with the laws of his conscience. This principle was unmistakably established in the Nuremberg trials. Such a precedent is a precious tool in the fight against the slavery resulting from the civic duty to kill.[8]

The McCarthyite assault on civil liberties evoked, for Einstein and most refugees from fascism, visions of the rise of Nazism twenty years earlier. Just as Communists, socialists, and Jews had been the Nazi scapegoats, Communists, liberals, and intellectuals were now pictured as enemies of American freedom. Initially McCarthyism was aimed at intellectuals who were allegedly in a position to betray the United States—atomic scientists and foreign policy specialists. It soon degenerated into a free-for-all of suspicion, accusation, and persecution of any who were alleged to have associated with Communists. Because of America's faulty understanding of communism, socialism, and the postwar aims of the Soviet Union, Americans had no clear idea of who the enemy was, and the epithet "Communist" soon came to mean anyone whose beliefs and behavior did not rigidly conform to "Americanism." Those who did not conform—individualists, intellectuals, foreigners, political nonconformists—saw their constitutional guarantees of freedom, justice, and equality under the law suspended. Those who were caught in the web of McCarthyism, as well as many who may have escaped overt persecution, lived in a nightmare state for years on end, never knowing if and when that Orwellian knock on the door at midnight might come.

During this period of anonymous denunication, guilt by association, and (as was sometimes the case) persecution caused by bureaucratic error due to mistaken identity, the basic freedoms guaranteed for all Americans were often subverted and sometimes nullified. The citizen's right to travel was frequently revoked. The individual could exercise his freedom of speech and right to dissent only at great peril. The guarantee of fair trial, equality under the law, and the right to confront one's accuser was often denied; the threat of prosecution was used to extort "cooperation" from frightened victims. Minority rights were trampled. The independence of the individual was further undermined by the threat of economic, political, and social reprisal. Countless innocent men and women lost their jobs because they refused to cooperate or because of an anonymous character slur. Those who saved their jobs often did so at the expense of their self-respect by cooperating with their inquisitors.

Security boards, designed to test the loyalty of government workers, blurred the distinction between dissent and subversion, and those whose ideas even vaguely coincided with some aspect of Communist ideology were vulnerable to purgation. The security boards were instituted to protect the alleged national interest, not individual rights, and they were invariably manned by zealots who were exempted from public accountability. The security officer for John Foster Dulles, Secretary of State under President Eisenhower, had a sign on his desk which read: "An ounce of loyalty is worth a pound of brains."[9]

Between 1950 and 1954 Senator Joseph McCarthy of Wisconsin was the most irresponsible and intimidating of the Red baiters. As Chairman of the Permanent

Subcommittee on Investigations on Government Operations, he became adept at manipulating the news media by making outrageous and generally unsubstantiated accusations. One of his favorite ploys was to quote derogatory comments from FBI loyalty reports which often contained hearsay and testimony from unreliable sources. His lists of facts exploited the American penchant for practical and concrete information while his antielitist rhetoric appealed to anti-intellectual sentiment. Coercion and guilt by association were among his favorite tricks, and his committee, like the House Committee on Un-American Activities, would grant immunity to witnesses who implicated friends and associates. Those who refused faced economic ruin because they would be cited for contempt of Congress. In the prevailing atmosphere, it was assumed that they were guilty of protecting Communists, or that they were themselves "fellow travelers."

Intellectuals were singled out for special attack because, as artists, scientists, educators, entertainers, and disseminators of news and information, they were molders of public opinion. For this reason, Einstein maintained, intellectuals had a double responsibility, as citizens and as members of a community targeted for persecution, to fight these political inquisitions. To remain silent was to become an accessory to the crime, but, Einstein sadly noted, "most intellectuals do not like to give expression to their convictions because they are financially dependent from a dull majority and from an economically privileged few who shun the light."[10]

In an atmosphere where very few individuals were capable of forming a clear idea of the nature of the real threat to American freedom, it became all the more urgent for responsible individuals to expose the investigations. At the time, the Communist threat to the United States and Western Europe was almost nonexistent. By 1950 the American Communist Party had lost most of its hard-won gains in the labor movement and was viewed as the embodiment of evil by much of the American public. In Western Europe the threat of Russian communism had provoked no such hysteria even though geographical proximity and economic and political upheavals in the aftermath of the war had rendered the European democracies much more vulnerable than the United States.

On occasion Einstein had been victimized by the dishonest methods of the American Communists. Although he deplored the investigations, he felt the behavior of the Communist Party had been irresponsible and had sowed mistrust in the community through their conviction that the end justifies the means. Nevertheless, even if a danger to the United States existed, the McCarthyite and other congressional investigations represented a far more serious threat to society because they violated the spirit of the Constitution. "As long as a person has not violated the 'social contract,'" Einstein wrote to a Princeton undergraduate in the autumn of 1953, "nobody has a right to inquire about his or her convictions."[11] These particular investigations, conducted by committees protected by congressional immunity, represented a move to destroy the rights of the individual and "ruin independently minded citizens economically and to intimidate them to such a degree that they are unable to exercise the criticism so necessary just now."[12]

Under the circumstances the only alternative was to refuse to cooperate with the investigators.

In May 1953 while a massive book-purging campaign was under way in the nation's libraries, Einstein was presented an award by Lord & Taylor honoring his nonconformity in scientific matters. He sarcastically commented in his acceptance speech that he was "an incorrigible nonconformist whose nonconformism in a remote field of endeavor no senatorial committee has as yet felt impelled to tackle."[13] This statement caught the attention of William Frauenglass, a Brooklyn high school teacher who was being investigated by the Committee on Un-American Activities. Frauenglass suggested to Einstein that a statement from him would be very helpful to intellectuals and the public in the fight against "this new obscurantist attack." Einstein replied on May 16, 1953, and the letter was published in the *New York Times* on June 12, just six days before the execution of Julius and Ethel Rosenberg. In the so-called Frauenglass Letter he openly challenged the witch-hunters to take action against him. In part, the letter read:

> The problem with which the intellectuals of this country are confronted is very serious. Reactionary politicians have managed to instill suspicion of all intellectual efforts into the public by dangling before their eyes a danger from without. Having succeeded so far, they are now proceeding to suppress the freedom of teaching and to deprive of their positions all those who do not prove submissive, i.e., to starve them out.
>
> What ought the minority of intellectuals to do against this evil? Frankly, I can only see the revolutionary way of non-co-operation in the sense of Gandhi's. Every intellectual who is called before one of the committees ought to refuse to testify, i.e., he must be prepared for jail and economic ruin, in short, for the sacrifice of his personal welfare in the interest of the cultural welfare of his country.
>
> However, this refusal to testify must not be based on the well-known subterfuge of invoking the Fifth Amendment against possible self-incrimination, but on the assertion that it is shameful for a blameless citizen to submit to such an inquisition and that this kind of inquisition violates the spirit of the Constitution.
>
> If enough people are ready to take this grave step they will be successful. If not, then the intellectuals of this country deserve nothing better than the slavery which is intended for them.[14]

Although he later regretted it, Einstein permitted Frauenglass to delete the paragraph concerning the Fifth Amendment.[15] While he understood the importance of the Fifth Amendment as a means for the individual to protect himself, he felt that it was an inappropriate defense under the prevailing circumstances because the various investigating committees were attempting to force citizens to inform against other citizens.

As expected, Einstein's letter created a furor. He had dared to articulate what many private citizens felt. Once again the Einstein home was flooded with mail, most of which enthusiastically supported his stand. To his Swiss biographer, Carl Seelig, he expressed regret that "[o]nly in a few letters was any attempt made to weigh the arguments carefully. Yet, on the whole, I have the impression that my letter did help somewhat to clear the political air. . . ."[16] The *New York Times* disagreed. In an editorial the following day, it stated: "To employ the unnatural and illegal forces of civil disobedience, as Professor Einstein advises, is in this case to attack one evil with another." Senator McCarthy was more blunt: "Anyone who advises Americans to keep secret information which they may have about spies and saboteurs is himself an enemy of America."[17] On June 18, 1953, the day the Rosenbergs were executed, J. Edgar Hoover, in response to the Frauenglass letter, again requested a report on Einstein.[18]

Otto Nathan recalls visiting Princeton on the day Einstein had given the *New York Times* permission to publish the letter to William Frauenglass. "Do you think I have to go to jail?" the worried scientist asked. Einstein and Nathan discussed at length whether or not to withdraw permission to the *Times*. Nathan was distressed about the letter, not only because it might lead to the jailing of his friend, whose health was precarious, but also because Nathan felt that the Fifth Amendment was a last straw for many victims of McCarthyism with families to support. Nathan agreed that, as a matter of principle, one should base one's defense upon the First Amendment, but he felt that in the prevailing climate such a defense was likely to result in imprisonment, and he believed that in such circumstances the Fifth Amendment was a legitimate defense.[19]

At the time of publication of the Frauenglass letter, Einstein was not sanguine, but later on he did make jokes with friends, expressing mock disappointment that McCarthy had chosen not to respond to his challenge. Erich Kahler later wrote, "I have never seen him so cheerful and so sure of his cause as during that time. His intention was to stir the conscience of the public. . . ."[20]

According to Senator Joseph McCarthy this man was an enemy of America. (Courtesy of Margot Einstein)

The most gratifying response to the Frauenglass letter came from Einstein's old friend and fellow rebel, Bertrand Russell, who wrote to the *New York Times* late in June:

> You seem to maintain that one should always obey the law, however bad. I cannot think that you have realized the implications of this position. Do you condemn the Christian Martyrs who refused to sacrifice to the Emperor? Do you condemn John Brown? Nay, more, I am compelled to suppose that you condemn George Washington and hold that your country ought to return to allegiance to Her Gracious Majesty, Queen Elizabeth II. As a loyal Briton, I of course applaud this view; but I fear it may not win much support in your country.[21]

Russell, whom Einstein affectionately called a "rascal,"[22] was one of the few prominent intellectual figures who shared Einstein's strong political views on both individual rights and the question of control of nuclear weapons.

After the publication of the Frauenglass letter, many victims of McCarthyism requested Einstein's intercession in their behalf, but he declined for reasons of age, increasing ill health, and the desire to avoid overexposure. As he explained to the broadcaster Raymond Swing, who had urged him to appear on Edward R. Murrow's television show "See It Now," "[i]n matters of public action—as in Art—economy seems very much needed, and the lack of economy would spoil the little bit I can do under the circumstances (my being a naturalized citizen and a Jew); this lowers, of course, considerably the point of saturation."[23] Nevertheless, several months later, a set of unique circumstances conspired to involve him in the case of McCarthy against Albert Shadowitz.

On December 7, 1953, Shadowitz was served a subpoena by McCarthy's Senate Subcommittee on Investigations because they were investigating an alleged Communist-dominated union in which Shadowitz, today a professor of physics, had been active during the Second World War. The committee claimed to be investigating communism and subversion in the government and in factories producing government materials. Employed as an engineer, first at the army's Aberdeen Proving Grounds from 1941 to 1943 and then from 1943 to 1951 at the Federal Telecommunication Laboratories of I. T. & T., Shadowitz learned one day that a union which would exclude Jews and Negroes was being formed at his plant. Immediately, he became involved in organizing a rival union, the Federation of Architects, Engineers, Chemists and Technicians. This soon merged with the United Office and Professional Workers of America, which subsequently was ousted from the CIO because Communists allegedly served on its executive board. Now, years later, McCarthy was hoping to prove it had ties with Moscow.

Shadowitz was unwilling to cooperate with the investigation because he hated McCarthyism, and he refused to invoke the Fifth Amendment because "it seemed to me that that was essentially an admission of guilt and saying that what I was trying to do was to save my own skin."[24] He decided, instead, to stand on his First Amendment right, which was to say, "Look, don't bother me. I have a right to think as I please. If I've done anything wrong, just bring charges and don't bother me about anything else that I've been doing."

The evening after he was served the subpoena Shadowitz remembered the Frauenglass letter, and feeling "insecure" about his plan of action, he decided to ask Einstein for advice. He tried telephoning, but learned the number was unlisted. In a moment of inspired desperation, he drove from his home in northern New Jersey to Princeton. Somehow he found the house, and when Miss Dukas answered, he asked to speak with Einstein.

"She looked at me and said, 'Do you have an appointment?'" Shadowitz recalls. "I answered no, and she said, 'Well, you can't just come in and speak to Professor Einstein.' I realized I hadn't really thought about it—it was sort of a stupid thing. Then she asked, 'What do you want with him?' I told her [about the subpoena] and that I wanted his advice on the course of action I should follow in my appearance before the committee. She looked at me for about a minute without saying a thing. I must have a very honest face, or something, because she then turned to me and said, 'O.K. come on in.' And she introduced me to Einstein."

Einstein, clad in a baggy sweatshirt, corduroys, and a pair of old slippers, led his visitor to the upstairs study. Shadowitz's first impressions were strong. "The thing that struck me about him was the gigantic size of his face. He had the biggest face that I've ever seen on any man. From the top of his head to his [chin] . . . the very longest face I've ever seen on a man. Aside from that, what struck me immediately was that he put you at ease. You were completely at ease. . . ."

While Shadowitz explained his situation, "Einstein listened very carefully without saying a word, and then, at the end, Einstein said that he thought this was the only proper way to behave, and I ought to recognize that, as a person who worked one way or another with ideas, I was an intellectual, and he thought it was a special responsibility of intellectuals to fight the sort of behavior that McCarthy was engaging in. It had grave risks, and a person ought to know this, but he ought to be prepared to go to jail if necessary because it was his duty to the rest of the people who were not intellectuals. He said he would advise me to go before the committee and definitely state that I would not use, under any circumstances, the Fifth Amendment; that I was refusing to answer all questions on the basis of the First Amendment and my right to think as I please. He said, if you could, because of the temper of the times, you should specifically disclaim the fact that you were a spy, but only if [this were true]. And he didn't ask me whether I could or I couldn't. . . . [Einstein continued]: If they had any knowledge of espionage on your part, they ought to charge you with that, and then you must try to defend yourself, but they have no right to try to extract this information from you *a priori*. . . ." Einstein never asked Shadowitz if he had been a Communist, because, as he wrote to another of McCarthy's victims: ". . . party membership is a thing which no citizen has any obligation to give an accounting for."[25]

"I was there a very long time," Shadowitz continues, "and finally it was clear to me that he was done, and then he said to me (and there was no urging on my part): 'If you take this path . . . then feel free to use my name in any way that you wish.' I was really shocked by that, because it was like a *carte blanche* check. . . ."

At the first session with the McCarthy committee Shadowitz was allowed only the company of his lawyer. McCarthy used these preliminary closed sessions to determine which cases would be best suited for purposes of publicity. Roy Cohn, who "was all smiles," opened the hearing with mundane questions about name, age, and address. However, the moment Shadowitz mentioned Einstein, "Roy Cohn dropped completely out and all the questioning from that point on was taken over by Joe McCarthy. . . . I think the question was 'Was I now a Communist?' I said, 'I refuse to answer that and I am following the advice of Professor Einstein.' Well, a hush came over the hearing, and McCarthy asked me if I knew Einstein. I said, 'Well, yes and no. I've met him but I couldn't really say I knew him.'" Throughout the remainder of the hearing Shadowitz maintained the position that any questions pertaining to his personal beliefs, politics, association with other people, reading, writing, or thinking violated his First Amendment rights. Although the committee had no jurisdiction over espionage cases, he voluntarily stated that he had never engaged in it. When it became obvious to McCarthy that Shadowitz was willing to go to jail rather than answer the questions of the committee, he told his assistant counsel to notify Shadowitz's current employer, the Kay Electric Company, to see if it would suspend him as General Electric had done to employees who invoked the Fifth Amendment. Then McCarthy dismissed Shadowitz after warning him that there would be a public hearing.

After this first session, Shadowitz, fearing that McCarthy was "out to get" Einstein, offered to stop citing Einstein's name. In a letter dated December 14, 1953, he gave an account of the committee's questions and his responses. He closed his letter by thanking Einstein for his generous support, adding, "I don't know how my wife and I could have stood up under the ordeal if it weren't for your support." Einstein responded the next day, congratulating him for sticking to his First Amendment rights. "I agree with you," he concluded, "also insofar as you declare voluntarily that you had nothing to do with spying or with any other disloyal activity. If possible it would be preferable to state this not as an answer to questions but as a spontaneous declaration. In this way you would make it clear that, in your opinion, the investigation as such is incompatible with the spirit of the law."[26]

The injection of Einstein's name into the case immediately transformed an otherwise routine case (for McCarthy) into a sensational affair. The day after the open hearing headlines proclaimed Einstein's intercession on Shadowitz's behalf. Editorials with titles like "The Ingratitude of Dr. Einstein" censored "the stateless individual" who had taken refuge in this country only to repay it by urging disrespect and violation of its laws. Letters written to Einstein were about evenly divided. Many Americans believed he had performed a heroic act by his refusal to be intimidated by McCarthy. The critical responses ranged from carefully worded pleas for him to cease his advocacy of disrespect for the law to a handwritten note telling him: "You should be shipped back to your homeland and a camp." One critic enclosed a printed copy of the "American Creed" which reads, in part: "I therefore believe it is my duty to my country to love it; *to support its Constitution;* to obey its laws; to respect its flag, and to defend it against all enemies." In the margin Einstein noted, "This is precisely what I have done."[27]

Along with letters commenting on his stand, came appeals from many other victims of investigations. Could he write something on their behalf? Could he appear at their hearing? Explaining that the value of his intercession was symbolic, Einstein declined. On January 14, 1954, he again wrote Shadowitz, who had asked Einstein to give a talk: "You must, however, consider that many people in a similar position are approaching me. What I have strictly to avoid is the impression that I am functioning as a kind of political organizer. It has to be clear that I am restricting myself to having publicly and clearly stated my conviction. If I would not restrict myself in this way my attempt to help a good cause somewhat effectively would be considerably frustrated. For this reason I can—also in your case—not function as 'man in the battle-line.'"[28]

The public hearing had been held six days earlier, on January 8, 1954, in which Shadowitz again was asked if he had been a Communist while working at Aberdeen. Shadowitz repeated his refusal to answer questions violating his freedom of thought, speech, and association, and again he raised the issue of McCarthy's jurisdiction to inquire into activities or associations of persons not employed by the federal government. On August 16, 1954, the Senate passed a citation of contempt against Shadowitz who had lost his job at Kay the previous March 17, the day after he successfully completed the development job he was working on. His case, which was to drag on for another year was lumped with the cases of two other individuals who had refused to cooperate with McCarthy—Corliss Lamont and Abraham Unger.

This was the last year of McCarthy's power. The Cold War tensions had begun to ease slightly, and the Korean War, his best political issue, had ended the preceding year. On February 24, 1954, Edward R. Murrow attacked the Senator on the television show "See It Now," and the favorable response indicated that McCarthy's support had begun to erode.[29] His downfall came suddenly in June after weeks of televised Army-McCarthy Hearings. McCarthy's belligerence, bullying of witnesses and opposing lawyers, and failure to substantiate his charges finally convinced the public that his tactics were a sham. Months later his colleagues censored his conduct, but characteristically they did so on side issues, and not on his unconstitutional practices.

On July 27, 1955, the indictment against Shadowitz, Lamont, and Unger was dismissed by the courts on the technicality that McCarthy's committee had been authorized to investigate fiscal matters and that this case was beyond its jurisdiction. Once again the courts avoided confronting the real issue of the citizen's First Amendment right to freedom of speech, thought, and association.

During his ordeal, Shadowitz paid two or three more short visits to Einstein, and on one occasion he brought along his father. "I was very embarrassed," Shadowitz recalled years later, "because the first thing that happened when we were ushered in was that my father grabbed hold of Einstein and kissed him."

Edith Shadowitz, who accompanied her husband on another visit to Einstein, explained her father-in-law's behavior: "Of course you have to know what it is to be a Jew and meet Einstein. He really was kind of like a superman to our Jewish community because he exemplified all those things which we would like to see in Judaism. . . . To Al's father this was *the* great Jew."[30] A quarter of a century later Albert Shadowitz views Einstein as a moral figure, devoid of selfish and aggressive tendencies: "What Gandhi must have meant to the Indians is what Einstein meant to me."

The case of Shadowitz, Lamont, and Unger was one of the principal challenges to the arbitrary behavior of the McCarthyites. The case became a cause célèbre of the Emergency Civil Liberties Committee which had been formed in October 1951 to aid individuals and causes in cases involving constitutional rights, because the American Civil Liberties Union had refused to aid Ethel and Julius Rosenberg on the pretext that civil liberties had not been at issue. Indeed, the ACLU, originally founded to defend pacifists during the First World War, had reversed its longstanding policy after the outbreak of the Korean War and had withdrawn its opposition to military conscription.

The ECLC was founded by Corliss Lamont, I. F. Stone, and numerous clergymen, educators, and professional men who felt that the ACLU, which had purged itself of Communists on its board, had become reactionary. From the start the ECLC was a favorite target of the anti-Communists who realized that if the committee could not be intimidated, it could at least be discredited in the eyes of the public. Despite the partially successful smear campaign waged against it, the ECLC managed, during the worst periods of the McCarthy era, to challenge successfully a number of unconstitutional practices of government officials.

On March 13, 1954, the ECLC sponsored a one-day conference in Princeton on the subject of academic freedom in honor of Einstein's seventy-fifth birthday. A great hue and cry was raised that many of the members of the ECLC were Communists, and a number of prominent civil libertarians publicly refused to attend. Norman Thomas, whose lifetime work for democratic socialism had often been exploited and betrayed by American Communists, wrote an open letter to Einstein explaining that his decision not to attend was based on the fact that leading members of ECLC "have shown through the years anything but a consistent love of liberty, in and out of the academic field. . . . I am thoroughly persuaded, as I think you are, that the test of freedom in America and indeed among thoughtful men everywhere is a capacity to oppose both Communism and the thing that in America we call McCarthyism."[31]

Einstein, who no longer attended such functions, replied to Thomas in a long friendly letter which provides an excellent statement of his attitude toward the Soviet Union and the McCarthyites. The Soviet Union, he wrote, was "politically underdeveloped" and its domestic policies were "abominable" to civilized people, but even well-intentioned criticism by foreigners could not help bring about progressive development, which must be effected by the Russian people themselves. He continued:

It seems to me, therefore, more useful to confine ourselves to the following question: How about the danger which America faces from its own Communists? Here is the principal difference of opinion between you and me. In short, I believe: America is incomparably less endangered by its own Communists than by the hysterical hunt for the few Communists there are here (including those fellow citizens whose red tinge is weaker, à la Jefferson). Why should America be so much more endangered than England by the English Communists? Or is one to believe that the English are politically more naïve than the Americans so that they do not realize the danger they are in? No one there works with inquisitions, suspicions, oaths, etc., and still "subversives" do not go unchecked. There, no teachers and no university professors have been thrown out of their jobs, and the Communists there appear to have even less influence than formerly.

In my eyes, the "Communist conspiracy" is principally a slogan used in order to put those who have no judgment and who are cowards into a condition which makes them entirely defenseless. Again, I must think back to the Germany of 1932, whose democratic social body had already been weakened by similar means, so that shortly thereafter Hitler was able to deal it the death-blow with ease. I am similarly convinced that these here will go the same way unless men with vision and willingness to sacrifice come to the defense.

Now you clearly see the difference of opinion. Who is right cannot be decided through a logical process of proof. The future will tell. . . .[32]

On the day of the conference Einstein refused to accept a gift of flowers from the organizers, saying, "You may bring flowers to my door when the last witch-hunt is silenced, but not before." Earlier, however, he had answered a series of questions on the meaning of academic freedom which served as a basis for the

Einstein and foreign students visiting America under the auspices of the American Field Service Program, summer 1952. (Courtesy of Margot Einstein)

conference discussions. He defined academic freedom as "the right to search for the truth and to publish and teach what one holds to be true. This right also implies a duty; one should not conceal any part of what one has recognized to be true." Any restriction with this right interferes with the dissemination of knowledge and impedes rational judgment and action. The current practices of the McCarthyites not only violate First Amendment rights, but intimidate even the private expression of beliefs. This violation of mutual trust threatens the ability of democratic government to survive. Everyone should fight these practices, regardless of personal risk. Intellectuals, as special targets of the witch-hunts because of their ability to influence public opinion, are especially obligated to fight any measure which violates the rights of the individual; to cooperate makes one an accessory to the crime of "invalidating the Constitution." The best way to assist the victims was, of course, to provide legal counsel and, when necessary, to find work for them.[33]

These were, as Otto Nathan has recently stated, "very bad years."[34] The American reputation as a haven for the oppressed was seriously weakened by the witch-hunts. Many European émigrés, who once had sought refuge in America from Hitler, returned to Europe because of McCarthyism. Others were driven into hiding or lived in fear that they would be the next victims of the anonymous informers. Edward R. Murrow noted on "See It Now," in January 1955 featuring Robert Oppenheimer, that because of the temper of the times and the McCarran Internal Security Act of 1950, prominent nuclear physicists like Szilard and Fermi would never have been permitted to enter the country. Oppenheimer, fresh from his own ordeal, added, "Perhaps not even Einstein."[35]

Even in the darkest times Einstein's loyalty to the democratic traditions and institutions of his adopted country never wavered. Despite his disgust with the direction of American society, he took pains to make sure that his public statements were constructive. A small incident from the spring of 1952 illustrates the careful manner in which he handled the responsibilities of a dissident.

Einstein's next-door neighbor, Mrs. Tiffin Harper (now Shenstone), was active in the American Field Service Exchange Program in which high school students from all over the world spent a year studying in America. Each year, in June, just before the visiting students returned home, they gathered for a farewell party. One afternoon in 1952 Einstein received several dozen young exchange students in his backyard. They asked him some particularly harsh questions about United States politics, and as Mrs. Shenstone recalls:

> I was terribly impressed [by the way he tried] to make these young people understand the problems. He was not allowing them to go back to their countries saying that Einstein agreed with all these things that were being said. It was a very big, wide-sweeping sort of understanding of the problems that he was trying to get across to them, instead of merely saying, "Oh, yes, it's perfectly awful." It was a very moving thing to see this man visiting with these young people. And, of course, they left absolutely ecstatic—this was the high moment of their trip to America.[36]

18

"Beware of Rotten Compromises"

For one like Einstein who had turned to science because of the independence it offered, the situation in America—indeed in international—science in the post-Hiroshima age was profoundly disturbing. The military domination of the fruits of scientific discovery and the McCarthyite assault on civil liberties had permanently altered the scientist's role in society and jeopardized his ability to think, investigate, and act independently. In his final years, Einstein became increasingly preoccupied with the problem of preserving the independence of the scientist.

The scientist is concerned with the discovery of truth and his work is the property of the entire human race, not to be hoarded by this or that nation or interest group. Anyone searching for scientific knowledge is entitled to freedom of inquiry regardless of his personal opinions and values. The scientist's gratification derives from his work, not from his national identity. Membership in the community of scientists makes him a natural internationalist. To perform his work properly, the scientist must have access to all information, and he must be free to discuss work in progress with his colleagues without restriction.

Before the Second World War, American scientific research had been relatively independent of the government. Most of the financial support for research came from universities and large private foundations. Group research began to develop in the 1930s because of the increasing degree of complexity of the equipment and the great increase in the numbers of students working with a professor. An example of this would be the early cyclotron work of E. O. Lawrence at Berkeley.

The early American research on atomic fission was financed by a few private institutions, and the military authorities only reluctantly agreed to contribute $6,000 after almost a year had elapsed since the first successful splitting of uranium. As late as the spring and summer of 1941, Vannevar Bush, fearful that the search for an atomic bomb might be fruitless, disappointed in the progress of the small American uranium project, and quietly hopeful that such a weapon might be impossible to build, had to be persuaded to intensify nuclear research.[1] Not until June 1942 did the United States make the large-scale commitment to develop atomic weapons. The success of the Manhattan Project permanently changed the relationship of government and scientific research, and after the onset of the Cold War arms race, there would be a perennial demand for weapons systems which would be obsolete almost before they were delivered. Scientific research, formerly a quest for a greater knowledge and understanding of nature became, when serving the government, a frenetic search for practical results which would increase man's illusion of power over nature and man, and scientists engaged in that research became highly specialized workers for the state.

The great influx of military funds enabled scientific research to proceed on a scale never before imagined, but at the same time the government began to exert an ever increasing influence on the life and activities of the scientists and the universities. Its interest was in "technical assistance, not wisdom." Where the intellectuals formerly had been, in the words of Lewis Cosner, "jealous guardians of moral standards that are too often ignored in the market place and the house of power,"[2] they were now increasingly dependent for their livelihood upon government and business. More and more the military overseers were able to dictate what was to be researched, who was to be funded, and what conditions of secrecy were to prevail. As the power of McCarthyism grew, the military and government were able to exert pernicious influence upon the attitudes, values, and loyalty of the scientific researchers.

Technical progress depends on, but is distinct from, the pursuit of scientific knowledge. The attempt to force specific technical advances while simultaneously tampering with the ability of the scientific thinker to pursue his work was bound to have adverse consequences. Scientific progress grows out of man's quest for knowledge, and only rarely does it come from a pursuit of practical objectives. "Science will stagnate," Einstein warned, "if it is made to serve practical goals."[3] In 1949 Einstein wrote to one correspondent: "Men really devoted to the progress of knowledge concerning the physical world . . . never worked for practical, let alone military, goals."[4] He conceded society the right to promote research through material assistance, but it should not interfere with the scientist's freedom of inquiry; great scientific advances are due to the work of gifted individuals and not to organizations and committees.

The Cold War and the enlistment of scientific research in the service of the politics of national interest caused security, as defined by the military, to become a paramount issue. Ever since the Manhattan Project precautions had been devised to insure the secrecy of sensitive research and the loyalty of the scientific workers. E. U. Condon had been sacked from the Manhattan Project by General Groves because he refused to submit to Groves's policy of compartmentalizing access to information. In the March 1946 issue of the *Bulletin of the Atomic Scientists,*

Condon wrote: "Because the scientific spirit is so completely opposite to the military spirit, science simply will not go forward under military domination." In the military hierarchy, the flow of ideas is from top to bottom, whereas, Condon pointed out, in scientific organizations, it is just the opposite.[5]

In an interview with a French journalist in June 1946 Einstein echoed the widespread dissatisfaction of nuclear scientists with the military by claiming that military procedures had been largely responsible for delaying the bomb's development by two years. "The professional soldiers," he is quoted as saying, "who today express themselves so loudly and arrogantly, displayed at the outset of the atomic scientific development a skepticism which often acted as a brake on research. Further, the exaggerated application of secrecy, the overly exclusive departmentalization of various scientific and research groups, and the behavior of the coordinating officers, who were ignorant of the new scientific discoveries, constituted the major causes of delay."[6] It was essential, Einstein maintained, that the individuals who controlled the distribution of the funds and the direction of the investigations possess a genuine understanding of the nature and requirements of research, and that political considerations not play a role in these decisions.

Einstein did not believe that scientists could be blamed for the political and military decision to bomb Hiroshima and Nagasaki, but he did agree with the mathematician Norbert Wiener that the scientist is not merely an expert, but is also responsible for anticipating the consequences of his work. If the fruits of his labors are incompatible with his ethical values, he is obliged, even at the risk of loss of employment, to refuse to participate. "Non-co-operation in military matters," Einstein flatly declared in January 1947, "should be an essential moral principle for all true scientists . . . who are engaged in basic research."[7]

Einstein recognized that the militarization of science was not an isolated problem, but was a direct consequence of the war mentality and could be ameliorated only when the threat of war was eliminated. As long as international anarchy prevailed, the escalating arms race would continue out of control. Since weapons development depends on scientific and technological advances, the military support of scientific research and development would continue apace. In addition to the unending pressure for practical results, requirements of secrecy would intensify the growing sense of national and personal insecurity. Noting this, Einstein warned early in the Cold War, "the civil rights of citizens are being sacrificed to the alleged cause of national interest."[8] Governmental interference in teaching and research, loyalty oaths, and political witch-hunts to ferret out real or imagined subversive elements would inevitably follow. Human values were being subordinated to political considerations.

Many years earlier Einstein had told students at the California Institute of Technology that modern science had not brought greater happiness to mankind even in times of peace because the mass of men had been "enslaved" to machines performing monotonous tasks while living in perpetual fear of unemployment. "If you want your life's work to be useful to mankind," he advised the students, "it is not enough that you understand applied science as such. Concern for man himself must always constitute the chief objective of all technological effort. . . ." Failure to keep human values paramount, he warned, would render the blessings of scientific progress a "curse" on all mankind.[9]

One of the most celebrated casualties of the McCarthy era was Robert Oppenheimer, the wartime Director of the Manhattan Project and Chairman of the General Advisory Committee of the Atomic Energy Commission from 1947 to 1952. In December 1953 he was stripped of his security clearance for alleged contact with Communists before the war. Of the twenty-four charges against him, all but one had been known at the time his 1947 security clearance was granted. The only new item dealt with his opposition in 1949 to the crash program to develop the hydrogen bomb and his alleged efforts to dissuade his colleagues from participating in the project. Nearly four years later, in the atmosphere of suspicion which characterized the McCarthy period, it was asked if there had been a deliberate delay in the development of the bomb and if Oppenheimer had been involved. The issue was exacerbated by the personal antagonism which existed between Oppenheimer and the Atomic Energy Commission's Chairman Lewis L. Strauss, the instigator of the action against the controversial physicist.

The Oppenheimer affair, destined to drag through the late spring and early summer of 1954, was a bizarre drama which mirrored the complex and tragic life of its central figure. Loved by his friends and despised by his enemies, Oppenheimer possessed an acute wit which occasionally earned the undying enmity of its victims, one of whom had been Strauss. The physicist Hans Bethe, who worked closely with Oppenheimer at Los Alamos, thinks that "Opje" was a great man. As a physicist, Bethe believes, Oppenheimer was not as original a thinker as some, but "he could often understand an entire problem after he had heard a single sentence." This talent may have been the source of many of his later woes, because he expected others to possess this same ability.[10]

In the late 1930s Oppenheimer flirted briefly with communism. He never belonged to the party and probably never seriously considered belonging. His brother Frank was a member, and his wife, Kitty, had been a fellow traveler during the Spanish Civil War. He was an active supporter of the Spanish Loyalists and a number of leftist causes which often were Communist fronts. When he learned of the fission of uranium in 1939, he immediately became so absorbed in problems relating to atomic energy that his political activities waned.

Late in 1942 General Groves selected Oppenheimer to direct the Manhattan Project. Routine army security investigators disclosed his involvement in Communist front groups and, had it not been for Groves's intercession on July 20, 1943, Oppenheimer's clearance would have been denied. Groves viewed his director's prewar activities as rather naïve but not dangerous. The two men enjoyed excellent rapport, and the general deemed Oppenheimer's remarkable abilities to organize and inspire the scientists under his direction indispensable to the success of the project. It should also be remembered that 1942–1943 marked the high point of the Grand Alliance, and the attitude in America toward communism was less hysterical than it became after the war.

That winter a Communist agent approached Haakon Chevalier, a close friend of Oppenheimer's, to suggest that he (the agent) would be willing to serve as conduit of information on atomic energy to America's Soviet allies. The agent asked Chevalier to enlist Oppenheimer in this enterprise. Although details of the story are murky, it is apparent that Chevalier refused to cooperate. A short while later, Chevalier informed Oppenheimer, who agreed that this would be treason, and the subject was dropped. Oppenheimer remained silent until a few weeks after his security clearance was granted. Then he volunteered a fabricated account of this incident to army security officers in which he alleged that three Manhattan Project scientists had been approached. His motivation can only be guessed at. Perhaps he wished to demonstrate that Groves's faith in him had been justified, or perhaps he thought his story would alert the security officers to the magnitude of the security problem facing them. Later, on at least two occasions, he altered and contradicted his story. For several months he resisted attempts to force him to divulge Chevalier's name, but finally in December 1943 Groves ordered him to do so and he complied. For the next several years Chevalier was harassed by investigators, lost his job, and eventually emigrated to France, completely baffled by his misfortune until the publication of the transcript of the Oppenheimer hearing in the summer of 1954.

Critics of Oppenheimer[11] contend that ever since he had yielded to Groves's request, Oppenheimer was a compromised man who owed his position of power to the continued good will of General Groves. This, his critics maintain, helps explain why Oppenheimer discouraged discussions at Los Alamos concerning the possible use of atomic weapons. A more objective appraisal would take into account the fact that at Los Alamos, in the spring and summer of 1945, there was a frantic push to complete construction of the first bombs, and serious discussion of the future use and control of atomic weapons was discouraged by General Groves, and to some extent by Oppenheimer. The work in Chicago had by that time been successfully completed, and scientists like Szilard and Franck were freer to contemplate the long-range implications of atomic weapons. It should also be noted that Szilard had, since 1939, a more acute appreciation of the political problems created by atomic science and technology than any other atomic scientist. Oppenheimer was far more reluctant to discuss political issues, and in the deliberations of the Interim Committee on May 31, 1945, he confined himself to a discussion of scientific and technological problems. He accepted, rather uncritically, the assumption of Groves and the policymakers that the bomb would be employed if it was ready.

After the war Oppenheimer became a national hero and the foremost adviser to the government on atomic energy, serving at one time or another on more than thirty governmental committees, and was the author of the report upon which the Acheson-Lilienthal Plan for the control of atomic energy was based.[12] His influence began to wane after his unsuccessful opposition to the crash program to develop the hydrogen bomb. In July 1952 he resigned from the General Advisory Commission, and thereafter his services were rarely sought by the Atomic Energy

Commission. At the height of McCarthyism in July 1953, Oppenheimer contributed an article to the *Bulletin of the Atomic Scientists*[13] in which he advocated greater openness of discussion of the atomic bomb within the United States government and among its citizens, and he proposed that the government share its knowledge with Great Britain. This approach, he believed, provided the best and healthiest defense for American society. His security clearance was scheduled to expire on July 1, 1954, but at the insistence of Lewis L. Strauss it was suspended in December 1953.

In August 1953 the Soviet Union successfully tested the first hydrogen bomb, half a year earlier than the United States. Senator McCarthy, convinced that only Soviet espionage could have beaten the American thermonuclear project, began to build a "case" against atomic physicists. On March 1, 1954, the United States' first hydrogen bomb test was carried out on Bikini Island. On April 6, McCarthy, invited by Edward R. Murrow to rebut charges made against the Senator on an earlier "See It Now" broadcast, charged that there had been an eighteen-month "deliberate" delay in the development of the hydrogen bomb. Five days later, on Sunday, April 11, 1954, the *New York Herald Tribune* ran a column by the Alsop brothers entitled: "Next McCarthy target: the leading physicists." The Alsops dismissed the McCarthy charge that the physicists had behaved traitorously, concluding that they had just made an honest mistake. That evening Abraham Pais received a telephone call at the Institute for Advanced Study from the director of the Washington Bureau of the Associated Press who wanted a statement from either Oppenheimer or Einstein. Pais was aware that the Oppenheimer hearing was about to commence, and in order to spare the Einstein residence from an invasion of newsmen he agreed to solicit a statement from Einstein.

At Mercer Street late that evening, when Pais explained the situation, Einstein burst out laughing, because, he then explained, the matter was so simple. All Oppenheimer had to do was to go to Washington, tell the officials they were fools, and return home. After further discussion, Einstein drew up a statement expressing his admiration for Oppenheimer as a scientist and as a human being which he telephoned to the AP in Washington.[14] This, of course, did not deter the newsmen and television cameras from descending upon the house when the story broke the next day. Einstein, walking home for lunch with Kurt Gödel, was surrounded by television cameras and newsmen. When Helen Dukas, who was preparing lunch, saw the journalists converging on the surprised physicist, she rushed outside to rescue him. Years later she described the pandemonium: "The newsmen were coming at him and I ran down there with my dirty apron shouting, 'Professor Einstein, they are newsmen, don't talk, don't talk.' They nearly pushed him into the bushes. [He refused to elaborate upon his AP statement.] They came after him and I slammed the door. They were mad. Later a friend told me they had already started the cameras and she heard me shouting."[15]

Most of the scientific community dismissed the charges against Oppenheimer as products of McCarthyism and gave him their full support. Forty leading scientists, including Einstein, expressed their convictions in the May issue of the

Bulletin of the Atomic Scientists. Einstein wrote simply: "The systematic and widespread attempt to destroy mutual trust and confidence constitutes the severest possible blow against society."[16] Privately Einstein advised Oppenheimer not to fight the AEC because he could not get justice, but would be playing into their hands. Instead, Einstein urged Oppenheimer to take the attitude that it was their loss, not his.

Months earlier, Oppenheimer had decided to fight for his rights and clear his name of the charge of disloyalty. The hearings, conducted by a special panel of the AEC, took place in April and May. Oppenheimer's personal life was raked over the coals, his flirtation with communism and the Chevalier incident were belabored endlessly. Oppenheimer was no longer the cocky, witty dominant figure; a humbling transformation had taken place.

The Oppenheimer hearing was a travesty of justice. John von Newmann, no friend of the accused, believed that in England Oppenheimer would have been created an earl and placed above censure in reward for his wartime services.[17] Technically, the trial was an informal hearing, but Oppenheimer's accusers turned it into a trial without due process of law. Information was withheld from his

Einstein and Robert Oppenheimer shortly after the latter's appointment to the directorship of the Institute for Advanced Study. (Courtesy of AIP Niels Bohr Library)

lawyer; there were delays in providing his counsel with transcripts; and the security agents of the AEC bugged offices where he sought legal advice.

The list of witnesses who testified reads like a who's who of American science. Among the scientists, only Edward Teller, father of the hydrogen bomb, spoke against reinstating Oppenheimer's security clearance. Teller had never forgiven the former director of the Manhattan Project for his opposition to the "super," and at the hearing he suggested that Oppenheimer's unwise judgment made him a security risk. Von Neumann, a fierce anti-Communist who would become a member of the AEC in the autumn of that year, testified on Oppenheimer's behalf. General Groves, like Teller, agreed that the man whose security clearance he had demanded in the middle of the war could no longer be trusted in peacetime with secrets he had helped assemble. (Groves also admitted that when he had devised his wartime plan to corner the world's supply of uranium, he had overlooked the possibility that the Soviet Union might have uranium ore.)

On June 1, 1954, the AEC special panel, by a vote of 2–1, opposed reinstating Oppenheimer's security clearance. The following day Einstein was among those who visited Oppenheimer's home to lend moral support. On June 30 the Atomic Energy Commission rejected Oppenheimer's appeal. This action had been taken, in the words of Lewis Strauss, "to safeguard [secret] information . . . and for no other purpose."[18]

The controversy surrounding this case has not abated after three decades. The hearing established that Oppenheimer had been guilty of indiscretions, lies, disloyalty to friends, especially Chevalier, and excessive political ambition. All these personal failings played into the hands of his enemies and exposed the real motives of his accusers. Clearly, the only valid issue before the Atomic Energy Commission was the question: Was Oppenheimer a security risk? Even Oppenheimer's opponents generally concede that his loyalty to the United States was beyond question. The fact that he was stripped of his clearance anyway underlines the threat McCarthyism posed to American society. If an individual can be innocent of charges against him, yet still be adjudged guilty because of personality flaws or because of political differences with powerful politicians, then the intent of the constitutional guarantee of impartial justice for all has been subverted. Although Lewis Strauss, like Senator McCarthy, claimed to be acting to protect American security, he was in reality waging a personal vendetta against a man he disliked, and he was sending an unmistakable message of intimidation to the intellectual community: "cooperate" with those in power, or be destroyed.

The Oppenheimer hearing exerted a profoundly dispiriting effect on the scientific community, particularly refugee scientists who were inclined to view McCarthyism as a fascist movement. Although the institute was not directly affected by the hearing, the entire sequence of events politicized the atmosphere there, and Lewis Strauss, who was also a trustee of the institute, was never forgiven for bringing inquisitorial methods against Oppenheimer.

By the time the ruling against Oppenheimer had been delivered, the institute was already on summer vacation, but the faculty, in anticipation of the negative decision, had taken steps to issue a statement of support for its director. Before Erwin Panofsky left Princeton that spring he said he would be willing to sign anything Einstein signed. This prompted one of his more conservative colleagues to comment that he was not at all sure he would entrust *his* vote to someone with Einstein's views. After much wrangling over the wording, all twenty-six active professors and professors emeriti signed a statement on July 1 which expressed complete confidence in Oppenheimer's loyalty, discretion, and concern for the welfare and security of the United States. They also expressed admiration for his public service and his work at the institute. Einstein would have preferred the statement to go further in defending the constitutional rights of the individual against politically motivated investigations.

While the hearings were in progress, Einstein and his colleagues feared that Strauss might attempt to remove Oppenheimer from his institute position as well. On May 19, Einstein wrote his friend, Senator Herbert Lehman, another trustee, that the faculty had been deeply upset by the "completely needless indignities" to which Oppenheimer had been subjected. Describing Oppenheimer as "by far the most capable Director the Institute has ever had," Einstein declared that apart from "the grave injustice which would be involved," it would be extremely difficult to replace such a man. Furthermore, he concluded, "[u]nder the present circumstances, a dismissal of Dr. Oppenheimer would arouse the justified indignation of all men of learning and do grave harm to the reputation of the Institute in this country and abroad."[19] In an unconvincing gesture of reconciliation, trustee Strauss proposed Oppenheimer's reappointment as director on October 1, 1954, and the motion was carried unanimously.

Something else was on trial that spring: Oppenheimer's generation of physicists. These men and women had opened the door to new sources of power and destruction, but many had learned to regret their success and had begun to fight the political, military, and economic forces which had come to depend on the new science. Oppenheimer symbolized their accomplishments, their dissidence, and their human frailty. Some of his prewar friends felt that after 1945 he had begun to see himself as "God." In like manner, the great achievements of science and technology during the war had resulted in the public image of the scientist as godlike. In the growing atmosphere of fear and distrust, the benefactor was soon transformed into the betrayer of man. Since 1954, and even more so since the Vietnam War, American society has been as ready to blame as to praise the work of the scientist. Society has thus far failed, by and large, to understand its own ethical responsibility in determining the appropriate uses of the fruits of the scientist's labors.

There also exists a great deal of confusion about the distinction between science, technology, and the quest for truth. Western civilization would become sterile very quickly if it abandoned the quintessentially human yearning to extend man's understanding of his world and himself. Science, which seeks to uncover the secrets of the physical and biological universe, has through its technological applications bestowed manifold blessings upon man from the conquest of disease to the increased production of food and the improvement in shelter. Many scientific and technological discoveries which have improved man's lot have, when applied differently, threatened his very existence. One need only cite a simple tool like the knife: so useful, but so deadly.

As the technical applications of scientific discovery became more lethal and as the scientist became more a servant of forces antithetical to the free-wheeling independence which true science requires to bear fruit, creative men of conscience faced a cruel dilemma. On the one hand, they could no more renounce that inner compulsion to search for truth than they could renounce their humanity. On the other hand, they could not countenance the immoral, antihuman application of their discoveries, nor could they tolerate the manipulation of their profession by philistine exploiters who cared nothing for the creative act but only for its final product.

The contrast in the response to McCarthyite persecutions by Oppenheimer and Einstein is instructive. It should be kept in mind that their external circumstances were very different. Einstein was retired, but even in his prime he had always taken an independent position and therefore was not as vulnerable to political repercussions. One of Einstein's aphorisms from this period was "Beware of rotten compromises." Oppenheimer unfortunately made rotten compromises in the course of his dealings with military security officials, and although he enjoyed a period of enormous power (during which time he made unique and patriotic contributions to the war effort of his country), in the end he paid a terrible personal price for his earlier compromising.

If Oppenheimer had heeded the advice Einstein gave to him and to other victims of McCarthyism and refused to go along with Strauss's inquisition, he would have been denied his position of influence—something he had already largely lost—but he would have been spared the ugly spectacle of the hearing which amounted to a trial of his private life. Refusal to cooperate would have sent a message to the witch-hunters that crude tactics of intimidation would not succeed, and Oppenheimer's example would have served those less celebrated victims of McCarthyism as an example of courage in the face of coercion.

Toward the end of 1954 *The Reporter* magazine asked Einstein to comment on their articles dealing with the situation of scientists in America. In light of the McCarthyite attacks upon intellectuals which had culminated in the security hearing of Robert Oppenheimer a few months earlier, Einstein, the former Patent Office technical assistant and would-be lighthouse keeper, replied:

> Instead of trying to analyze the problem, I should like to express my feeling in a short remark: If I were a young man again and had to decide how to make a living, I would not try to become a scientist or scholar or teacher. I would rather choose to be a plumber or a peddler, in the hope of finding that modest degree of independence still available under present circumstances.[20]

The so-called plumber statement received wide circulation and was so completely misinterpreted that a decade after Einstein's death Max Born still mistakenly believed that Einstein had lost his love for science after the bombing of Hiroshima. (Born quickly admitted his error after receiving a clarifying letter from Otto Nathan.)

Einstein's love for pure science, a field which in his youth had offered so much independence, remained undimmed, and in fact was the cause of his intentionally provocative remarks. Einstein believed that unless "the practices of the ignoramuses who, based on their official position of power, tyrannize the professional intellectuals"[21] were resisted by scientists and intellectuals, the spiritual life of the community would become impoverished. Since intellectuals lacked political power, they had no choice but to resort to passive resistance and, like Rabbi Hillel who was a woodchopper and Spinoza who refused a professorship at the University of Heidelberg, they would be well advised to consider entering an occupation which would not be subject to political meddling.

An editorial in the *New York Times* charged Einstein with exaggerating the impact of security measures on science and scholarship and warned that the Soviet Union would soon take a "commanding lead" over the United States if his advice were to be followed. Other editorials were less dispassionate as Einstein was labeled a "bonehead" by one newspaper and a "babe in the woods [who] ought to stay out of the woods" by another.[22] Not everyone was offended, however. The members of Chicago Local 130 of the Plumbers and Steamfitters Union sent him a plumber's working card which Einstein gratefully accepted as proof that his remark had not been offensive to plumbers and peddlers.

Einstein's seemingly irresponsible remark was, in fact, a very serious response to a problem that weighed especially heavily upon his conscience in his final years. What he was saying was that the scientist must be independent to search for truth in his own peculiar fashion without fear of interference, as long as he does not violate the social contract. In addition, the scientist must assume responsibility for the applications by others of his discoveries. If he cannot countenance the technical applications of his discoveries, he must desist from that work voluntarily, even if this brings on financial and social ruin. He must also work to enlighten society so that mankind collectively can understand the implications of scientific discoveries and can appreciate its own collective responsibility for the humane applications of the fruits of research.

What Einstein did not say or imply in the "plumber statement," or in any other statement, was that the scientist (or the artist or anyone else) should renounce the quest for truth because of man's frequent abuse of the results of that quest. The search must go on or the spiritual life of society would perish.

19

"Even Age Has Beautiful Moments"

instein came to resemble, in the eyes of the public, an Old Testament Prophet in the last years of his life. "He became more and more patriarchal in appearance," one colleague from the institute remembers. "I used to watch him as he walked across the field here [in front of Fuld Hall] . . . even on cold wintry days. He was letting his hair grow longer and longer and his mustache was becoming more and more shaggy. He was, in his last years, a very venerable figure and looked more like a typical sage."[1] One child who saw the celebrated 1947 Halsmann photograph asked, "Is that the Lord?" Another youngster who saw Einstein in New York exclaimed, "There's Gandhi!"[2]

There was a sculptured beauty in his aging face; his eyes, filled with compassion, belied an impression of remoteness in his gaze. Sometimes this quality produced a hypnotic effect. In 1950 John Kemeny brought his fiancée to meet Einstein. When Kemeny was called to the telephone for several minutes, she told Einstein she knew nothing about her husband's field and asked if he thought it was a mismatch. Einstein answered that he felt it was better if husband and wife were not in the same field and therefore not in competition with each other. "But she hardly remembers that," Kemeny says, "because although [Einstein's answer] went on for about five minutes, Einstein was sitting in front of the window and there was something in his very low and somewhat hypnotic voice and that beautiful silvery hair. . . . The light through the window came through his hair and she was absolutely hypnotized, and she can barely remember anything that Einstein said."[3]

His daughter Margot has said that the features of his face became finer and more sensitive with age. In photographs taken of Einstein in his last years, one is drawn to the beauty and sadness in his eyes. Eva Kayser speaks of these photographs "where he looks straight ahead and you see his eyes fully. His eyes had an incredible depth; they looked far beyond everything that was visible. There was something sad [inside] and in certain moments they reflected the age-old misery of the Jews. . . . They spoke of his great wisdom. . . . There is something akin to the self-portraits of the very old Rembrandt. Margot and Rudi [Kayser] used to say, 'Rembrandt might have painted him had he known him.'"[4]

Painters and sculptors eagerly sought him as a subject. On one occasion, by way of small talk, a passenger on a train who did not recognize the famous person sitting next to him asked his neighbor what his profession was, and Einstein replied, "Model." Another time, a sculptress who was a friend of the family convinced Einstein to sit for her. Unknown to him, she was recording their discussions in illegible handwriting, which, after her death, was found to be indecipherable, and in order to prolong the conversations, she worked at an extremely slow pace. Finally, Einstein remarked in exasperation, "This bust is the robe of Penelope; it will never be finished."[5]

In his later years, Einstein accepted his fame with an air of bemusement. Sometimes he became annoyed by autograph hunters, photographers, and newsmen, but when admirers stopped him on the street, he invariably had a friendly quip and a smile. After one such incident he told his walking companion, Ernst Straus, "Well, the old elephant has gone through his tricks again."[6] Once when the family tomcat Tiger had released his perfume indoors, Einstein jokingly complained to Margot: "A man has to work so hard so that something of his personality stays alive. A tomcat has it so easy, he has only to spray and his presence is there for years on rainy days."[7]

To the very end of his life Einstein could be seen walking to the institute, or in the vicinity of the nearby Marquand Park with friends like Kurt Gödel and Saxe Commins. Dorothy Commins remembers Einstein and her husband were "like two kids" walking around the park, discussing literature, philosophy, and the world situation. A deep friendship developed in the later years, and when Commins suffered a heart attack in the summer of 1953, Einstein was one of his first visitors after he was released from the intensive care unit. Princeton was experiencing one of its most wretched heat waves, and Commins was distressed that Einstein had walked down to the hospital. "Professor Einstein," he said with embarrassment, "this is an imposition on you." Einstein smiled and replied, "Where there is love, there is no imposition." Mrs. Commins said later, "Saxe never got over it. I think it helped to pull him out."[8]

Einstein had always enjoyed walking in fields and woods with Margot. Sometimes he was silent, other times he explained things from nature to her in a clear and simple way. Once he told her with a touch of sadness, "When one had once an idea, people are always waiting for one to have a new idea. It's ridiculous. One cannot always have ideas. It comes once in a lifetime that you have an idea."[9]

In old age, the man who had been a solitary and dreamy child remained a dreamer. At the dinner table he was usually very quiet, often drifting away in thought while absentmindedly balancing the cutlery—ever the physicist conducting experiments. Once he and an assistant were having lunch with Margot, who expressed concern that her parakeet seemed lonely and listless. When the assistant suggested she should get it a mate, Einstein, who had been silent, piped up: "All of that is an illusion. Having a mate is an illusion." Another time he was eating dinner alone with his daughter. She realized that he was lost in thought, and she, too, remained quiet. Toward the end of the silent meal he looked up at her and said softly, "*Ist dies nicht schon?* [Is this not beautiful?]" The silence and the tranquillity of the moment had moved him deeply.[10]

Drawing by Margot Einstein in the 1950s. Einstein also made a drawing of Margot at the same time, but he disliked the result and destroyed it before she could see it. (Courtesy of Margot Einstein)

Einstein turned seventy-five on March 14, 1954. Newsmen gathered outside his door were disappointed by the lack of celebration and by Einstein's attitude that "birthdays are for children." Many friends and colleagues dropped by the house with a present and a brief word of congratulations, but when Saxe Commins greeted him with "Many returns of the day," Einstein raised his hands and replied, "*Ach, Gott, nein.* It's time to go."[11] One little girl, Anne Fankhauser, cut out some paper flowers for him, but just as she presented them to him, the florist delivered a large box with long-stemmed roses. Einstein looked at them and quipped, "They send you the coffin right along with it." Then he turned to Anne and said, "I like your flowers much better than those roses."[12] Congratulatory letters from friends and strangers all over the world poured in, prompting Einstein to respond to one such message: "This 75th birthday has a little similarity with the well-achieved atomic explosion. I shall have to drudge for a long time in order to clean up the rubble."[13]

The correspondence with Elizabeth, Queen Mother of Belgium, interrupted by the war, had been resumed in 1951. Two weeks after his seventy-fifth birthday, Einstein thanked her for the friendly understanding she showed him on "this strange occasion."

> All manner of fable is being attached to [my] personality, and there is no end to the number of ingeniously devised tales. All the more do I appreciate and respect what is truly sincere.
>
> Strange that science, which in the old days seemed rather harmless, should have evolved into a nightmare that causes everyone to tremble. And fear is the worst counsel of all. Swords still fail to register the slightest inclination to be beaten into plowshares.[14]

Late in 1954 the paths of Einstein and Dr. Albert Schweitzer crossed. They had been introduced to each other in Berlin in the twenties, and although they never met again they did exchange letters on two or three occasions. In an unpublished essay written in 1953, Einstein had hailed the great doctor as the only Westerner "who has had a moral effect on this generation comparable to Gandhi's. As in the case of Gandhi, the extent of this effect is overwhelmingly due to the example he gave by his own life's work."[15]

In honor of Schweitzer's eightieth birthday to be celebrated in January 1955, Einstein wrote in the preceding July:

> It seems to me that the work in Lambarene has been to a considerable extent an escape from the morally petrified and soulless tradition of our culture—an evil against which the individual is virtually powerless.
>
> He has not preached and he has not warned and he did not dream of it that his example would become an ideal and a solace to innumerable others. He simply acts out of inner necessity.
>
> There must be, after all, an indestructible good core in many people. Or else they would never have recognized his simple greatness.[16]

In November 1954, a close family friend, Dr. Erna Fankhauser, was killed in an automobile accident. At the time of her death she had been teaching German and Latin at the Hun School in Princeton. She had always greatly admired Schweitzer and had assigned one of his books to her German classes. Several of her students made a collection among themselves and raised $50 which they took to E. R. Squibb and Company to buy antibiotics to send to Schweitzer as a memorial to their popular teacher. When the pharmaceutical company learned of the purpose of the drugs, they gave the students $500 worth of a brand-new antibiotic. Knowing of Dr. Fankhauser's friendship with Einstein, the students asked him to send a covering letter along with the drugs to Dr. Schweitzer explaining the reason for the gift. "An outstanding woman and teacher here suddenly lost her life in an accident," he wrote. "Surviving friends and colleagues tried to find a way to give expression to their admiration for the deceased. The contribution for your beneficial and admirable activity which you are now receiving was felt by those concerned to be the most appropriate way.

"This shows that discerning people everywhere are able to recognize a way out of the aberrations of our time. Thus one sees that your silent example has a deep-reaching effect. We may all rejoice in that."[17]

The medicine reached Schweitzer at the time of his eightieth birthday, and in February he thanked Einstein for his symbolic role in the Hun School gift. "Even without writing each other," Schweitzer reflected, "we are in mental communication, for we respond to our dreadful times in the same way and tremble together for the future of mankind. When we met in Berlin we could not have imagined that such a bond would ever exist between us. . . . Strange how our names are so often linked in public. I like it that we have the same given name. . . . I cannot grasp nor understand the fact that I should exert any influence in our time. It accompanies me like a mystery on the final stretch of my life. . . ."[18]

In the fall of 1954 Einstein became very ill with pneumonia and anemia which caused a weakness in the legs and heart and palpitations when walking. He was confined to the house until the end of the year, and by Christmastime he could report to a friend that he was much better, adding, characteristically, that "I am really quite happy with this simplification of my life."[19] He still had his cluttered study, littered with books and papers, where he would sit in a comfortable chair writing or calculating, with a blanket over his knee. Early in 1955 his health stabilized, and a visitor at the end of January reported that he did not appear to be ill, but "he moves creakily."[20]

Inevitably, as he grew older, references to aging and death slipped into his personal letters. Two weeks after Maja's death, he wrote to Hans Mühsam: "When we went on our long and beautiful hikes in that accursed Berlin, we were still at an age when one doesn't really believe in getting old, even though one knows it in one's own mind."[21] A year later he wrote Besso in Switzerland: "After all, it's a good thing that this individual life with all its tensions and problems does stop at some point. Instinctively one postpones thinking about this, even though one's reason says 'yes.' How pitiable must those people have been who thought up the idea of individual survival after death!"[22]

Ernst Straus "in a tactless moment" once asked Einstein how the aging process had affected his thinking. Einstein replied that he had just as many ideas as in earlier years, but that he found it increasingly difficult to decide which ideas ought to be pursued and which should be discarded. "In short," writes Straus, "he thought that his nose had grown less certain."[23] On one occasion Einstein wrote to an old friend, "Old age produces in the brain something that feels like a spider's web." But, he added, "Luckily, nature out there remains forever fresh."[24]

Responding to the annual New Year's greeting from the Queen Mother of Belgium, Einstein wrote in 1954:

> In one's youth every person and every event appear to be unique. With age one becomes much more aware that similar events do recur. Later on one is less often delighted or surprised, but also less often disappointed than in earlier years. This is how we notice that it is our way of looking that has changed, rather than the variegated world outside.
>
> One feels that there isn't much that one can achieve by one's endeavors, and one acquires a taste for the role of the understanding and possibly consoling onlooker.[25]

As his life drew to a close, he once told his daughter, "Margot, you will see for yourself, even age has very beautiful, beautiful moments."[26]

The institute celebrated the twenty-fifth anniversary of its incorporation in April 1955, and Einstein, appearing frail and tired, attended the quiet dinner. Louise Morse was seated next to him, and she remembers that he felt poorly and through most of the dinner, at which he consumed only a specially prepared broth, he spoke in German with the institute's librarian, Miss Sachs, because he was too tired to carry on an extended conversation in English. At one point, however, he spoke to Mrs. Morse about racial prejudice in Princeton and was especially sharp in his criticism of the discriminatory policies of the university.[27] The institute dinner was his final public appearance.

Einstein affixed his signature to a public appeal for the last time on April 11. As had so often been the case in the past, this final gesture was a call for the abolition of war. The appeal, known as the Einstein-Russell Manifesto, bluntly warned the world to disarm or perish. It had been conceived and written by Bertrand Russell and was subsequently signed by nine other leading scientists from the United States, Great Britain, France, Japan, and Germany (Max Born), all but two of whom were Nobel Laureates. Appealing "as human beings, to human beings," the signers asked the world community: "Shall we put an end to the human race; or shall mankind renounce war?"[28] The manifesto called upon scientists of all nations to convene a conference of scientists to open channels of cooperation in an effort to end the East-West nuclear arms race. It was made public three months after Einstein's death, and led directly in July 1957 to the first Pugwash Conference on Science and World Affairs at which, for the first time since 1945, scientists from the East and West met to discuss the problems of nuclear arms.

On April 11 he was visited by Israeli Ambassador Abba Eban and Consul Reuven Dafni to discuss a statement for radio broadcast on the occasion of Israel's seventh anniversary of independence. Einstein had viewed with growing alarm the East-West confrontation in the Middle East, especially the policy of the Eisenhower administration which sought to win the sympathy of the Arab states "by sacrificing Israel." The Israeli consul in New York had invited him to make a statement about the cultural and scientific achievements of Israel, but he felt the political situation was so dangerous that he preferred to make "a somewhat critical analysis of the policies of the Western nations with regard to Israel and the Arab states. . . ." Deeply worried about the future survival of Israel, he was even more distressed by the global ramifications of the seemingly small conflict in the Middle East, and he wished to warn the world that war between Arabs and Jews could escalate to World War III. After Eban and Dafni left, he began to draft the address.[29]

On Tuesday, April 12, Einstein paid his final visit to the institute. After his assistant, Bruria Kaufman, had fussed over him as much as she dared, she asked: "Is everything comfortable?"

He replied, smiling, "Yes, everything is comfortable. But I am not." It was his only reference to his pain. They then worked together for the customary two hours before returning home for lunch.[30]

On Wednesday Dafni returned to Princeton for further consultations. Within two hours of Dafni's departure, Einstein was attacked by severe abdominal pains which his Princeton physician Dr. Guy Dean diagnosed as a small leak from his aneurysm into the tissue behind the aorta. He gave Einstein a sedative, and later that evening he returned with Einstein's old friends Dr. Bucky and Dr. Rudolf Ehrmann, who had come from New York more as friends than doctors. They appraised the patient of the situation and decided to give him another sedative. He slept well, but awoke Thursday morning with more pain. Another doctor, Frank Glenn, a cardiac and aortic surgeon, was brought in for consultation that afternoon, and Einstein vehemently rejected surgery to prevent further bleeding; "It is tasteless to prolong life artificially," he protested.[31] By Thursday, an old gall bladder condition, which had occasionally caused him pain in recent years, began causing abdominal pain, but as there was no swelling and pain in the upper abdominal region of the gall bladder, it was not judged to be an emergency.

On Friday morning, the pain was still acute, and he was showing signs of dehydration and was unable to take fluids by mouth. When the doctors recommended hospitalization, Einstein, who did not want a special fuss made over him, objected. He only agreed to go when they convinced him that the strain of taking care of him at home was too great for Helen Dukas. (This was typical of Einstein. In the past, when he had been ill, he would refuse to disturb a doctor. Helen Dukas then would call Dr. Bucky and Dr. Ehrmann and ask them to come to Princeton and pretend that they had just popped in for a visit. Einstein, who was not fooled, remarked to Miss Dukas on one occasion, "I can't die without the help of the doctors.")[32] By Friday evening his condition had improved significantly and he received several visitors, both family and friends. On Saturday he asked for his glasses and on Sunday he requested his calculations and unfinished draft for his Israel Day speech. Margot was also a patient in the hospital, and when she was brought in to see him, she was at first unable to recognize his pale and pain-wracked face. Hans Albert, summoned from Berkeley, arrived Saturday afternoon. Otto Nathan journeyed down from New York. Einstein faced death with serenity, although he did want to know if it would be painful. To the very end, he spoke of war and peace, science, and personal matters. His spirits remained undimmed and, despite the pain, he still was able to tease his saddened visitors with a smile and a quip.

By Sunday evening his condition appeared to have improved, and his doctors hoped that the bleeding would cease. Otto Nathan left his bedside at about 8:00 P.M., not realizing that the end was near. Einstein had been alert and wanted to work on his calculations, but he was in especially great pain when he tried to work. In one of his last conversations with Nathan, Einstein had motioned to his heart and said he felt in there that he was close to success with his unified field theory. But on this evening, for the final time, Nathan and Einstein discussed the threat against civil liberties in America and the danger of rearming Germany.[33]

Dr. Dean visited his room at 11:00 P.M. and found him sleeping soundly. Shortly after one o'clock Monday morning, April 18, Einstein, still sleeping, began to mumble something in German which the attending nurse could not understand. At 1:15 A.M. Einstein gave two deep breaths and died.

Einstein had hated the thought that his grave might be turned into a shrine and, accordingly, his remains were cremated in a small private ceremony at which Otto Nathan spoke a few words recalling Goethe's famous lines at Schiller's death. His ashes were then scattered.

Michele Besso had died in March 1955, and on March 21 Einstein had written a moving letter to Besso's sister and son describing the long-ago days of their youthful friendship in Switzerland before the First World War, their musical evenings, their work together in the Patent Office, and the "unforgettable charm" of their discussions of physics and other subjects on their way home from work during the period Einstein was formulating his early great ideas. "And now he has preceded me briefly in bidding farewell to this strange world," he continued. "This signifies nothing. For us believing physicists the distinction between past, present, and future is only an illusion, even if a stubborn one."[34]

20

Morning Air

"If a plant cannot live according to its nature, it dies; and so a man."
Thoreau,
"On the Duty of Civil Disobedience"

Almost everyone agrees upon the goodness of Einstein's character, even those who most belittled his public comments on political matters. In fact, so beguiling is the character of Einstein, that the biographer, if he wishes to present a reasonably objective account of his life, worthy of the spirit of the subject, must, like Odysseus, order himself tied to the mast of his craft to resist the Siren's song of hero worship. The evidence of his kindness, generosity of spirit, and gentle humor is too overpowering to ignore. From the old laborer at the institute who told Margot Einstein after her father's death that he was a great man "because he always greeted me first" when he passed on his way to work[1] to the royal family of Belgium, Einstein was the same simple, unassuming person, without aggressions or passions, unconcerned by the attitudes and opinions of others, and at peace with himself. To such a man, helping others came naturally.

To a greater degree than is true of most mortals, he was free of human foibles, but he was no plaster saint. By his own admission he failed twice in marriage, and his relations with his sons were often difficult. His great inner strength and independence perhaps contributed to his disinclination to close personal relations, but this was nevertheless very difficult for others to understand. One of his assistants, who was on vacation, once received a letter from him that contained one line of personal greetings and a page and a half of equations; even many years later, this absence of personal interest in the life of his co-worker remained a painful memory. I asked Valentine Bargmann to comment on this apparent absence of interest in the lives of his fellow workers. Professor Bargmann recalled that Einstein's phone conversations were conducted with "severe economy"; the

(Courtesy of Library of Congress)

problem was discussed, and when the discussion was completed, there was no small talk, but a return to work. Bargmann did not feel slighted; rather, he suggested that great thinkers like Einstein were great in part because they concentrate so intensely on what they are doing.[2]

Einstein could also be childish and unkind, as in the embarrassing fight with Elsa, witnessed by Otto Nathan, over the issue of wearing socks to the party in his honor given by President Dodds. Margot Einstein remembers similar arguments about luggage before embarking on voyages. Sonja Bargmann once attended a lecture with Einstein by the sculptor Archipenko. They were sitting in the front row, and Einstein, believing that a practicing artist should not analyze his work, made a number of schoolboy remarks to Mrs. Bargmann ridiculing the lecturer. His caustic jibes, although inappropriate and rude, were quite funny, and much to her embarrassment, she could not contain her laughter.[3]

It is true that Einstein disliked his fame and scorned the notion that there is such a thing as a great man, and that he scrupulously refused to exploit his renown for personal gain. It does not follow that he was above using his fame as leverage in negotiations in matters of principle (the Brandeis affair) or in an effort to assist a worthy friend or colleague in a time of crisis (the negotiations with Flexner over a position for Walter Mayer at the institute in 1932).[4]

Throughout his life, he was absorbed by his scientific work. If the world had left him alone, he would have quietly pursued his researches to his last breath. Except for relations with his sons, he was rarely if ever depressed by personal matters. Margot Einstein viewed him with the eyes of an artist. "He was a person full of harmony," she told me; "he lived in his own world, and this saves people."[5] What could distress him and wrench him away from his science was an acute and austere social conscience that apparently was first stirred to action by the advent of the First World War.

His ethical outlook had been shaped by the Jewish tradition, stripped, he noted, of its priestly additions. From an early age he had rejected externally imposed authority and had made for himself a life that was remarkably independent of such authority. He believed that every individual should be permitted the opportunity to develop his qualities without interference from society, provided the development of this potential did not intrude upon the rights of another to do the same.

In his lifetime there was a general consensus—originally a consequence of his pacifist activities since 1914—that Einstein personally was the kindest of mortals, that he never failed to champion the noblest ideals, but that he was a hopeless novice in the "real world" and his dreams for a more just and decent world— desirable though they may be—were woefully impractical and unrealistic. Whether articulated or not, the feeling existed that since politicians did not meddle in science, a scientist ought not to intrude in practical politics. Once this perception of Einstein developed, it permitted his critics to praise his character while dismissing his message out of hand. Indeed, almost all but the most vicious enemies—Nazis, McCarthyites, racists—damned him with faint praise when he spoke out on matters of truth and justice.

Einstein was the first to admit that he was not a political creature, that he lacked the patience, the discipline, the training, and the temperament to deal with the day-to-day practical workings of politics. He never was in a position to make decisions that would influence the lives of thousands and millions of others. Therefore, he obviously never experienced firsthand the pressures, the responsibility, and the conflicting demands of competing constituencies. Even his admirers sometimes wished he would curb his tongue.

Nevertheless, the ideas he put forward were not the product of wishful thinking. The thorough and careful study that preceded formation of his ideas should not be overlooked. If they did not find favor among the cold warriors, it does not follow that Einstein was naïve or out of his element any more than were Antigone, Thoreau, Tolstoy, Gandhi, or Martin Luther King, whose philosophy of noncooperation with evil Einstein exemplified. This philosophy, so simple to articulate, so difficult to understand and live by, holds that man's primary allegiance is to universal laws. If the state legislates immoral laws, one must follow one's conscience and repudiate those dictates of the majority, which are immoral. Thoreau writes, ". . . any man more right than his neighbors constitutes a majority of one already."[6]

A significant portion of this study of Einstein's life during the Princeton years has been devoted to the attempt to clear away the lazy prejudices and misperceptions of those who seek to dismiss Einstein's political activity out of hand. Much effort has been expended to reconstruct as carefully as possible the climate of the times, the forces at work, and the actions of those people who did possess the power to shape our destiny. Einstein's ideas, opinions, and actions are viewed against this backdrop. Whether his ideas—specific ones, or taken as a whole—appeal to the reader or not, it seems difficult to sustain the myth that they were the product of a naïve, well-meaning old saint who should have restricted his activities to the narrow confines of his area of expertise. Instead, we see in Einstein a man without personal ambition whose political ideas represent a lifelong effort to discover ways to achieve greater justice and decency in a world that has been brought to the edge of extinction by technological progress unaccompanied by progress in the realm of human affairs.

At the same time, one must ask: How do we assess the performance of the "experts" who have possessed power in this century? Have their policies succeeded? Is the world a safer, better place in which to live in 1985 than in 1918? Or 1945? To those who share Einstein's profound concern about the dangers of nuclear war, the answer can only be negative. The political experts—whether Soviet or American—are men of great personal ambition whose devotion to the advancement of the cause of their particular country generally precludes objective appraisal of the total world situation; nor are they concerned to find out what would be the best way to achieve world peace rather than Soviet or American aims. Since the end of the Second World War and the dawning of the nuclear age, these men have seen no alternative route to follow but that of the Cold War arms race which may lead toward total annihilation. They claim that "deterrence"—a policy designed to scare your enemy while reassuring your own citizens[7]—has thus far prevented nuclear war. To a growing number of people this precarious armed stalemate affords no sense of security whatsoever. If there is a posterity, will its wisest and most just historians dismiss as naïve Einstein's post-Hiroshima efforts to achieve lasting worldwide peace and total international disarmament through the creation of a supranational world authority?

Thoreau's refusal to pay his taxes did not succeed in abolishing slavery, but the legacy of this act of conscience, the essay "On the Duty of Civil Disobedience," influenced Tolstoy, Gandhi, and King, and thereby has changed and is still changing the world in ways unimagined even by that Concord visionary whose attitudes so perplexed his neighbors more than a century ago. In his lifetime, Einstein and those who shared his convictions failed to abolish war and the anarchy of the nuclear arms race. Like Thoreau, they too have left a legacy which, if the human race is to survive, must soon triumph. As Thoreau has written: ". . . It matters not how small the beginning may seem to be: what is once well done is done forever."[8]

Whether this or that idea of Einstein's is judged to be right or wrong, one cannot escape a sense of admiration for his ideas in general. What I admire most is the spirit that motivated all his actions—a love for life and a passionate commitment to truth and justice in human affairs. One searches in vain for an ulterior motive in the political and social pronouncements of Albert Einstein.

Sir Isaiah Berlin suggests that Einstein's "deep humanity and sympathy with the victims of political oppression, social discrimination, economic exploitation . . . were in part, perhaps, a compensation for his difficulty in forming close personal relationships."[9] Perhaps Berlin is correct. It seems to me, however, that Einstein's "deep humanity" and identification with victims of injustice represent a far more positive impulse than compensation alone. It was the very essence of his character to identify with those whose freedom to pursue their God-given destiny had been violated. He had been blessed with a strong intellect and a great heart, and he had, from his earliest years, worked to achieve that independence of thought and action that alone could nourish his special gifts. Infringement of this independence by others was intolerable. Infringement of the independence of anyone else was just as intolerable and must be opposed by the same uncompromising zeal with which he would defend his own autonomy. His daughter once said he was a small piece of nature, a small part of the whole. How could he defend and enjoy the fruits of his freedom and independence if he did not also defend with equal determination the right of others both living and, as yet, unborn, to enjoy similar opportunities?

John Kemeny was one of Einstein's last assistants. I once asked him what it had meant to him to have known Einstein. Kemeny, who had been a very young man when they collaborated, replied: "I think everybody who knew Einstein well had his life changed by that. It set a standard that you wish you could live up to and you absolutely know you can't. Not just because your brains aren't as good as Einstein's, but to be that good and to be that humble and that kind a human being and that tolerant of human short-comings is a standard I know I couldn't live up to."[10]

In one sense, Kemeny speaks for all who knew Einstein well. In another sense, however, I think he sells himself short. Granted, few among us can reasonably aspire to match Einstein's special scientific exploits. And on the universal plane of human qualities, Einstein sets, indeed, an imposing standard. But the example of his life presents a challenge to posterity—a challenge to each individual to make the most of the gift of life, to achieve that independence of thought and action which permits the free and glorious development and expression of curiosity. Unquenchable fascination with nature, with life, with the cosmos produces a being at once unique, independent, and in harmony with the music of the spheres. Such a person cannot tune out the discord of exploitation and injustice. He can only respond in a unique and unselfish way. Whether he is great as a scientist, artist, doctor, or teacher, he will surely be a great human being. And Einstein, for all his greatness as a scientist, was, above all, a human being, a great human being.

The qualities of character whose flowering in Einstein have made him the rarest of mortals are, paradoxically, those that are common to us all as a matter of birthright—the possibility to revere all life and to aspire to achieve the promise of one's God-given potential. Accordingly, I would like to conclude with a passage from Thoreau that never fails to remind me of Einstein:

> For my panacea, instead of one of those quack vials of a mixture dipped from Acheron and the Dead Sea, which come out of those long shallow black-schooner wagons which we sometimes see made to carry bottles, let me have a draught of undiluted morning air. Morning air! If men will not drink of this at the fountain-head of the day, why, then, we must even bottle up some and sell it in the shops, for the benefit of those who have lost their subscription ticket to morning time in this world. But remember, it will not keep quite till noonday even in the coolest cellar, but drive out the stopples long ere that and follow westward the steps of Aurora.[11]

NOTES

INTRODUCTION

1. Albert Einstein, *Einstein on Peace,* ed. Otto Nathan and Heinz Norden (New York: Simon and Schuster, 1960), p. 639.

2. Albert Einstein, *Ideas and Opinions,* based on *Mein Weltbild,* ed. Carl Seelig, and other sources, new translations and revisions by Sonja Bargmann (New York: Crown Publishers, Inc., 1954), p. 225.

3. Albert Einstein, *The Human Side: New Glimpses from His Archives,* selected and edited by Helen Dukas and Banesh Hoffmann (Princeton: Princeton University Press, 1979), p. 52.

4. Einstein to Hermann Broch, September 1945, quoted in Banesh Hoffmann and Helen Dukas, *Albert Einstein: Creator and Rebel* (New York: The Viking Press, 1972), p. 254.

5. "Zu Spinoza's Ethik" written by Einstein, ca. 1920, Einstein Archives.

6. Baruch Spinoza, *Ethic,* part IV, proposition XXXV, in *Spinoza: Selections,* ed. John Wild (New York: Charles Scribner's Sons, 1958), p. 313.

7. Albert Einstein, *Autobiographical Notes: A Centennial Edition,* trans. Paul Arthur Schilpp (LaSalle and Chicago: Open Court Publishing Company, 1979), p. 5.

8. *Human Side,* p. 89.

9. Ibid., p. 23.

10. Albert Einstein, Preface to *Albert Einstein: A Biographical Portrait,* Anton Reiser (pseudonym of Rudolf Kayser) (New York: Albert and Charles Boni, 1930), p. v.

1

1. Mrs. Randolph Frothingham to Honorable A. Dana Bogdan, Chief Visa Division, Department of State, November 19 and 22, 1932. See the Albert Einstein FBI files, section 1.

2. Albert Einstein, *Ideas and Opinions,* based on *Mein Weltbild,* ed. Carl Seelig, and other sources, new translations and revisions by Sonja Bargmann (New York: Crown Publishers, Inc., 1954), pp. 108, 7–8, and for a slightly different translation, see Albert Einstein, *Einstein on Peace* (hereafter *EoP*), ed. Otto Nathan and Heinz Norden (New York: Simon and Schuster, 1960), pp. 206–207.

3. *New York Times,* December 4, 6, 7, 11, 1932.

4. *EoP,* p. 211.

5. Gordon A. Craig, *Germany 1866–1945* (New York: Oxford University Press, 1980), pp. 646–647.

6. Lucy Dawidowicz, *The War Against the Jews 1933–1945* (New York: Holt, Rinehart and Winston, 1975), p. 71.

7. Ibid., p. 254.

8. *EoP,* p. 213.

9. "To the Prussian Academy" written by Einstein, April 7, 1933, Einstein Archives.

10. *EoP*, pp. 217–218.

11. Joseph Haberer, *Politics and the Community of Science* (New York: Van Nostrand Reinhold Co., 1969), pp. 130–133. Hitler is quoted in Edward Yarnell Hartshorne, Jr., *The German Universities and National Socialism* (Cambridge, Mass.: Harvard University Press, 1937), p. 112.

12. *EoP*, p. 220.

13. Philipp Frank, *Einstein: His Life and Times* (New York: Alfred A. Knopf, 1947), p. 241.

14. Ibid., p. 232.

15. Ibid.

16. Ibid., p. 228.

17. Interview with Margot Einstein, May 3 and 4, 1978.

18. Albert Einstein, *The Human Side: New Glimpses from His Archives*, selected and edited by Helen Dukas and Banesh Hoffmann (Princeton: Princeton University Press, 1979), p. 115.

19. Interview with Margot Einstein, May 3, 1978.

20. Einstein to Max Born, May 20, 1933, in *The Born-Einstein Letters: Correspondence Between Albert Einstein and Max and Hedwig Born from 1916 to 1955* (New York: Walker and Co., 1971), p. 114.

21. Einstein to Maurice Solovine, April 23, 1933, in *Lettres à Maurice Solovine* (Paris: Gauthier-Villars, 1956), p. 66.

22. See Herbert Parzen, "The Magnes-Weizmann-Einstein Controversy" in *Jewish Social Studies*, vol. 32 (July 1970), p. 206.

23. Jewish Telegraphic Agency, July 3, 1933, quoted in Ronald W. Clark, *Einstein: The Life and Times* (New York: Thomas Y. Crowell Co., 1971), p. 482.

24. *EoP*, p. 95.

25. Einstein to Rabbi Stephen S. Wise, June 6, 1933, Einstein Archives; Einstein to Lord Ponsonby, *EoP*, p. 226.

26. *EoP*, p. 229.

27. *EoP*, pp. 230–233.

28. *EoP*, p. 246.

29. *EoP*, p. 214.

30. Lecture by Robert J. Schulmann, Historian of the Einstein Papers Project, March 24,

1983. Fritz Stern, "Einstein's Germany" in *Albert Einstein: Historical and Cultural Perspectives: The Centennial Symposium in Jerusalem*, ed. Gerald Holton and Yehuda Elkana (Princeton: Princeton University Press, 1982), p. 332, writes: "Like so many thinkers of the 1920s, Einstein underestimated the force of the irrational . . . in public affairs. That is what so ill-prepared them for an understanding of fascism. In their innocence they thought that men were bribed to be fascists, that fascism was but frightened capitalism; in its essence, it was something much more sinister and elemental. In his social commentary, Einstein left out the very thing he once called 'the most beautiful experience we can have: the mysterious.' " It should be noted that intellectuals like Einstein were not the only ones who misread fascism in the 1920s. The statesmen of western Europe and the United States—with very few exceptions—continued to delude themselves until 1939. In the 1930s Einstein was far more flexible and perceptive than most thinkers or statesmen regarding the menace of fascists.

31. *EoP*, p. 236.

32. Clark, *Einstein: The Life and Times*, pp. 494–495.

33. Albert Einstein, "Paul Ehrenfest In Memoriam," in Albert Einstein, *Out of My Later Years* (Westport, Conn.: Greenwood Press, 1970), pp. 236–239. Also see: Martin J. Klein, *Paul Ehrenfest: The Making of a Theoretical Physicist* (Amsterdam: North Holland Publishing Co., American Elsevier Publishing Co., 1970), and *Paul Ehrenfest: Collected Scientific Papers*, ed. Martin J. Klein (Amsterdam: North Holland Publishing Co., New York: Interscience Publishers Inc., 1959).

34. *EoP*, pp. 238–239.

35. Ernst Straus, "Reminiscences" in *Albert Einstein: Historical and Cultural Perspectives: The Centennial Symposium in Jerusalem*, ed. Gerald Holton and Yehuda Elkana (Princeton: Princeton University Press, 1982), p. 420.

36. Einstein to Leo Szilard, September 15, 1928, Einstein Archives.

37. Quoted in G. J. Withrow, ed., *Einstein: The Man and His Achievement* (London: British Broadcasting Corp., 1967), p. 21.

2

1. Albert Einstein, *Autobiographical Notes: A Centennial Edition*, trans. Paul Arthur Schilpp (LaSalle and Chicago: Open Court Publishing Co., 1979), p. 3. (Hereafter this essay will be referred to as Schilpp.)

2. Lucy Dawidowicz, *The War Against the Jews 1933–1945* (New York: Holt, Rinehart and Winston, 1975), pp. 221–222.

3. Quoted in Banesh Hoffmann, "Einstein and Zionism" in *General Relativity and Gravita-*

tion, ed. G. Shaviv and J. Rosen (New York: John Wiley and Sons: Jerusalem: Israel Universities Press, 1975), p. 235.

4. Schilpp, pp. 3, 5.

5. Anton Reiser, *Albert Einstein: A Biographical Portrait* (New York: Albert and Charles Boni, 1930), p. 30.

6. Banesh Hoffmann and Helen Dukas, *Albert Einstein: Creator and Rebel* (New York: The Viking Press, 1972), p. 20.

7. Maja Einstein-Winteler, Unpublished Biography of Albert Einstein, p. 15, Einstein Archives.

8. Schilpp, p. 9.

9. Albert Einstein, *Ideas and Opinions,* based on *Mein Weltbild,* ed. Carl Seelig, and other sources, new translations and revisions by Sonja Bargmann (New York: Crown Publishers, Inc., 1954), p. 292.

10. Schilpp, p. 5.

11. Schilpp, p. 13.

12. Hoffman and Dukas, *Einstein: Creator and Rebel,* p. 25.

13. Philipp Frank, *Einstein: His Life and Times* (New York: Alfred A. Knopf, 1947), p. 15.

14. Einstein to Ernestina Marangoni, August 16, 1946 (this letter is written in imperfect Italian), Einstein Archives.

15. Albert Einstein, *The Human Side: New Glimpses from His Archives,* selected and edited by Helen Dukas and Banesh Hoffmann (Princeton: Princeton University Press, 1979), p. 13.

16. Carl Seelig, *Albert Einstein: A Documentary Biography* (London: Staples Press, 1956), pp. 14–15. A copy of the extensive corrections and annotations to the Seelig biography

made by Helen Dukas can be found in the Einstein Archives. The English translation is particularly unreliable. Regarding Hans Byland's use of the phrase "impudent Swabian," she wrote: "The word 'Swabian' is not to be taken literally. In Switzerland the Germans are—or were—all called Swabians." Einstein was Bavarian.

17. Schilpp, p. 15.

18. Hoffmann and Dukas, *Einstein: Creator and Rebel,* p. 36.

19. Ibid., p. 32.

20. Schilpp, pp. 15, 17.

21. *Albert Einstein, Michele Besso: Correspondence 1903–1955,* translation, notes and introduction by Pierre Speziali (Paris: Hermann, 1972); *Lettres à Maurice Solovine* (Paris: Gauthier-Villars, 1956).

22. Maja Einstein-Winteler, Unpublished Biography, p. 23, Einstein Archives. Also Reiser, *Einstein: A Biographical Portrait,* p. 66.

23. Einstein to a Young Student, December 25, 1929, Einstein Archives.

24. Pierre Speziali, "Einstein's Friendship with Michele Besso" in *Einstein: A Centenary Volume,* ed. A. P. French (Cambridge, Mass.: Harvard University Press, 1979), p. 13.

25. Martin J. Klein, *Paul Ehrenfest: The Making of a Theoretical Physicist* (Amsterdam: North Holland Publishing Co., American Elsevier Publishing Co., 1970), p. 296.

26. Reiser, *Einstein: A Biographical Portrait,* p. 75.

27. Einstein to Besso, late 1913, in *Besso Correspondence,* p. 50.

28. Albert Einstein, *Einstein on Peace,* ed. Otto Nathan and Heinz Norden (New York: Simon and Schuster, 1960), p. 2.

3

1. Albert Einstein, *Einstein on Peace* (hereafter *EoP*), ed. Otto Nathan and Heinz Norden (New York: Simon and Schuster, 1960), p. 3.

2. Lewis Feuer, *Einstein and the Generations of Science* (New York: Basic Books, Inc., 1974), p. 48. Solovine's observation was made to Otto Nathan on August 19, 1957.

3. *EoP,* p. 55.

4. Interview with Margot Einstein, May 3, 1978.

5. Einstein to Heinrich Zangger, July 7, 1915, Einstein Archives. Quoted by Abraham Pais, *"Subtle is the Lord . . .": The Science and the Life of Albert Einstein* (New York, Oxford University Press, 1982), p. 241. Philipp Frank, *Einstein: His Life and Times* (New York: Alfred

A. Knopf, 1947), pp. 124–125; quoted by Pais, *"Subtle is the Lord . . .,"* pp. 301–302.

6. Martin J. Klein, *Paul Ehrenfest; The Making of a Theoretical Physicist* (Amsterdam: North Holland Publishing Co., American Elsevier Publishing Co., 1970), p. 312.

7. Hannah Arendt, *The Origins of Totalitarianism* (Cleveland and New York: Meriden Books, World Publishing Company, 1958), p. 36.

8. Arthur Hertzberg, Introduction to *The Zionist Idea: A Historical Analysis and Reader* (Westport, Conn.: Greenwood Press, 1970), p. 60.

9. Albert Einstein, *Ideas and Opinions* (hereafter *IaO*), based on *Mein Weltbild,* ed. Carl

Seelig, and other sources, new translations and revisions by Sonja Bargmann (New York: Crown Publishers, Inc., 1954), p. 171.

10. Kurt Blumenfeld, "Einstein on Zionism" in *Jewish Frontier*, (June 1939), p. 45.

11. Banesh Hoffmann, "Einstein and Zionism" in *General Relativity and Gravitation*, ed. G. Shaviv and J. Rosen (New York: John Wiley and Sons; Jerusalem: Israel Universities Press, 1975), p. 237.

12. *IaO*, p. 186.

13. *IaO*, p. 185.

14. Erich Kahler, *The Jews Among the Nations* (New York: F. Unger Publishing Co., 1967), p. 117.

15. Isaiah Berlin, "Einstein and Israel" in *Albert Einstein: Historical and Cultural Perspectives; The Centennial Symposium in Jerusalem*, ed. Gerald Holton and Yehuda Elkana, (Princeton: Princeton University Press, 1982), p. 284.

16. See Anne Roiphe, *Generation Without Memory: A Jewish Journey in Christian America* (New York: The Linden Press, Simon and Schuster, 1981), pp. 102–103.

17. Robert Oppenheimer to Francis Fergusson, November 1, 1925, in *Robert Oppenheimer: Letters and Recollections*, ed. Alice Kimball Smith and Charles Weiner (Cambridge, Mass.: Harvard University Press, 1980), p. 87.

18. Leopold Infeld, *The Quest: The Evolution of a Scientist* (New York: Doubleday, Doran and Co., 1941), p. 290.

19. *New York Times* (hereafter *NYT*), May 21, 1920.

20. Louis de Broglie, "My Meeting with Einstein at the Solvay Conference of 1927" in *Einstein: A Centenary Volume*, ed. A. P. French (Cambridge, Mass.: Harvard University Press, 1979), p. 14.

21. Quoted by Pais, *"Subtle is the Lord . . .,"* p. 310.

22. Ibid., p. 311.

23. Interview with Eva Kayser, March 7, 1979.

24. Albert Einstein, *The Human Side: New Glimpses from His Archives*, selected and edited by Helen Dukas and Banesh Hoffmann (Princeton: Princeton University Press, 1979), p. 22.

25. Anton Reiser, *Albert Einstein: A Biographical Portrait* (New York: Albert and Charles Boni, 1930), p. 170.

26. Interview with Eva Kayser, March 7, 1979.

27. *NYT*, March 12, 1944.

28. Lincoln Barnett, "On his Centennial, the Spirit of Einstein Abides in Princeton" in *Smithsonian* (February 1979), p. 74.

29. Hoffmann, "Einstein and Zionism" in *General Relativity*, p. 237.

30. Blumenfeld, "Einstein on Zionism," p. 46. Kurt Blumenfeld to Chaim Weizmann, March 15, 1921, Weizmann Archives, Rehovot, Israel.

31. See Einstein to President John Hibben, November 14, 1920; Einstein to Max Warburg, December 8, 1920; Einstein to Felix Frankfurter, May 28 and 29, 1921; and Trip to America 1921 Folder, Einstein Archives.

32. Herbert Parzen, "The Magnes-Weizmann-Einstein Controversy" in *Jewish Social Studies*, vol. 32 (July 1970), pp. 191–192.

33. *NYT*, April 4 and 3, 1921.

34. Einstein to Besso, May 28, 1921, in *Albert Einstein, Michele Besso: Correspondence 1903–1955*, translation, notes and introduction by Pierre Speziali (Paris: Hermann, 1972), p. 163.

35. *NYT*, April 13, 1921.

36. Parzen, "The Magnes-Weizmann-Einstein Controversy," p. 192.

37. Albert Einstein, *About Zionism* (New York: The Macmillan Co., 1930), p. 48.

38. Chaim Weizmann to Einstein, March 14, 1949, copy in Einstein Archives.

39. *Human Side*, p. 63.

40. Vera Weizmann, *The Impossible Takes Longer: The Memoirs of Vera Weizmann, Wife of Israel's First President* as told to David Tutaev (London: Hamish Hamilton, 1967), p. 102.

41. Citation from honorary degree awarded to Einstein by Princeton University, May 9, 1921.

42. *Philadelphia Evening Bulletin*, May 10, 1921.

43. Letter from Ernest Heller, Princeton University, Class of 1922, to JS, July 11, 1977.

44. Einstein to Oswald Veblen, April 1930, Einstein Archives. See Pais, *"Subtle is the Lord . . .,"* p. vi.

45. Interview with Valentine Bargmann, April 1, 1979.

46. *IaO*, pp. 3–7.

47. *NYT*, July 8, 1921; July 11, 1921; July 12, 1921.

48. *NYT*, July 31, 1921.

49. Reiser, *Einstein: A Biographical Portrait*, p. 166.

50. Ippei Okamoto, "Einstein's 1922 Visit to Japan," manuscript in Einstein Archives.

51. See Pais, *"Subtle is the Lord . . . ,"* pp. 502–512 for an excellent account of how the Nobel Prize was awarded to Einstein.

52. Einstein's Travel Diary, February 3, 1923, Einstein Archives.

53. Banesh Hoffmann and Helen Dukas, *Albert Einstein: Creator and Rebel* (New York: The Viking Press, 1972), pp. 151–152.

54. Einstein to Maurice Solovine, Pentecost 1923, in *Lettres à Maurice Solovine* (Paris:

Gauthier-Villars, 1956), p. 44.

55. Hoffmann, "Einstein and Zionism" in *General Relativity*, p. 241.

56. Quoted in Frederic Grunfeld, *Prophets Without Honor: A Background to Freud, Kafka, Einstein and Their World* (New York: Holt, Rinehart and Winston, 1979), p. 152.

57. See Robert L. Oldershaw, "Gravity and Levity" in *Bulletin of the Atomic Scientists* (August–September 1981), p. 54. Oldershaw writes that Einstein told the sculptor Robert Berks: "Were I wrong, one professor would have been quite enough."

58. Frank, *Einstein: His Life and Times*, p. 162.

59. *EoP*, p. 155.

60. *EoP*, p. 131.

61. Millikan to Amos A. Fried, March 4, 1932, Millikan Papers, California Institute of Technology, quoted by Ronald W. Clark, *Einstein: The Life and Times* (New York: Thomas Y. Crowell Co., 1971), p. 454.

62. *EoP*, p. 163.

63. Abraham Flexner, *An Autobiography* (New York: Simon and Schuster, 1960) (revised edition of *I Remember, I Remember*), pp. 235–249.

64. Ibid., pp. 250–251.

65. Einstein to Solovine, March 4, 1930, in *Lettres à Maurice Solovine*, p. 57.

66. See Pais, "*Subtle is the Lord . . .*," p. 493.

67. Flexner, *Autobiography*, p. 252. Flexner reversed the German idiom.

4

1. Helen Dukas had become Einstein's secretary on Friday, April 13, 1928. Shortly before, Einstein had suffered a heart attack in Switzerland and was confined to bed for several weeks. Elsa was searching for a secretary to handle the large volume of mail, but she could not advertise the position in the newspapers because of Einstein's fame. She was the honorary president of an organization supporting orphan children in Palestine, and the chief secretary of the organization was the older sister of Helen Dukas. The elder Miss Dukas and Elsa enjoyed a special rapport because Elsa hailed from the same small town as Frau Dukas, whom she remembered with fondness. Elsa mentioned her plight to Helen Dukas's sister, and, because Helen's employer had just declared bankruptcy, she was available for the job.

Helen was horrified when she learned of this because she knew nothing about physics and because she was quite frightened at the prospect of meeting and working for such an important person. When she arrived at the Einstein residence on April 13, 1928, Elsa immediately gave her tea and cake and reassured her that she would not have to do anything with physics. "My husband is very nice to all people. He wouldn't say a hard word to anybody."

At the time, his doctor was examining Einstein, and when the doctor emerged, he admonished the frightened new secretary, "Visitors not longer than a quarter of an hour." Einstein was lying in bed, and when Elsa introduced Helen, he gave her his hand and said, "Here is an old children's corpse . . ." Miss Dukas recalled fifty years later: "Then I felt at ease. That was the great thing. It was quite unconscious; he just treated everybody the same. . . . I remember how frightened I was the first day, and how I lost that fear. It had nothing to do with losing respect. He put me at ease, and he put everybody at ease like that because everybody was the same to him." Interview with Helen Dukas, January 19, 1977.

2. Flexner to Einstein, October 13, 1933, copy in Einstein Archives.

3. *The Princeton Herald*, October 13, 1933.

4. *The Daily Princetonian*, October 17, 1933.

5. Antonina Vallentin, *The Drama of Albert Einstein* (New York: Doubleday and Co., 1954), p. 235.

6. Albert Einstein, *Einstein on Peace* (hereafter *EoP*), ed. Otto Nathan and Heinz Norden (New York: Simon and Schuster, 1960), p. 245. Annemarie Clark, "Princeton—or the Exile in Paradise" in *National Zeitung*, Basel, Switzerland, February 5, 1937. Quoted by Frederick Spring Osborne, in *The Princeton Packet*. The article, without a date, is in my possession.

7. Interview with Eleanor Drorbaugh, April 20, 1977.

8. Stephen S. Wise to Judge Julian Mack, October 18 and 20, 1933, in *Stephen S. Wise: Servant of the People*, Selected Letters ed. Carl Hermann Voss (Philadelphia: Jewish Publication Society of America, 1969), pp. 195–196.

9. Flexner to Franklin Delano Roosevelt, November 3, 1933, copy in Einstein Archives.

10. Einstein to Eleanor Roosevelt, November 21, 1933, Einstein Archives.

11. Frieda Sarsen Bucky, "You Have to Ask for Forgiveness . . .: Albert Einstein, as I Remember Him" in *The Jewish Quarterly*, vol. 15, no. 4 (Winter 1967–1968), p. 34.

12. Einstein to the Board of Trustees of the Institute for Advanced Study, December 1933 or

January 1934; Flexner to Emil Hilb, December 4, 1933, Einstein Archives.

13. Letter, Norman Gort, Princeton University, Class of 1935, to JS, August 14, 1977.

14. Interview with Helen Dukas, December 26, 1978.

15. H. D. Thoreau, *Walden: Or Life in the Woods* (New York: Signet Paperback ed., 1960), p. 60. *New York Times* (hereafter *NYT*), April 19, 1955.

16. Interview with Robert Strunsky, October 11, 1977. Interview with Alan Shenstone, March 15, 1977.

17. Interview with Gerhard Fankhauser, November 2, 1977. Interview with Louise Morse, April 15, 1977. Interview with Hubert Alyea, June 13, 1977. Letter, Nancy Panofsky to JS, October 29, 1977.

18. Letter, Charles W. Bray III to JS, October 13, 1977.

19. Letter, Charles E. Shain, Princeton University, Class of 1936, to JS, June 12, 1977.

20. Letter, Hans Panofsky to JS, October 29, 1977.

21. Letter, John B. Oakes, Princeton University, Class of 1934, to JS, June 27, 1977.

22. Letter, Laurence Fenninger, Princeton University, Class of 1936, to JS, June 16, 1977.

23. Letter, Gordon S. Mosher, Princeton University, Class of 1940, to JS, June 9, 1977. Letter, Joel T. Loeb, Princeton University, Class of 1937, to JS, June 12, 1977.

24. Einstein to Max Born, March 22, 1934, in *The Born-Einstein Letters: Correspondence Between Albert Einstein and Max and Hedwig Born from 1916 to 1955* (New York: Walker and Co., 1971), p. 122.

25. Bucky, "You Have to Ask . . .," p. 34.

26. Interview with Helen Dukas, January 19, 1977.

27. James Blackwood, "The Einsteins as Neighbors," unpublished monograph in my possession.

28. Interview with James C. Sayen, June 13, 1977.

29. Interview with Eleanor Delanoy by Elric Endersby, 1971. Courtesy of the Princeton History Project.

30. Interview with Mary Hicks, May 9, 1977.

31. Interview with Eleanor Delanoy by Elric Endersby, 1971. Courtesy of the Princeton History Project.

32. Interview with Helen Dukas, November 9, 1977.

33. *EoP*, p. 257.

34. Letter, Henry Rosso to JS, April 25, 1977.

35. Einstein to Frederico Carlos Jgel, March 12, 1953, Einstein Archives.

36. Poem by Einstein, April–May 1938, Einstein Archives.

37. Einstein to Tyffany Williams, August 25, 1946, and September 19, 1946, Einstein Archives.

38. Interview with Eugene Wigner, June 6, 1977.

39. Interviews with Margot Einstein, July 21, 1978; Beatrice Delong, April 22, 1977; John Kemeny, November 21, 1977.

40. Leopold Infeld, *The Quest: The Evolution of a Scientist* (New York: Doubleday, Doran and Co., 1941), p. 282.

41. *NYT*, December 22, 1936.

42. Interview with Otto Nathan, November 28, 1982.

43. Abraham Pais, *"Subtle is the Lord . . ." The Science and the Life of Albert Einstein* (New York: Oxford University Press, 1982), p. 301.

44. Interview with Otto Nathan, April 10, 1982.

45. Einstein to Vero Besso, March 21, 1955, in *Albert Einstein, Michele Besso: Correspondence 1903–1955*, translation, notes and introduction by Pierre Speziali (Paris: Hermann, 1972), p. 538. Quoted by Pais, *"Subtle is the Lord . . .,"* p. 302. When Otto Nathan, as executor of Einstein's literary estate, gave permission for the publication of this letter in the *Besso: Correspondence,* he was unaware of the extent of Einstein's aversion to the publication of personal matters. Later, Nathan came across a letter written by Einstein to Philipp Frank, who was then engaged in writing his biography of Einstein. In the letter, Einstein refused to show Frank his diaries because the contents were too personal. Einstein even felt that the publication of the details of Newton's life two hundred years after the English physicist's death represented an invasion of privacy. Interview with Otto Nathan, November 11, 1982. Because the letter to Vero Besso has been published, I have chosen to make use of it, although, not without a sense of discomfort.

46. Banesh Hoffmann quoted in *The Princeton Packet,* March 14, 1979.

47. Infeld, *Quest*, p. 282.

5

1. Robert Oppenheimer to Frank Oppenheimer, January 11, 1935, in *Robert Oppenheimer: Letters and Recollections*, ed. Alice Kimball Smith and Charles Weiner (Cambridge, Mass.: Harvard University Press, 1980), pp. 190–191.

2. Saunders MacLane, "Oswald Veblen, 1880–1960: A Biographical Memoir" published for the National Academy of Sciences of the United States by Columbia University Press, 1964, pp. 332–333. Also, Herman Goldstine, *The Computer from Pascal to von Neumann* (Princeton: Princeton University Press, 1972), pp. 77–80. Constance Reid, *Hilbert,* with an appreciation of Hilbert's mathematical work by Hermann Weyl (Berlin, Heidelberg, New York: Springer-Verlag, 1970), pp. 160–161.

3. Albert Einstein, *Einstein on Peace,* ed. Otto Nathan and Heinz Norden (New York: Simon and Schuster, 1960), p. 43.

4. Interview with Otto Nathan, May 25, 1983.

5. Daniel J. Kevles, *The Physicists: The History of a Scientific Community in Modern America* (New York, Alfred A. Knopf, 1978), pp. 162–163. Einstein to Else Cartan, June 21, 1950, Einstein Archives.

6. Albert Einstein, *Autobiographical Notes: A Centennial Edition,* trans. Paul Arthur Schilpp (LaSalle and Chicago: Open Court Publishing Company, 1979), p. 83.

7. Otto Stern to Res Jost, quoted by Abraham Pais, "Einstein, Newton and Success" in *Einstein: A Centenary Volume,* ed. A. P. French (Cambridge, Mass.: Harvard University Press, 1979), p. 37.

8. Lecture by Abraham Pais, April 3, 1981. Freeman Dyson, *Disturbing the Universe* (New York: Harper & Row, 1979), p. 62, notes that the physicist Richard Feynman believed that "Einstein had failed [in his later] work because he stopped thinking in concrete physical images and became a manipulator of equations. . . . [The later theories] failed because they were only sets of equations without physical meaning."

9. Interview with Banesh Hoffmann, May 9, 1977. Interview with John Wheeler, November 13, 1977.

10. Poem by Einstein written on Bruria Kaufman's notes in the 1950s, Einstein Archives.

11. Interview with Valentine Bargmann, April 11, 1977.

12. Interview with Margot Einstein, May 3, 1978.

13. Inscription by Einstein for the Bargmanns' copy of *Albert Einstein: Philosopher-Scientist,* ed. Paul Arthur Schilpp (Evanston, Ill.: Library of Living Philosophers, 1949).

14. *New York Times,* March 12, 1944.

15. Interview with Abraham Pais, November 27, 1977.

16. Ernst Straus, "Working with Einstein" in *Some Strangeness in the Proportion: A Centennial Symposium to Celebrate the Achievements of Albert Einstein,* ed. Harry Woolf (Reading, Mass.: Addison-Wesley Publishing Co., 1980), p. 482.

17. Interview with Bruria Kaufman, January 10, 1979.

18. Aphorism quoted by Ernst Straus in *Helle Zeit, Dunkele Zeit,* ed. Carl Seelig (Zurich: Europa Verlag, 1956), p. 73.

19. Valentine Bargmann, "Recollections of an Assistant of Einstein," April 1979 (English version not published), p. 6.

20. Banesh Hoffmann, quoted by Gerald Holton, "What, Precisely, Is Thinking?" in French, *Einstein: A Centenary Volume,* p. 153.

21. Bargmann, "Recollections," p. 8.

22. Banesh Hoffmann, "Working with Einstein" in *Some Strangeness in the Proportion,* pp. 476–477.

23. Interview with Valentine Bargmann, December 27, 1978.

24. Leopold Infeld, *The Quest: The Evolution of a Scientist* (New York: Doubleday, Doran and Co., 1941), p. 302, and pp. 307–321 for an account of the writing of *The Evolution of Physics.*

25. Poem by Einstein, May 31, 1938, Einstein Archives.

26. Interview with Valentine Bargmann, December 12, 1979.

27. Frances Margaret Blanshard, *Frank Aydelotte of Swarthmore,* ed. and with a Preface by Brand Blanshard (Middletown, Conn.: Wesleyan University Press, 1970), pp. 311–312.

28. Abraham Flexner to Frank Aydelotte, August 28, 1939, in Blanshard, *Aydelotte,* p. 318.

29. Einstein to Samuel Leidesdorf, November 3, 1937, Einstein Archives.

30. Einstein to Samuel Leidesdorf, December 16, 1937, Einstein Archives.

31. Einstein to Samuel Leidesdorf, February 14, 1939, Einstein Archives.

32. Einstein to Dr. Gustav Bucky, May 30, 1950, Einstein Archives.

33. Abraham Flexner to Frank Aydelotte, August 28, 1939, in Blanshard, *Aydelotte,* p. 318.

6

1. Einstein to Stephen S. Wise, March 5, 1936, Einstein Archives.

2. Arthur D. Morse, *While Six Million Died: A Chronicle of American Apathy* (New York:

Random House, 1967), pp. 235 and 112.

3. Letter, E. G. Gifford to JS, June 16, 1977.

4. Interview with Otto Nathan, March 27, 1982.

5. Poem by Einstein to Alfons Goldschmidt, winter 1935–1936, Einstein Archives.

6. Einstein to Stephen S. Wise, July 3, 1934, Einstein Archives. Wise to Einstein, July 12, 1934, copy in Einstein Archives.

7. Gordon A. Craig, *Germany: 1866–1945* (New York: Oxford University Press, 1980), pp. 586–589. Hannah Arendt, *The Origins of Totalitarianism* (Cleveland and New York: Meriden Books, World Publishing Company, 1958), pp. 370–371.

8. Einstein to Charles Wagner, September 12, 1949, Einstein Archives.

9. Interview with Otto Nathan, November 28, 1982.

10. See Edward W. Said, *The Question of Palestine* (New York: New York Times Books, 1979), pp. 15–20, for the Palestinian view of the legitimacy of the Balfour Declaration.

11. Susan Lee Hattis, *The Bi-National Idea in Palestine During Mandatory Times* (Haifa: Shikmona Publishing Co., 1970), p. 40.

12. Albert Einstein, *Ideas and Opinions* (hereafter *IaO*), based on *Mein Weltbild*, ed. Carl Seelig, and other sources, new translations and revisions by Sonja Bargmann (New York: Crown Publishers, Inc., 1954), p. 172.

13. Einstein to Chaim Weizmann, November 25, 1929, Einstein Archives. See also Ronald W. Clark, *Einstein: The Life and Times* (New York: Thomas Y. Crowell Co., 1971), pp. 402–403.

14. See Bernard Wasserstein, *The British in Palestine: The Mandatory Government and the Arab–Jewish Conflict, 1917–1929* (London: Royal Historical Society, 1978), p. 239.

15. *IaO*, p. 190.

16. *IaO*, p. 172.

17. Einstein to Chaim Weizmann, May 12, 1938, Einstein Archives.

18. Einstein to Maurice B. Hexter, July 5, 1938, Einstein Archives.

19. Einstein to Chaim Weizmann, October 27, 1923, Einstein Archives.

20. Nicholas Bethell, *The Palestine Triangle: The Struggle Between the British, the Jews and the Arabs 1935–1948* (London: André Deutsch, 1979), p. 52.

21. Barnet Litvinoff, *Weizmann: Last of the Patriarchs* (London: Hodder and Stoughton, 1976), p. 209.

22. Walter Laqueur, *A History of Zionism* (New York: Holt, Rinehart and Winston, 1972), p. 550.

23. Henry L. Feingold, *The Politics of Rescue: The Roosevelt Administration and the Holocaust, 1938–1945* (New Brunswick: Rutgers University Press, 1970), p. 114.

24. Ibid., p. 142.

25. Interview with Otto Nathan, April 10, 1982.

26. Feingold, *Politics of Rescue*, p. 148. Also see Morse, *While Six Million Died*, p. 268.

27. Einstein to Besso, October 10, 1938, in *Albert Einstein, Michele Besso: Correspondence 1930–1955*, translation, notes and introduction by Pierre Speziali (Paris: Hermann, 1972), pp. 330–331.

28. Feingold, *Politics of Rescue*, p. 159.

29. Interview with Otto Nathan, April 10, 1982.

30. Morse, *While Six Million Died*, pp. 61–62.

31. Einstein to Eleanor Roosevelt, July 26, 1941, Einstein Archives.

7

1. Philipp Frank, *Einstein: His Life and Times* (New York: Alfred A. Knopf, 1947), pp. 173–174.

2. Albert Einstein, *Einstein on Peace* (hereafter *EoP*), ed. Otto Nathan and Heinz Norden (New York: Simon and Schuster, 1960), p. 290.

3. *EoP*, p. 622.

4. The difficulty a nonscientist encounters when trying to comprehend a scientific problem is a critical issue which will be discussed again in the chapters dealing with the efforts after 1945 to achieve international control of atomic energy. The myth that $E = mc^2$ opened the door to the atomic bomb and that Einstein is, therefore, the "father" of the bomb is due to a misunderstanding of the science involved. The result has been an

error which does a historical injustice to Einstein—a regrettable, but not a disastrous, mistake. The consequences of the faulty understanding of the science and long-term implications of the atomic bomb by the politicians, the military, and the public in 1945 and after are of an entirely different order of magnitude. The politicians failed to listen to the warnings of the scientists, and the scientists failed in their efforts to explain to the politicians the complexity of the science involved and the very dangerous long-term consequences of atomic energy in a world accustomed to solving its problems by violence. The mutual antipathy between the politicians and the scientists complicated the communication problem. If the nightmare applications of the fruits of science are to be controlled before they destroy humanity, then this obstacle must be overcome.

What should be emphasized here—and cannot be emphasized too greatly—is the difficulty faced by a nonscientist in understanding the workings of science. Clearly, without such an understanding, wise political, economic, and social decisions on the implications of scientific developments are not possible. (This idea will be developed more fully in Chapters 11–13.)

5. Interview with Eugene Wigner, June 6, 1977.

6. *EoP*, p. 285.

7. *EoP*, p. 295.

8. *EoP*, p. 296.

9. *EoP*, pp. 297–302. Ronald W. Clark, *The Greatest Power on Earth: The International Race for Nuclear Supremacy* (New York: Harper & Row, 1980), pp. 72–137.

10. *EoP*, p. 286.

11. Aeschylus, *Prometheus Bound*, lines 103–106, trans. David Grene in *Greek Tragedies:* Volume I, ed. David Grene and Richmond Lattimore (Chicago: University of Chicago Press, 1960), p. 69.

8

1. *New York Times* (hereafter *NYT*), October 2, 1940.

2. Einstein to Miss Clara Jacobson, May 7, 1945, Einstein Archives.

3. Einstein to Elizabeth, Queen Mother of Belgium, August 11, 1937, Einstein Archives.

4. Interview with Tiffin Harper Shenstone, March 18, 1977.

5. Letter, G. B. Calkins, Princeton University, Class of 1939, to JS, July 11, 1977.

6. Interview with Lily Kahler, June 9, 1977.

7. Frieda Sarsen Bucky, "You Have to Ask Forgiveness . . .: Albert Einstein as I Remember Him," in *The Jewish Quarterly*, vol. 15, no. 4 (Winter 1967–1968), p. 33.

8. Ernst Straus, "Albert Einstein: The Man," Memorial Talk at the University of California, Los Angeles, May 1955, pp. 14–15.

9. Interview with Margot Einstein, January 15, 1979.

10. A. P. French, "Einstein: A Condensed Biography" in *Einstein: A Centenary Volume*, ed. A. P. French (Cambridge, Mass.: Harvard University Press, 1979), p. 61.

11. Interview with Eva Kayser, March 7, 1979.

12. Interview with Margot Einstein, May 4, 1978.

13. Albert Einstein, *The Human Side: New Glimpses from His Archives*, selected and edited by Helen Dukas and Banesh Hoffmann (Princeton: Princeton University Press, 1979), p. 35.

14. Interview with Margot Einstein, May 4, 1978.

15. Albert Einstein, *Einstein on Peace* (hereafter *EoP*), ed. Otto Nathan and Heinz Norden (New York: Simon and Schuster, 1960), pp. 185–186.

16. Freud to Einstein, May 3, 1936, in Ernest Jones, M.D., *The Life and Work of Sigmund Freud—Volume 3: The Last Phase, 1919–1939* (New York: Basic Books, Inc., 1957), pp. 203–204.

17. Alexander Moszkowski, *Conversations with Einstein* (New York: Horizon Press, 1970), pp. 185, 186.

18. *Forum* (June 1930), p. 374.

19. *EoP*, p. 261.

20. Einstein to L. Caspar, April 9, 1932, Einstein Archives.

21. Carl Seelig, *Albert Einstein: A Documentary Biography* (London: Staples Press, 1956), p. 114.

22. "My Credo," recorded for the German League for Human Rights in 1932, quoted in *Einstein: 1879–1979*, Exhibition Catalogue of the Jerusalem Einstein Centennial Symposium, March 1979 (Jerusalem: Raphael Haim Hacohen Press, Ltd., 1979), p. 49.

23. *NYT*, April 1, 1934.

24. *Human Side*, p. 78.

25. Ibid., pp. 51–52.

26. Ibid., pp. 76–77.

27. Ibid., p. 76.

28. Banesh Hoffmann, "Unforgettable Albert Einstein," *Reader's Digest* (January 1968), p. 110.

29. Anton Reiser, *Albert Einstein: A Biographical Portrait* (New York: Albert and Charles Boni, 1930), pp. 202–203.

30. Interview with Gaby Casadesus, May 2, 1977.

31. A. Barjansky to Margot Einstein, May 9, 1959, copy in Einstein Archives.

32. Poem by Einstein to Emil Hilb, April 18, 1939, Einstein Archives.

33. Letter, Barbara L. Rahm to JS, August 28, 1977.

34. Interview with Gaby Casadesus, May 2, 1977.

35. Interview with Margot Einstein, May 3, 1978.

36. Interview with Eva Kayser, March 7, 1979.

9

1. Albert Einstein, *Einstein on Peace* (hereafter *EoP*), ed. Otto Nathan and Heinz Norden (New York: Simon and Schuster, 1960), p. 319.

2. John Lewis Gaddis, *The United States and the Origins of the Cold War, 1941–1947* (New York: Columbia University Press, 1972), pp. 34–42, discusses the widespread, uncritical portrayal by the American press of Stalin and the Soviet regime during 1942 and 1943. On p. 43 Gaddis notes that Americans have a ". . . peculiar habit of regarding moral excellence as a prerequisite for wartime collaboration."

3. *Life* magazine, March 29, 1943, p. 40.

4. *EoP*, pp. 322–324.

5. Einstein to Dr. Frank Kingdom, September 3, 1942, Einstein Archives.

6. Arthur D. Morse, *While Six Million Died: A Chronicle of American Apathy* (New York: Random House, 1967), p. 52.

7. Einstein to Otto Juliusburger, summer 1942, Einstein Archives.

8. Ibid., September 30, 1942, Einstein Archives. See Albert Einstein, *The Human Side: New Glimpses from His Archives,* selected and edited by Helen Dukas and Banesh Hoffmann (Princeton: Princeton University Press, 1979), p. 81.

9. Interview with Alan Shenstone, March 15, 1977.

10. Albert Einstein, *Out of My Later Years* (Westport, Conn.: Greenwood Press, 1970), pp. 265–266.

11. See Chapter 12, pp. 187–188, for more on Einstein's attitude toward Germany within the context of the Cold War.

12. *EoP*, p. 578. Ronald W. Clark, *Einstein: The Life and Times* (New York: Thomas Y. Crowell Co., 1971), p. 573, writes: "[H]is natural, and later almost paranoiac, distrust of the Germans, a distrust which he finally appreciated

had paved the road to Hiroshima . . ." Apart from his insensitivity to the trauma all Jews experienced during and after the Hitler years, Clark appears to have overlooked the fact that the Germans were to be distrusted in 1939, and that by no stretch of the imagination can it be said that Einstein's 1939 letter to President Roosevelt paved the road to Hiroshima. See Chapter 11.

13. *Human Side,* p. 114.

14. Vannevar Bush to Frank Aydelotte, December 30, 1941, quoted in Clark, *Einstein: The Life and Times,* p. 565.

15. Visa investigation on Einstein in regard to the visa application of Hans Heller, FBI files, section 2, pp. 175–175A. The report is dated March 24, 1942.

16. Brigadier General Sherman Miles to J. Edgar Hoover, July 30, 1940. J. Edgar Hoover to Brigadier General Sherman Miles, August 15, 1940. FBI files, section 1.

17. FBI files, section 2, p. 76.

18. Einstein to Otto Juliusburger, September 13, 1943, Einstein Archives.

19. Einstein to David Rothman, April 14, 1944, Einstein Archives.

20. Mark Van Doren to Julian Boyd, November 18, 1943: Julian Boyd to Dorothy Pratt, November 22, 1943, Princeton University Archives.

21. Banesh Hoffmann and Helen Dukas, *Albert Einstein: Creator and Rebel* (New York: The Viking Press, 1972), p. 209.

22. Julian Boyd to Dorothy Pratt, February 11, 1944, Princeton University Archives.

23. Letter from George Cook to JS, June 15, 1977.

24. Interview with Helen Dukas, November 9, 1977.

25. Leo Szilard, April 18, 1955. Transcript in Einstein Archives.

10

1. Albert Einstein, *Autobiographical Notes: A Centennial Edition,* trans. Paul Arthur Schilpp (LaSalle and Chicago: Open Court Publishing Company, 1979), pp. 21, 23, 31.

2. Albert Einstein, *Ideas and Opinions* (hereafter *IaO*), based on *Mein Weltbild,* ed. Carl Seelig, and other sources, new translations and revisions by Sonja Bargmann (New York: Crown Publishers, Inc., 1954), p. 349.

3. *IaO*, p. 282.

4. *IaO*, p. 323.

5. Aphorism quoted by Ernst Straus in *Helle Zeit, Dunkele Zeit,* ed. Carl Seelig (Zurich: Europa Verlag, 1956), p. 72.

6. *IaO*, p. 40.

7. Einstein to Maurice Solovine, March 30, 1952, quoted by Gerald Holton in "What, Precisely, Is Thinking?" in *Einstein: A Centenary Volume,* ed. A. P. French (Cambridge, Mass.: Harvard University Press, 1979), pp. 162–163.

8. Quoted by Gerald Holton, "Mach, Einstein, and the Search for Reality," *Daedalus* (Spring 1968), pp. 658–659. From Einstein's essay "Über den gegenwärtigen Stand der Feld-Theorie," in the *Festschrift* for Aurel Stodola, 1929, Orell Füssli Verlag (Zurich and Leipzig).

9. *New York Times* (hereafter *NYT*), April 25, 1929.

10. Albert Einstein, "Statement to the Spinoza Society of America," September 22, 1932, Einstein Archives.

11. *IaO*, pp. 46–47.

12. Einstein to Professor V. T. Aaltonen, May 7, 1952, Einstein Archives.

13. Einstein to E. P. St. John, March 9, 1943, Einstein Archives.

14. Einstein to Vivian Phelips, August 25, 1937, Einstein Archives.

15. Einstein to Catherine Hayden Salter, July 14, 1945, Einstein Archives.

16. *IaO*, p. 48.

17. *Time* magazine, September 23, 1940, p. 46.

18. See folder "Symposium on Science, Philosophy, and Religion—1940," Einstein Archives.

19. Einstein to a man who forgot to sign his name; letter filed under Chapman-Cohen, August 7, 1941, Einstein Archives.

20. Einstein to M. M. Schayer, August 5, 1927, Einstein Archives.

21. Einstein to Hans Mühsam, March 30, 1954, Einstein Archives.

22. *IaO*, pp. 38–40.

23. *IaO*, p. 46.

24. Einstein to Reverend Paul Keppel, March 4, 1953, Einstein Archives.

25. Einstein to Michele Besso, January 6, 1948, in *Albert Einstein, Michele Besso: Correspondence 1903–1955*, translation, notes and introduction by Pierre Speziali (Paris: Hermann, 1972), p. 392.

26. Conversation with Einstein recorded by Raymond G. Swing, no date, but probably between 1945 and 1950, Einstein Archives. See correspondence with Swing regarding November 1954 television program "This I Believe."

27. *IaO*, p. 9.

28. *IaO*, p. 8.

29. *IaO*, p. 186.

30. *IaO*, p. 10.

31. Albert Einstein, *Einstein on Peace* (hereafter *EoP*), ed. Otto Nathan and Heinz Norden (New York: Simon and Schuster, 1960), p. 502.

32. *IaO*, p. 187.

33. *IaO*, pp. 151–158. All quotations until next footnote are from this essay.

34. Albert Einstein, *The Human Side: New Glimpses from His Archives*, selected and edited by Helen Dukas and Banesh Hoffmann (Princeton: Princeton University Press, 1979), p. 95.

35. Message for Ben Schemen Dinner, March 1952, Einstein Archives.

36. *Human Side*, p. 27.

37. Alexander Moszkowski, *Conversations with Einstein* (New York: Horizon Press, 1970), p. 68.

38. *IaO*, p. 66.

39. Philipp Frank, *Einstein: His Life and Times* (New York: Alfred A. Knopf, 1947), p. 185.

40. Quoted by Virgil Hinshaw, "Einstein's Social Philosophy" in *Albert Einstein: Philosopher-Scientist*, ed. Paul Arthur Schilpp (Evanston, Ill.: Library of Living Philosophers, 1949), p. 650. Also see *NYT*, June 20, 1932, p. 17. This was Einstein's answer to a question posed by *Youth,* a publication of the Young Israel of Williamsburg, N.Y.

41. *IaO*, p. 9.

42. Interview with Margot Einstein, July 21, 1978.

43. *EoP*, p. 639.

44. Albert Einstein, *Out of My Later Years* (Westport, Conn.: Greenwood Press, 1970), p. 19.

45. Einstein to Valentin Bulgakov, November 4, 1931, Einstein Archives. Note that *Human Side* on p. 83 describes Bulgakov as a "troubled young man in Prague." Actually, he was Director of the Tolstoy Museum in Moscow and was a secretary to Tolstoy for a brief period before the latter's death in 1910.

11

1. Einstein to Otto Juliusburger, September 6, 1944, Einstein Archives.

2. Support of the view that Stalin did not follow an aggressive Marxist-Leninist foreign policy committed to the subversion of the world order lies in his treatment of the Communist parties outside the Soviet Union. Stalin compelled them to choose between obedience to Moscow or success at home; without such a policy, there might have been several noncapitalist societies in Western Europe. Only the Chinese and Yugoslavian Communist parties succeeded, and both had strong leaders who defied Stalin. See Daniel J. Yergin, *Shattered Peace: The Origins of the Cold War and the National Security State* (Boston: Houghton Mifflin Company, 1977), p. 311.

3. Yergin, *Shattered Peace,* p. 84.

4. *Robert Oppenheimer: Letters and Recollections,* ed. Alice Kimball Smith and Charles Weiner (Cambridge, Mass.: Harvard University Press, 1980), p. 271.

5. Quoted in Martin J. Sherwin, *A World Destroyed: The Atomic Bomb and the Grand Alliance* (New York: Alfred A. Knopf, 1975), p. 110.

6. "President Truman Did Not Understand," *U.S. News and World Report,* August 15, 1960, p. 69. Also see Sherwin, *A World Destroyed,* pp. 200–202, and Joseph I. Lieberman, *The Scorpion and the Tarantula: The Struggle to Control Atomic Weapons* (Boston: Houghton Mifflin Company, 1970), p. 76.

7. President Truman appointed the Interim Committee to advise him on the use of atomic weapons. Secretary of War Henry L. Stimson was Chairman. Other members were: George L. Harrison, President of the New York Life Insurance Company; Ralph Bard, Undersecretary of the Navy; William L. Clayton, Assistant Secretary of State; Vannevar Bush, Chairman of the National Defense Research Committee; Karl T. Compton, President of MIT, representing the Office of Scientific Research and Development; James B. Conant, President of Harvard University and Chairman of the National Research Council; and Byrnes, who was President Truman's personal representative.

8. See Lieberman, *The Scorpion and the Tarantula,* p. 72; "The Interim Committee Discusses the Bomb: Minutes of May 31, 1945," in *The Atomic Bomb: The Critical Issues,* ed. Barton J. Bernstein (Boston: Little, Brown and Co., 1976), p. 22; and Barton J. Bernstein, "The Atomic Bomb and American Foreign Policy: The Route to Hiroshima," in *The Atomic Bomb: The Critical Issues,* p. 105.

9. Richard G. Hewlett and Oscar E. Anderson, Jr., *The New World, 1939–1946, Volume I, A History of the United States Atomic Energy Commission* (University Park: Pennsylvania University Press, 1962), p. 358. Bernstein, "The Atomic Bomb and American Foreign Policy," in *The Atomic Bomb: The Critical Issues,* p. 105. Lieberman, *The Scorpion and the Tarantula,* pp. 79–83.

10. The Franck Report is printed in Alice Kimball Smith, *A Peril and a Hope: The Scientists' Movement in America: 1945–1947* (Chicago: University of Chicago Press, 1965), pp. 560–572. It is also printed in *The Atomic Age: Scientists in National and World Affairs: Articles from the "Bulletin of the Atomic Scientists,"* ed. and with introduction by Morton Grodzins and Eugene Rabinowitch (New York: Basic Books, Inc., 1963), pp. 19–27.

11. Franck Memo of April 21, 1945, quoted by Alice Kimball Smith in "Behind the Decision to Use the Atomic Bomb: Chicago 1944–1945," *Bulletin of the Atomic Scientists* (October 1958), p. 294.

12. "Truman at Potsdam," ed. Robert H. Ferrell, in *American Heritage* (June–July 1980), p. 42. Truman's diary entry is dated July 25, 1945.

13. Gar Alperovitz, "Atomic Diplomacy" in *The Atomic Bomb: The Critical Issues,* p. 76.

14. Barton J. Bernstein, "The Atomic Bomb and American Foreign Policy: The Route to Hiroshima" in *The Atomic Bomb: The Critical Issues,* p. 113. Richard J. Barnet, *Roots of War* (New York: Atheneum, 1972), p. 17, points out that in his *Memoirs* Truman denounced hunting because one ought not shoot at animals who cannot shoot back. Elsewhere in the same volume, he justifies the use of the atomic bomb on moral grounds.

15. In his diary on March 15, 1945, Henry Stimson noted that President Roosevelt had heard rumors that the scientists had sold him a "lemon." See Lieberman, *The Scorpion and the Tarantula,* p. 59. In 1947 Stimson wrote: "The entire purpose [of the $2 billion spent on the Manhattan Project] was the production of a military weapon; on no other ground could the wartime expenditure of so much time and money have been justified." Henry L. Stimson, "The Decision to Use the Atomic Bomb" in *The Atomic Bomb: The Critical Issues,* p. 4. The day after Hiroshima was bombed, Marston Morse, Einstein's colleague at the Institute for Advanced Study, who was working at the Pentagon at the time, asked the general for whom he was working why the bomb had been used without warning, and received the answer: "We spent two billion dollars on it, didn't we?" Interview with Marston Morse, April 15, 1977.

16. Gregg Herken, *The Winning Weapon: The Atomic Bomb in the Cold War 1945–1950* (New York: Alfred A. Knopf, 1980), p. 24. In June 1951 when prospects for developing the hydrogen bomb began to be favorable, Robert Oppenheimer, at a conference held at the Institute for Advanced Study of many leading atomic scientists, said: ". . . it is my judgment in these things that when you see something that is technically sweet you go ahead and do it and you argue about what to do about it only after you have had your technical success. That is the way it was with the atomic bomb." Quoted by Robert Jungk, *Brighter Than a Thousand Suns: The Moral and Political History of the Atomic Scientists* (London: Victor Gollancz, Ltd., 1958), p. 289. Valentine Bargmann has suggested that the "gadget" might be a name invented by the scientists to enable them to speak about the bomb

without getting into trouble. This seems to be a plausible explanation but, even if it is the case, one wishes a somewhat more neutral name had been chosen.

17. Oppenheimer, Teller, and some of the Russian scientists who worked on the hydrogen bomb had been students of Max Born in Göttingen. Writing in the June 1957 issue of the *Bulletin of the Atomic Scientists*, p. 191, Born said: "It is satisfying to have had such clever and efficient pupils, but I wish they had shown less cleverness and more wisdom."

18. Frank Oppenheimer is quoted on a documentary television show produced for Public Television, "The Day of Trinity," ca. 1980. See *Oppenheimer Letters*, ed. by Smith and Weiner, pp. 294–296.

19. Sherwin, *A World Destroyed*, p. 237.

20. *Sunday Express* (London), August 18, 1946. See also *New York Times*, August 19, 1946. This probably was his opinion; however, as there is apparently no other record of this attitude, the interview in the *Express* must be accepted with caution.

21. Albert Einstein, *Einstein on Peace*, ed. Otto Nathan and Heinz Norden (New York: Simon and Schuster, 1960), p. 434. The American public, like the policymakers, had apparently become largely inured to mass destruction, and after the fire bombings of Dresden and Tokyo had occasioned little moral outrage in the United States, it appeared that, in the words of the historian Barton J. Bernstein, "there were few, if any, moral restraints on what weapons were acceptable in war." (Bernstein, "The Atomic Bomb and American Foreign Policy" in *The Atomic Bomb: The Critical Issues*, pp. 114–115.) Late in 1945, the noted writer Lewis Mumford wrote that the most remarkable fact about postwar life was that "mass extermination has awakened so little moral protest." (Quoted in Herken, *The Winning Weapon*, p. 311.) One common line of reasoning held that the destruction of Hiroshima and Nagasaki was not all that much dissimilar to the damage inflicted by the fire bombings of Dresden and Tokyo by conventional air attacks. Max Born, in disputing that contention, asked: ". . . can a big crime be justified by the statement that we are accustomed to committing many smaller crimes?" Max Born, "Man and the Atom," *Bulletin of the Atomic Scientists* (June 1957), p. 189.

22. Fyodor Dostoevsky, *The Brothers Karamazov*, trans. David Magarshack (New York: Penguin Books, 1970), pp. 287–288.

12

1. For a discussion of the activities of the Interim Committee, see previous chapter.

2. Gregg Herken, *The Winning Weapon: The Atomic Bomb in the Cold War 1945–1950* (New York: Alfred A. Knopf, 1980), p. 153.

3. Albert Einstein, *Einstein on Peace* (hereafter *EoP*), ed., Otto Nathan and Heinz Norden (New York: Simon and Schuster, 1960), p. 386.

4. *EoP*, p. 337.

5. *EoP*, pp. 347–352.

6. Joseph I. Lieberman, *The Scorpion and the Tarantula: The Struggle to Control Atomic Weapons* (Boston: Houghton Mifflin Co., 1970), p. 156.

7. Herken, *The Winning Weapon*, p. 71.

8. Otto Nathan believes Einstein erred in calling his idea for a supranational authority a "world government" because the term is misleading and was easier for his opponents to criticize. Nathan prefers "world authority," which he feels is a less threatening, more accurate description of the international agency which was not intended to govern the world, but to accomplish and enforce disarmament and world peace. Interview with Otto Nathan, March 27, 1982.

9. *EoP*, p. 398. Interview with Otto Nathan, April 10, 1982.

10. *EoP*, p. 436.

11. *EoP*, p. 442.

12. Comment about film *Where Will You Hide?* 1948, Einstein Archives.

13. Figures are from John Lewis Gaddis, *The United States and the Origins of the Cold War, 1941–1947* (New York: Columbia University Press, 1972), p. 80. According to Gaddis, the figure for the Soviet casualties is a "conservative estimate."

14. Richard J. Barnet, *The Giants: America and Russia* (New York: Simon and Schuster, 1977), p. 95.

15. Interview with Janet McClosky, October 10, 1977.

16. Einstein to Henry Offerman, November 3, 1942, Einstein Archives.

17. Gaddis, *United States and the Origins of the Cold War*, p. 300.

18. Equating Stalin with Hitler is irresistible, but dangerously misleading. That his crimes against the people of Russia were as monstrous as Hitler's crimes is beyond dispute, but the two prototypical totalitarian dictators are so different

in style, temperament, and particularly their goals, that they must be dealt with separately.

19. Adam B. Ulam, *Stalin: The Man and His Era* (New York: The Viking Press, 1973), p. 319.

20. Lieberman, *The Scorpion and the Tarantula,* p. 406. It should be noted that physicists in Russia knew that research on atomic weapons was being conducted during the war because of the abrupt cessation of the publication of articles on nuclear physics in the scientific journals after 1940, and the disappearance of leading nuclear physicists in America and England. What the Soviet physicists could not deduce, of course, was the actual structure of the Manhattan Project, the technological approach to the development of atomic weapons, and the degree of success of the project. Soviet espionage was able to provide some of this information.

21. For the Baruch plan, see Lieberman, *The Scorpion and the Tarantula,* pp. 260–386; and Herken, *The Winning Weapon,* pp. 151–191.

22. Jeremy Bernstein, "Master of the Trade," part II (Profile of Hans Bethe), in *The New Yorker,* December 10, 1979, p. 92.

23. FBI files, section 4, p. 564.

24. FBI files, section 4, p. 628. The report is dated December 13, 1946.

25. *EoP,* pp. 403–404. The date is apparently ca. February 13, 1947.

26. FBI files, section 4, pp. 647–648. The report is dated February 14, 1947.

27. Memorandum to D. M. Ladd from J. C. Strickland, March 4, 1947. FBI files, section 4, pp. 655–656.

28. Memorandum to D. M. Ladd from V. P. Keay, March 12, 1947. FBI files, section 4, pp. 657–658.

29. FBI files, section 8, p. 107.

30. Herken, *The Winning Weapon,* pp. 224, 401. At the meeting Oppenheimer had said, "I feel we have blood on our hands." Truman replied, "Never mind. It'll all come out in the wash." Quoted by Nuel Pharr Davis, *Lawrence and Oppenheimer* (New York: Simon and Schuster, 1968), p. 258.

31. Interview with Otto Nathan, May 15, 1982.

32. Einstein to Otto Juliusburger, March 31, 1943, Einstein Archives.

33. Albert Einstein, *The Human Side: New Glimpses from His Archives,* selected and edited by Helen Dukas and Banesh Hoffmann (Princeton: Princeton University Press, 1979), pp. 55, 38.

34. Richard Hofstadter, *Anti-Intellectualism in American Life* (New York: Alfred A. Knopf, 1963), pp. 426–430.

35. Herken, *The Winning Weapon,* p. 339.

36. "Memorandum by William T. Golden to the Secretary of State," June 9, 1947, in *Foreign Relations of the United States of America: 1947* (Washington, D.C.: U.S. Government Printing Office, 1973), vol. I, pp. 487–489.

37. Interview with Bruria Kaufman, January 10, 1979.

38. *EoP,* p. 572.

39. See James Franck's comments to the Emergency Committee of the Atomic Scientists in 1947, quoted in Robert Jungk, *Brighter Than a Thousand Suns: The Moral and Political History of the Atomic Scientists* (London: Victor Gollancz, Ltd., 1958), p. 44.

40. Isaiah Berlin, "Einstein and Israel" in *Albert Einstein: Historical and Cultural Perspectives: The Centennial Symposium in Jerusalem,* ed. Gerald Holton and Yehuda Elkana (Princeton: Princeton University Press, 1982), p. 290.

41. Jungk, *Brighter Than a Thousand Suns,* p. 243.

42. Ernst Straus, "Reminiscences" in *Centennial Symposium in Jerusalem,* p. 418.

43. Interview with Otto Nathan, May 25, 1983.

44. Albert Einstein, *Ideas and Opinions,* based on *Mein Weltbild,* ed. Carl Seelig, and other sources, new translations and revisions by Sonja Bargmann (New York: Crown Publishers, Inc., 1954), pp. 225–227.

45. Quoted in Herken, *The Winning Weapon,* p. 270.

13

1. Daniel J. Yergin, *Shattered Peace: The Origins of the Cold War and The National Security State* (Boston: Houghton Mifflin Co., 1977), pp. 275–276.

2. Ibid., pp. 288–289.

3. Quoted by John Lewis Gaddis, *The United States and the Origins of the Cold War, 1941–1947* (New York: Columbia University Press, 1972), p. 351; from the Truman Public Papers: 1947, pp. 178–179.

4. Ronald Steele, *Walter Lippmann and the American Century* (Boston: An Atlantic Monthly Press Book, Little, Brown and Company, 1980), p. 439.

5. Richard J. Barnet, *Roots of War* (New York: Atheneum, 1972), p. 258. See also Adam B. Ulam, *Stalin: The Man and His Era* (New York: The Viking Press, 1973), p. 632.

6. Barnet, *Roots of War,* p. 60.

7. Steele, *Lippmann,* p. 425.

8. Barnet, *Roots of War,* pp. 285–286.
9. FBI files, section 5, p. 788. See also FBI files, section 5, pp. 746–747, 850.
10. FBI files, section 1, September 5, 1946. Contained in report to H. B. Fletcher from V. P. Keay, February 13, 1950.
11. FBI files, section 5, pp. 735–736.
12. Albert Einstein, *Einstein on Peace* (hereafter *EoP*), ed. Otto Nathan and Heinz Norden (New York: Simon and Schuster, 1960), p. 343.
13. Einstein to Edwin Lindsay, July 18, 1953, Einstein Archives.
14. Elenore Lester and Frederick E. Werbell, "The Lost Hero of the Holocaust: The Search for Sweden's Raoul Wallenberg" in *New York Times Magazine,* March 30, 1980, p. 21.
15. Dorothy Thompson to Einstein, May 20, 1947, letter in Einstein Archives.
16. Einstein to Stalin, November 17, 1947, Einstein Archives.
17. Semen Tsarapkin to Einstein, December 18, 1947, letter in Einstein Archives.
18. Einstein to Guy von Dardel, December 22, 1947, Einstein Archives.
19. Aleksandr I. Solzhenitsyn, *The Gulag Archipelago, 1918–1956: An Experiment in Literary Investigation* (New York: Harper & Row, 1973), Volume I, p. 240, and Volume II, p. 189. Adam B. Ulam, *A History of Soviet Russia* (New York: Praeger Publishers, 1976), pp. 191–195.
20. Ulam, *Stalin,* p. 105.
21. See *EoP,* pp. 440–455, or Albert Einstein, *Out of My Later Years* (Westport, Conn.: Greenwood Press, 1970), pp. 156–175.
22. Quoted in Yergin, *Shattered Peace,* p. 365.
23. *EoP,* pp. 464–467.
24. *EoP,* p. 522.
25. George Kennan, *American Diplomacy 1900–1950* (Chicago: University of Chicago Press, 1951), pp. 89–90.
26. *EoP,* pp. 425–426.
27. Quoted by Gregg Herken, *The Winning Weapon: The Atomic Bomb in the Cold War 1945–1950* (New York: Alfred A. Knopf, 1980), p. 244, from David E. Lilienthal, *The Journals of David E. Lilienthal: Atomic Energy Years, 1945–1950* (New York: Harper & Row, 1964), p. 391.

28. Harrison Brown quoted in *EoP,* p. 431. Also see Harrison Brown, "An Early Brief Encounter" in *Bulletin of the Atomic Scientists* (March 1979), pp. 17–19.
29. Einstein to Sidney Hook, April 3, 1948, Einstein Archives.
30. Einstein to Jerome Davis, August 28, 1948, Einstein Archives. Einstein to Vincent Sheean, January 22, 1952, Einstein Archives.
31. Einstein to Norman Thomas, March 10, 1954, Einstein Archives. Quoted by W. A. Swanberg, *Norman Thomas: The Last Idealist* (New York: Charles Scribner's Sons, 1976), pp. 369–370.
32. Einstein to Henry A. Wallace, January 26, 1949, Einstein Archives.
33. *EoP,* p. 439.
34. *EoP,* p. 507.
35. Herken, *The Winning Weapon,* p. 284.
36. The real fruits of Soviet espionage were: (1) the Russians discovered the low opinion America held of the capabilities of Russian technology; and (2) they also learned of General Groves's plan to corner the world's supply of uranium 235. In short, the damage to American security by Soviet espionage was much less significant than the domestic anti-Communist hysteria it engendered during the McCarthy era. The result of Soviet espionage was not Soviet atomic weapons, but a serious weakening of American civil liberties. See Herken, *The Winning Weapon,* p. 341.
37. Richard A. Falk in Robert Jay Lifton and Richard A. Falk, *Indefensible Weapons: The Political and Psychological Case Against Nuclearism* (New York: Basic Books, 1982), p. 203.
38. Joseph I. Lieberman, *The Scorpion and the Tarantula: The Struggle to Control Atomic Weapons* (Boston: Houghton Mifflin Co., 1970), p. 139.
39. Robert Jungk, *Brighter Than a Thousand Suns: The Moral and Political History of the Atomic Scientists* (London: Victor Gollancz, Ltd., 1958), p. 266.
40. *EoP,* p. 521. *EoP* mistakenly dates this speech February 13, 1950.
41. Quoted in "Einstein at Seventy," by Alfred Werner, written March 5, 1949, p. 9. Copy in Einstein Archives.

14

1. Interview with Samuel Howell, June 8, 1977.
2. Einstein to Frau Planck, November 10, 1947, Einstein Archives. Translation from Ronald W. Clark, *Einstein: The Life and Times* (New York: Thomas Y. Crowell Co., 1971), pp. 603–604.
3. Einstein to Millicent Bingham, September 1945, Einstein Archives.
4. Albert Einstein, *Einstein on Peace*

(hereafter *EoP*), ed. Otto Nathan and Heinz Norden (New York: Simon and Schuster, 1960), pp. 367, 577.

5. Ernst Straus, "Reminiscences" in *Albert Einstein: Historical and Cultural Perspectives: The Centennial Symposium in Jerusalem,* ed. Gerald Holton and Yehuda Elkana (Princeton: Princeton University Press, 1982), p. 419.

6. Interview with Judge Philip Forman, April 18, 1977.

7. Message for Conference of National Urban League, September 16, 1946, Einstein Archives. Letter written to Lester B. Granger, Executive Secretary, National Urban League.

8. Anton Reiser, *Albert Einstein: A Biographical Portrait* (New York: Albert and Charles Boni, 1930), p. 187.

9. Albert Einstein, *Out of My Later Years* (Westport, Conn.: Greenwood Press, 1970), p. 133.

10. Address at Wall of Fame, World's Fair, 1940, Einstein Archives.

11. Interview with Margot Einstein, May 3, 1978.

12. Helen Dukas to Abraham Pais, April 30, 1955, quoted by Pais in "*Subtle is the Lord . . .*": *The Science and the Life of Albert Einstein* (New York: Oxford University Press, 1982), pp. 475–476.

13. Interview with Banesh Hoffmann, May 9, 1977.

14. Einstein to Gustav Bucky, May 30, 1950, Einstein Archives.

15. Bertrand Russell, *The Autobiography of Bertrand Russell, 1914–1944* (Boston: Little, Brown and Co., 1967), p. 341. *EoP*, p. xv. In *EoP* Russell erroneously gives the date as 1943, and Pais in "*Subtle is the Lord . . .*" repeats it on p. 13.

16. Herman Goldstine, *The Computer from Pascal to von Neumann* (Princeton: Princeton University Press, 1972), p. 173. Interview with Herman Goldstine, November 14, 1977. Straus, "Reminiscences" in *Centennial Symposium in Jerusalem,* pp. 420–422.

17. Interview with John Kemeny, November 21, 1977.

18. Frances Margaret Blanshard, *Frank Ayde-*

lotte of Swarthmore, ed. and with a preface by Brand Blanshard (Middletown, Conn.: Wesleyan University Press, 1970), pp. 341–342.

19. Abraham Pais, "The Princeton Period," *Physics Today* (October 1967), pp. 42–47.

20. Interview with Eugene Wigner, June 6, 1977.

21. Interview with Atle Selberg, June 15, 1977.

22. Interview with Atle Selberg, June 16, 1977. Professor Selberg said he had been told this story, and although he could not vouch for its authenticity with certainty, he believed it to be true.

23. Leopold Infeld, *Why I Left Canada, Reflections on Science and Politics* (Montreal: McGill–Queen's University Press, 1978), p. 147.

24. Interview with Lily Kahler, June 2, 1977.

25. Interview with Eugene Wigner, June 6, 1977.

26. Interview with John Kemeny, November 21, 1977.

27. Pais, "*Subtle is the Lord . . .*," p. 8.

28. Interview with Eugene Wigner, June 6, 1977.

29. Pais, "*Subtle is the Lord . . .*," p. 474.

30. Einstein to Gertrude Warschauer, March 26, 1950, Einstein Archives.

31. Interview with Sonja Bargmann, April 12, 1977.

32. Einstein to Max Born, September 7, 1944, in *The Born-Einstein Letters: Correspondence Between Albert Einstein and Max and Hedwig Born from 1916 to 1955* (New York: Walker and Co., 1971), p. 148.

33. Amiya Chakravarty to Einstein, October 4, 1949, letter in Einstein Archives.

34. Amiya Chakravarty to Einstein, November 9, 1949, letter in Einstein Archives.

35. Interview with Otto Nathan, March 27, 1982, and May 25, 1983.

36. Einstein to Bice J. Rusconi-Besso, August 11, 1953, Einstein Archives.

37. Interview with Margot Einstein, May 5, 1978.

15

1. Hearing Before the Anglo-American Committee of Inquiry on Jewish Problems in Palestine and Europe, Washington, D.C., State Department Building, vol. 5, January 11, 1946, pp. 118–135. Bartley Crum, *Behind the Silken Curtain* (Port Washington, N.Y.: Kennikat

Press, Inc., 1969), pp. 24–28. Richard Crossman, *Palestine Mission: A Personal Record* (New York: Harper and Brothers, 1947), p. 39.

2. Stephen S. Wise to Einstein, January 14, 1946. Einstein to Stephen S. Wise, January 14, 1946, Einstein Archives.

3. Nicholas Bethell, *The Palestine Triangle: The Struggle Between the British, the Jews and the Arabs 1935–1948* (London: André Deutsch, 1979), p. 208.

4. Ibid., p. 237.

5. Einstein to Hans Mühsam, April 3, 1946, Einstein to Richard Crossman, June 3, 1946, Einstein Archives.

6. Einstein to Hans Mühsam, January 22, 1947, Einstein Archives.

7. Einstein to Hans Mühsam, April 11, 1947, Einstein Archives.

8. Einstein and Leo Baeck to the *New York Times* (hereafter *NYT*). Letter dated April 12, 1948, and published in *NYT* on April 18, 1948.

9. Einstein to Lina Kocherthaler, May 4, 1948, Einstein Archives. Translation from Ronald W. Clark, *Einstein: The Life and Times* (New York: Thomas Y. Crowell Co., 1971), p. 605.

10. Einstein to Hans Mühsam, September 24, 1948, Einstein Archives.

11. Einstein to Hans Mühsam, February 26, 1949, Einstein Archives.

12. Albert Einstein, *Einstein on Peace* (hereafter *EoP*), ed. Otto Nathan and Heinz Norden (New York: Simon and Schuster, 1960), p. 637.

13. *The Daily Princetonian,* September 20, 1954.

14. Einstein to Louis D. Brandeis, March 4, 1935, Einstein Archives. Einstein to David Eisenberg, February 24, 1945, Einstein Archives.

15. Abram L. Sachar, *A Host at Last* (Boston: Little, Brown, and Co., 1976), p. 15.

16. Einstein to Israel Goldstein, May 14, 1946, Einstein Archives.

17. Einstein to Israel Goldstein, July 1, 1946, Einstein Archives.

18. Einstein to Stephen S. Wise, June 29, 1946, Einstein Archives.

19. Einstein to Felix Frankfurter, August 20, 1946, and September 2, 1946, Einstein Archives.

20. Einstein to Hans Mühsam, January 22, 1947, Einstein Archives.

21. Sachar, *A Host at Last,* p. 18.

22. Einstein to James Franck, May 21, 1947, Einstein Archives.

23. *NYT,* June 23, 1947.

24. Interview with Otto Nathan, March 27, 1982.

25. Einstein to Hans Mühsam, March 24, 1948, Einstein Archives.

26. Interview with Abraham Pais, November 27, 1977.

27. Einstein to Dr. Ludwig Freund, July 23, 1935, Einstein Archives.

28. Einstein to Chaim Weizmann, May 19, 1948, Einstein Archives.

29. Abba Eban, *My Country: The Story of Modern Israel* (New York: Random House, 1972), p. 115.

30. Interview with Helen Dukas, February 2, 1977.

31. *EoP,* pp. 572–573.

32. Interview with Otto Nathan, April 10, 1982.

33. Interview with Margot Einstein, July 21, 1978.

34. Yitzak Navon, "On Einstein and the Israeli Presidency" in *Albert Einstein: Historical and Cultural Perspectives: The Centennial Symposium in Jerusalem,* ed. Gerald Holton and Yehuda Elkana (Princeton: Princeton University Press, 1982), p. 295. See also Abraham Pais, *"Subtle is the Lord . . ." The Science and the Life of Albert Einstein* (New York: Oxford University Press, 1982), p. 11.

35. *EoP,* p. 574.

16

1. Albert Einstein, *Einstein on Peace* (hereafter *EoP*), ed. Otto Nathan and Heinz Norden (New York: Simon and Schuster, 1960), p. 523.

2. Phoenix office, FBI to J. Edgar Hoover (hereafter JEH), February 19, 1950, FBI files, section 1.

3. D. M. Ladd to JEH, February 15, 1950, FBI files, section 1. See Richard Alan Schwartz, "The FBI and Dr. Einstein," *The Nation,* vol. 237, no. 6 (September 3–10, 1983), pp. 168–173, for an excellent account of the contents of the FBI files on Einstein. Note that Schwartz deciphers Hoover's handwriting thusly: "I have seen somewhere Einstein was the one who suggested Fuchs [*sic*] assignment to live in England" (p. 169).

4. FBI files, section 8, p. 5.

5. FBI files, section 6, pp. 1053 and 1081.

6. Emma Rabbeis to State Department, February 25, 1950, and Report to JEH, July 31, 1950, FBI files, section 1.

7. Army Intelligence Report, FBI files, section 1.

8. JEH to Assistant Chief of Staff, G-2, October 23, 1950, FBI files, section 1.

9. Army Intelligence Report, January 25, 1951, FBI files, section 1.

10. FBI files, section 8, pp. 6–13; and FBI files, section 10 (September 1, 1954).

11. FBI files, section 10.

12. W. F. Kelley to JEH, September 14, 1950, FBI files, section 1.

13. INS memorandum to W. W. Wiggins, June 14, 1950, FBI files, section 1.

14. *EoP*, pp. 181–182.

15. *EoP*, pp. 483–491 and 511–512.

16. Newark office of FBI to JEH, December 5, 1951; Philadelphia office of FBI to JEH, December 17, 1951; JEH to Newark office of FBI, January 10, 1952; JEH to Commissioner of INS, February 12, 1952; all in FBI files, section 1.

17. Thirteen-page summary report from FBI to INS, February 23, 1952, p. 3; FBI files, section 1.

18. Newark office of FBI to JEH, August 30, 1951, FBI files, section 1. FBI files, section 2.

19. D. M. Ladd to JEH, February 15, 1950, FBI files, section 1.

20. Einstein to Gertrud Warschauer, July 15, 1950, Einstein Archives.

21. *EoP*, pp. 538–539.

22. *EoP*, p. 554.

23. *EoP*, p. 435.

24. *EoP*, pp. 521, 539.

25. Albert Einstein, *Ideas and Opinions* (hereafter *IaO*), based on *Mein Weltbild*, ed. Carl Seelig, and other sources, new translations and revisions by Sonja Bargmann (New York: Crown Publishers, Inc., 1954), pp. 151–158. All quotations until footnote 26 are from this essay.

26. *IaO*, p. 52.

27. *IaO*, p. 158. See Chapter 10 for a discussion of Einstein's ideas on education.

28. *IaO*, p. 158; *EoP*, p. 450.

29. *EoP*, pp. 450–451; Interview with Otto Nathan, May 8, 1981; and *EoP*, p. 533.

30. For the following discussion, see Daniel J. Yergin, *Shattered Peace: The Origins of the Cold War and the National Security State* (Boston: Houghton Mifflin Co., 1977), especially pp. 196–201.

31. Yergin, *Shattered Peace*, p. 197.

32. See comment by Max Born quoted in footnote 21, Chapter 11.

33. See Richard Hofstadter, *Anti-Intellectualism in American Life* (New York: Alfred A. Knopf, 1963).

34. Niccolo Tucci, Profile, *The New Yorker*, November 22, 1947, p. 54.

35. As a scientist, Einstein's work required a high degree of specialization. There is, however, a difference between specialized knowledge and narrow specialization which focuses so intently upon a single subject that any wider perspective is lost in the process. Of the consequences of narrow specialization, Einstein once wrote: ". . . our age takes a more skeptical view of the role of the individual than did the eighteenth and the first half of the nineteenth century. For the extensive specialization of the professions and of knowledge lets the individual appear 'replaceable,' as it were, like a part of a mass-produced machine." Foreword to *Galileo Galilei: Dialogue Concerning the Two Chief World Systems, Ptolemaic and Copernican;* trans. Stillman Drake (Berkeley: University of California Press, 1967), pp. vii, ix.

36. See Adam Ulam, *The Rivals: America and Russia Since World War II* (New York: The Viking Press, 1971), p. 141.

37. George F. Kennan, *Memoirs: 1950–1963*, Vol. II (Boston: Little, Brown and Co., 1972), pp. 134–138.

38. FBI files, section 3.

39. FBI files, section 5, p. 852.

40. Einstein to Judge Irving R. Kaufman, December 23, 1952; Einstein to President Harry S. Truman, January 11, 1953, Einstein Archives.

In the fall of 1954, Irwin Edelman, a former Communist who had twice been expelled from the party, sent Einstein a copy of his manuscript on the Rosenberg trial. Einstein was very impressed by the research and exchanged a number of letters with Edelman. Although he disagreed with Edelman on a great many subjects (the Stalinist Purges, Hegelian philosophy, the American Communist Party) he agreed that the Rosenbergs' legal defense had been "lamentable . . . bordering on treachery." (Einstein to Edelman, September 8, 1954.) He also noted that the "indictment was based on the testimony of a man who wanted and was able to save his life by becoming a witness for the prosecution." (Einstein to Edelman, February 8, 1955.)

In reference to the execution of the Rosenbergs, Einstein noted sardonically: "It is one of the shortcomings of the death penalty that it kills, generally speaking, not only the persons but also the public interest in their case." (Einstein to Edelman, September 8, 1954.) In 1931 Einstein explained his opposition to legal executions in terms of human fallibility and the irreversibility of the act: "I am not for punishment at all, but only for measures that serve society and its protection. In principle I would not be opposed to killing individuals who are worthless or dangerous in that sense. I am against it only because I do not trust people, i.e. the courts." (Einstein to Valentin Bulgakov, November 4, 1931, quoted in *Albert Einstein, The Human Side: New Glimpses from His Archives*, selected and edited by Helen Dukas and Banesh Hoffmann [Princeton: Princeton University Press, 1979], p. 84.)

See the Rosenberg file in the Einstein Archives.

41. Newark office of FBI to JEH, April 22, 1953, FBI files, section 7.

42. Letter to JEH, April 21, 1953, FBI files, section 7.

43. Ronald Steele, *Walter Lippmann and the American Century* (Boston: An Atlantic Monthly Press Book, Little, Brown and Co., 1980), pp. 486–487, and 569–580.

17

Opening quote: Albert Einstein, *Einstein on Peace* (hereafter *EoP*), ed. Otto Nathan and Heinz Norden (New York: Simon and Schuster, 1960), p. 604.

1. *EoP*, pp. 589–590.

2. "It goes without saying that the perversion of justice which manifests itself in all the official trials staged by the Russian government, not only those of Prague, but also the earlier ones since the second half of the Thirties, deserve unconditional condemnation." Einstein to Daniel James, editor of *The New Leader*, January 15, 1953, Einstein Archives.

3. Daniel J. Yergin in *Shattered Peace: The Origins of the Cold War and the National Security State* (Boston: Houghton Mifflin Co., 1977), pp. 407–408, points out that the Korean War served as a catalyst to escalate American arms build-up. Prior to the Korean fighting, Truman often had trouble getting his growing military budgets passed by Congress. Even so, Einstein felt that military appropriations in the years immediately preceding the Korean War were excessive, and the budgets after the outbreak of war were that much worse.

4. *EoP*, p. 596.

5. Quoted in *Gandhi on Non-Violence*, ed. Thomas Merton (New York: New Directions Publishing Corp., 1965), p. 24.

6. Ibid., p. 34.

7. *EoP*, pp. 542–543.

8. *EoP*, p. 543.

9. Richard J. Barnet, *Roots of War* (New York: Atheneum, 1972), p. 87.

10. Einstein to Guy Raner, November 9, 1951, Einstein Archives.

11. Einstein to Richard Kluger, September 17, 1953, Einstein Archives.

12. Einstein to Edwin Lindsay, July 4, 1953, Einstein Archives.

13. *EoP*, p. 546.

14. *EoP*, pp. 546–547.

15. Einstein to Corliss Lamont, January 1954, Einstein Archives.

16. *EoP*, pp. 547, 550.

17. *New York Times*, June 13 and 14, 1953.

18. FBI files, section 7.

19. Interview with Otto Nathan, May 25, 1983.

20. Erich von Kahler, "Einstein the Man (On the Occasion of his 75th Birthday)," published in *Die Weltwoche* (Zurich), March 12, 1954; English translation furnished by Lily Kahler.

21. *EoP*, p. 550.

22. Einstein to Michele Besso, December 12, 1951, in *Albert Einstein, Michele Besso: Correspondence 1903–1955*, translation, notes and introduction by Pierre Speziali (Paris: Hermann, 1972), p. 453.

23. Einstein to Raymond Swing, March 29, 1954, Einstein Archives.

24. The following material was drawn from an interview with Albert Shadowitz, November 18, 1977.

25. Einstein to Corliss Lamont, January 2, 1954, Einstein Archives.

26. Albert Shadowitz to Einstein, December 14, 1953; Einstein to Albert Shadowitz, December 15, 1953, Einstein Archives.

27. See letter to Einstein from William H. Hirschaut, December 19, 1953, Einstein Archives.

28. Einstein to Albert Shadowitz, January 14, 1954.

29. In May 1953 Murrow visited Einstein to arrange the radio hookup for the broadcast of his acceptance speech for the Lord & Taylor Award on nonconformity. As Helen Dukas was showing him to the door, she said she thought McCarthy was like Hitler. Murrow replied that there was an important difference in that McCarthy had neither wealthy backers nor a police force behind him. (Interview with Helen Dukas, December 20, 1979.)

30. Interview with Edith Shadowitz, November 18, 1977.

31. Norman Thomas to Einstein, March 9, 1954, in W. A. Swanberg, *Norman Thomas: The Last Idealist* (New York: Charles Scribner's Sons, 1976), p. 369.

32. Einstein to Norman Thomas, March 10, 1954, Einstein Archives. Quoted in Swanberg, *Norman Thomas*, pp. 369–370.

33. *EoP*, pp. 551–552.

34. Interview with Otto Nathan, November 28, 1982.

35. "See It Now" (television program), "J. Robert Oppenheimer," 4th ed., show # 18, January 4, 1955.

36. Interview with Tiffin Harper Shenstone, March 18, 1977.

18

Title: Undated aphorism in Einstein Archives, ca. 1950.

1. Daniel J. Kevles, *The Physicists: The History of a Scientific Community in Modern America* (New York: Alfred A. Knopf, 1978), p. 325.

2. Robert Barnet, *Roots of War* (New York: Atheneum, 1972), p. 44. Steve J. Heims, *John von Neumann and Norbert Wiener: From Mathematics to the Technologies of Life and Death* (Cambridge, Mass.: The MIT Press, 1980), p. 179. Lewis Cosner quoted in Heims, p. 330.

3. Albert Einstein, *Einstein on Peace* (hereafter *EoP*), ed. Otto Nathan and Heinz Norden (New York: Simon and Schuster, 1960), p. 402. For a pessimistic appraisal of contemporary "Big Science," see Hyman Hartman, "Reflections on Einstein's 100th Birthday" in the *Bulletin of the Atomic Scientists* (December 1979), p. 9. Hartman concludes: "I have seen a dramatic decay in pure science over the last ten years: the poetry and the philosophy are missing; the young are apathetic; budgets and profits have priority; the technical mediocrities spawned in the 1960s now dominate; and government funding is mission oriented. It is ironical that as we celebrate Einstein's birthday we are burying his legacy of play and passion."

4. *EoP*, p. 510.

5. E. U. Condon, "An Appeal to Reason" in Morton Grodzins and Eugene Rabinowitch, *The Atomic Age: Scientists in National and World Affairs: Articles from the "Bulletin of the Atomic Scientists"* (New York: Basic Books, Inc., 1963), p. 358.

6. *EoP*, p. 383.

7. *EoP*, p. 401.

8. *EoP*, p. 423.

9. *EoP*, p. 122.

10. Bethe quoted by Bernstein in "Master of the Trade," *The New Yorker*, December 10, 1979, p. 72.

11. For instance, Robert Jungk, *Brighter Than a Thousand Suns: The Moral and Political History of the Atomic Scientists* (London: Victor Gollancz, Ltd., 1958), pp. 139–156, and Haakon Chevalier, *The Story of a Friendship* (New York: George Braziller, 1965), p. 190.

12. See discussion of Oppenheimer-Acheson-Lilienthal Report in Chapter 12, pp. 189–191.

13. J. Robert Oppenheimer, "Atomic Weapons and American Policy," in Grodzins and Rabinowitch, *The Atomic Age*, pp. 188–196.

14. Abraham Pais, *"Subtle is the Lord . . ." The Science and the Life of Albert Einstein* (New York: Oxford University Press, 1982), pp. 10–11.

15. Interview with Helen Dukas, November 9, 1977.

16. *EoP*, p. 607. See also *Bulletin of the Atomic Scientists* (May 1954), p. 190.

17. Herman Goldstine, *The Computer from Pascal to von Neumann* (Princeton: Princeton University Press, 1972), p. 318.

18. Quoted in Philip M. Stern, *The Oppenheimer Case: Security on Trial* (New York: Harper & Row, 1969), p. 406.

19. Einstein to Senator Herbert Lehman, May 19, 1954, Einstein Archives.

20. *EoP*, p. 613. See discussion in *EoP*, pp. 613–614.

21. Einstein to Arthur Taub, November 24, 1954, Einstein Archives.

22. See "Plumber File" in the Einstein Archives.

19

1. Interview with Homer Thompson, October 25, 1977.

2. Interview with Helen Dukas, December 26, 1978.

3. Interview with John Kemeny, November 21, 1977.

4. Interview with Eva Kayser, March 7, 1979.

5. Interview with Lily Kahler, June 2, 1977.

6. Ernst Straus, "Albert Einstein: The Man," Memorial Talk at the University of California, Los Angeles, May 1955, p. 14.

7. Interview with Margot Einstein, January 15, 1979.

8. Interview with Dorothy Commins, December 13 and 16, 1977.

9. Interview with Margot Einstein, July 21, 1978.

10. Interview with Bruria Kaufman, January 10, 1979. Interview with Margot Einstein, July 21, 1978.

11. Interview with Dorothy Commins, November 17, 1977.

12. Interview with Gerhard Fankhauser, November 2, 1977.

13. Einstein to Paul Arthur Schilpp, March 27, 1954, Einstein Archives.

14. Albert Einstein, *Einstein on Peace*

(hereafter *EoP*), ed. Otto Nathan and Heinz Norden (New York: Simon and Schuster, 1960), pp. 603–604.

15. Unpublished statement written for the European reedition of *Mein Weltbild,* 1953, Einstein Archives.

16. Einstein's contribution to Albert Schweitzer's *Festschrift* (80th Birthday), published January 1955, Einstein Archives.

17. Einstein to Albert Schweitzer, December 1954, Einstein Archives.

18. Albert Schweitzer to Einstein, February 20, 1955, copy in Einstein Archives.

19. Einstein to Gertrud Warschauer, December 28, 1954, Einstein Archives.

20. Letter from Princeton University undergraduate to his father, January 26, 1955, copy in possession of JS.

21. Einstein to Hans Mühsam, July 9, 1951, Einstein Archives.

22. Einstein to Michele Besso, July 17, 1952, in *Albert Einstein, Michele Besso: Correspondence 1903–1955,* translation, notes and introduction by Pierre Speziali (Paris: Hermann, 1972), p. 474.

23. Ernst Straus, "Memoir," in *Einstein: A Centenary Volume,* ed. A. P. French (Cambridge, Mass.: Harvard University Press, 1979), p. 32.

24. Einstein to Gertrud Warschauer, December 26, 1953, Einstein Archives.

25. Einstein to Elizabeth, Queen Mother of Belgium, January 1954, Einstein Archives.

26. Interview with Margot Einstein, July 21, 1978.

27. Interview with Louise Morse, April 15, 1977.

28. *EoP,* pp. 632–635.

29. *EoP,* pp. 637, 638–640.

30. Murray Kempton, "The Professor," *New York Post,* April 19, 1955.

31. Helen Dukas to Abraham Pais, April 30, 1955, quoted in Abraham Pais, "*Subtle is the Lord . . .": The Science and the Life of Albert Einstein* (New York: Oxford University Press, 1982), p. 477.

32. Interview with Helen Dukas, January 19, 1977.

33. Interview with Otto Nathan, November 28, 1982. See also Nathan's Introduction to *EoP,* p. vii.

34. Einstein to Vero Besso and Bice Rusconi-Besso, March 21, 1955, in *Besso Correspondence,* p. 538. Also quoted in Banesh Hoffmann and Helen Dukas, *Albert Einstein: Creator and Rebel* (New York: The Viking Press, 1972), pp. 257–258.

20

Opening quote: Henry David Thoreau, "On the Duty of Civil Disobedience" in Henry David Thoreau, *Walden: Or Life in the Woods and On the Duty of Civil Disobedience* (New York: A Signet Classic, 1960), p. 234.

1. Interview with Margot Einstein, May 4, 1978.

2. Interview with Valentine Bargmann, September 15, 1983.

3. Interview with Sonja Bargmann, September 15, 1983.

4. See Abraham Pais, "*Subtle is the Lord . . .*": *The Science and the Life of Albert Einstein* (New York: Oxford University Press, 1982), pp. 492–493.

5. Interview with Margot Einstein, May 4, 1978.

6. Thoreau, "On the Duty of Civil Disobedience," p. 230.

7. Richard Falk, "Nuclear Intentions," in Robert Jay Lifton and Richard Falk, *Indefensible Weapons: The Political and Psychological Case Against Nuclearism* (New York: Basic Books, Inc., 1982), p. 170.

8. Thoreau, "On the Duty of Civil Disobedience," p. 230.

9. Isaiah Berlin, "Einstein and Israel," in *Albert Einstein: Historical and Cultural Perspectives: The Centennial Symposium in Jerusalem,* ed. Gerald Holton and Yehuda Elkana (Princeton: Princeton University Press, 1982), p. 289.

10. Interview with John Kemeny, November 21, 1977.

11. Thoreau, *Walden: Or Life in the Woods and On the Duty of Civil Disobedience,* p. 97.

INDEX

Aarau, Switzerland, Einstein in, 29
Academic freedom, Einstein on, 278–279
Acheson, Dean, 182
Albert, King of Belgium, 14–15, 75
Albert Einstein Foundation for Higher
　Learning, 241–243
Albert Einstein: Philosopher-Scientist
　(Schlipp), 227
Alexander, James, 82, 92–93, 223
Alpert, George, 242–243
American Field Service Program, 278–
　279
Anderson, Marian, 221
Anglo-American Committee of Inquiry on
　Palestine, 234–237
Annalen der Physik, 31
Annals of Mathematics, 83
Anti-Relativity Company, 54
Anti-Semitism, 65, 75
　in American universities, 47, 101,
　　240–244
　in Britain, 110
　in Germany, 24–25, 38–39
　in U.S., 47, 101, 111, 240–244
Arabs
　Israel attacked by, 238–239
　in Palestine, 53, 102–110, 234–239
Arms race, 170–173, 251
Atlantic Monthly, 183
Atomic bomb, 117–123, 147–148, 169–
　180
　Bikini test of, 189
　Briggs committee and, 122
　as defensive weapon, 170, 179
　demonstration proposed for, 172, 173,
　　177
　"E = mc²" and, 117–119
　Einstein as "father" of, 117
　Einstein on use of, 179
　in Hiroshima and Nagasaki raids, 151,
　　175, 178–180
　international sharing proposed for,
　　170–175
　Japan considered as target for, 172–
　　179

letters warning about, 117, 120–122
Soviet possession of, 212–213, 262
See also Manhattan Project
Atomic energy
　Acheson-Lilienthal plan for, 190
　"E = mc²" and, 118–119
　Einstein on control of, 191–200
　Einstein's security clearance and, 147–
　　148
　Einstein's skepticism about, 117–118
　experimental discoveries in, 118
　funding of research on, 281–282
　international control proposed for,
　　182–186, 190–194
　politicians' ignorance on, 195
　scientists' self-censorship and, 119,
　　123
　scientists vs. politicians on, 190–198
　security and, 147–148, 282, 285–288
　U.S. policy on, 181–182
Atomic Energy Commission, 184, 193,
　213–215, 223, 250
　Oppenheimer case and, 285–288
Atomic Energy for Military Purposes
　(Smyth Report), 182
"Atomic War or Peace" (Einstein), 183
Attlee, Clement, 234, 236
Autobiographical Notes (Einstein), 25–
　27, 30, 227
Aydelotte, Frank, 92–94, 147–148, 225,
　234

Baeck, Leo, 146–147, 238
Balfour, Arthur James, Lord, 40, 103
Balfour Declaration, 40, 103
Bamberger, Louis, 57, 65, 92, 95
Bargmann, Sonja, 86, 228–229, 303
Bargmann, Valentine, 51, 86–89, 91,
　121, 126, 137, 147, 149, 228, 301–
　302
Barnet, Richard, 202
Baruch, Bernard, 190–191
Beethoven, Ludwig van, Einstein on, 136
Begin, Menachem, 237–238
Belgium, 14–17

Ben-Gurion, David, 107, 110, 233, 240, 247
  Weizmann and, 245
Bergmann, Peter, 88, 147
Berlin
  blockade of, 209
  Einstein in, 32–38, 54–55
  Physics Colloquia in, 55
  scientists in, 83
Berlin, Sir Isaiah, 198, 305
Berlin, University of, 32, 34
Besso, Michele, 31, 34, 80, 112–113, 159, 297–298, 300
Bethe, Hans, 212, 284
Bevin, Ernest, 233
Bible, Einstein on, 156
"Bivector Fields" (Einstein and Bargmann), 149
Blumenfeld, Kurt, 40–41, 46
Bohr, Niels, 84–85, 118, 170–171, 174
Books and Authors War Bond Committee, 149–150
Born, Max, 12, 71, 229, 290–291
Boyd, Julian, 149–150
Brandeis, Louis D., 46–47, 108, 240
Brandeis University, 241–244
Briggs, Lyman J., 122
Brit Shalom, 105–106
Broch, Hermann, 2, 126
Brothers Karamazov, The (Dostoevsky), 180
Bucky, Frieda, 137
Bucky, Gustav, 71–72, 94, 130, 222, 299
Buell, Mrs. Raymond Leslie, 64
Bulletin of Atomic Scientists, 212, 282, 286–287
Bunche, Ralph, 239
Bush, Vannevar, 123, 147–148, 194, 282
Byland, Hans, 29–30
Byrnes, James F., 170–173, 176, 182, 189–190, 213

California Institute of Technology, 5, 55–58
Capitalism, 188
  Einstein on, 161, 257–258

Casadesus, Robert and Gaby, 137
Central Intelligence Group (CIG), 201
Chadwick, James, 118
Chakravarty, Amiya, 229
Chevalier, Haakon, 285
Chico (Einstein's dog), 130–131
Churches, Einstein's distrust of, 156–157
Churchill, Winston, 17, 142, 145, 189
  atomic bomb and, 171, 175
  atomic energy sharing and, 171
  Eastern Europe and, 168
City College of New York, 49
Clemence, S. M., 226
Cleveland Plain Dealer, 251
Cold War, 167, 186–215
  propaganda exchange in, 202–203, 211
  Soviets as seen in, 189
  spying in, 212–213
  Truman policy in, 202, 259–262
  U.S. democracy weakened in, 260
Columbia University, 49
Commins, Saxe and Dorothy, 294, 296
Committee for Foreign Correspondence, 193
Communism
  Einstein and, 5–6, 252–254, 270, 277–278
  socialism vs., 259
  in U.S., 203, 270
  U.S. misunderstanding of, 261–262
Compton, Arthur H., 172–173
Condon, E. U., 282–283
Conservatives, Einstein opposed by, 5–6, 54–55
Cook, George, 150–151
Crossman, Richard, 235, 237
Curie, Marie, 20

Dafni, Reuven, 299
Dardel, Guy von, 206–207
Delong, Adelaide, 78–79
Democracy, Einstein and, 161, 257
Depression, Great, 55–56, 261
Disarmament, Einstein on, 56–57
Dodd, William, 102
Dodds, Harold W., 82–83, 91–94
Dostoevsky, Feodor, 134–135, 180

Dreyfus, Bertha, 218
Dreyfus Affair, 39
Dukas, Helen, 8, 12, 61–62, 65, 75, 78,
    79, 130–132, 147, 150–151, 204,
    219, 228–231, 274
  citizenship of, 125
  Einstein's estate and, 231
  Einstein's health and, 222, 299
  as Einstein's intermediary, 130, 286
  Einstein's seventieth birthday and, 226
  FBI and, 251–253, 262
  Israel presidency and, 245–246

Eastern Europe, 218
  post-war boundaries for, 168
  Soviet Union and, 168–169, 187,
    208
Eban, Abba, 245–247, 299
Eddington, Arthur Stanley, 42–43
Education, 161–163
  Einstein on, 162–163
  general vs. specialized, 163
  German, 25, 161–162
  independent thought as goal of, 163
  real life and, 163
  trades and, 163
  in U.S., 162
$E = mc^2$, Einstein's discovery of, 117,
    119
Egypt, 239
Ehrenfest, Paul, 17–18, 32, 34, 38, 43,
    47
Ehrenfest, Tatiana, 47
Ehrmann, Rudolf, 299
Einstein, Albert
  animals and, 130–131
  appearance of, 44, 68–69, 80
  assistants and, 87–90
  childhood of, 23–28
  childishness of, 303
  children and, 78–79, 219
  citizenship of, 8, 28, 125, 219
  daily routine of, 88, 222
  death and, 221–222, 297–300
  diet of, 36, 99, 221
  as dreamer, 294–295
  early physics papers of, 31–32

education of, 25–31, 161–162
English language and, 48–49, 68, 70,
    89, 126, 228–229, 298, 300
fame and, 44–46, 51, 303
health of, 221–222, 297–300
homesickness of, 217–218
human welfare as concern of, 163–
    165, 301–306
individualism of, 25, 29–30
informality of, 34, 44, 68, 70
Jewish jokes and, 245
last European public appearance of,
    18–19
as lecturer, 32, 34, 70
and letters warning about atomic
    bomb, 117, 120–122
literary tastes of, 134–135
mail received by, 76–78
marriages of, 31, 34, 36, 79–80
mathematics and, 25, 28, 30, 87
military power sharing urged by, 171,
    183–186
moral courage of, 44, 52
offhand remarks of, 50–52
as old man, 293–300
organized groups avoided by, 41
philosophy and, 135
"plumber statement" of, 290–291
poetry of, 3, 9, 78, 85, 86, 90, 99,
    136–137
as portrait subject, 293–295
public image of, *see* Einstein's public
    image
publicity avoided by, 61, 75–76
reading aloud by, 132, 231
remuneration of, 47, 59
safety of, 17, 61–62
seventieth birthday of, 226–227
seventy-fifth birthday of, 296
smoking and, 222
solitude and, 3–4, 19–21
as speaker, 46, 48–50
thinking and, 19–20, 86–89
walks of, 67–68, 294–295
will of, 229–231
Einstein, Bernhard Caesar (grandson),
    231

Einstein, Eduard "Tetel" (son), 31, 34,
    132–134, 218
Einstein, Elsa (second wife), 6–8, 12,
    61, 65–66, 71–74, 79
  Einstein's fame and, 45
  Einstein's finances and, 46, 59
  Einstein's health overseen by, 36
  Einstein's safety and, 17
  illness and death of, 79–80
  Ilse's death and, 72
  marriage of, 36, 79–80
  Mercer Street home and, 79
  sciatica attack of, 74
  society life enjoyed by, 36
Einstein, Hans Albert "Aden" (son), 21,
    31, 34, 127, 218, 222, 231, 300
Einstein, Hermann (father), 24, 26, 28,
    31
Einstein, Ilse (daughter), 36, 72
Einstein, Jacob (uncle), 24
Einstein, Lina (cousin), 218
Einstein, Maja, *see* Winteler, Maja Ein-
    stein
Einstein, Margot (daughter), 12, 36, 72–
    73, 79, 87, 129–132, 139, 165,
    218–219, 221, 229–231
  animals and, 130–131
  citizenship of, 125
  and Einstein as old man, 293–300
  Einstein's estate and, 231
Einstein, Mileva Marie (first wife), 31,
    34, 53, 218
Einstein, Pauline (mother), 24
Einstein, Robert (cousin), 127
Einstein Archives, 112
Einstein on Peace, 16, 242
Einstein-Russell Manifesto, 298
Einstein's Attempt to Overthrow Physics
    (Thurring), 54
Einstein's public image, 4, 42–46
  as absentminded, 67–68
  general relativity theory verification
    and, 42–44
  as mysterious, 44–45
  in Princeton, 67–69
Elizabeth, Queen of Belgium, 14, 62,
    75, 120, 256, 267, 296, 298

Emergency Civil Liberties Committee,
    277–279
Emergency Committee of Atomic Scien-
    tists, 191–194, 209, 211–213
  FBI and, 191–193
Ethics (Spinoza), 3
Evolution of Physics, The (Einstein and
    Infeld), 90

Faisal, King of Syria and Iraq, 103
Fankhauser, Anne, 296
Fankhauser, Erna, 297
Faulkner, William, 229
Federal Bureau of Investigation (FBI),
    192–193
  on Einstein, 203–204, 250–257
  Einstein investigated by, 250–253,
    262, 265
  and INS investigation of Einstein,
    253–255
Federation of Atomic Scientists, 183–184
Fenninger, Laurence, 70
Fermi, Enrico, 118, 172–173
Fight Against War, The (Einstein), 8
First World Congress Against War and
    Fascism, 254
Flexner, Abraham, 57–59, 65–66, 82,
    90–95
  anti-Semitism and, 65
  Einstein's complaints about, 66–67,
    92–95
  Einstein shielded by, 63, 65–66
  faculty relations with, 91–95
  resignation of, 94
  Roosevelt's invitation to Einstein re-
    jected by, 65–66
Forman, Philip, 219
Forrestal, James, 208
Förster, Wilhelm, 35
France
  1922 visit to, 52
  Sykes-Picot agreement and, 103
  Vichy government in, 144
Franck, James, 173–174, 182
Franck Report, 173
Frank, Philipp, 10, 34, 36, 44, 55, 118,
    255–256

Frankfurter, Felix, 102, 241
Frauenglass, William, 271
Frauenglass Letter, 271–273
Freud, Sigmund, 132–134
Frisch, Otto, 118
Frothingham, Mrs. Randolph, 6
Fuchs, Klaus, 213, 249, 251
Fuld, Mrs. Felix, 57, 65

Gandhi, Mohandas K., 226, 229, 268
Geist, Raymond B., 6–7
General Advisory Commission of Scientists, 213–215
Germany, 23–25, 141–146, 151, 187–188
  anti-Semitism in, 24–25, 38–39
  atomic energy research in, 118, 122–123
  education in, 25, 161–162
  Einstein on, 34, 145–146, 218–219
  Einstein on disarmament of, 188
  Kristallnacht in, 109
  nationalism in, 23, 35
  in Nonagression Pact with Soviet Union, 142–143
  Nuremberg Laws in, 101
  rearmament of, 14
  unification of, 23
  West, 188–189
  World War I defeat and, 38, 42
  see also Hitler, Adolf; Jews, German; Nazis, Nazism; Weimar Republic
God, Einstein on, 155–159
Gödel, Kurt, 222–224, 286, 294
Goethe, Johann Wolfgang, 135
Golden, William T., 196–197
Goldman, Hetty, 94
Goldstein, Israel, 241–243
Goldstine, Herman, 226
Great Britain
  anti-Semitism in, 110
  Einstein on Palestine policies of, 234–235
  Jewish immigration to, 109–110
  1921 visit to, 52
  Palestine and, 102–110, 233–238
  Peel Commission in, 107

Greece, 201–202
Gromyko, Andrei, 190, 237
Grossmann, Marcel, 31
Groves, Leslie, 169, 172–173, 177
  atomic energy policy and, 181–182, 190, 194–196
  Oppenheimer and, 284–285

Haber, Fritz, 35
Habicht, Conrad, 31
Hahn, Otto, 10, 118
Halsman, Philippe, 242
Harriman, Averell, 169
Harvard University, 47, 101–102
Hasenohrl, Friedrich, 11
Hebrew University, 13, 53, 231, 240
  Einstein's fundraising for, 48, 240
Heisenberg, Werner, 84
Heuss, Theodor, 146
Hibben, John Grier, 49, 56
Hindenburg, Paul von, 7
Hitler, Adolf, 7–10, 14, 55, 97–102, 141–146
  absolute authority of, 8, 99
  appointed as chancellor, 7
  Einstein's criticism of, 8
  Einstein's pacifism and, 14–17
  non-Jewish attacks on, 97
  self-defeating war plans of, 141–142
Hoffmann, Banesh, 80, 88–89, 150, 222
Hofstadter, Richard, 195
Honorary degrees, 220
Hoover, J. Edgar, 148, 250–253, 255
Hopkins, Alfred, 137
House Un-American Activities Committee, 203, 254, 270–271
Hull, Cordell, 98
Hussein, Sharif, 102–103
Hydrogen bomb, 213–215, 249, 285–286
  Einstein on, 215

Ideas and Opinions (Einstein), 228
Immigration and Naturalization Service (INS), 252–255
India, 229
Individuality, Einstein on, 160–161
Infeld, Leopold, 67, 79–80, 89–90, 226

Institute for Advanced Study, 5–6, 57–
    59, 81–83, 90–96, 222–226, 298
  Aydelotte as head of, 147
  campus of, 90–91
  computer project at, 223–225
  Economics and Politics School at, 93
  Einstein as isolated in, 83
  Einstein's acceptance of position at,
    58–59
  Einstein's retirement from, 222–223
  faculty of, 81–82, 91–92
  faculty power and relations at, 91–96
  flexibility of, 58
  formation of, 57–58
  Jews at, 92–93
  mathematics as initial field for, 57–58
  members of, 58
  Oppenheimer and, 225, 288–289
  Princeton University's relations with,
    82–83, 91–92, 94, 96
  salaries at, 58–59
  World War II and, 147
Interim Committee on Atomic Weapons,
    172–173, 177
Irgun, 107, 237–238
Isolationism, Einstein on, 56, 101
Israel, 238–240, 245–247
  Einstein and presidency of, 245–247
  Einstein on, 239–240
  Palestinian Arabs in, 240
  see also Palestine; Zionism, Zionists
Italy, 28–29

Japan
  military deterioration of, 175–176
  1922 visit to, 52
  in World War II, 151, 170–180
Jews, 38–42, 74–75, 92–93
  affection of, for Einstein, 98
  assimilation of, 39
  Eastern European, 39–40, 97
  Einstein's charity work for, 98–100,
    244
  Einstein's support of, 65, 70
  emigration by, 39–40, 98
  morality and, 160
  non-German, and Nazi terror, 14

  pogroms and, 39
  as rebels, 165
  Soviet, 144
  in U.S., 97–101
  U.S. apathy about, 101
  in Western Europe, 39
  World War II atrocities against, 145–
    146
  see also Israel; Palestine; refugees;
    Zionism, Zionists
Jews, German, 24–25, 97–98
  emigration as difficult for, 101, 109
  Nazi attacks on, 8–12, 108–109
  Nuremberg Laws and, 101
  Weimar Republic and, 38
Joliot-Curie, Frédéric, 118–119
Judaism, 24–26, 28, 41
  individualism and, 160–161
Juliusburger, Otto, 145–146, 149, 167

Kahler, Erich, 126, 222
Kaiser Wilhelm Institute of Physics, 32,
    118, 122, 218
Kaufman, Bruria, 87, 299
Kayser, Eva, 132, 139
Kayser, Ilse Einstein (daughter), 36, 72
Kayser, Rudolf (Anton Reiser), (son-in-
    law), 4, 26, 72, 136, 243, 294
  on Einstein in Patent Office, 31
Kemeny, John, 78–79, 87–89, 222, 227,
    293, 305–306
Kennan, George, 209, 262
Keren Hayesod, 46–48
Kollwitz, Käthe, 8
Korean War, 256
Krieck, Ernst, 11–12

Lamont, Corliss, 276–277
Laski, Harold, 242–243
Laue, Max von, 11, 32, 55, 83, 85, 253
Lawrence, Ernest O., 172–173, 281
Lazrus, S. Ralph, 242–243
League of Nations, 51–52, 101
Lehman, Herbert, 289
Lehman, Irving, 77
Leiden, University of, 38, 49, 55
Leidesdorf, Samuel, 92–94

Lenard, Philipp, 11, 54
Lincoln University, 220
Lippmann, Walter, 202, 208, 265–266
Lloyd George, David, 40, 103
Loeb, Jacques, 194
Long, Breckenridge, 111–113, 145
Lorentz, H. A., 38, 43
Los Angeles University of International
 Relations, 57
Lowe, E. A., 93
Lowell, A. L., 47

Maariv, 245, 247
Maass, Herbert N., 61
McCarthy, Joseph, 249, 269–270, 286
 downfall of, 276
McCarthyism, 213–215, 267–279
 civil liberties and, 269, 277–279
 Einstein on, 270–279
 Einstein on civil disobedience as re-
  sponse to, 268–269, 271
 Fifth Amendment and, 271–274
 First Amendment and, 272–276, 279
 historical background of, 259–262
 intellectuals and, 270–276
 Oppenheimer and, 279, 284–290
 pacifism and, 268–269
Mack, Julian, 65
McMahon, Sir Henry, 102–103
Manchester Guardian, 105
Manhattan Project, 169–172, 176–178,
 282, 284–285
 as self-perpetuating, 170, 177
 Smyth report on, 182
"Manifesto to Europeans," 35
"Manifesto to the Civilized World," 35
Mann, Thomas, 126–127, 145, 249
Marshall Plan, 208–209
Materialism and Empiriocriticism
 (Lenin), 207–208
Maurice Schwartz Yiddish Art Theater,
 98
Mayer, Walter, 12, 14, 59, 61
May-Johnson Bill, 183–184
Meaning of Relativity, The (Einstein),
 49
Meir, Golda, 236

Meitner, Lise, 118
Michelson-Morley experiments, 50
Miles, Sherman, 148
Miller, Dayton C., 50
Millikan, Robert, 55–58
Mitrany, David, 93
Morality, 159–160
 determinism and, 159–160
 Einstein on, 156, 159–160
 Jews and, 160
 myths and epics as basis for, 156
 and rejection of personal God, 159
Morgenthau, Henry, 66, 114–115, 145
Morse, Marston, 94–95, 223
Moszkowski, Alexander, 134–135
Mozart, Wolfgang Amadeus, 136, 139
Mufti of Jerusalem, 104–107
Mühsam, Hans, 236–237, 239–240, 242,
 244, 297
Murrow, Edward R., 276, 279, 286
Music, 25–27, 29–30, 64, 135–139, 226
 Einstein's improvisation of, 139
 Einstein's piano playing and, 137–139
 Einstein's public performances of, 137,
  139
 Einstein's violin playing and, 135–137

Nahon, Alfred, 14–16
Nathan, Otto, 62–63, 75, 80, 84, 123,
 184, 194, 291
 Brandeis University and, 241–244
 Einstein's final illness and, 300
 Einstein's Jewish activities and, 98–99
 on Einstein's political thought, 198
 Einstein's will and, 229–231
 Jewish refugees and, 112–114
 McCarthyism and, 272, 279
 at World Congress of Intellectuals,
  209–210
National Security Council, 212–213
Nature, 3–4, 294
Navy, U.S., 119, 149, 203
Nazis, Nazism, 7–12, 55, 97–102, 205
 Einstein's property attacked by, 9
 Einstein's theories attacked by, 90
 Jews attacked by, 8–12, 14, 108–109
 purge of, 99–101

Roosevelt administration and, 98, 102
  science and, 10–12
Nehru, Jawaharlal, 229–231
Nernst, Walter, 11, 35
Newark Star-Ledger, 65
New York Herald Tribune, 286
New York Times, 7, 48, 64, 70, 98–99,
  102, 210, 238
  on Einstein, 51–52, 291
  Frauenglass Letter and, 271–273
New York World Telegram and Sun, 8
Nicolai, Georg Friedrich, 35
Nissen, Rudolf, 221
Nobel Prize, awarded to Einstein, 31–32,
  53
Norden, Heinze, 123
North Atlantic Treaty Organization
  (NATO), 211

Okamoto, Ippei, 52
Old Lyme, Conn., 79
"Olympia Academy," 31
One Hundred Authors Against Einstein,
  54
Oppenheim, Paul, 126
Oppenheimer, Frank, 178, 284
Oppenheimer, Robert, 81, 170, 172–173,
  177–178, 226
  atomic energy control and, 190, 194–
  195
  hydrogen bomb and, 213–215, 285–
  286
  as Institute director, 225, 288–289
  McCarthyism and, 279, 284–290
"Our Debt to Zionism" (Einstein), 107–
  108
Out of My Later Years (Einstein), 227–
  228
Oxford University, 55, 59

Pacifism, 6–8, 141, 268–269
  conscientious objection and, 268–269
  Einstein's "two percent" speech on, 56
  Hitler as exception to, 14–17
  in World War I, 35–36
Pageant, 220–221

Pais, Abraham, 44, 85–87, 222, 227,
  245
  Oppenheimer and, 286
Palestine, 9, 40, 233–239
  anti-Jewish riots in, 104–105
  Arab Legion in, 238
  Arabs in, 53, 102–110, 234–239
  binational solution for, 105–110, 235–
  236, 239
  British in, 102–110
  civil war in, 238
  Einstein on, 53, 105–108
  Einstein on statehood for, 235–236
  German refugees and, 102, 109–110
  Haganah in, 236, 238
  history of, 102–110
  immigration to, 102, 107, 109–110,
  233–238
  increased terrorism in, 109–110
  Irgun in, 107, 237–238
  1923 visit to, 53–54
  1939 White Paper on, 109–110, 233,
  236
  partition proposed for, 107–108, 233–
  239
  Passfield Paper and, 105
  Peel Commission and, 106
  statehood and, 107–110, 233, 235–238
  terrorism in, 237
  see also Israel; Zionism, Zionists
Panofsky, Erwin, 67, 126, 226
Pasadena, Calif., 7–8
Patent Office, Berne, Einstein at, 19–20,
  31–32
Pauli, Wolfgang, 223
Pauling, Linus, 249
Pepper, Claude, 218
Photoelectric effect, 31, 53, 84
Planck, Max, 2, 9–10, 32, 35, 55, 83,
  85
  death of, 218
  Nazis and, 10
Politics, 97, 101
  Einstein on, 191–200
  Einstein's ideas rejected on, 196–197
Ponsonby, Lord, 14, 16
Potsdam Conference, 169, 174–175

Prague, Einstein in, 32
Princeton, N.J., 61–64, 217–231
  Einstein in, 61–96, 126–131, 217–218
  Einstein's friends in, 126
  Einstein's residence in, 63–64, 79
  history of, 61–62
  Jews in, 74–75
  local visitors to Einstein in, 64–65
  Mercer Street home in, 79
  postwar growth of, 217
  racism in, 219–220
  refugees in, 74–75
  society in, 64, 68, 74–75
Princeton Herald, 62–63, 75, 219–220
Princeton University, 47, 49–51, 63
  Einstein and undergraduate activities
    at, 70
  Einstein's lectures at, 49–50
  racism at, 219–220
Prussian Academy of Science, 7, 9–11,
    34, 59
  Einstein's election to, 32
  Einstein's resignation from, 9–10

Quantum theory, 84–85
  Einstein's objections to, 84–85

Rabbeis, Emma, 251–252
Rabi, Isidor I., 174, 226
Rabinowitch, Eugene, 212
Racism, Einstein on, 219–221
Rahm, Barbara L., 137
Refrigerator, Einstein's patent on, 119
Refugee Assistance Fund, 18–19
Refugees, European, 12, 71, 74–75, 97–
    102, 109–115, 127
  Allied inaction on, 145
  Anglo-American conference on, 145
  Einstein's affidavits for, 264
  Einstein's aid to, 112–114
  employment for, 12, 19
  German, 12, 19, 98, 101–102, 109–
    115
  Palestine and, 102, 109–110
  visas for, 101–102, 111–113
Reiser, Anton, *see* Kayser, Rudolf

Relativity
  attacks on, 54
  ether experiments and, 50–51
  experience and, 154
  special, 32
Relativity, general theory of, 53, 87
  verification of, 42
Religion
  cosmic, 158
  determinism and, 155–156
  Einstein and, 155–159
  morality tied to epics and myths in,
    156
  science and, 157–159
  see also Judaism
Reporter, 290
"Report to the Secretary on the Acquies-
    cence of this Government in the Mur-
    der of the Jews," 114–115
Robertson, H. P., 226
Roentgen, Wilhelm, 35
Rolland, Romain, 16
Roosevelt, Eleanor, 66, 112–114, 215
Roosevelt, Franklin D., 65–66, 111, 145
  atomic bomb research and, 122–123
  Eastern Europe and, 168–169
  Jewish refugees and, 111, 115
  letters on atomic bomb sent to, 117,
    120–122
  Nazism and, 98, 102
Rosenberg, Ethel and Julius, 264–265,
    277
Rosso, Henry, 75–76
Royall, Kenneth, 209
Russell, Bertrand, 223, 273
Russian War Relief, 143–144
Rutherford, Ernest, 18–19, 117–118

Sachar, Abraham, 241–242
Sachs, Alexander, 120–123, 148
Sailing, 72, 79, 125, 131–133
Saranac Lake, 79, 113–114, 131–132,
    150–151, 182
Schroedinger, Erwin, 55, 85
Schweitzer, Albert, 296–297
Science
  Einstein's study of, 27–28

religion and, 157–159
research conditions for, 19–20, 281–282
"Science and Religion" (Einstein), 157–158
Scientific and Cultural Conference for World Peace, 254–255
Scientific theory, 153–155
  experience and, 153
  imagination in, 154
  rationality and, 155
  simplicity as virtue in, 153
  wonder and, 154–155
Scientists, 173–174
  Einstein and independence of, 281–291
  military and, 281–290
  politicians vs., 190–198
"Scottsboro Boys," 56
Seeley, Evelyn, 8
Seelig, Carl, 271
Senate Permanent Subcommittee on Investigations on Government Operations, 269–270, 273–276
Shadowitz, Albert, 273–277
Shapley, Harlow, 254
Shatara, F. I., 108
Shenstone, Mrs. Tiffin Harper, 279
Sitter, W. de, 43
Smyth Report, 182
Socialism
  communism vs., 259
  Einstein and, 161, 185, 257–258
Solovine, Maurice, 13, 31, 36, 53, 59, 154
Soviet Union
  Allies and, 142–145, 168–175, 187
  atomic bomb developed by, 212–213, 262
  atomic energy and, 190–191
  Eastern Europe and, 168–169, 187, 208
  Einstein on, 143–144, 204–206, 210, 267, 277
  Einstein as seen in, 208
  Germany and, 142–144
  Jews in, 144

peace propaganda of, 203
post-war repression in, 207
preventive war proposed against, 208, 212
Wallenberg and, 205–207
world government rejected by, 205
Spain, 148
Spinoza, Baruch, 2–3, 155–156
Stalin, Joseph, 187–189
  atomic bomb and, 175–177, 187
  on capitalism, 188
  Eastern Europe and, 168–169, 187, 208
  post-war repression of, 207
  Wallenberg letter from Einstein to, 206–207
  World War II and, 142–144
State Department, 169
  atomic energy policy and, 196–197, 199
  "final solution" and, 145
  Jewish immigration and, 111–114
Steele, Ronald, 265–266
Stern, Otto, 85
Stimson, Henry, 169–170, 176
Stone, I. F., 277
Strassmann, Fritz, 118
Straus, Ernst, 19, 21, 87–88, 131, 154, 219, 294, 298
  on Einstein's political thought, 98
Strauss, Lewis, 225, 286–289
Strong, George, 148
Study Group of German Natural Philosophers, 54
Swabia, 23–24
Swing, Raymond Gram, 183, 273
Swiss Federal Institute of Technology (ETH), 28–30, 32
Sykes-Picot agreement, 103
Symington, Stuart, 208
Szilard, Leo, 118–122, 150–151, 183–184, 209
  atomic bomb opposed by, 171–174, 182
  atomic bomb warning letter and, 120–122
  atomic energy controls and, 191–192

Einstein visited by, 120–122, 150–151
Manhattan Project and, 170–171, 285

Talmey, Max, 28
Tel Aviv, Einstein as honorary citizen of, 53
Teller, Edward, 120–122, 213, 288
Thomas, Norman, 210, 277–278
Thompson, Dorothy, 206
Thoreau, Henry David, 304–306
Thurring, Bruno, 54
Time, 158, 188
Tinef, 132
Tolstoy, Count Leo, 134–135
"To the Heroes of the Warsaw Ghetto" (Einstein), 146
Truman, Harry S., 169–171, 174–179, 194, 264
  atomic bomb and, 174–179
  Cold War policy of, 256–257, 259–262
  Eastern Europe and, 187
  Einstein on, 256–257
  "get tough" policy of, 189–190
  Greek crisis and, 201–202
  Palestine and, 234–236
Truman Doctrine, 202
Truth, Einstein on, 165
Tucci, Niccolo, 261

Uncertainty principle, 84–85
Unger, Abraham, 276
Unified field theory, 53, 84–85, 225, 300
United Jewish Appeal, 244
United Nations, 173, 184
  Atomic Energy Commission of, 190
  atomic energy control and, 190–191
  Palestine and, 236–239
United Nations World, 208
United States, 119–123
  Advisory Committee on Uranium and, 122–123
  anti-Communists in, 188–189
  anti-intellectualism in, 126
  atomic energy policy of, 181–182
  Cold War weakening of democracy in, 260

education in, 162
Einstein and politics in, 97, 101
Einstein as stranger in, 125
Einstein on militarism in, 215
Einstein's criticism of values in, 125–126
Jewish immigration to, 109–115
Jews in, 97–101
national character of, 260–261
1921 tour of, 49–52
1924 immigration law in, 110–112
1930–1931 trip to, 56
Palestine and, 234–238
racism in, 219–221
in World War II, 143–151, 168–180
Urey, Harold C., 192

Veblen, Oswald, 8, 50–51, 81–82, 90–95, 223
Versailles, Treaty of, 42
Völkischer Beobachter, 11
Von Neumann, John, 82, 91, 223–225, 287

Wallace, Henry, 210–211
Wallenberg, Raoul, 205–207
War Refugee Board, 115, 205
War Resisters International, 6–7, 105
Washington *Times Herald,* 193, 251
Watch Hill, R.I., 71–74
Weber, Heinrich, 30
Weimar Republic, 5, 38
  economic problems in, 54–55
  Einstein's support of, 38
  Jews and, 38
Weizmann, Chaim, 13, 46–49, 98, 105–110
  American Zionists and, 46–47
  Faisal's meeting with, 103
  as Israeli president, 245
  Palestine partition and, 109
Weizmann, Vera, 49
Weizsäcker, C. F. von, 122
West, Andrew F., 49
Weyl, Hermann, 82–83, 90, 91, 226
"Why Socialism?" (Einstein), 257–258
Wiener, Norbert, 283

Wigner, Eugene, 120, 226–227
Winteler, Jost, 29
Winteler, Maja Einstein (sister), 24, 29,
    127–130, 132, 231
    Einstein and, 127–130
Winteler, Paul (brother-in-law), 29, 127,
    130, 231
Wise, Stephen S., 14, 65–66, 108, 113–
    114, 149, 234–236
    Einstein's correspondence with, 99
    Einstein's reliance on, 98
Woman Patriot Corporation, 5–6
Workers' International Relief, 6
World Antiwar Committee, 254
"World as I See It, The" (Einstein), 160
World Congress Against Imperialist War,
    6
World Congress of Intellectuals, 209–
    210
World government
    economics and, 185–186
    Einstein's advocacy of, 167, 183–186,
    208–210
    as only hope for peace, 186
    proposed structure and function of,
    183–186
    Soviets and, 205

World War I, 34–38, 102
World War II, 141–151, 168–180
    Allies in, 141–145, 168–175, 187
    atrocities against Jews in, 145–146
    Einstein's scientific work in, 147–149
    end of, 151, 175–180
    second (Western) front in, 141, 144–
    145
    U.S. in, 143–151, 168–180
World Zionist Organization, 40, 105
    American branch of, 46–48

Yalta Conference, 168

Zinn, Walter, 119
Zionism, Zionists, 8, 39–42, 46–49
    Arabs and, 104–110
    background of, 39–40
    binational solution and, 105–106
    blind nationalism of, 106–107
    Einstein and, 40–42
    Einstein's American tour for, 46–49
    original goals of, 40
    politicization of, 40
    statehood as goal of, 233
Zionist Union of Germany, 40
Zurich, Einstein in, 30–32